DIARY OF AN AIR WAR

Allied Flights Over Fortress EUROPE In WWII

Gerrit Zijlstra

A Teenage Witness in the Netherlands

EAKIN PRESS ★ Austin, Texas

Contents

Preface

It might have been easier for me to write a preface if I had written a book about my own experiences, but I could only have done so if I had kept a diary during those war years, when I was a schoolboy who was very much concerned with the war. Maybe I was aware of the seriousness of the situation because my parents took Jewish people in the house to hide them from the Nazis, soon after the occupation of our country. Everybody knew what would be the outcome if they were found.

I remember I never left the house without carrying my binoculars with me in order not to miss anything of the air war that daily raged overhead. That was more exciting than any Wild West book could have been. Living near the German border and near the German fighter-base Twenthe, and with a highway behind our back-garden leading to Germany on which much German military traffic passed, one can easily understand that we received frequent visits — not only from the bombers that more than once mistook our town for a German town, but also from "Jabo's" (fighter-bombers) as Thunderbolts, Spitfires, and Typhoons kept a close watch on the road traffic. Although many events are engraved in my memory, the absence of the exact dates kept me from making an account of my experiences that, if I had kept a diary, might have made a small contribution to the many stories that have already been written about those hectic days.

Instead I stated, many years after the war, collecting all data I could lay my hands on to make a daily account of the operations of the 8th and 9th U.S. Army Air Forces. I finally completed a handy reference work, at first with no intention to have it issued as a book. However, the more I proceeded with the subject the more I thought it not only useful for my own sake but for all who kept a keen interest in what really happened in those days. I also wanted to insert a lot of detailed information about the aircraft taking part and about the targets, etc. The index at the back of the book refers to pages where one can find type of aircraft, first operational flights, why certain targets were important, the history of V-weapons, and so on.

The book was issued earlier in a very limited edition in 1977. The reactions I received from those in possession of the book convinced me that there still exists a great interest in the exploits of airmen in the Second World War.

I want to thank the people of the Imperial War Museum in London for their assistance in helping me to find the necessary data and who made it possible to check the data I had already collected by reading numerous books and magazines.

In the library of the KLM at Schiphol I consulted the weekly reviews in the 1940–1945 issues of *Flight* and *The Aeroplane*. Last but not least, I want to thank my friend Dick Muller for helping me to collect many of the photographs printed in the book.

Introduction

It was a bright Sunday afternoon and many families in our town, which was situated in the Netherlands near the German border, took the opportunity to take a walk in this exceptionally beautiful weather so late in the year. They ignored the constant rumbling in the distance, far beyond the German border, preferring to forget, at least for this afternoon, that there was a war going on.

My friend and I listened to that rumbling, which we knew was the heavy anti-aircraft artillery of the Germans. And this meant that the American flyers were in the air.

We decided to go into the countryside to look for leaflets which we had already begun collecting since the first ones were dropped by the RAF in 1939. Living at the edge of the town it took us only a few minutes to leave the houses behind us, and while we walked along a country road we heard the distant thunder growing louder and louder.

Suddenly a constant roar drowned the guns, and I realized that the bombers were coming. I always took my binoculars with me and I searched the sky. And there they were! High up in the blue came the Flying Fortresses, majestically proceeding in tight formations. But then I saw more: I saw lots of tiny black specks everywhere in the sky, darting around the bombers, even flashing through their formations. And I also saw parachutes . . .

All of a sudden the air was torn apart by the horrible noise of bombs coming down and we jumped into a ditch beside the road (fortunately it was dried up). The bombs came down all around us and we were covered with mud. I turned myself on my back because, amid all that misery, I still didn't want to miss the sight of those bombers, proceeding in their tight formations as if the sky were not filled with steel, fire, and horror.

I saw a Fortress falling, just like a leaf, nose down, and then the big machine straightened out, dived again and then straightened out again . . .

A few moments later a Fortress took a more direct way to the ground. More parachutes blossomed up in the sky.

We cheered up when we saw a German fighter, trailing a large plume of smoke, racing overhead in the direction of Twenthe Airfield, its pilot obviously hoping to reach it in time.

It was all over just as suddenly as it all started. We crawled on our feet again and looked at the thick clouds of smoke from the burning houses, drifting in our direction.

The date was October the 10th, 1943. Little did we know that the US Army Air Force had entered its most critical phase in the European warfare, culminating in the Schweinfurt raid four days later. We would never have believed that after that raid, even the continuance of daylight operations had come to hang in the balance. To us it was an ever-increasing power that day after day droned over our heads which could not be stopped any more on its way to ultimate victory. Those airplanes were our only visible contact with the free world in those days.

I still remember one afternoon in April, 1944, when I was standing with my father in our garden, looking at a large procession of bombers on their way to Germany. The B-17s were flying at an extreme low altitude and I saw my father shaking his head while he said: "Those boys are really risking their necks."

And I knew how to explain those words. They expressed great concern and also admiration for that, in fact, so-small army of young boys who had the courage to penetrate so far into hostile territory where one of the most powerful armies in the world was waiting to annihilate them.

This whole period left an indelible impression on me, and after the war had become another chapter in our gloomy history I read numerous books, magazines, and articles about the subject.

Many books have been written about the airwar, indeed: heroic epics, accounts of battles, accounts of actions of some special outfit. Only a few tried to get near the feelings of the human beings, often barely in their twenties, who had to do their jobs in those vulnerable machines, thousands of feet above the earth, in the face of an enemy whose fighting capabilities no one could deny.

I started to write down everything I read to make a connection between all data. In doing so, I hoped to be able to form a complete whole of the major activities of the 8th and 9th Air Forces, in chronological order with background information where necessary. It became a daily account of the struggle of an Air Force to gain air superiority over Europe, which goal was finally reached, however, at the cost of thousands of men and machines.

That some fighter or bomber groups are more often mentioned than others does not mean that their share in the total war effort was of more importance.

The successes, the disasters, and the losses came to all who participated in one of the most cruel battles in history, where every man in each unit devoted himself to the job that had to be done.

Too often they had to pay the highest price: their lives. They paid it for all of us . . .

Chronology

1942

20 February	Officers of the USAAF disembark in England in order to arrange the reception of American combat flying units which are to be based in the UK.
18 June	With the arrival of General Spaatz the USAAF is officially stationed in Great Britain.
1 July	The first B-17 Flying Fortress lands in the United Kingdom.
4 July	The first American attack from England on airfields in Holland. The aircraft are Douglas Bostons, borrowed from the RAF.
9 July	Lightnings land at their base in England. Before the end of the year they will be sent to North Africa.
17 August	Mission n°1: 12 Fortresses attack the marshalling yards at Rouen.
19 August	The first German aircraft has been shot down by an 8th Air Force fighter pilot, the latter flying in support of the Dieppe operations.
6 September	First American bomber losses in combat.
29 September	The Eagle Squadrons (American pilots who had voluntarily joined the RAF) are formally taken over by 8th Air Force Command and organized into the 4th Fighter Group.
7 October	The first B-24 Liberator Group, the 93rd, has become operational.
9 October	First operational sortie of B-24 Liberators.
7 November	First mission of the B-17 "Memphis Belle."
23 November	German fighter pilots change their method of attack by starting their head-on attacks. B-17s and B-24s being inadequately equipped against these kind of attacks. Not before August 1943 both types will be equipped with a nose-turret.
30 December	The 305th BG tries out the "Box Formation" after its

xi

commander Curtis Le May had experimented in this respect. This type of formation became standard for the duration of the war.

1943

11 January	The 56th Fighter Group arrives in England and with the group come the first Republic P-47 Thunderbolts to this country.
21 January	The Combined Chiefs of Staff issue their "Casablanca Directive" giving the primary objectives for the time being. On top of the list are the German submarine construction yards.
27 January	The first American bomber mission to a target in Germany.
8 March	The first Medium Bomber Group, the 322nd, equipped with a B-26 Marauders arrives in England.
10 March	First operational sortie of the P-47 Thunderbolts.
1 April	The 4th Fighter Group flies its last sorties with the Spitfire. From now on they will fly the P-47 Thunderbolt.
8 April	Two new Thunderbolt groups, the 56th and the 78th FG join the 4th on operational status.
14 May	B-26 Marauders of the 322 BG make their first assault from the UK. The target is Ijmuiden on the Dutch coast.
17 May	The B-17 "Memphis Belle" has completed the last mission of her tour and is sent back to the States for a Stateside tour. Eleven B-26 Marauders of the 322nd BG were on the way to Ijmuiden when one aborts the mission due to technical malfunctioning. Of the remaining ten aircraft not one will return to England.
13 June	A simultaneous attack on Kiel and Bremen results in the first heavy loss of 26 bombers. One of the shot down Fortresses had a Brigadier General on board. The first U.S. General to be killed in action in Europe.
16 July	After the disastrous mission on May 17th, the 322nd BG is operational again, together with three other medium bomber groups.
13 August	Three North African-based 8th Air Force bomber groups take part in a mission to Wiener-Neustadt, covering a distance of 1,200 miles.
17 August	Mission 84: Two aerial task forces bomb Regensburg and Schweinfurt. After bombing the Messerschmitt factory the Regensburg force continues to North Africa, while the Schweinfurt forces returns to England after bombing the

ball-bearing factories. Sixty heavy bombers go down in the fierce air battles.

For the first time radar equipment is used when an 8th Air Force bomber drops two tons of bombs on Frankfurt with the aid of an H2S installation in a trial attack.

At night the RAF delivers the first blow to the V-weapon production at Peenemünde.

27 August	B-17 Fortresses make their first attack on the rocket launching sites on the French coast.
3 September	A new Liberator group is out on its first mission with the new B-24H with a power-operated nose-turret.
27 September	The first H2S-equipped bomber mission is flown.
10 October	236 B-17s are dispatched to bomb Münster. In the ensuing air battles 39 Fortresses go down.
14 October	Target: Schweinfurt. 291 Fortresses meet near disaster when 60 bombers are shot down, 5 crash in England and another 12 are written off after landing. German losses: 38 fighters. No deep penetration will take place before long-range fighters are available.
15 October	The first fighter group equipped with the P-38 Lightning becomes operational.
16 October	A new Tactical Air Force is established in England. General Brereton assumes command of the newly formed 9th Air Force. Four medium bomber groups are taken over from the 8th Air Force.
11 November	The first 9th Air Force fighter group receives its P-51B Mustangs.
1 December	9th Air Force P-51s make their first sortie.
5 December	First bomber escort mission by P-51 Mustangs.
15 December	Both American and British Tactical Air Forces come under the command of Ai Chief Marshal Sir Trafford Leigh Mallory. Those tactical air forces are committed to operation "Overlord," the planned invasion of the continent.

1944

1 January	The first "Carpet Bagger" mission is flown: dropping supplies to underground movements, dropping agents, etc.
6 January	A new organization, the "United States Strategic Air Forces" (USSTAF) is established to coordinate the operations of the 8th Air Force from England with the 15th Air Force from Italy.
20 February	Plan "Argument" coordinates precision bombing attacks by

8th and 15th Air Forces against aircraft manufacturing targets in order to gain air superiority before the planned invasion of the continent. When 1,003 heavies of the 8th Air Force take off for the execution of the plan is that the beginning of "Big Week," following the deliberate policy to force the Luftwaffe into combat. Fighters are now from a defensive to an offensive force.

3 March	American fighters appear over Berlin for the first time. The 9th Air Force 416th BG, the first to be equipped with the A-20 Havoc flies its first mission.
4 March	American bombers attack Berlin for the first time.
6 March	The mission to Berlin is the most costly so far undertaken: 69 bombers and 11 fighters are lost.
10 March	Medium bombers, so far mainly engaged in actions against the rocket-launching sites, will from now on more concentrate on targets in connection with the coming invasion.
1 April	Schaffhausen in Switzerland is erroneously bombed by 38 B-24s.
18 April	IX Air Support Command and XIX Air Support Command of the 9th Fighter Command are redesignated IX and XIX Tactical Air Command, a more fitting title for the kind of operations they are to carry out after D-Day.
May	The month of May saw a great increase in the intensity of attacks on transportation targets and of sealing off the intended landing area.
12 May	The 8th and 15th Air Force and RAF Bomber Command open a huge campaign against German oil facilities.
6 June	D-Day: The invasion in Normandy, supported by overwhelming air power. From now on the air forces will operate in close cooperation with the ground forces.
13 June	The first V-1s are launched. Of the eleven V-1s launched, four came down on London. Squadrons of the 9th AF start to use the landing strips in France on a regular scheduled basis.
21 June	Berlin is the target for a force of 1,311 heavy bombers with an escort of 1,190 fighters. The first shuttle mission by the 8th Air Force to Russia takes place with 114 B-17s and an escort of 70 P-51s.
22 June	Large forces of German aircraft bomb the American aircraft that landed in Russia with devastating results.
18 July	Heavy air attacks on Caen in preparation of an attempt for a break-out by the ground forces.

25 July	A breakthrough at St. Lô is made under overwhelming air power, after weather had made such an attack impossible on the previous day. Armed column-cover will be given by fighter-bombers during the drive into France.
28 July	Me-163 jets make their introduction in the air war.
15 August	American troops land in southern France.
17 August	Heavy air assaults on German troops in the Falaise pocket.
25 August	Paris is liberated.
29 August	The first Me-262 is destroyed in action by an American P-47 pilot.
6 September	A new type of aircraft, the A-26 Invader, joines the mediums of the 9th AF in an attack on Brest.
7 September	Antwerp is taken by the British.
8 September	The V-2 rocket missile is fired for the first time, coming down in a suburb of Paris.
10 September	Luxembourg is liberated.
14 September	Maastricht in Holland is liberated.
17 September	Operation "Market Garden." Also the beginning of the "Battle of Arnhem."
18 September	The 8th Air Force flies a mission in support of the beleaguered city of Warsaw.
25 September	After the British and Polish troops had withdrawn across the Rhine at night the Battle of Arnhem had ended. This marked the end of operation "Market Garden."
21 October	Aachen surrenders.
16 December	The Germans start operation "Greif" or better known as the Ardennes Offensive, or the "Battle of the Bulge."
24 December	The 8th Air Force sends the largest bomber force into Germany that ever crossed its border: 2,034 heavy bombers set off to attack airfields and communication centers.

1945

1 January	Operation "Bodenplatte," well over 1,000 German fighters attack Allied airfields.
31 January	The end of the Ardennes Offensive.
14 February	B-17s bomb Dresden, which town received already a terrible bombardment from the RAF on the previous night.
22 February	All available American and British bombers and fighters attack transportation targets to wreck German communications. Operation "Clarion" is meant to resume the offensive toward the Rhine.
4 March	B-24s bomb Basle and Zürich in Switzerland. General

7 March	Spaatz flies to Switzerland to make formal apologies. Cologne is captured. American troops cross the Rhine when they find the bridge at Remagen still intact.
9 March	Bonn is captured.
21 March	In close connection with the intended great airborne and land assault over the Rhine the Allied Air Forces start their enormous operation to isolate the Rhur. Airfields are the primary targets.
24 March	Operation "Varsity" starts: the big airborne and land assault across the Rhine under cover of overwhelming air power.
4 April	The last of nearly 70 B-17s that made an emergency landing in Sweden arrives in that neutral country.
7 April	German pilots of the Sonderkommando Elbe try to stop the bombers by ramming.
12 April	Brunswick and Schweinfurt are captured.
23 April	Stuttgart is captured.
30 April	Berlin is taken by the Russians. Munich and Bremen are captured by the Allies.
1 May	Food drops above Holland. The last drops take place on 6 May.
9 May	The unconditional surrender of Germany which ends all hostilities.

Germany

1 Berlin
2 Brandenburg
3 Rostock
4 Warnemünde
5 Lübeck
6 Kiel
7 Hamburg
8 Braunschweig
9 Hildesheim
10 Hannover
11 Dümmer Lake
12 Bremen
13 Bremerhaven
14 Wilhelmshaven
15 Emden
16 Münster
17 Gelsenkirchen
18 Hamm
19 Dortmund
20 Essen
21 Krefeld
22 Düsseldorf
23 Cologne
24 Düren
25 Bonn
26 Koblenz
27 Wiesbaden
28 Mainz
29 Ludwigshafen
30 Freiburg
31 Stuttgart
32 Karlsruhe
33 Mannheim
34 Frankfurt
35 Schweinfurt
36 Nürnberg
37 Augsburg
38 München
39 Regensburg
40 Plauen
41 Jena
42 Gotha
43 Erfurt
44 Kassel
45 Leuna
46 Merseburg
47 Halle
48 Leipzig
49 Chemnitz
50 Dresden
51 Breslau
52 Stettin

The Netherlands

1 Amsterdam
2 Den Helder
3 Ijmuiden
4 Haarlem
5 The Hague
6 Rotterdam
7 Arnhem
8 Nijmegen
9 Enschede
10 Zwolle
11 Leeuwarden

Belgium

1 Brussels
2 Antwerp
3 Ostende
4 Malmedy
5 Bastogne

France

1 Paris
2 Lille
3 Dunkirk
4 Calais
5 Boulogne
6 Abbeville
7 Amiens
8 Dieppe
9 Le Havre
10 Rouen
11 Caen
12 St Lô
13 St Malo
14 Brest
15 Lorient
16 St Nazaire
17 Nantes
18 Tours
19 Le Mans
20 Orléans
21 Bordeaux
22 Marseilles
23 Toulon
24 Lyon
25 Mulhouse
26 Strasbourg
27 Nancy
28 Metz
29 Rheims
30 Chartres
31 Cherbourg

Italy

1 Rome
2 Foggia
3 Genoa
4 Turjn
5 Milan

Switzerland

1 Berne
2 Basle
3 Schaffhausen

Austria

1 Vienna
2 Salzburg

Czechoslovakia

1 Prague
2 Brüx

Poland

1 Warsaw
2 Posen
3 Danzig
4 Gdynia

Hungary

1 Budapest

Roumania

1 Bukarest
2 Ploesti

Bulgaria

1 Sofia

Albania

1 Tirana

FORTRESS EUROPE
With targets of the 8th and 9th Air Force and the maximum ranges of Allied fighter planes.

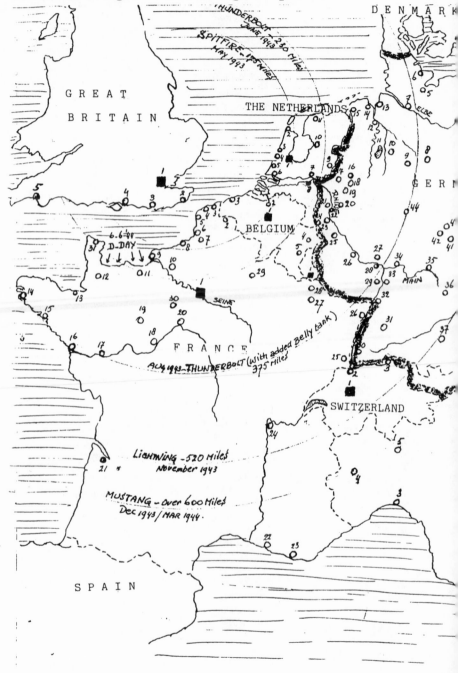

Boundary of
Germany, Sept 19

Part I

1942

Friday, 20 February

A Douglas DC–3 landed in England after a long and dangerous over-water flight from Lisbon. German aircraft were keeping a constant watch over the Bay of Biscay to intercept traffic to and from Britain. And this time it would certainly have paid off to stop this aircraft from reaching England, but no Luftwaffe long-range patrol aircraft did show up.

Seven officers of the United States Army Air Force (USAAF) disembarked in order to arrange the reception of American combat flying units, soon to be based in England. Leading the party was General Ira C. Eaker. General Eaker was no stranger for the British, for he had already spent many weeks in England in previous years to make a careful study of British air operations.

Already, early in 1941, an agreement had been made between the Americans and the British that in case of a war against the Axis in Europe and Japan, Germany would be the principal enemy. Therefore, to start the offensive a strong American air force had to be built up in England.

Although the British were very skeptical about the idea because of bitter experiences in the past, the Americans chose to concentrate on daylight attacks with the general aim to carry out missions against precise targets vital to the Axis war effort. Their faith lay in their bombers, which were faster and much more heavily armed than the British nightbombers.

Thursday, 18 June

Major General Carl Spaatz, veteran pilot of the First World War, arrived in England to take command of the Army Air Forces in Great Britain. With his arrival, the 8th Air Force was officially stationed in Great Britain.

Monday, 29 June

Twelve RAF Bostons were dispatched to carry out an attack on the marshalling yards at Hazebrouck. One of the Bostons was manned by a crew of the USAAF. The pilot was Captain Kegelman.

Wednesday, 1 July

The first of what will become a tremendous stream of Army Air Force aircraft touched down at Prestwick in Scotland after a ferry flight of 2965 miles. It was a Boeing B–17E Flying Fortress of the 97th Bomber Group of the 8th Air Force.

Saturday, 4 July

The first American attack from England was carried out by the 8th Air Force. The date seemed favorable to start the offensive as it was the American Independence Day.

Six aircraft of the 15th Bombardment Squadron (Light), using Douglas Bostons borrowed from the RAF's 226th Squadron, formed part of a force of twelve aircraft. So it was not an all-American force that took off from Swanton-Morley early in the morning at 07:11 hours.

Four flights of three aircraft, with at least one experienced RAF crew of the 226th in each flight, crossed the North Sea on their way to the Low Countries, where they would make low-level attacks on four different air-fields.

The Bostons flew very low to avoid detection by enemy radar. Near the Dutch coast the flights split, two of them going in northerly direction. These two flights immediately ran into heavy anti-aircraft fire. Most probably the batteries had been warned by the vessels the Bostons had passed.

Murderous flak was met by the three Bostons approaching the airfield of De Kooy. The leading RAF aircraft escaped, but both American Bostons were hit. One of them crashed in flames. The other one received a direct hit in the engine; a propellor flew off and a fire started. For a moment, the pilot, Captain Kegelman, lost control and the aircraft touched the ground. However, it bounced back up again and Kegelman managed to keep the aircraft in the air. He jettisoned his bombs. At the same moment, he saw the gunners of a flak tower aiming at him. He turned his bomber in their direction and opened fire with the nose-guns at close range.

The flight back home was made at sea level, but fortunately the fire in his disabled engine went out.

When the Bostons neared the airfield at Bergen, the pilots had no diffi-culty in identifying their target. Bursting flak shells paved their way to the airfield. One Boston with an American crew was fatally hit and went down after it dropped its bombs.

The airfield at Haamstede was bombed without losses.

The fourth flight was unable to identify the assigned target and returned to base without bombing.

4

Also one of the RAF Bostons failed to return.

For his exploits, Captain Kegelman received the DFC. It was the first 8th Air Force's combat-earned medal.

Monday, 6 July

B–17 Fortresses of the 97th Bomb Group took possession of their new base, Polebrook. Two squadrons of the group were based here, whereas the two other squadrons of the group went to the nearby airfield at Grafton Underwood.

Thursday, 9 July

Part of the 1st Fighter Group P–38 Lightnings landed at their base at Goxhill in Lincolnshire. One of the three squadrons had to remain at Reykjavik in view of possible German air attacks on Iceland.

Sunday, 12 July

A six-plane formation of the 15th Squadron headed for the airfield Abbeville/Drucat. This time, the Bostons flew at a medium altitude of 8500 feet. Flak was thrown up and two bombers were damaged, but all returned safely to their base.

After this raid the 8th Air Force procured some Bostons from the RAF and from then on the 15th Squadron aircraft carried the white star on the blue disc.

Sunday, 26 July

Six pilots of the 31st Fighter Group of the 8th Air Force, the first complete AAF group in the United Kingdom, joined a Canadian squadron of the Biggin Hill Wing in a sweep over northwestern France. Three squadron commanders were among the six pilots. One of them, a lieutenant colonel, was shot down and taken prisoner.

The 31st Fighter Group had been equipped with the P–39 Airacobra in the United States, but when the group moved to Europe their planes had been left behind and so they were flying Spitfire V's.

Sunday, 9 August

The 31st Fighter Group of the 8th Air Force was out on a patrol when they encountered a Ju–88 over the Channel. Two Spitfires attacked but the pilots could only claim a damaged enemy aircraft.

Friday, 14 August

Two P–38 Lightnings of the 8th Air Force's 1st Fighter Group, stationed at Iceland, were engaged in a mock-combat with a P–40 when they suddenly spotted a German four-engine FW–200.

First the P–40 registered several hits, and then one of the P–38s came in and the *Scourge of the Atlantic* was finished off. The first victory for the 1st Fighter Group had been scored.

Sunday, 16 August

Via the Greenland-Iceland route, the last Fortresses of the new 301st Bomb Group arrived at Prestwick, Scotland. With the bombers came the P–38 Lightnings. The fighters navigated on the bombers during the Atlantic crossing. Usually four P–38s with one B–17 in the lead made the long journey to England.

Monday, 17 August

Eighteen B–17 Fortresses of the 97th Bomb Group thundered along the runway at Polebrook in the English Midlands and lifted into the air. Mission No. 1 was on and the target was Rouen.

At 1539 hours the striking force of two flights of six B–17s each set course to the marshalling yards at Rouen while a decoy force of six Fortresses flew along the Channel coast, some ten miles off the French coast.

The sky was clear with unlimited visibility over the continent. A strong escort of four squadrons of the RAF's new Spitfire IXs rode along with the bombers.

The 12 B–17s climbed to 23,000 feet with General Eaker riding in the *Yankee Doodle,* lead bomber of the second flight. The first flight of six planes was led by *Butcher Shop* carrying the group commander, Colonel Frank Armstrong. His co-pilot was Major Paul W. Tibbets, who would make an even more historic mission three years later when he was the pilot of the bomber that dropped the atomic bomb on Hiroshima.

The bombers reached their objective and more than 36,900 pounds of explosives were unloaded. Nearly half of the bombs were complete misses.

Five RAF squadrons of Spitfire V's gave withdrawal support. Very few German fighters were seen and only three Me–109s made an attack, but they caused no losses to the bombers. Two Messerschmitts were claimed to be destroyed, but also two Spitfires failed to return.

After the Germans started their operation "Barbarossa," they had only two fighter forces left to guard the Channel coast, Jagdgeschwader 2 guard-

ing the area from Cotentin to Paris, and Jagdgeschwader 26 covering the
northern area. Each was composed of some 100 aircraft.

Tuesday, 18 August

Reinforcements of the 8th Air Force came in with the B–17Fs, landing
at Prestwick. These were the Fortresses of the 326th Squadron, part of the
92nd Bomb Group. They made a non-stop flight from Gander in Newfoundland to Prestwick in Scotland, covering a distance of 2119 miles.

Wednesday, 19 August

As a support to the raid on Dieppe, the 8th Air Force dispatched 24 Fortresses of the 97th Bomb Group on their second mission to Abbeville, the
home of the yellow-nosed Messerschmitts, "Göring's elite" of JG 26. Escorting British fighter pilots watched the perfect formation of heavy bombers flying in the clear, thin air.

The bombing caused considerable damage to the parked German aircraft.
The Luftwaffe did not interfere because its fighters were too much involved in the Dieppe battle to pay attention to the Fortresses. All returned
to their base.

The 31st Fighter Group received its battle-baptism and flew 123 sorties
in support of the Dieppe operations, resulting in many encounters with the
Luftwaffe.

The 8th fighter pilots brought down their first German fighter aircraft: a
FW–190 was shot down by a Spitfire flown by Lt. Junkin. After his victory over the battle area, Junkin was shot down himself, but he was
rescued from the Channel.

The 31st Group learned the art of air fighting the hard way and lost six
aircraft in the battle.

Thursday, 20 August

Twelve B–17 Fortresses were out on their third mission. They proceeded
to the marshalling yards at Amiens. Spitfires escorted the bombers. Eleven
bombers dropped their load on the yards and, again, all returned safely to
their base.

Still, no losses had been suffered by the 8th Air Force heavies, and this
undoubtedly made not only the crews but also the 8th commanders over-
confident in view of the coming events. More than ever, the commanders
were convinced of their right judgment for high-level precision-bombing in
daylight. Few, if any, then thought of the possibility that the future might

have such disastrous events in store that the continuation of daylight attacks would come to hang in the balance.

Friday, 21 August

The twelve Fortresses of the 342nd and 412th Squadrons of the 97th Bomb Group were sixteen minutes late for their rendezvous with the RAF fighter escort, composed of three Spitfire squadrons, including a squadron of the 31st Fighter Group. Consequently, the escort, with its limited fuel capacity, was only able to accompany the bombers half way across the North Sea. The twelve B–17s were left alone in the sky when they neared the Dutch coast.

At that moment the bombers were recalled, but due to a delay in communication, the information did not reach the bomber commander until he had crossed the coast and was committed to his target, the Wilton Shipyard at Rotterdam.

The unprotected Fortresses were also observed by the German fighter controller and 20 to 25 FW–190s took the air to intercept the bombers. During the twenty minutes that the engagement lasted the German pilots showed a marked respect for the concentrated firepower of the Fortresses. They didn't close in on the bombers, but preferred to concentrate on a Fort lagging behind.

A cannonshell wounded the pilot, while the co-pilot was so seriously injured that he was to die soon after.

Yet all bombers returned to base. They claimed two German fighters shot down.

The German fighter pilots were still insufficiently prepared for the fight against the formations of B–17s with their fighter escort.

Monday, 24 August

The 8th Air Force dispatched twelve Fortresses on the fifth mission. This time the bombers set course to Le Trait to attack the shipyards.

The bombers suffered no losses, but apparently no damage was done to the shipyards either. Out of a total of 48 bombs dropped, twelve were plotted to have fallen within 500 yards of the aiming point.

No German fighters rose to challenge the bombers.

Thursday, 27 August

Nine Fortresses of the 8th Air Force were on the way to the shipbuilding yards at Rotterdam. Spitfires provided escort and the bombers suffered no losses.

The Luftwaffe fighters didn't show up.

8

Friday, 28 August

Eleven B–17 Fortresses crossed the French coast and headed for the aircraft factories at Méaulte. Protecting Spitfires accompanied the bombers, but the Luftwaffe didn't show much interest, and no enemy aircraft was met. Again all bombers made it back home.

Saturday, 29 August

The 8th Air Force sent out thirteen Fortresses to bomb the airfield at Courtrai. Actually, twelve B–17s dropped their bombs. Again, all aircraft landed safely at their base.

The 8th Air Force 1st Fighter Group flew its first combat mission from England when two P–38 Lightnings took off to intercept enemy aircraft nearing the British coast. No German planes were sighted, so the Lightnings returned to their base at Ibsley, Hants.

Two more sorties were made later on the day, but no contact was made.

Tuesday, 1 September

Thirty-two P–38 Lightnings of the 8th Air Force carried out a fighter sweep.

Saturday, 5 September

The largest US striking force to date set out on a mission to Rouen. Thirty-seven Fortresses escorted by RAF Spitfires were going to revisit the marshalling yards.

The 97th Bomb Group led with 25 new B–17F bombers (the E-models went to a training center), and in its wake followed the 301st Bomb Group, making its first mission with twelve Fortresses.

There was little opposition, yet many bombs fell outside the target area, especially those dropped by the inexperienced 301st Bomb Group, causing destruction of French houses and homes. 140 French civilians were killed, and twice that number injured.

In all, 31 aircraft dropped their bombs, the others being unable to drop on account of mechanical failures.

Sunday, 6 September

A force of thirty B–17 Fortresses was heading for the Potez aircraft factory at Méaulte. Trailing the 22 Fortresses of the 97th Bomb Group was the 92nd with eight B–17s on its first operational mission. The group had dispatched fourteen bombers, but six had aborted for various reasons.

Meanwhile, a second strike force of thirteen Fortresses of the 301st Bomb Group carried out a diversion attack on the fighter airdrome at St. Omer. Two B–17s bombed St. Omer/Ft. Rouge, which they mistook for the assigned airfield St. Omer/Longuenesse.

Shortly before they made their attacks, twelve A–20s of the 15th Light Bombardment Squadron visited the homebase of JG 26 at Abbeville.

When the bombers turned away from Méaulte both groups came under determined attacks by yellow-nosed Focke Wulfs and, despite the efforts of the supporting Spitfires to ward off the German fighters, two Fortresses went down. The first bomber of the 8th Air Force to be lost in combat went down over Flasselles under heavy attack from three Focke Wulfs. Four men bailed out and their chutes were seen to open. The second B–17 was last seen near Beachy Head, struggling toward Dover. British Air Sea Rescue searched the area in vain. Apart from these losses, many bombers returned with considerable battle damage. The bombing was more accurate than on the previous attack.

Monday, 7 September

Adverse weather was the main cause of the poor bombing by 29 B–17s on the Wilton Shipyard near Rotterdam. Only seven Fortresses succeeded in dropping on the target. German fighters rose to meet the bombers. Their attacks were mainly directed against the 97th Bomb Group, but all bombers returned safely.

Saturday, 12 September

The 4th Fighter Group was activated at Bushey Hall, headquarters of the 8th Fighter Command. The group was composed of the three RAF Eagle Squadrons, based at Debden and Great Sampfort in Essex. The 71st, 121st, and 133rd Squadrons became the 334th, 335th, and 336th Squadrons respectively.

For the time being, the group remained under RAF Flying Control. The official transfer to the USAAF was to take place later in the month with an official ceremony.

Monday, 21 September

The 4th Fighter Group flew a shipping reconnaissance mission. While attacking a flak ship, one of the pilots of the 335th Squadron was shot down. He was the first pilot of the group to be killed in action.

10

Saturday, 26 September

After a prolonged period of unsuitable bombing weather, the 8th Air Force dispatched 26 bombers to attack the Maupertuis Aircraft Factory at Cherbourg, while nineteen Fortresses set course to the Poujean Aircraft Factory at Morlaix. P–38 Lightnings escorted the bombers. However, the targets were not bombed because the weather was so bad that all bombers returned to their bases.

The atrocious weather proved to be fatal for eleven pilots of the 336th Squadron, 4th Fighter Group, when they became lost over the continent. Faulty navigation and interference of German fighters added to the cause of the disaster.

Since they were flying the new Spitfire IX's, it also meant a setback for the remaining pilots of the squadron. Spitfire IX's were scarce and so they were to be confined to the MK V's again.

Only one of the pilots managed to come back, although he crash-landed his aircraft at Kingsbridge.

Tuesday, 29 September

Hitherto, the 8th Air Force had a strength of four fighter groups. The 31st Fighter Group, flying Spitfires, saw the most action. They were to make 1286 sorties prior to being removed to Africa. The 1st and the 14th Fighter Groups were both equipped with the P–38 Lightning. The 14th would soon fly its first operational mission. The 52nd Fighter Group was flying Spitfires.

The four groups would continue to operate under 8th Fighter Command until the 10th of October, the date after which all four groups were removed to North Africa to take part in the planned invasion there.

The Eagle Squadrons were formally taken over by 8th Fighter Command and organized into the 4th Fighter Group. The Spitfires went with the pilots, and only the RAF roundels were replaced by the star insignia.

Friday, 2 October

Persistent bad weather, and an order that all combat activity of the 8th Air Force had to take second place to the processing of units destined for Operation Torch in North Africa, had discouraged further operations.

But on this day the sky was clear and the weather seemed ideal for bombing, and therefore 32 Fortresses of the 8th Air Force took a heading to the Avions Potez factory at Méaulte, the third time that this target was visited by the B–17s.

And it was the second time that the bombers arrived over the German fighter airfield at St. Omer/Longuenesse where six Fortresses unloaded. Heavy fighter opposition was met and, although a protecting screen of 400 fighters tried to keep the Germans away from the bombers, they occasionally succeeded in pressing home their attacks against the Fortresses. The 301st Bomb Group especially received its share of the Luftwaffe attacks. Yet the bombers sustained no losses and all returned to their bases.

Meanwhile a diversion was flown by thirteen B–17s of the 92nd Bomb Group along the French coast.

P–38 Lightnings of the 14th Fighter Group started their operational career with fighter sweeps in coordination with RAF units.

Led by a wing-commander of the RAF, the 4th Fighter Group flew its first fighter sweep over France. In an encounter with the Luftwaffe over Calais, the Spitfires destroyed three Focke Wulfs.

Saturday, 3 October

The 4th Fighter Group had its headquarters moved from Bushey Hall to Debden.

Wednesday, 7 October

Two heavy bombardment groups of the 8th Air Force became operational: the 306th and the 93rd Bomb Groups. The 93rd Group was equipped with the B–24 Liberator. Two of its squadrons made the first non-stop formation flight from Gander to Prestwick.

Friday, 9 October

For the first time, B–24 Liberators were aloft in a clear blue sky with 24 aircraft to form the rear of a stream of 108 heavy bombers droning on toward their target, the transportation complex at Lille. Another novice group that made the mission was the 306th Bomb Group. A heavy escort of RAF and USAAF fighters flew along with the bombers. The escort included the 1st Fighter Group with its three P–38 squadrons, and the 4th Fighter Group, flying Spitfires.

The German fighters were again up in force to meet the bombers. Seven Fortresses flew a diversionary sweep to Cayeux. Only 69 bombers attacked the primary target at Lille. Two aircraft bombed the alternative target, the Courtrai/Wevelghem airfield in Belgium; six others attacked the last-resort target, the airfield at St. Omer; two heavies bombed Roubaix; and 33 bombers, including fourteen B–24 Liberators, made abortive sorties.

Again, as during the mission on October 2nd, the German fighters evaded the British and American fighters to concentrate on the bombers, and three Fortresses and one Liberator went down. Many bombers received damage and not only by German fighter action, but also from heavy and accurate flak. One Liberator that made it back contained approximately 200 holes of various sizes.

One Fortress of the freshman 306th Group, leading the rear squadron, had one engine feathered and lost speed. Another Fortress of the squadron stayed with the straggler for protection, and thus also lagged behind the rest of the group. German pilots were always eager to exploit such advantageous opportunities, and both Fortresses were subjected to persistent attacks of Focke Wulfs. Though heavily damaged, both Fortresses made it back. One B–17 of the same 306th Group did not have that much luck: a direct flak hit sent it down.

German losses, as claimed by the American crews (56 destroyed, 26 probables, and 20 damaged), were considered as firmly exaggerated and caused Intelligence officers to take a revised look at the method of evaluating gunner claims, since numerous gunners could claim the same aircraft. To be counted as destroyed, an enemy aircraft had to be reported as having lost a wing or tail section, completely in flames, or the pilot observed abandoning the aircraft. In fact, the maximum possible score during this mission was two enemy aircraft destroyed.

Approximately 147 tons of 500-pound high-explosive bombs and over eight tons of incendiaries were dropped on Lille. Of 588 high-explosive bombs, only nine were plotted within 1500 feet of the aiming points. This can partly be explained by the heavy fighter attacks sustained by the bombers over the target, but also by the inexperience of at least two of the groups.

Wednesday, 14 October

Twelve Spitfires of a squadron of the 4th Fighter Group were out on a patrol when they observed three flak ships off Hook of Holland. All three ships were attacked.

Thursday, 15 October

Spitfires of the 4th Fighter Group escorted 12 Bostons on a mission to Le Havre.

Wednesday, 21 October

Submarines had become the main concern of the 8th Air Force, and they would continue to stay on top of the target list until June, 1943, although it was not clear in the fall of 1942 if attacks on submarine bases would be effective in reducing the menace.

After a period of foul weather, cancelling eleven initiated missions, 66 Fortresses and 24 Liberators set off on a mission to attack the enemy submarine base at Lorient Keroman, a small fishing port southwest of Lorient. The weather was very bad and the majority of the bombers returned at an early stage. Only the Fortresses of the experienced 97th Bomb Group succeeded in reaching the target.

The Germans appeared to be taken completely by surprise. There was no air alarm and the anti-aircraft guns only went into action after the last bomb had been dropped. However, the German Air Force was alert and waiting for the bombers at the coast. Yellow-nosed Focke Wulfs made a series of violent attacks from the rear in an attempt to find a blind spot, safe from both dorsal and ball turrets. Sometimes they attacked in a formation of three aircraft, opening fire at 800 yards at flight level and then breaking away. Three Fortresses went down and another six were damaged.

Fifteen B–17s arrived over the target and thirty high explosives, each bomb weighing one ton, were dropped from an altitude of 17,500 feet instead of the usual altitude of between 22,000 and 27,000 feet. With a few exceptions, most of the bombs fell in the target area. Ground observers reported five bombs hitting the central block of shelters; however, they didn't penetrate more than five feet.

This was the last mission with the 8th Air Force for the 97th Bomb Group. This most experienced group was soon to be transferred to North Africa.

Saturday, 7 November

Four heavy bomb groups became operational: the 91st, 303rd, 305th, and 44th Bombardment Groups.

The 8th Air Force dispatched 68 aircraft to bomb the submarine base at Brest. The 91st Bomb Group joined the mission, making its maiden trip, though insufficiently trained. But they were fortunate enough not to run into trouble and all bombers returned without losses. Only 34 bombers dropped their bombs on the base.

One of the Fortresses that flew its first mission with the 91st Bomb Group was the *Memphis Belle* of the 324th Squadron. This B–17 would become one of the most publicized aircraft of the war.

The 44th Bomb Group had only become partially combat ready. The group was equipped with the B–24 Liberator. Eight of its aircraft made a diversional flight. General Hodges, commanding the 2nd Wing, witnessed the first operational flight in one of the B–24s, and it happened to be this bomber that lost its way in the clouds and finally touched down on Great Ashfield, an airfield still under construction.

November 7, 1942. An early B–24 Liberator of the 44th Bomb Group, based at Shipdham, Norfolk. (Official USAF Photo)

Sunday, 8 November

The 8th Air Force dispatched 38 heavy bombers to fly a mission to Lille. Thirty Bombers made an attack and dropped 293 500-lb. high explosives on the Hillemmes Shops at Lille. Meanwhile, eleven Fortresses of the 91st Bomb Group flew a diversion to the airfield at Abbeville.

Monday, 9 November

The theory of being able to attain more accuracy on precise targets if bombings were conducted at low altitudes was tried out in an attack against the submarine installations at St. Nazaire.

Forty-seven heavy bombers of the 8th Air Force crossed the English coast and thundered at 500 feet over the wavetops to avoid detection by radar. Cotentin was skirted, and then the bombers started their climb before turning sharply on a course that brought them right onto the target.

Flak was intense and accurate; some fifty heavy anti-aircraft guns filled the sky with explosives. The first to go through the barrage was the 91st Bomb Group. The Fortresses came in at 10,000 feet and all but one were damaged (including the B–17 *Memphis Belle*).

The twelve Liberators of the 44th and 93rd Bomb Groups flew at 18,000 feet, above the barrage. They escaped practically unscathed though several crewmembers returned with frostbite. Their flying clothes proved to be inadequate for the freezing conditions at high altitudes.

Then came the trailing 306th Bomb Group, flying even lower than 10,000 feet, and they plunged into the middle of the exploding shells. Three bombers were blown out of the sky.

Twenty-two aircraft were severely damaged. The bombing results were poor, and a repetition of the experiment was not justified.

The flak at St. Nazaire was to be increased considerably in the months to come, and the city would become notorious for its deadly flak.

Spitfires of the 4th Fighter Group escorted Bostons to Le Havre.

Thursday, 12 November

The 319th Bomb Group (Medium) had only recently arrived in the United Kingdom. After a brief period of practicing low-level flying over the English countryside, they were ordered to join the 12th Air Force in North Africa.

A flight of the group's B–26 Marauders took off from its British base to commence the long flight to Africa. Bad weather and equally bad navigation brought the Marauders over Cherbourg in what was in fact their first appearance over occupied Europe.

The reception committee was ready, and two Marauders, including the commander's aircraft, were shot down, while a third, badly shot up, managed to reach England where it crashlanded at Warmwell.

Saturday, 14 November

The 8th Air Force unleashed 34 heavy bombers to strike on the submarine pens at St. Nazaire. Twenty-four Bombers arrived over their target and this time they dropped their bombs from about four miles high. All bombers returned safely.

Tuesday, 17 November

Thirty-five heavy bombers out of the 63 dispatched by the 8th Air Force attacked the submarine base at St. Nazaire. Sixteen B–17s were from the 303rd Bomb Group and their debut was not successful because they were unable to locate the target—due to cloud conditions—and they all turned back to their base without bombing. The Fortresses that did bomb were met with intense flak, but this time there were no losses.

Wednesday, 18 November

Sixty-five heavy bombers of the 8th Air Force were scheduled to attack the submarine installations at La Pallice. As it turned out, nineteen bombers dropped on La Pallice, while thirteen aircraft turned to Lorient.

A second trial of the freshman 303rd Bomb Group brought nineteen of its bombers over what they thought was La Pallice. However, they mistook St. Nazaire for their assigned target, making a navigational error of about 100 miles.

One of the bombers attacking La Pallice was shot down. Twenty-six bombers flew a diversionary sweep.

Saturday, 21 November

A B–24 Liberator of the 330th Squadron, 93rd Bomb Group, piloted by the squadron commander, Major Ramsey, flew a patrol over the Bay of Biscay when it encountered five Ju–88s. It obviously looked a very easy prey to the Germans, for they made a nonchalant approach. In doing so, they made a fatal mistake and two Ju–88s were shot down and a third was damaged. The Liberator escaped.

Sunday, 22 November

The 8th Air Force sent 76 bombers out on a mission to attack the submarine base at Lorient. As the bombers neared their target, they found it covered by clouds. Only eleven bombers were able to find a gap in the clouds and they dropped their bombs on the target.

The bombers involved were all of the 303rd Bomb Group, which group could certainly use this heartening feature after the failure of the two previous missions.

Monday, 23 November

Poor weather conditions with heavy clouds all the way were encountered by the 58 heavy bombers dispatched by the 8th Air Force to attack the submarine base at St. Nazaire. Many Fortresses of the 91st and 306th Bomb Groups aborted the mission and turned back to England, leaving 36 bombers to continue to their target.

The German raid warning system brought the Luftwaffe fighters up in force, and the Germans had radically changed their method of attack. Oberst Egon Mayer, a distinguished fighter pilot and skilled tactician, commanding the attacking fighters, developed the head-on attack. Having studied the largely unsuccessful efforts made so far to stop the bombers, he ordered a frontal attack, leading one element personally. This tactic caught the bombers in their most vulnerable spot.

At this time the B–17s had one 30-cal. hand-operated gun, firing through one of four eyelets just off center; some mounted two 50-cal. side nose-guns. In either case, a blind spot was left in front which neither the upper turret nor the ball turret could reach. The B–24 was equipped with 50-cal. side-nose guns and a single 50-cal. center nose-gun mounted to fire below horizontal only. This also left a blind spot which the upper turret could not cover.

However, the head-on attack demanded from the attacker a high degree of skill and training to make effective use of the short time allowed by the very rapid rate of closure.

In the months ahead, losses would increase, and many times bomber crews would have to face the enemy's frontal attack just over the target; in fact, the Germans made their attacks to break up the bomb run. It was not to be until August and September, 1943, that improved B–17s and B–24s arrived in the theater complete with power-driven turrets in the nose. Yet it was not only the defensive armament against frontal attacks that was lacking, but also the protection of the crews against these attacks. Of all the armor plating, twenty-seven heavy pieces in a Fortress, none protected the crew from frontal attack.

Firing well-aimed bursts with their cannon from dead ahead, the Luftwaffe fighters came flashing in with flights of three aircraft, hammering on the reduced formations of four to five aircraft, and immediately two B–17s of the 91st Bomb Group tumbled down, taking with them the commanders of the 322nd and 323rd Squadrons, together with the group's navigator, bombardier, and gunnery officer. Two others were badly hit, and one of them crashed while attempting to reach its base, Bassingbourn, killing three of the crew.

One bomber of the 306th Bomb Group was badly hit by flak and lagged behind the formation. To increase the defensive firepower, another Fortress

18

of the same group deliberately dropped behind to stay with the stricken bomber. The German fighters jumped on their prey and during twelve long minutes, both Fortresses fought off the attackers. Both made it back home.

A Fortress of the 303rd Bomb Group didn't have that luck: it went down over the target in flames.

The 305th Bomb Group, making its first mission, escaped the attackers and returned unscathed.

November 23, 1942. Activity for the next mission at the Shipdham Liberator Base. (Official USAF Photo)

Saturday, 5 December

The 93rd Bomb Group of the 8th Air Force was ordered to move to North Africa, where it would stay until the end of February, 1943. Only one squadron stayed behind and this squadron, the 329th, was added temporarily to the strength of the 44th Bomb Group.

Sunday, 6 December

Thirty-six heavy bombers of the 8th Air Force set off on a mission to Lille where they would visit the Hellemmes shop. Spitfires of the 4th Fighter Group accompanied the bombers. One bomber was lost.

Meanwhile, the full 44th Bomb Group was out on a diversionary mission to attack the airfield at Abbeville. A few miles from the French coast a recall message was received, but only by the 66th and 67th Bomb Squadrons. They cancelled the mission.

That left only the 68th Squadron to proceed to the target with six air-

19

craft. All six unloaded their charges and turned off the target. At this moment, some thirty Focke Wulfs dove on the bombers and one of the Liberators went down ablaze and the other five were damaged.

One of the pilots earned the DFC by bringing his plane back to base in spite of being badly injured in the head and shoulders by a 20mm. shell that exploded in the cockpit.

Twenty-four Liberators of the 93rd Bomb Group left Alconbury to land in Portreath, Cornwall. Here the bombers were to refuel to start the next day on their long over-water flight to Oran for their detachment to the North African forces for a period of about ten days. So the crews were told; however, those "ten days" would grow into eighty-one days. Long-range bombers were badly needed in order to attack the Axis' supply ports.

Heretofore squadrons and groups formed cohesive teams as a defensive unit against fighter attacks, but the wing as a whole did not exist as a combat unit. When General Kuter took over the 1st Bombardment Wing, he started immediately to evolve a system of formations which were to become the prototype for operations in the theater. The idea was Colonel Curtis Le May's, who had been experimenting with formations to find the best solution for maximum defensive firepower against German fighter attacks.

Saturday, 12 December

In spite of a favorable weather forecast, cloud conditions proved to be so bad that most of the bombers dispatched turned back to their base.

Only the 306th and 303rd Bomb Groups pressed on, taking a heading to a secondary target: the marshalling yards at Rouen. Only the 303rd Group was able to bomb, and seventeen aircraft delivered their load. Both to and from the target, the group was subjected to persistent German fighter attacks and two of the bombers were shot down. One of them made an emergency landing in a French field, and the bomber *Wulf Hound* survived this landing fairly unscathed. This presented the Germans with the first Flying Fortress which they were to use to develop fighter tactics against this type of bomber.

As bombing results were in no small measure dependent on clear visibility at this stage of the war, operations were extremely limited due to the persistently unfavorable conditions during this winter, with only one cloudless or almost cloudless sky in twenty days.

Sunday, 20 December

One hundred one heavy bombers of the 8th Air Force crossed the Channel and droned on to their target, the major Luftwaffe servicing base at

Romilly-sur-Seine, which meant a penetration of 200 miles into enemy-held territory. Twelve squadrons of escorting Spitfires of the RAF and AAF flew with the bombers to the limit of their range, yet this was still not further than Rouen.

And that was exactly the point where the Germans were waiting for the bombers. Almost the entire fighter force located in northwestern France was thrown into the battle. The escort had barely turned back at about 1150 hours, when an estimated sixty German fighters, mostly FW–190s from the Pas de Calais area, approached the 91st Bomb Group.

The Luftwaffe fighters came in well above the bomberstream. Then they peeled off and closed in from the front, either slightly above, dead level, or slightly below. One Fortress of the 91st Bomb Group hit the ground near Vascoeuil, a few moments later followed by a Fortress of the same group, losing altitude rapidly, with a number of German fighters following it down.

At about 1205 hours, the enemy planes were relieved by fifty to sixty fresh fighters from Caen/Bougie, Paris, and possibly Evreux. These fighters accompanied the bombers almost to the target, which was reached between 1240 and 1245 hours. At that time, a number of Me–109s joined the battle, some of them approaching from 10 or 11 o'clock, flying through the formation, and diving out at 3 o'clock. A few minutes before reaching the target, a bomber of the 306th Group went down.

Sixty Fortresses and twelve Liberators bombed their assigned target, unloading 153 tons of high explosives and twelve tons of incendiaries. Considerable damage was done to hangars, barracks, and aircraft.

On the return trip, the bomber formation suffered almost continuous attacks from fighters, most of which had obviously taken part in the earlier stages of the engagement and were now making second sorties. It was only when seven squadrons of RAF Spitfires arrived to provide withdrawal support that the Germans broke off their attacks and turned back. Meanwhile, two Fortresses of the 306th Bomb Group had been shot down in the vicinity of Paris, while another bomber crashed into the sea. It was the sixth bomber lost in the mission. Another 29 bombers were damaged. One of the bombers to survive was *Memphis Belle*.

The commander of the 44th Liberator Group, Major Algene Key, received a DSC for his leadership of the group in this mission. Major Key was a well-known aviator, who had helped to set a world endurance record in 1935.

Wednesday, 30 December

Seventy-seven heavy bombers were on their way to bomb the submarine base at Lorient.

A revised formation was tried out by the 305th Bomb Group after its commander, 35-year-old Colonel Curtis LeMay, had experimented in this respect and found the best solution for utmost protection in the "box" formation: staggered squadrons within a group, and the squadrons composed of staggered 3-plane elements. The concentrated combined firepower of such a formation seemed the best way to keep the enemy fighters at distance.

The system was to prove its value as soon as the bombers arrived at Lorient and started their bomb runs, for at the same moment the German fighters rushed to the bombers and started their head-on attacks.

One Fortress of the 91st Bomb Group plunged to earth and with it yet another squadron commander. A bomber of the 306th Group was shot down when it separated from the 305th Bomb Group after the bomb run. A Fortress of the 305th, trying to come to its aid, was also shot down.

Only forty bombers attacked of which three were shot down. Many abortives occurred on these missions because of frozen equipment, supercharger failure, and other malfunctions.

Part II

1943

1

JANUARY

Saturday, 2 January

Four B–24 Liberators of the 329th Squadron 93rd Bomb Group (a special experimental squadron of the 8th Air Force) made the first blind operation over manufacturing cities north of the Ruhr. However, the bombers were recalled because the cloud cover proved to be insufficient to protect the bombers with their valuable equipment, which could, under no circumstances, be allowed to fall into German hands. All further air operations were hampered by snow and other bad weather conditions.

Sunday, 3 January

Eighty-five heavy bombers of the 8th Air Force crossed the Channel coast and headed in a southwesterly direction to the submarine base at St. Nazaire. The leading formation was the 305th Bomb Group and on board one of the aircraft was Brigadier General Hansell, commander of the 1st Wing. He joined the mission to get an impression of the effectiveness of LeMay's new tactics. With staggered formations ranging from 20,000 to 22,000 feet, a long, straight-in approach was made to obtain the best bombing results.

But the Germans had a novelty also, and for the first time the flak batteries used a technique, called the "predicted barrage," in which flak was thrown up throughout a limited area through which it had been calculated the attacking aircraft would have to fly. Moreover, the flak had become effective by now at altitudes above 20,000 feet.

To make circumstances even more uncomfortable for the bombers, strong adverse winds nearly doubled the time of the bombing run, during which time the crews were exposed to the heaviest anti-aircraft fire they had ever encountered. Two bombers were brought down.

And not only the flak took its toll. As soon as the protective Spitfire escort withdrew the Luftwaffe fighters appeared and three bombers were shot down.

A fourth bomber was intercepted by six FW–190s while it was limping home after having been badly shot up by flak. Part of the underside of the nose had been shot away, and with it the navigator and bombardier had disappeared. With two engines feathered, the unlucky aircraft lagged behind the returning formation at an altitude of 1500 feet. As soon as the Focke Wulfs attacked, four parachutes were seen separating from the Fortress. In a steady descent, *Son of Fury* went down until it settled in the water. Till the very moment that the water closed over the upper turret, the gunner's fire was seen streaming at the Focke Wulfs, which kept on coming to strafe their victim. The gunner who went down with his ship was T/Sgt Arizona Harris, and he was awarded a posthumous DSC.

Though bombing had been good, with 342 1000-lb. bombs placed in the target area, again little had been done to eliminate the submarine danger. Seven bombers failed to return from the mission, and two others crashlanded in England. 47 bombers were damaged. One of the bombers to return in one piece was *Memphis Belle*.

Eight B–24 Liberators of the 44th Bomb Group followed a formation of Fortresses on the return flight, on a course that took them out over the Atlantic. Unfortunately, they were off course and in the deteriorating weather they failed to observe Lands End and flew up the Irish Sea. The low fuel capacity of the Liberators did not allow such a miscalculation, and as soon as land was sighted, the bombers turned east to look for the first available airfield. Several ran out of gas completely and made forced landings. Many crashed and only a few managed to make a normal landing.

Monday, 11, January

Aboard the *Queen Elizabeth,* the 56th Fighter Group arrived in England. This group had been formed two years previously. In June, 1942, they received the first production P–47B Thunderbolts, and their task was to try the new breed of Republic out and to discover all its shortcomings. As with most new aircraft many problems manifested themselves, but after Republic's surgeons had cured the malfunctions and after many problems had been solved, the 56th Fighter Group started to like their aircraft and had all faith in its behavior in combat.

The fact that the sound construction of the Thunderbolt saved many a pilot's life in a crash landing undoubtedly added to the popularity of the aircraft among its pilots. The airducts, running at the bottom of the aircraft from engine to supercharger, acted as a buffer in a belly-landing, and the pilot knew that the aircraft would not disintegrate around him with the impact.

The 56th Fighter Group was, in fact, the only fighter group in the 8th Air Force to be entirely equipped with the Thunderbolt until the end of hostilities.

The 56th was an elite unit composed of pre-war pilots. Its leader was the very experienced 28-year-old Major Hubert Zemke.

Wednesday, 13 January

The 8th Air Force dispatched 72 Fortresses, and in four staggered eighteen-plane formations the bombers set course to the locomotive works at Lille to deliver the hitherto heaviest attack against this target. Sixty-four heavy bombers arrived over the city and unloaded approximately 125 tons of bombs on or near the target. As a result, the repair and locomotive construction work was seriously interrupted.

The lead formation was again the 305th Bomb Group, and the lead Fortress was *Dry Martini II,* named after its pilot, Captain Allen V. Martini. Captain Martini did not make this mission through illness, and his place was taken by Major Taylor. The aircraft also carried Brigadier General Hansell.

Over Lille, the yellow-nosed Focke Wulfs displayed their usual tactics and made their head-on attacks on the lead group the moment it began concentrating on the bomb run. A cannon shell exploded in the cockpit of *Dry Martini II*, instantly killing the pilot, Major Taylor.

One Fortress of the 305th Group did not return from the mission. Two B–17s of the 306th Bomb Group also failed to return. Both aircraft were believed to have collided over Belgium.

Spitfires of the 4th Fighter Group escorted twelve Bostons to St. Omer. On the return trip, the Spits picked up the bombers coming back from Lille.

Sixteen heavy bombers flew a diversionary mission.

Thursday, 21 January

The Combined Chiefs of Staff issued their CCS 166/1/D, better known as the "Casablanca Directive," for the bomber offensive from the United Kingdom. It aimed for

> the progressive destruction and dislocation of the German military, industrial and economic system and the undermining of the morale of the German people to a point where their capacity for armed resistance is fatally weakened.

Primary objectives for the time being were:

1. German submarine construction yards.
2. German aircraft industry.
3. Transportation.
4. Oil plants.
5. Other targets in enemy war industry.

At the Casablanca Conference, the whole matter of daylight bomber raids was discussed and the value of it questioned in both British and American circles. The British had always stuck to the opinion that the daylight bombing assaults had to result in prohibitive losses while a much more valuable contribution to the all-out effort could be provided by joining the British in their night assaults. General Eaker, sent to the Conference by General Arnold, defended the strategy of continuing daylight raids and one of his successful achievements was a directive that called for a combined day-and-night offensive by the strategic bomber forces of both the USAAF and RAF respectively.

Friday, 22 January

Spitfires of the 4th Fighter Group escorted twelve Bostons to St. Omer when German fighters appeared to intercept the formation. In the ensuing dogfights, four FW–190s were claimed to be shot down over the Channel.

Saturday, 23 January

Fifty-four heavy bombers of the 8th Air Force headed out for an assault on the Lorient port and the submarine base at Brest. The Luftwaffe fighters were ready to meet the bombers, and this time they tried out another tactic—a simultaneous attack from both sides and from above the formation, obviously in an attempt to disperse and confuse the defensive fire. The trick paid off, and four Fortresses of the 303rd Bomb Group plunged earthward. A fifth B–17 of the same group was shot down by flak.

Another victim of flak was a B–17, which had only one engine running by the time it reached the English coast. The Captain ordered his crew to bail out, and managed to land the bomber in a small field at Dawlish. This bomber would return to its base in two weeks, during which time, contrary to the usual procedure, the aircraft was put in flyable condition on the spot. In the meantime, an improvised 2250-foot-long runway was made from which the B–17 could take off again.

Wednesday, 27 January

Soon after dawn, heavy bombers of the 1st and 2nd Bombardment Wings of the 8th Air Force flew in tight formations on a northeasterly heading across the North Sea. The bombers winged across the outer defenses of the Frisian Islands on their way to their first target in Germany.

The primary target was Vegesack on the Weser; however, en route the weather conditions grew worse and worse, and 53 heavies turned to Wilhelmshaven.

Above the Frisian Islands, some light flak was thrown up, which grew in intensity as they neared the target port.

The bombers flew at 25,000 feet, and leading the formations was the 306th Bomb Group. In the lead aircraft was Colonel Frank Armstrong, who also had flown in the lead aircraft on the first mission of the 8th to Rouen.

The target was not only obscured by a thin layer of overcast, but also by a smokescreen. Flak over the target was ineffective and generally inaccurate. The bombs were dropped over the dock area through gaps in the clouds. Two Fortresses, unable to drop their bombs on Wilhelmshaven, delivered their load on Emden on the return flight. Results of the bombing were uncertain because of frozen bomb release mechanisms and frozen cameras.

The German fighters were up in force, but their attacks were not as effective by far as those encountered by the more experienced Luftwaffe pilots over France. For the first time, twin-engine aircraft were observed, although they didn't attack.

A force of 27 B-24 Liberators of the 44th Bomb Group made a navigational error and the men were unable to locate their target, Wilhelmshaven. The Luftwaffe traced the bombers and sent one down over Terschelling. A Focke Wulf was fatally hit by the Liberator gunners and the fighter crashed into another B-24, both aircraft going down. A few minutes later, a FW-190 was sent down, to dive straight into a small village.

From this mission, two Liberators and one Fortress failed to return. Seven German fighters were claimed by the gunners of the bombers.

January 27, 1943. The *Eight Ball,* just arrived at her base at Molesworth after her first mission to Germany. (Official USAF Photo)

29

2

FEBRUARY

Tuesday, 2 February

Bombers of the 8th Air Force set out to visit the marshalling yards at Hamm, however, they encountered such poor weather that all returned before reaching the target. These abortions occurred many times, and it had a frustrating and demoralizing effect on the crews.

Thursday, 4 February

Eighty-six heavy bombers of the 8th flew in combat formation over the North Sea. Briefed for an attack on the marshalling yards in Hamm, the bombers took a southerly course upon crossing the north German coast, thus shortening their stay over hostile territory.

Once again, heavy clouds prevented the execution of the intended assault and the bombers turned to Emden instead. Here 39 Fortresses dropped their loads, while the others attacked a convoy just off the coast.

The formations became somewhat separated and the intercepting German fighters took their toll. For the first time, twin-engine Me–110s and Ju–88s joined the Me–109s and FW–190s in the battle. One FW–190 slammed head-on into a Fortress of the 305th Bomb Group. In all, five bombers went down, four of them shot down by the German fighters.

Sunday, 14 February

Another attempt was made to strike on the marshalling yards at Hamm, and again the city escaped a treatment by the 8th Air Force because the 74 bombers ran into heavy cloud conditions, whereupon they aborted the mission at the enemy coast.

Monday, 15 February

Twenty-two B–24 Liberators left the English coast behind when they set course to Dunkirk to carry out an attack on the German raider *Tojo*, which was reported to be in dock there.

Led by the 67th Squadron of the 44th Bomb Group, the Liberators started a long, straight approach to their target to make sure that the eggs were delivered with the utmost accuracy. This undoubtedly also helped the German anti-aircraft crews to make accurate calculations in preparation of the most effective reception. Moreover, the Germans may well have been on the alert already because of an attack by RAF Bostons in the morning.

At 1540 hours the leading aircraft dropped its bombs, followed by the others. But the flak opened up and the entire nose-section of the lead aircraft was shot away and with it, the bombardier and navigator. For several moments the bomber continued its flight, but then it rolled over and started a steep dive during which the right wing came off. An explosion tore the big bomber to pieces. Another B–24 was struck by the debris of the exploding aircraft, yet the pilot managed to put the bomber down on Sandwich Flats at the English coast. German fighters picked off another Liberator after it had already been crippled by flak.

To make things even worse, the *Tojo* escaped to live another day.

Tuesday, 16 February

Eighty-nine heavy bombers neared the French coast for a renewed visit to St. Nazaire, or "Flak City" as it was called by the crews. And again, as the bombers arrived, the city lived up to its evil reputation. And it was not merely the flak that was notorious, but also the skill of the fighter pilots of JG 2 and JG 26. Upon arrival the bombers had to face both hazards.

Sixty-five bombers struck the target, yet the chief objectives, the U-boat basin locks, were completely missed. Eight heavies went down, and thirty others were damaged.

For one instant, the pilot of one of the B–24s lost control of his plane, but it was sufficient to have it collide with a Liberator flying below. Both aircraft exploded and the pieces of both aircraft whirled through a formation of Fortresses.

Friday, 26 February

After following a northerly course, the heavies of the 8th turned to Bremen; however, on arrival near the target area, they found it completely covered by an overcast. Course was set to Wilhemshaven, which city was in the clear. But it also meant a longer flight over enemy territory, and the Germans were well prepared to challenge the intruders. Even fighters from bases as far south as Flushing were called to the scene.

New defensive techniques were tried out and the bomber crews realized that the Germans were going to try every means to destroy their opponents. High-explosive charges attached to parachutes were fired in the path of the bombers by anti-aircraft guns, obviously also intended to unnerve the pilots and to have them break up their formation.

An Me–109 was reported attempting to drop bombs on the B–17s (a similar attack had been reported on the St. Nazaire mission of the 16th). Seven bombers were shot down, including two Liberators of the 44th Bomb Group, though the group that suffered most was the 305th Bomb Group, which group also lost the only bomber to fall victim to the flak.

Wilhelmshaven received the 150 tons of bombs destined for Bremen from the 63 bombers that arrived over the city.

Spitfires of the 4th Fighter Group escorted twelve RAF Venturas when they were out to attack a German raider off Dunkirk.

Saturday, 27 February

Very efficient fighter cover by Spitfires of the RAF contributed to the safe return of the 8th Air Force bombers, attacking the U-boat base at Brest with a force of sixty aircraft.

The Germans successfully employed a new trick in sending a recall radio message to the bombers. One flight of bombers already nearing the target, actually returned on this fake message.

The same German raider that was attacked the previous day received a new treatment under the watchful eye of 4th Group Spitfires.

3

MARCH

Thursday, 4 March

At dawn, the bombers of the 8th Air Force set out to the marshalling yards at Hamm. To confuse the enemy defenses, a northeasterly route was maintained as if Bremen or Wilhelmshaven were going to be the targets.

Fourteen B–24 Liberators flew a diversion. They followed a similar route but for a longer distance, at the same time looking for shipping targets.

Some fifty miles off the English coast, the Fortresses took a southeasterly course and crossed the Dutch coast. Above Holland, the weather thickened and the bomber groups became separated. The 306th Group abandoned the mission and returned to England. Two groups, the 303rd and the 305th, turned south and came upon clearer skies whereupon they decided to go to Rotterdam. 28 bombers dropped on the shipbuilding yards.

One group of fourteen Fortresses of the 91st, flying above the clouds, found itself out of visual contact with the other groups, but because of dense contrails all over the sky, the men believed the other formations to be still ahead of them. However, when visibility improved and the vapor trails disappeared, it was clear to the formation leader, the 22-year-old Major Paul Fishburne in *Chief Sly II,* after scanning the sky without seeing a single trace of any group, that he was all alone with his small group of Fortresses. Under these circumstances, it would have been fully justified to turn back, but Fishburne decided to continue on to the target and, out of the force of 71 heavy bombers dispatched, only his small force headed forward into Germany.

He soon broke into clear weather. The Germans had obviously not expected the Americans to fly through the cloud banks and only when the bombers neared their target were the first signs of the German opposition encountered. But this could not prevent the little force from making an excellent bomb run. A flak barrage was thrown up, but it was on the return trip that the Germans were fully alerted. Luftwaffe fighters rushed to the B–17s and they attacked with a vengeance. The bombers were outnumbered by a ratio of 5:1 and they had to sustain attacks from between 10 and 2 o'clock.

Experiences like these made it clear to air force leaders that small formations had only a small chance of survival once they tried a deep penetration into enemy territory. Four B–17s were shot down. One of them, with three engines dead, tried to reach the English coast. It didn't make it, and ditched into the North Sea. The impact was so heavy that the bomber broke into four parts. Both pilots and the ball-turret gunner drowned. The seven other crew members were picked up by a British minesweeper.

Saturday, 6 March

Sixty-three heavy bombers arrived over the port area of Lorient. Exceptionally clear weather enabled the 8th bombers to strike with good results. Heavy flak brought down three bombers.

A diversionary sweep was carried out by fifteen Liberators. With a heavy Spitfire escort, they turned to the U-boat base at Brest. The fighters were usually placed in a position to defend the bombers from head-on attacks, while the rearward defence of the bomber formations was the responsibility of the bombers.

March 6, 1943. B–17 Fortresses deliver their payload on Lorient. (Photo Imperial War Museum, London)

34

Monday, 8 March

The railway yard at Rennes was cut at both ends after 67 B–17 Fortresses had dropped their load. Rail communications with the Brest peninsula, and in particular with the submarine bases, were seriously disorganized, Rennes being the strategic key to the whole railway network of Brittany. On the credit side were the nearly 300 civilian casualties.

With the main force of Fortresses heading for Rennes, sixteen B–24 Liberators set out to the railyards at Rouen. Escort was furnished by Spitfires of the RAF plus two squadrons of the 4th Fighter Group.

Luftwaffe fighters appeared and their attack was well planned and well executed. Near Rouen, the fighters of JG 26 deliberately jumped on the escort. With their Spitfires embroiled in a violent battle with the German fighters, the Liberators continued to the target and started the bomb run. A formation of FW–190s approached swiftly, making a head-on pass, and in a single pass the lead bomber was hit and plunged down in flames, followed by his number two. In the ensuing confusion, the other bombers scattered their bombs as far as ten to fifteen miles from the target. Both aircraft shot down were from the ill-fated 44th Bomb Group.

The first medium bomber group, the 322nd, arrived at Great Saling. The group was equipped with the B–26 Marauder, and it formed the first unit of the 3rd Bombardment Wing of the 8th Air Force. They were to practice low-level attacks.

Wednesday, 10 March

For the first time, P–47 Thunderbolts took off from Debden for their first operational sorties. The fourteen Thunderbolts of the 4th Fighter Group took part in a fighter sweep over Walcheren.

Trouble with the VHF radios had already considerably delayed the delivery of P–47s and on this mission, flying at about 30,000 feet, intercommunication was made virtually impossible by radio interference caused by the 2000 hp engines. For successful fighter tactics this problem had to be solved, and it was not to be until 8 April that the P–47s came into action again. Luckily, no German aircraft were met on this mission, and the Thunderbolts took a course home from Dunkirk.

Friday, 12 March

The 8th Air Force dispatched 72 aircraft to bomb the marshalling yards at Rouen. Sixty-three heavies made an attack and dropped their loads on the yards. All bombers returned to their bases.

Eighteen bombers flew a diversionary sweep.

Saturday, 13 March

Eighty heavy bombers were briefed to bomb the marshalling yards at Amiens. Forty-four aircraft actually dropped their bombs on the yards, while thirty others turned to targets of opportunity, including the Abbeville/Drucat airfield.

Sixteen Bombers were out on a diversion mission. Again all bombers landed back at their bases.

Thursday, 18 March

In a clear sky with unlimited visibility, 97 bombers of the 8th Air Force droned along a carefully planned course to avoid the Frisian Islands as they headed to the Bremer Vulkan Schiffbau at Vegesack. Seventy-three B–17s and 24 B–24s, with the Liberators trailing some 2000 feet below the Fortresses, were near Heligoland when the German fighters made their appearance. A running fight developed all the way to the target and again on the return trip, some fighters following the bombers sixty to eighty miles beyond the coastline.

The leading force was the 303rd Bomb Group. As soon as it started the bomb run, heavy and accurate flak was met. Bombing was done by squadrons, and when the bombardier of *The Duchess,* leadship of the 359th Squadron, was less than a minute from his release point, he was mortally wounded by a shell exploding near the nose of the bomber. Yet he managed to crawl back to his bombsight and dropped the bombs with the other aircraft of the squadron releasing on his aim. For his exploit, the bombardier posthumously received the Medal of Honor, the highest decoration for bravery in the US, and the first to go to an 8th Air Force crewmember.

The Liberators of the 93rd Bomb Group, flying near Heligoland, formed an attractive target for the German fighters, and one B–24 was shot down. It was the group's first mission after their stay in North Africa, where they lost eight bombers. The 93rd Group received the title "Ted's Travelling Circus" because of their employment in various roles and theaters.

For the first time a new device was used, the automatic flight control equipment (AFCE), which enabled the bombardier to fly the aircraft on the bomb run by linking up with the automatic pilot. The accuracy of the bombing was appraised highly; however, from the air the results were highly overestimated as were the interpretation reports, both failing to measure the quality of the destruction, although they were accurate enough to identify the points of damage inflicted. (This can be said of the entire effort against the building yards during the first half of 1943.)

Two bombers were lost. Not *The Duchess,* for this Fortress even survived all the bitter struggles in 1943, and she would be retired after 59 missions.

Monday, 22 March

Eighty-four out of the 102 dispatched by the 8th Air Force struck the U-boat yards in Wilhelmshaven. The German fighters were up, and again they tried the tactic of air-to-air bombing.

It was near Heligoland that an Me–109, piloted by Lt. Heinz Knoke, dropped a 500-pound high-explosive bomb from an altitude of 30,000 feet on a Fortress formation. The bomb exploded in the middle of the formation. The wing of one of the Fortresses was torn off and the bomber tumbled down to crash into the sea.

The 93rd Bomb Group commander, Col. Timberlake, had a narrow escape when a cannonshell missed his head by barely six inches.

The other Liberator group, the 44th, lost one aircraft, shot down by flak near Wilhelmshaven. In all, three bombers failed to return from the mission.

Sunday, 28 March

The marshalling yards at Rouen were again subjected to attacks by the 8th Air Force bombers. Seventy heavies dropped their bomb loads. One bomber didn't make it home.

Wednesday, 31 March

The 8th Air Force dispatched 102 bombers to fly a mission to Rotterdam. Only 33 aircraft carried out an attack on the shipyards. Luftwaffe fighters took the air to intercept the American bombers. They kept on coming until the bombers neared the British coast. One heavy bomber was lost.

4

APRIL

Thursday, 1 April

The 4th Fighter Group flew fourteen sorties with the Spitfire on a patrol along the coast. It was their last mission with the Spit; from then on they would exclusively fly the P–47C Thunderbolt. The group was allowed to keep one Spitfire.

Sunday, 4 April

The 8th Air Force set out on a mission to the Renault motor factories at Billancourt. Leading the bomber formations was the 305th Bomb Group. Ninety-seven fortresses assembled at 5000 feet after the first plane took off at 1100 hours. It took two hours before the four groups left Beachy Head behind on a steadily climbing course, until they crossed the French coast near Dieppe at an altitude of 25,000 feet. Spitfires rode along with the bombers.

Even when the bombers reached Paris, there was still no sign of the Luftwaffe and the 305th Bomb Group, the first to arrive over the target, could pick out the factory undisturbed. Only moderate and inaccurate flak was thrown up. Smoke towered up to some 4000 feet when at least nineteen factory buildings were hit by bombs of the 305th Group. Eighty-five fortresses dropped their bombs, and when the last B–17 left the target area, 81 of the 251 tons of high explosives had descended on the factory, denying to the Germans approximately 3075 trucks (according to German documents).

Over the target, the bombers were without escort and they were only five minutes out on their homeward flight when the Luftwaffe appeared: 50 to 75 FW–190s came rushing in, making coordinated frontal attacks by

38

waves of four to seven aircraft. Intervals of 1000 to 1500 yards between waves gave the bombers no chance to reposition after evasive manoeuvering. The Germans concentrated on the low squadron of the leading 305th Group. And although *Dry Martini 4th* bore the brunt of the initial successive attacks, the Fortress survived, but three other B–17s from the same squadron were less fortunate and went down. The air battle raged for fifty minutes and cost the 8th four bombers.

Monday, 5 April

One hundred four heavy bombers were dispatched to fly a mission to Antwerp to bomb the aircraft factories in the city. Just before they reached the target, the Focke Wulfs of JG 26 arrived on the scene and started their head-on attacks. This time it was the 306th Bomb Group on which the Germans concentrated their attacks and four Fortresses went down.

Eighty-two bombers managed to attack the target; however, not only the target was hit. Many bombs descended on a village which was heavily struck.

One of the Fortresses seriously damaged by cannon fire carried Brigadier General Frank Armstrong, flying as an observer. But this Fortress returned to its base. Hauptmann Fritz Geisshardt, Commander of III JG 26, a very successful and skilled fighter pilot, was mortally wounded in this battle.

Thursday, 8 April

Two new P–47 Thunderbolt groups, the 56th and 78th Fighter Groups, joined the 4th Fighter Group on operational status. The first operational mission was a sweep over the Pas de Calais area. Led by the experienced 4th Fighter Group, the 24 Thunderbolts flew at an altitude of 30,000 feet without getting the sight of an enemy fighter. Not even flak was met, and all aircraft returned safely.

Tuesday, 13 April

Thirty-six P–47 Thunderbolts from two squadrons of the 4th and one mixed squadron of the 78th Fighter Group took off to fly a sweep over northwestern France in company of a strong force of RAF Spitfires. It was early afternoon when the Thunderbolts flew at 30,000 feet, proceeding to St. Omer. There was, again, no sign of enemy fighters or flak.

Yet one Thunderbolt did not return to the base. Engine failure forced the pilot to bail out. RAF Air-Sea Rescue was quickly on the spot and picked up the pilot some twelve miles northeast of Calais. Four pilots of the 56th Fighter Group had joined the 4th Group in order to get experience.

39

In the evening, the Thunderbolts took the air again to pay a visit to the French coast. Twelve aircraft from each group assembled over Debden. En route, the commander of the 56th Group, Hubert Zemke, got oxygen regulator trouble and he was forced to turn back. His deputy, Major David Schilling, took over. This time, only slight flak was encountered, but again no sign of the Luftwaffe.

Over Dunkirk at 31,000 feet, one 56th Group Thunderbolt was in trouble when the engine quit, but the pilot managed to glide across the Channel to make a successful belly-landing in England.

Again, a large force of RAF Spitfires accompanied the inexperienced American fliers.

Thursday, 15 April

The sun was already low on the horizon when sixty Thunderbolts of the three fighter groups crossed the French coast on an evening mission. Some confusion arose among the 56th Group pilots when they mistook a large formation of fighters coming in from the east for Focke Wulfs, until the white recognition bands showed that they were Thunderbolts of the 4th and 78th Fighter Groups.

Two P–47s of the 4th Group had been forced to turn back due to mechanical failure. The remaining ten aircraft, heading the sweep, were led by Major Donald Blakeslee, a former Eagle Squadron pilot. Near Flushing, the Thunderbolts spotted three Focke Wulfs flying at 10,000 feet, and Blakeslee led his flight into the attack. One FW–190 dived away, a manoeuvre the Germans still had to learn never to do in front of a Thunderbolt. The heavy P–47 easily caught up with the German fighter and after a few bursts the Focke Wulf dived straight into the outskirts of Ostende. One more Focke Wulf was destroyed by a 4th Group Thunderbolt, whereas, also, one of their P–47s was shot down.

And this was not the only Thunderbolt that failed to return. Two others were forced down due to engine failure, a common feature in the Thunderbolts' early days, happening with discouraging, though decreasing, frequency.

At this time, the P–47 still had no auxiliary fuel tanks and its range was not much further than that of the Spitfire. Only in May would extra tanks be fitted, and by that time the P–47 could be shared among the long-range fighters.

Friday, 16 April

The 8th Air Force bombers were sent out again, and, of the 83 dispatched, 59 attacked the port area of Lorient. The 305th Bomb Group, especially, demonstrated accurate bombing. The Fortresses of the group severely hit a dock power station in spite of a dense smokescreen laid to hide the target. Luftwaffe fighters rushed to the bombers and the 91st Bomb Group took most of the punishment. One bomber went down.

Meanwhile, a force of fifteen B–24 Liberators turned to the port facilities at Brest. Fighters of JG 26 closed in from the rear of the formation and three bombers were knocked down by the Focke Wulfs.

Saturday, 17 April

The largest formation of 8th Air Force heavy bombers to date was crossing the North Sea, flying in two combat formations. Each formation comprised three group boxes of 18 to 21 aircraft. Course was set to Bremen where the bombers were going to deliver a blow to the Focke Wulf aircraft factories. Leading the force of 115 Fortresses was the 91st Bomb Group with the 306th Bomb Group in the low position. The top of the leading box was composed of aircraft from different groups. The vertical distance between the highest and the lowest elements was 3000 feet.

Still over the North Sea, a German plane spotted the bomberstream, so the German Fighter Control got an early warning of their position, altitude, and course, almost one hour before the bombers reached the coast.

The overwhelming German fighter assault started when the Fortresses neared their target. Wave after wave the Focke Wulfs flashed head-on to the bombers, blasting away at the first combat boxes. The fighter pilots were specially trying to shoot the formation leaders out of the sky, in which effort they didn't succeed owing to their, at this time, still poor markmanship, and also to the fact that the bombers kept their tight defensive formation.

Over the target, a murderous flak barrage greeted the bombers. The German fighter pilots totally neglected the flak and kept on hammering at the Fortresses. In spite of the harassing circumstances, the 91st and 306th Bomb Groups managed to place their bombs right on the target, though at a terrible cost. The entire low squadron of the 91st Group was destroyed: six bombers came down in the target area. The ill-fated 306th Bomb Group received another shattering blow: ten out of the sixteen aircraft were shot out of the sky.

Obviously, the more scattered formation maintained by the leading wing accounted in part for the fact that this wing suffered all the losses. During previous months, much thought had been given to the need for a compact formation and by this month, the 8th was able to fly a fifty-four-plane combat wing in such a way that any fighter coming in from the front was met by a solid wall of fire.

Half of the factory was destroyed by a large amount of bombs descending on the target. To the loss of sixteen Fortresses, an additional 48 bombers came back with damage in various degrees. One of the bombers that made it back again to England was the B–17 *Memphis Belle*.

Gunners of the Fortresses claimed 63 enemy fighters destroyed, but after the war, German records revealed that a maximum of ten fighters was possible.

During the first quarter of 1943, one-fourth of the total German fighter strength was located in Germany and the western front. During the second quarter, it would rise to one-third, and after that period it would further increase.

The increase in quantity and in effectiveness of the Luftwaffe fighter force made the need for long-range escort fighters urgent.

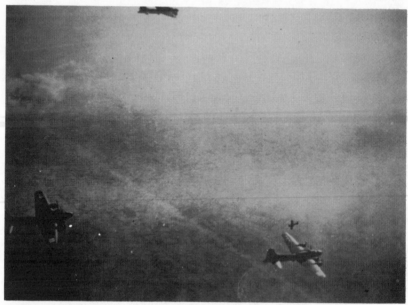

April 17, 1943. The air battle over Bremen. (Official USAF Photo)

Thursday, 29 April

Four more fightersweeps had been flown by the American P–47 groups during the last half of April and so far they had passed uneventfully. However, this day the Luftwaffe was alert.

The three fighter groups despatched 36 Thunderbolts each. The 4th and 78th Fighter Group returned without engaging the enemy. The 56th Group flew a sweep over the area The Hague–Woensdrecht-Blankenberghe at an altitude of 28,000 feet. The group passed Woensdrecht and then turned north. At that moment, the German fighters dived suddenly on the two low squadrons, and one Thunderbolt was sent into the ground.

The 61st Squadron, flying topcover, was called to assistance by the Group Leader Major Schilling, but he called in vain. Again there was no inter-communication possible.

Another Thunderbolt was so heavily damaged that the pilot bailed out over the Dutch coast. Two P–47s lost for no losses to the enemy was the sad picture with which the 56th Fighter Group had to turn home.

In most cases, the German fighters did not scramble when Allied fighters ranged overhead. They preferred to use their fighters against the American bombers, penetrating their territory in ever-increasing numbers.

The 8th Air Force had by this time six heavy bomber groups.

5

MAY

Saturday, 1 May

When the bombers of the 8th Air Force neared St. Nazaire they found the U-boat base covered by 7/10 cloud, which hampered accurate bombing considerably.

But this was not the only setback, for on the return flight the 306th Bomb Group made a gross navigational error which brought the group nearer to the French coast than the planned course indicated. Through a gap in the murk, they saw a landmark which they assumed to be Lands End. The Fortresses started their descent until heavy anti-aircraft fire made the crew well aware that they were far from their destination and that they were descending in the defenses of the Brest peninsula. They had to pay dearly for their mistake, and especially the 306th Group suffered heavily. Seven Fortresses were shot down.

Twenty-four Liberators flew a diversionary sweep.

Monday, 3 May

More than 200 Thunderbolts and Spitfires set out to fly a fighter sweep. They proceeded over a solid blanket of clouds as far as the eye reached. Not a single Luftwaffe fighter rose to challenge the invaders.

Tuesday, 4 May

For the first time Thunderbolts escorted the bombers when the 8th Air Force set out to attack the Ford and General Motors factories at Antwerp. Six squadrons of P-47s of the 4th and 56th Fighter Groups joined six squadrons of RAF Spitfires. The Thunderbolts provided high cover and withdrawal support.

44

Luftwaffe fighters rose to intercept the bombers. A Focke Wulf was shot down by the Thunderbolts while the Spitfires also sent one down and probably destroyed one other. Three Spitfires were lost and the one Thunderbolt that failed to return was probably a victim of engine failure. Sixty-five Fortresses out of the 79 dispatched were able to carry out an accurate attack, thanks to a diversionary force and also to the excellent fighter cover. All bombers made it back home.

Bad luck again for the 56th Fighter Group, giving withdrawal support. Over Walcheren they got the sight of an aircraft and in the supposition that it was an Me–109 the Thunderbolts attacked and shot it down. Alas, it was a Spitfire. Aircraft recognition was certainly a subject of which most American pilots knew not much more than that it existed.

Thirty-three bombers flew a diversionary feint over the Channel escorted by three Thunderbolt squadrons of the 78th Fighter Group.

After this mission more bomber groups would join the four pioneering Fortress groups on operations. Apart from the 92nd Bomb Group, which was back on operations after its commitment to training duties, four new bomber groups had arrived in England during April, while another seven Fortress groups were planned to arrive in the next two months.

Thursday, 13 May

Three new bomber groups, the 94th, 95th, and 96th Groups, were briefed to fly their first combat mission to the airfield at St. Omer. The 96th Bomb Group, already late in assembly, aborted the mission. They lost one of their aircraft over the Channel when it encountered mechanical failure. That left only 31 B–17s out of the 72 dispatched to proceed to the target.

Meanwhile, 88 bombers of the 8th ran into trouble when they were on the way to the aircraft factories at Méaulte. German fighters harassed the bombers all the way to the target and three heavies went down under their persistent attacks.

Thirteen RAF squadrons provided cover, while Thunderbolts flew 124 offensive sorties.

Friday, 14 May

Seventeen B–24 Liberators, loaded with incendiaries, followed in the wake of the 109 B–17 Fortresses, droning on across the North Sea toward the German North Sea ports. Course was set along the Danish-German border to upset the German defenses and, maybe, because of this, only light flak was met over the target, the shipyard at Kiel. The Luftwaffe fighters approached the bombers upon reaching the coast and it was again the un-lucky 44th Liberator Group that drew the heaviest German attacks. Flying below the low group of the second combat wing, the B–24s had to make a longer bomb run than the Fortresses, because their incendiaries made a shorter trajectory than bombs and had consequently to be dropped at a later stage. Heavily battered by the German fighters, the Liberators lost five of their number before even reaching the release point. Three Fortresses were also lost.

Hell's Angels was a Fortress that made it back, herewith completing its tour of 25 missions. The bomber would fly another 23 missions before go-ing back to the US on a stateside tour.

Two smaller forces made diversionary attacks to keep the German Fighter Command off balance. Thirty-eight B–17 Fortresses headed to a motor transport vehicle plant in Antwerp, while a force of 34 Fortresses turned to the fighter field at Courtrai, where hangars, dispersal areas, and runways were hit. 118 P–47 Thunderbolts of the 4th, 56th, and 78th Fighter Groups shepherded the bombers, flying at an altitude of 31,000 feet. Five miles from the coast the P–47s slid into battle formation, fanning out and taking a line-abreast position.

Near the target, the German fighters came rushing in. Yellow- and red-nosed Focke Wulfs became engaged in a violent battle with the Thunder-bolts, ranging from 24,000 feet to 20,000 feet. Three Thunderbolts were shot down. The Germans lost two FW–190s. Three Fortresses failed to re-turn from both missions to Belgium.

A few minutes before 1000 hours the first B–26 took off to start the first assault by Marauder medium bombers from the United Kingdom. The twelve Marauders of the 322nd Bomb Group headed for the electrical generating plant near Ijmuiden on the Dutch coast. The bombers crossed the North Sea a few feet above the wavetops to avoid radar detection and they crossed the Dutch coast near Leiden. Light flak opened up and one Marauder was hit in an engine, while part of the rudder was torn off. The pilot managed to keep his plane airborne and flew back to England, a fea-ture considered as quite an achievement with a Marauder.

Flying through heavy flak at 100 to 300 feet, the bombers arrived over the target at 1100 hours and dropped their 500-lb. bombs with 30-second delay fuses. However, not one of the bombs hit the plant.

Ground fire followed the bombers and all but one were damaged. Near his base, the pilot of one of the damaged bombers ordered his crew to bail out. Before the pilot could free himself from the aircraft, it dived into the ground.

Fighter escort was not provided on this mission since it was thought im-possible to give sufficient cover on such a low-level mission. No German fighters interfered, which was not surprising since the largest bomber force in the history of daylight offensives was in the air.

Saturday, 15 May

The growing strength of the 8th Air Force made it possible to concentrate with sufficient numbers on various targets at a time, which helped to confuse the defenses.

One hundred thirteen heavy bombers of the 1st Wing arrived over Wilhelmshaven. However, a solid overcast proved to be a better defense than anti-aircraft batteries and the bombers turned to secondary targets Heligoland, Düne, and Wangerooge Islands, where 76 bombers dropped their loads. It was here that the Germans started their interception and, in tenacious head-on attacks, they knocked five Fortresses down. One of them, *Spareball,* was shot down over Holland. The Germans lost at least eight Me–109s.

Eighty heavies of the 8th also found heavy clouds above their target, Emden, but through gaps 50 bombers were able to drop, resulting in widespread bombing. The only loss was a bomber that received a direct flak hit, causing it to explode.

The 78th Fighter Group lost one aircraft in a fighter sweep, when the engine of the P–47 quit over the Channel. The pilot was never found.

Sunday, 16 May

The 78th Fighter Group encountered the Luftwaffe when they were out on a fighter sweep. One German fighter was shot down.

Monday, 17 May

While the main force of 159 Fortresses of the 1st and 4th Wings headed for Lorient, 39 Liberators of the 2nd Wing made a 700-mile trip to Bordeaux. They flew the stretch at an altitude of 2500 feet to avoid the enemy radar. When climbing to bombing altitude, the lead aircraft developed trouble with one of the engines. It was *Suzy Q,* one of the last surviving aircraft of the original batch of bombers of the 44th Bomb Group. The group took part in this mission with 21 B–24s, while the other 18 were of the 93rd Bomb Group.

The bombers arrived over Bordeaux at an altitude of 22,000 feet. Only light flak was met and accurate bombing was possible. Considerable damage was inflicted in the port area. One bomber with mechanical trouble diverted to neutral Spain.

The bombers heading for Lorient ran into vicious Luftwaffe resistance. The leading 305th Bomb Group neared the Keroman submarine shelters when three Fortresses were shot out of the formation. Fifteen minutes later, the 4th Wing Fortresses arrived over the port area, where they received a murderous welcome from flak and fighters. Another two Fortresses went

47

down. But this could not deter the others from dropping and the bombs hailed down on the harbor installations and on a power station, which was hit.

One of the Fortresses that touched down at its base after the mission was *Memphis Belle*. She had completed the last mission of her tour and she was to be sent back to the States to be used as a morale booster.

Take-off was at 1056 hours and after assembling, the eleven B–26 Marauders flew without fighter escort at an indicating 210 m.p.h. across the North Sea at fifty feet above the water. The target was again the power station at Ijmuiden. Some thirty miles off the Dutch coast, one of the Marauder pilots reported that one of his generators was malfunctioning, whereupon he aborted the mission. On turning back, the Marauder climbed to 1000 feet and at this altitude the bomber was clearly visible on the radar screens of the RAF, so doubtless on the German screens as well. After crossing the coast, the formation was planned to split into two forces, six Marauders going to Ijmuiden and the other four were to head to a generating plant near Haarlem.

A navigational error caused the landfall to be made some thirty miles south of the planned crossing. A sudden change in course in southerly direction in order to evade a formation of German destroyers undoubtedly caused this error. This brought the formation over the mouth of the Maas, one of the most heavily defended spots in the Low Countries. Here Group Commander Colonel Stillman's B–26 received a hit that sent his plane down to crash in the dunes at Rozenburg. A moment later, flak brought the second Marauder down, which crashed into the Maas near Maassluis. The remaining Marauders droned on in a northeasterly direction, which meant that they were off-course.

With their leader gone, the deputy leader manoeuvred to a position to take control of the flight, but he collided with another B–26 which tried to evade the deadly flak. Both aircraft crashed near Bodegraven. Fragments of the wreckages of both aircraft hit the Marauder flying behind them and, heavily damaged, the bomber made a belly-landing.

The remaining five bombers ranged in confusion over the countryside and ran into the defenders of Amsterdam. They dropped bombs on a gasholder and then turned west. However, four of them were so badly shot up that they didn't come much farther than the coast before they crashed into the sea.

The only remaining Marauder hurried home, but some fifty miles off the Dutch coast the bomber was intercepted by three Me–109s, coming in from the front. The Marauder had no chance and crashed into the sea. It was from this aircraft that two surviving gunners were picked up by a British destroyer after five days of hardships in a dinghy. Twenty other crewmembers survived as prisoners of war.

48

After this mission, operations ceased for the 322nd Bomb Group for the first two months. As a result of the loss of this entire force, the USAAF would change their tactics of the medium bombers from low altitude to medium altitude (10,000–15,000 feet), out of range of automatic anti-aircraft weapons.

After training, combat missions would resume on 16 July.

May 17, 1943. The B–17 *Memphis Belle* and her crew have safely returned from the last mission of their tour. (Official USAF Photo)

May 17, 1943. The *Memphis Belle* in flight over England before returning to the United States on June 9, 1943. (Official USAF Photo)

49

Wednesday, 19 May

One hundred twenty-three heavy bombers of the 8th Air Force took a northeasterly direction, going to pay a renewed visit to Kiel. In the meantime, 64 heavies took a heading to the submarine yards at Flensburg.

The latter force was able to accomplish a very accurate bombing, unhindered by Luftwaffe fighters. Fifty-five Fortresses placed their bombs well within the assigned area and they returned without losses. The Luftwaffe directed its attention to the Kiel force, striking at the bombers shortly after they had dropped on the U-boat yards. The 305th Bomb Group, heading the formations, again bore the brunt of the German assault and four of its aircraft were destroyed. In all, six Fortresses failed to return from this mission.

Twenty-four B–17s flew a diversionary sweep to The Hague. Escorting Thunderbolts of the three fighter groups crossed the coastline near Ijmuiden, turned to The Hague, and then took a heading to the coast again. While crossing the coast, the Thunderbolts were jumped by four German fighters, but there were no losses on either side.

Friday, 21 May

The 8th Air Force dispatched two forces for an attack against Emden and Wilhelmshaven. The 1st Wing, with the 91st Bomb Group in the lead position, was on the way to Wilhelmshaven with a force of 77 Fortresses, while Emden was going to be visited by 46 Fortresses of the 4th Wing.

This time the Luftwaffe took the air to challenge both forces and the fighters concentrated on breaking up the bombing runs. At both the targets these tactics paid off. At Emden, the target even escaped completely unscathed, not only because of the successful German fighter attacks, but also because of the inexperience of the 4th Wing bomber crews. Five of its bombers were shot down.

Only a few German fighters were met by the bombers of the 1st Wing when they approached the German coast. But at the Initial Point, before turning to the target, some 40 to 60 German aircraft arrived and they took position with twenty to thirty fighters on each side of the leading bomber formation. Upon reaching the target, the German escort peeled off and the next moment they came rushing in on the bombers, head-on in waves of four, six, and eight planes at a time. Seven or eight separate attacks were made during the bomb run. Again, air-to-air bombing was tried by several aircraft. Some fighters used rocket-guns and large-caliber cannon. Seven bombers of the 1st Wing went down. Bombs were scattered over a wide area.

Thunderbolts of the 4th Fighter Group flew a sweep in the area of Ostende.

50

Thursday, 27 May

This time enemy action was not responsible for the disaster that struck the 95th Bomb Group. While loading bombs into a Fortress, several 500-pounders inexplicably detonated and within a second 18 men were killed, 21 seriously injured (one of them would die later on), and 14 were slightly injured. Four B–17s were completely destroyed and eleven damaged.

May 27, 1943. Beyond the wrecked QW–Q stood the B–17 that exploded. (Official USAF Photo)

Saturday, 29 May

A record number of 279 bombers was dispatched by the 8th Air Force to strike on targets in France. 169 Fortresses of the 1st Wing went for the U-boat base at St. Nazaire, while 38 B–17s of the same wing were on the way to the U-boat base at La Pallice.

Seventy-two Fortresses of the 4th Wing, accompanied by two P–47 groups, headed for the naval storage depot with connected marshalling yards at Rennes. This diversion force was the first to cross the French coast and the Luftwaffe was ready for the reception. Equipped with auxiliary fuel tanks, the German fighters flew along with the Americans until the Thunderbolts were forced to withdraw because of fuel shortage. From that moment onward, the Germans pressed home their head-on attacks. One B–17 of the 95th Bomb Group collided with another Fortress in the formation and both went down. Six bombers were shot down before the Spitfires of the RAF appeared near the coast to give withdrawal support.

51

With their auxiliary tanks empty, the Focke Wulfs and Messerschmitts flew back across Cotentin and ran into the Fortresses of the 1st Wing. The St. Nazaire force lost eight aircraft, including three B–17s of the 379th Bomb Group out on its first mission. All three were brought down by the notorious guns of St. Nazaire.

The Fortresses of the 1st Wing had a new breed in their midst. It was the YB–40, a heavily armed B–17. But as it happened, fighter opposition was moderate and seven of the flying dreadnoughts had little chance to prove their ability. However, a few aspects became all too clear. Due to the added weight in the rear section, the aircraft was tail-heavy. Even more troublesome was the fact that the heavy aircraft forced the formations to reduce speed after the bombs had been released in order to keep pace with the leading YB–40s.

Five new B–17 groups had become operational this month: the 94th, 95th, 96th, 351st, and 379th Bomb Groups. The new groups were organized into the 4th Bombardment Wing.

The first D-models of the P–47 Thunderbolt had arrived this month.

Hitherto the 8th Air Force had lost 188 heavy bombers.

May 29, 1943. P–47Cs of the 56th Fighter Group in formation over England. (USAAF Photo)

52

6

JUNE

Friday, 11 June

After ten days of bad weather over European targets the 8th Air Force was up again with a strong force. Still, no long-range fighters were available and to make matters worse, half of the bomber force had been operational for barely a month and could hardly be considered as experienced. 252 Bombers flew in a northeasterly direction, climbing for altitude as they took up a course via Heligoland to the submarine pens and docks at Bremen.

Through aborts, 218 B-17s were left spreading between 22,000 and 24,000 feet. Nearing Bremen they found their target obscured by clouds. 168 bombers headed for Wilhelmshaven and thirty went for Cuxhaven. German fighters appeared in force, but they waited until the bombers were near their target before starting the assault.

Upon starting the bomb run, flak opened up and the air commander, Chuck Marion, had both No. 1 and No. 2 engines of his B-17 knocked out. The German fighters started their coordinated head-on attacks. Their primary aim was to destroy the aim of the bombardiers. During the attack, at least three collisions were narrowly avoided. A Focke Wulf attempted to roll while passing over a bomber, but its wing chopped across the nose of the B-17.

The leader of the low group had one engine shot out; in fact, every plane in the lead squadron had at least one feathered propeller. As a consequence, the bombing accuracy at Wilhelmshaven was very poor: of the 417 tons dropped, only a few inflicted real damage but none hit the target, the U-boat building yards.

On the way back, a lone FW-190 deliberately rammed a Fortress head-on, instantly killing fighter and bomber crews. Seven out of the eight bombers lost were of the leading combat wing. One Fortress, named *Dangerous Dan*, was flown back and safely landed by the top-turret gunner on directions of the heavily wounded pilot, the co-pilot having been knocked unconscious by shell fragments.

Saturday, 12 June

8th Air Force fighter groups carried out two fighter sweeps and on both occasions they ran into the Luftwaffe fighters. During the first encounter the 78th Fighter Group claimed three enemy aircraft destroyed for the loss of two Thunderbolts. The second encounter brought the first air victory for the 56th Fighter Group. Flying a high-altitude sweep at 20,000 feet and cruising over Ostende, the Thunderbolts met twelve FW–190s and in the brief engagement one Focke Wulf was shot down.

Sunday, 13 June

Before this day was over, the 8th Air Force would lose 26 heavy bombers. A simultaneous attack on Kiel by the 4th Wing and on Bremen by the 1st Wing was planned in order to split the German fighter force.

Early in the morning the Fortresses of the 4th Wing took off. Eighteen aircraft of the 95th Bomb Group were leading the force. The commanding aircraft, with Captain H. A. Stirwalt at the controls, carried Brigadier General Nathan Bedford Forrest as an observer. When the sixty B–17s neared the harbor area and U-boat building yards, they found the Luftwaffe waiting. Me–109s, Me–110s, and cannon-firing FW–190s were thrown into the battle and, as usual, the first assault was against the leading formation. The first to go down with an engine in flames was the Fortress with the general, the first US general to be killed in action in Europe.

The attacks were pressed with vigor and tenacity, but the small force fought its way through the swarms of German fighters. One Fortress, totally out of control, smashed into another B–17. After bombing the target, the broken and scattered remnants of the force headed for home under constant fighter attacks. The 95th Bomb Group had its rows depleted by ten aircraft which left only six bombers to struggle back to England.

The 94th Group was only about thirty miles off the British coast and the crews were busy dismantling and cleaning their weapons in the assumption that their hardships were over, when all of a sudden, twelve black-painted Ju–88 nightfighters jumped the bombers and within moments nine Fortresses dived into the sea.

Of the sixty bombers that went out this morning, 22 failed to return.

Meanwhile 102 heavy bombers of the 1st Wing ran into very slight opposition. Flak was met and a dense smokescreen obscured the target at

54

Bremen. Four bombers were brought down. The inexperience of two of the seven groups participating may have contributed to the poor bombing.

At 0900 hours, Colonel Zemke took his 56th Fighter Group into the air for a sweep in the area Gravelines-Knocke. Flying at 27,000 feet, the pilots observed some twenty FW–190s, climbing from Ypres in a north-westerly direction.

At the head of a section of the 61st Sqadron, Zemke dropped down to attack the rear of the enemy formation at an altitude of 20,000 feet. In quick succession, he destroyed two Focke Wulfs; the third was shot down by 2 Lt. Robert S. Johnson.

Without a single loss, the 56th Fighter Group returned to its base.

Tuesday, 22 June

The 8th Air Force unleashed the first major attack of American daylight bombers against a major target deep in the heavily defended Ruhr area: the Chemische Werke Hüls, operated by I. G. Farben. 235 Fortresses of the 1st and 4th Bombardment Wing flew their usual route over the North Sea, as if bound for the north German ports. After about one hundred miles out, the bombers turned to take a southeasterly heading across Holland.

On this bright morning, the Germans crowded into the streets of Hüls to watch the large formations of planes, which they took for German because no alarm had sounded and no guns were firing. Within ten minutes, 186 people were killed and 1000 were wounded. 500 tons of bombs came down on the synthetic rubber plant, producing 30 percent of the nation's output. So effective was this bombardment that the entire plant was shut down for one month for repairs, although most of the damage was to buildings rather than to vital equipment. After the bombing swarms of German fighters appeared and in the ensuing battles sixteen Fortresses were lost.

The German fighter control was confused as a result of a bomber force approaching the southern coast of Holland. After crossing the coast, the bombers followed the southern border of the Wester Schelde, flying at an altitude of 23,000 feet. The primary task of this force of 42 B–17s of the 381st and 384th Bomb Groups, on their first combat mission, was to draw the German fighters away from the main force. Their target was Antwerp, where they were planned to attack the Ford and General Motors factories.

A rendezvous with Typhoons and Thunderbolts should have been made at North Foreland, but no fighter escort was in evidence. The only escort arrived about thirty miles west of Antwerp when the German fighters approached the bombers. They displayed their usual tactics and four B–17s were downed.

Above the target the bombers ran into heavy flak. Most of the thousand-pounders fell short of the target due to the inexperience of the bombardiers. On the way back, 23 squadrons of Spitfires, three squadrons of Typhoons and eight squadrons of Thunderbolts picked up the bombers for withdrawal support.

A force of twelve B–25 Mitchell bombers of the RAF, escorted by Spitfires, carried out a diversionary attack on Rotterdam. They drew the German fighters in that area, which were unable to refuel in time to meet the bombers of the 8th.

Twenty-one Fortresses of the freshman 100th Bomb Group made a diversionary flight over the North Sea, though they were too late to confuse the German controller.

Friday, 25 June

The heavy bombers of the 8th were unable to keep their tight formations when they tried to find their way through the towering banks of clouds that separated them from their primary target, Hamburg. Formations scattered all around the mountainous clouds. Some groups abandoned the mission and turned back to England with their bombs. Other groups dropped their load on targets of opportunity.

The German Air Force took advantage of the perilous situation and hunted after the ragged bomber formations and they managed to pick off 18 out of the 167 bombers ranging all over the area. American gunners claimed 62 German aircraft destroyed and, though this figure was likely exaggerated, it certainly gives an impression of the intensity of the various battles.

Late in the evening, the 93rd Bombardment Group departed with its Liberators to North Africa to take part in the planned operation against Ploesti.

Saturday, 26 June

In a clean, bright afternoon sky, a large formation of 246 heavy bombers proceeded to France. Flying at an altitude of 20,000 feet above the Channel, the pilots scanned the sky searching for their Spitfire escort but, although twenty squadrons were planned, none appeared. But the Luftwaffe did not show up either, until the bombers reached a point just south of Rouen. There the yellow-nosed Focke Wulfs of the "Abbeville Kids" came rushing to the bombers, concentrating their attacks on the low group of the lead wing. It meant that the unlucky 384th Bomb Group bore the brunt of the assault and five Fortresses would not return to their base at Grafton-Underwood. These five bombers made the total loss for the 8th Air Force.

At Poissy-sur-Seine, the formations broke into individual group units to

56

attack the Villacoublay Airfield in Paris. However, before the bombers reached their target, a large cloud darkened the sky over Paris and obscured the target. Only twelve B–17s dropped on an aircraft factory at Villacoubly and 39 bombers unloaded on Tricqueville Airfield. Another five dropped on targets of opportunity, and all other bombers turned on a heading to England without bombing.

Forty-eight P–47 Thunderbolts of the 56th Fighter Group took off at 1812 hours from a forward base to increase range. They headed out over the Channel for the continent to pick up the bombers for withdrawal support. Nearing Forges, it became clear to the Thunderbolt pilots that their big friends were in big trouble. They rushed to the scene and plunged into a battle that was going to range half-way across the Channel. But their eagerness to join in the combat was no sufficient substitute for their lack of experience, and when Goering's elite had to withdraw because they were out of ammunition and fuel, it was a battered 56th Group that turned back. Four P–47s were shot down, and five others were badly damaged. One of them was in such a bad shape that the pilot abandoned his aircraft over the sea.

One of the badly shot-up Thunderbolts was nursed back by 2nd Lt. Robert Johnson. Still over the continent, a Focke Wulf slid behind the tail of his fighter. The Focke Wulf had his cannon shells expended in the earlier battles, but still had plenty of 30-caliber bullets to pour into the Thunderbolt. Several times the German pilot pulled his plane alongside the P–47 to examine the damage, wondering how such a wreckage could stay in the air. He then manoeuvred his Focke Wulf behind the P–47 and started blazing away again, until he ran out of ammunition. For a while, both aircraft flew a tight formation; then the German fighter rocked its wings, accelerated and made a climbing turn back to the continent.

Johnson managed to make a safe landing at Manston. The German pilot was the successful veteran Oberst Egon Mayer of JG 2.

Meanwhile twelve Bostons of the RAF with Spitfire escort carried out an attack on the home base of the "Abbeville Kids."

Sunday, 27 June

The 44th Bomb Group of the 8th Air Force departed to North Africa to participate with its Liberators in the planned Ploesti raid.

Monday, 28 June

The 8th Air Force dispatched 191 bombers on a mission to the submarine pens at St. Nazaire. Led by the 303rd Bomb Group, 158 Fortresses carried out one of their most successful, and also one of their last, attacks against this notorious city. Thunderbolts accompanied the Fortresses. Eight B–17s failed to return.

A diversionary task force of fifty Fortresses was dispatched against the Beaumont-le-Roger Airfield at Brussels. The bombers took off at midday. The formation climbed to an altitude of 20,000 feet in a clear, blue sky, and proceeded to its Initial Point, where the bombers turned on a course that led them directly across the heart of the city in order to avoid the main flak area. One group erroneously dropped its bombs on a square park in the town. It so happened that the bombs descended on the adjoining building where German troops were housed, resulting in 1200 casualties among them.

After the bombing, a few German fighters appeared but they soon turned back. Thunderbolts picked up the bombers and escorted them home.

Tuesday, 29 June

A persistent heavy overcast kept the 8th Air Force from continuing to their assigned target, the Gnome-Rhône aero-engine plant at Le Mans. Only the 4th Bombardment Wing was able to pick out the target and of the 232 bombers dispatched only 74 Fortresses unloaded, with only a few of the bombs actually hitting the plant. Two B–17s dropped on targets of opportunity but all others, two forces, returned without bombing.

Wednesday, 30 June

The 389th Bomb Group was the last heavy bomb group of the 8th Air Force to depart to North Africa. Counting the Liberators leaving Portreath this day, the 8th contribution to the forthcoming Ploesti mission was 124 Liberators. However, before that mission would take place, many of the bombers would fly missions to Italian targets in connection with the Allied invasion of Sicily.

7

JULY

Thursday, 1 July

To house the steady flow of aircraft coming in from the United States, the number of airfields in the United Kingdom occupied by the 8th Air Force had increased to 58, and this figure would rise until the end of the year to 66 airdromes, occupied both by the 8th and 9th Air Forces.

Today command of the 8th Bomber Command was taken over by Brigadier General F. L. Anderson.

Thunderbolts of the 78th Fighter Group became entangled in a dog-fight with the Luftwaffe over Schouwen, Holland. The Americans claimed four German fighters shot down. One of their own aircraft was lost and this Thunderbolt took the group commander, Colonel Arman Peterson, down to crash near Ouddorp.

56th Fighter Group Thunderbolts passed over Rotterdam and then turned in a southerly direction. Near St. Omer, the pilots observed more than twenty Me–109s flying below them. However, their Thunderbolts were too low on fuel to take advantage of the situation, so they headed for home.

Sunday, 4 July

The first anniversary of American air operations against Germany was celebrated with a threefold attack on targets in France. 275 Fortresses were involved. 121 B–17s of the 1st Wing set out on a mission to the aircraft engine plant in Le Mans, where 105 of them dropped their loads. In spite of effective fighter escort, four Fortresses of this force were lost.

Seventy-one B–17s of the 1st Wing were dispatched to strike the S.N.C.A. de l'Ouest aircraft factory at Nantes. 145 tons of bombs were dropped by 61 bombers, scoring eighteen direct hits on the target from

25,000 feet: on a building only 650 square feet. German fighters rose to intercept the bombers and, in the ensuing battle, three Fortresses were shot down.

The third attack was made by 83 B–17s, dispatched by the 4th Wing. These aircraft turned to the stubborn U-boat base at La Pallice. Here one bomber went down. The Fortresses returned at mid-afternoon.

Thunderbolts of the 56th Fighter Group flew a patrol to Le Touquet.

Tuesday, 6 July

Thunderbolts of the 56th Fighter Group flew an uneventful patrol to Rotterdam.

Saturday, 10 July

In the hope that a break in the clouds would enable the bombers to deliver a blow against the major air depot at Villacoublay, the 8th Air Force sent 286 Fortresses to France. And as had happened so many times in the past, the forecasters had shown too much optimism. Only two groups were able to bomb: 34 Fortresses dropped on the airfield at Caen and 36 aircraft gave the airfield at Abbeville a treatment. All others delivered their loads in the Channel. Three Fortresses were lost.

Wednesday, 14 July

Once again the Fortresses of the 8th set out on a mission to the Focke Wulf workshop at Villacoublay, and this time they booked better results. 101 B–17s delivered a shattering blow to the factory. Luftwaffe reaction was as had been anticipated, and three Fortresses were shot down.

Le Bourget Airfield was visited by 52 aircraft at a cost of four B–17s.

Meanwhile 53 Fortresses headed towards the airfield of Amiens. Thunderbolts of the 78th Fighter Group shepherded the bombers. The Luftwaffe took to the air and soon thereafter the German fighters were embroiled in a violent battle with the Thunderbolts. Three of their Focke Wulfs went down, but the Thunderbolts lost an equal number. One FW–190 collided with a Fortress after a head-on pass, cutting off the propeller from the B–17's No. 3 engine. A wing of the fighter was knocked off and the Focke Wulf cartwheeled over the Fortress, heavily damaging skin and tailfin with the debris of the German fighter flying around. Miraculously, the Fortress stayed in the air and was escorted back to England by eight Thunderbolts. The bomber made a belly-landing at Manston. A gun barrel of the Focke Wulf was still embedded in the wall of the radio room. One

Fortress of the Amiens force failed to return, making the total bomber loss for the day eight aircraft.

July 14, 1943. The Focke Wulf assembly and repair shops at Villacoublay airfield after the Fortresses had paid their visit. Numbers on the photo denote hits on hangars *(1, 2,* and *7),* repair buildings *(3, 5,* and *6),* bomb and fuel storage areas *(9* and *4),* and heavy flak position *(8).* (Official USAF Photo)

Friday, 16 July

Four B–26 Marauder groups of the 3rd Bombardment Wing were on operational status now. One of these groups, the 322nd, resumed operations after the disastrous low-level attack on the 17th of May. The other three groups were the 323rd, 386th, and 387th Bomb Groups.

61

The crews had meanwhile been trained in medium-altitude attacks, employing an altitude of 12,000 to 15,000 feet. This would help greatly to improve the shaken confidence in the aircraft. Moreover, on missions to France and the Low Countries, the bombers would no longer be all by themselves, but sufficient fighter escort would be furnished.

Eighteen B–26 Marauders of the 323rd Bomb Group opened their new operational career with an attack on the marshalling yards at Abbeville. Sixteen of them dropped their bombs and, though the results made this bombing a far cry from a precision attack, there were no losses and that was an encouraging start. Yet in spite of ending the war with the lowest loss rate in an excellent service career, the reputation of the Marauder would remain doubtful. Flak was thrown up, and German fighters tried to interfere, but many squadrons of RAF Spitfires kept the enemy aircraft at a distance.

Saturday, 17 July

A record number of 332 heavy bombers headed toward targets in northwestern Germany. Weather en route was worsening, and most of the bombers decided to turn back. Twenty-one of them dropped their bombs on an aircraft factory near Amsterdam.

One B–17 was hit by flak and it soon started to lag behind the formation. An Me–109 spotted its prey and poured its fire into the Fortress, knocking out one of the only two engines which were still running. With no chance to reach the English coast, the pilot ditched his aircraft near the Dutch coast. An RAF launch managed to pick up the crew.

Only 34 Fortresses continued on to Germany where they attacked targets of opportunity.

Saturday, 24 July

The 8th Air Force heavy bombers had been grounded for one week because of bad weather over the occupied countries and Germany. For the last three months, murky weather had closed in northwestern Europe for most of the time. However, weather forecasters had promised this part of Europe would be in the clear today.

From three airdromes in England, 324 heavy bombers started their takeoff roll. With a 30-second interval, the heavies thundered along the runways and climbed into a solid overcast. Assembling was above the clouds and this always-complicated procedure was made easier by means of three beacons, the so-called splasher beacons (British medium-frequency radio stations).

Fifteen Fortresses failed to rendezvous on time, and returned. Three long columns of B–17s flew at below 500 feet to the departure point to start the longest American mission over Europe to date. The 1st Bombardment Wing was to fly a 1200-mile round-trip to the magnesium, aluminium, and nitrate works of Nordisk Lettmetal at Heroya.

The Fortresses of the 4th Bombardment Wing were out on a 1900-mile round-trip to the harbor installations at Bergen and Trondheim. These Fortresses were equipped with extra wingtanks. Heading the formations was the 384th Bomb Group. The North Sea was crossed at 2500 feet to be assured of the most economical fuel consumption. Over the Skagerrak, the Heroya-bound force climbed to bombing altitude at 16,000 feet, above a solid cloudcover at 10,000 feet. Well off the coast of northern Denmark, the smaller force, composed of the 4th Wing Fortresses, was on a northerly course to follow the west coast of Norway to Bergen and Trondheim. When the bombers arrived over Bergen, they found it completely obscured by clouds and, as the policy prescribed, no bombing over occupied countries in such a case was allowed. Therefore, no attempt was made to bomb. The 41 bombers arriving over Trondheim had a better opportunity to hit the target, and 79 tons of bombs descended on the harbor installations.

One hundred sixty-seven Fortresses droned on to Heroya above a solid cloud deck, stretching as far as the eye could see. As they came near the target, the bombers turned to start the bomb run and at that very moment they passed the edge of the cloud deck and from 16,000 feet up they could clearly distinguish their target. Bombs hailed down and 151 direct hits were placed, while 580 bombs came down within the target area. The nitrate plant was put out of use for at least three and one-half months. The still-unfinished aluminium and magnesium plants were abandoned for the duration of the war.

Moderate flak was thrown up and one B–17 of the 381st Bomb Group had to leave the formation. This damaged Fortress, *Georgia Rebel,* limped to Sweden, where she crash-landed near Vannacka. She was the first of nearly seventy B–17s to force-land in neutral Sweden before the war was over.

Only a few Ju–88s appeared on the return flight.

July 24, 1943. Fortresses of the 303rd Bomb Group flying over a solid undercast to their target in Norway. (Official USAF Photo)

July 24, 1943. Bombs on their way toward the important aluminium factory at Heroya. The target is indicated by a *broken white line*. (Official USAF Photo)

July 24, 1943. The end of the road for the *Georgia Rebel,* the first of nearly seventy B–17s to land in Sweden before the war's end. (Photo courtesy Swedish government)

Sunday, 25 July

In the early afternoon, large formations of the 8th heavies made for northwestern Germany where one combat wing from the 1st Bombardment Wing was going to the submarine construction yards at Kiel, while the other Fortresses of the 1st Wing carried their loads to Hamburg. B–17s of the 4th Wing were on their way to an aircraft factory at Warnemünde.

Cloud conditions not predicted by the forecasters caused many groups to drop on targets of opportunity. Only the Fortresses heading for Kiel were able to attack their assigned target in good visibility and 67 bombers dropped on the U-boat base.

The Luftwaffe rose in strength when the bombers neared Hamburg. The Luftwaffe pilots were longing for revenge after the RAF had started the battle of Hamburg during the night. A smokepall of some 15,000 feet still hung over the city to bear testimony to the horrors suffered by their compatriots.

Again the groups flying in the low position were in trouble and, from the 384th Bomb Group in the leading wing, seven Fortresses fell victim to the increasingly effective mass attacks of the German fighters. Nineteen

Fortresses were lost: fourteen shot down by the German fighters and five brought down by anti-aircraft guns.

These heavy losses were suffered in spite of diversionary missions flown by medium bombers of the 3rd Wing (8th Air Support Command) and RAF light bombers to targets in Holland, Belgium, and northwestern France. 218 Bombers out of 323 dispatched by the 8th Air Force made attacks on various targets; 68 of them dropped on Hamburg.

Foul weather conditions during the previous week had impeded the operations of the medium bombers; however, today favorable forecasts gave reason to expect a successful medium-level attack on the coke ovens at Ghent in Belgium by thirteen B–26 Marauders of the 323rd Bomb Group.

RAF Spitfires engaged the German interceptors and in the ensuing melee they lost four aircraft for one Me–109 shot down. However, the Marauders escaped unharmed, though the very poor bombing show left also the coke ovens practically unscathed.

The 322nd and 386th Bomb Groups flew a diversionary mission.

Monday, 26 July

A heavy overcast made assembling for the 303 Fortresses, dispatched by the 8th Air Force, a very hazardous affair and several groups were recalled. As a result, only 199 bombers climbed on a heading to Germany. One of the assigned targets was at Hannover, and two combat wings involving 92 Fortresses delivered 208.85 tons of high explosives and incendiaries on the two factories of the Continental Gummi Werke. Although considerable damage was done, with a consequent production loss, recovery would be rapid and it was not until March, 1945, that the plant would be completely knocked out of action. Twenty-one direct hits were placed on buildings, and a smoke column rose to just below the bombers.

German fighters reacted in force, delivering their main attacks as usual at the leading formations. One of the Fortresses of the 92nd Bomb Group, *Ruthie II*, was struck by a frontal attack of an FW–190, mortally wounding the pilot. The top-turret gunner, whose left arm was severed just below the shoulder, was pushed out of the aircraft via the nose door, after the navigator had adjusted the parachute. This saved the life of the gunner, who was directly taken to a German hospital. The co-pilot landed the aircraft at an RAF airfield.

Meanwhile, 54 Fortresses attacked the assigned targets at Hamburg and 53 B–17s turned to targets of opportunity. Twenty-four bombers were lost. Thirteen were shot down by German fighters, seven were downed by anti-aircraft fire, and of four bombers the cause of their loss was unknown. Again, no fighters escorted the bombers; only three heavily armed Fortresses (YB–40s) went along.

Diversionary flights were undertaken by Marauders of the 8th Air Support Command and by Bostons and Typhoons of the RAF. The airfield at St. Omer/Longuenesse was well cratered after eighteen Marauders of the 323rd Bomb Group had paid their visit.

Tuesday, 27 July

The 323rd Bomb Group set out on a mission to strike an enemy airfield and this time the airfield at Tricqueville was to be on the receiving end of the bombs, dropped by seventeen Marauders. Again, the bombers returned without loss, largely due to the excellent protection of RAF Spitfires. The Spits, on the other hand, became fully employed and this time they had more luck than on the 25th. Nine Focke Wulfs were sent down for the loss of one Spitfire. The pilot was picked up from the sea by Air-Sea Rescue.

Wednesday, 28 July

Two forces, altogether 302 heavy bombers, were dispatched by the 8th Air Force to carry out missions deep in Germany, to Kassel and Oschersleben. The objectives to be visited were the aircraft factories in these cities. The Oschersleben force was composed of Fortresses of the 4th Wing. The 94th Bomb Group was leading the wing and in one of its planes, *Sour Puss*, rode the commander, Colonel Frederick Castle.

The 120 bombers executed a feint by maintaining a course to the much-bombed coastal targets before turning in a southeasterly direction. They ran into adverse weather conditions and the formations became dispersed and, in consequence, they became very vulnerable to German fighter attacks. And the Germans were intended to hit hard this time, producing every device at their command, including aerial bombing, large-bore cannon, and the most threatening of them all: rockets. The battle raged chiefly in the Heligoland area. Fifteen Fortresses went down. One B–17 was hit and crashed into two other bombers, causing the destruction of all three.

Several formations turned back, more or less in confusion. In fact, only the 94th Bomb Group, with a few B–17s of the 96th, in all fifteen bombers, with thirteen Fortresses from the 388th Bomb Group in their wake, droned on into the heart of the Reich. The only chance of finding their target depended on finding a gap in the clouds. But luck stayed with the 94th and, through a small hole in the 9/10 cloud over Oschersleben, the lead bombardier recognized a crossroad a few miles from the aiming point. Although the bombs were dropped on estimated time of arrival, photos taken next day would reveal an excellent concentration of hits on the target, causing an estimated loss of production of approximately one month.

The 182 Fortresses of the 1st Wing met the same weather conditions as the bombers of the 4th, and their bombing results were generally ineffective. Me–109s intercepted a Fortress formation, firing rockets, which caused a lot of damage though all bombers stayed in the air, struggling on to reach the Dutch coast where they knew the fighter escort would take over. In all, 22 8th Air Force bombers failed to return.

One hundred five P–47 Thunderbolts picked up the returning bombers about 260 miles from the English coast at a point near Emmerich. The Thunderbolts were equipped with jettisonable belly tanks. The tanks were of the older type, 205-gallon tanks, which could only be loaded to half capacity and which were not to be used above 23,000 feet. But the tanks could take the Thunderbolts across the Channel and their appearance at a point thirty miles deeper in Germany than they had ever been, caught some sixty German fighters by surprise at the moment that they were launching heavy attacks against the returning bomber formations. The P–47s of the 4th Fighter Group destroyed nine German fighters for the loss of one of their number.

The YB–40 had meanwhile proved to be a failure. Being too heavy to climb or to keep speed with the standard B–17 it also could not justify its existence by the number of enemy aircraft shot down. Moreover, it was just as vulnerable as the other B–17s.

Marauders of the 323rd Bomb Group flew a mission to Zeebrugge, where the coke ovens were bombed. Meanwhile, the 322nd and 386th Groups flew a diversion to the A.G.O. Flugzeugwerke, producing FW—190s.

July 28, 1943. German soldiers guard this Flying Fortress of the 92nd Bomb Group that crashlanded near Hengevelde in Holland. (Photo from *Air Combat 1939–1945)*

Thursday, 29 July

After an abortive mission on the 25th, the Fortresses of the 4th Wing headed to Warnemünde again to bomb the Heinkel factories, also engaged in Focke Wulf production. This time they achieved better results and eighteen of the 27 buildings were blasted by excellent bombing of 54 Fortresses, being about half the force dispatched by the 4th Wing. Forty-eight of its bombers struck on targets of opportunity. The 1st Wing paid a renewed visit to the submarine base at Kiel and 91 Fortresses dropped 207.9 tons of bombs on the shipyard, which load was accompanied by 767,000 propaganda leaflets. Ten heavy bombers were lost, and in a fight with Focke Wulfs one Thunderbolt of the 56th Fighter Group went down.

For the fifth day in succession the Marauders of the 323rd Bomb Group set out on a mission. An airfield at St. Omer was bombed. All Marauders returned to their base.

Friday, 30 July

Early in the morning, 186 Fortresses climbed into a clear sky and, after assembling both wings, headed for the same target: the Fieseler aircraft components and assembly plant at Kassel. 134 bombers arrived over the city and dropped their load.

Heavy enemy resistance was encountered and twelve Fortresses went down. One of the B–17s, badly shot-up, with a large part of its tail section missing, miraculously managed to land in England with jammed throttles and a flat tire. It was the B–17 *Patches,* and this time *Patches* would not be patched anymore because more than a thousand holes were counted. Six of the ten men on board were wounded, including the pilot.

The P–47 Thunderbolts rendezvoused with the returning bomber force at Bocholt in Germany, just beyond the Dutch border. And as on the 28th, they surprised the enemy fighter force which had not yet become accustomed to fighter penetrations beyond the coastal fringe. One pilot of the 78th Fighter Group, Captain Charles P. London, destroyed two German fighters, bringing his total score to five which made him the first "ace" of the 8th fighter pilots. Major Eugene Roberts, commanding the 84th squadron of the 78th Fighter Group shot down two FW–190s and an Me–109 to become the first 8th Air Force pilot with three victories on a single mission. One hundred seven Thunderbolts were involved and the Germans again made the mistake of diving as an evasive action, which didn't work in front of a Thunderbolt.

Seven Thunderbolts were lost, whereas 25 German fighters were claimed to be destroyed, including five by the 4th Fighter Group. The 56th

Fighter Group came to grips with some sixty German fighters, mostly Messerschmitts, and, in violent dogfights ranging from 23,000 feet to the deck, the Thunderbolts destroyed three Luftwaffe fighters for the loss of two of their own.

One P–47 made its way home at zero feet. The fighter first encountered a locomotive which was shot up, and then a gun position west of Rotterdam was treated likewise. It was in fact the first strafing action of a Thunderbolt and it would not by any means be the last.

The 386th Bomb Group flew its first operational mission. Twenty-one Marauders were dispatched, but only eleven B–26s managed to bomb the airfield at Woensdrecht. The German fighters were determined to deal with the bombers and they dived through the Spitfire escort. One Marauder was shot down and seven others were damaged.

Saturday, 31 July

The 322nd Bomb Group set out on its first operational mission to an enemy target since their disastrous mission on May 17th. RAF Spitfires accompanied the Marauders when they headed for Tricqueville airfield. FW–190s tried to interfere. One of them was shot down by a Marauder gunner. Only three bombers were slightly damaged.

The 386th Bomb Group was going to visit Abbeville/Drucat airfield.

USAAF heavy bombers had dropped 50 percent more bombs in July than in June, yet their effective strength was down to 275 bombers at the end of this month. In six operations from 24–30 July, the heavy bomber force lost 88 aircraft; that was 8.5 percent of those listed as attacking or less than 5.3 percent of the planes dispatched. If only the targets in Germany are taken into consideration, these figures become even worse.

8

AUGUST

Sunday, 1 August

103 aircraft from the three Liberator groups, the 93rd, 44th, and 389th Bomb Groups, took off from their bases in North Africa to join the 76 B–24s of the 9th Air Force in a low-level attack on the oil refineries at Ploesti. Fifty-three bombers were lost; thirty of these were from the three 8th Air Force groups.

Monday, 2 August

The 8th Air Force sent two medium bomber groups to France to attack several airfields. Both the 322nd and 386th Bomb Group ran into the heaviest flak so far encountered and several Marauders were severely damaged but they all made it home.

Tuesday, 3 August

Major General William E. Kepner took over command of 8th Fighter Command.

Wednesday, 4 August

Thirty-three B–26 Marauders of the 322nd Bomb Group arrived over the shipyards at Le Trait to carry out one of the most successful attacks made so far by the medium bombers. Havoc was created against the installations, with nearly all bombs falling in the target area.

Monday, 9 August

The airfield at St. Omer/Ft. Rouge was again visited by the 8th medium bombers of the 322nd and 386th Bomb Groups. Adverse weather prevented good bombing and the aircraft became separated in the heavy clouds. One Marauder of the 386th Group encountered two Spitfires who had not been informed about the presence of a Marauder in that area, and the RAF pilots tragically mistook the bomber for an enemy aircraft and shot it down.

Sixteen P–47 Thunderbolts of the 353rd Fighter Group flew their first operational mission. The P–47s were accompanied by 32 Thunderbolts of the experienced 56th Fighter Group. In late evening, they made a sweep over Holland and Belgium, led by the renowned leader of the "Wolf Pack," Colonel Hubert Zemke.

Thursday, 12 August

The 390th Bomb Group made its maiden trip as part of a force of 243 heavy bombers, heading for targets in the Ruhr like Bochum, Bonn, Gelsenkirchen, and Recklinghausen. 131 Thunderbolts with auxiliary tanks slung under their bellies flew along the bomberstream.

However, weather intervened again and even where gaps were found in the heavy clouds, the targets were in many cases hidden behind a smoke-screen. Only two groups were able to bomb their assigned targets. Formations became separated and many bombers turned to targets of opportunity. Such circumstances always gave the Luftwaffe ample chances to raise their score considerably, and they were not going to make an exception this time. In fact, the 8th Air Force had to take one of the severest blows in its existence—25 Fortresses were knocked down.

Very heavy opposition was encountered by the bombers of the 1st Wing near Gelsenkirchen. The 384th Bomb Group lost five B–17s. Leading the force to Gelsenkirchen was a Fortress piloted by Major Theodore Milton of the 351st Bomb Group, and riding with him was Captain Clark Gable, taking films for use in a gunnery training film.

Enemy airfields were still on top of the target list for the medium bombers and today the Marauders went to Poix Nord.

Friday, 13 August

The three North African-based 8th Air Force bomber groups dispatched 69 Liberators to take part in a mission to the Me–109 plants at Wiener-Neustadt. Over the Adriatic, the trailing elements of the 9th Air Force abandoned the mission, so it became an entirely 8th Air Force affair.

72

Flying through heavy clouds, the bombers had to cover a distance of over 1200 miles. They achieved complete surprise, and the leading 389th Bomb Group saw no flak nor enemy fighters. Only the 44th Group encountered some German fighters making ineffective passes at the bombers, both over the target and on the return trip. They met only light flak. The target was severely hit, causing a loss in production.

Sunday, 15 August

To impede the movement of German troops into Russia and Italy, plan "Starkey" was designed to give the Germans the idea that an amphibious assault in the Pas de Calais area was impending. The 8th Air Force's contribution consisted of attacks in northwestern France, Belgium, and Holland. The objectives were mainly airfields, because in this way another very important object was served: the campaign against the Luftwaffe. Many novice crews took part in these operations, considered as "milk runs" in comparison to the penetration flights into Germany.

Escorted by Thunderbolts, 327 heavy bombers set out to airfields in France and Holland. 290 of them actually dropped their bombs. 91 Fortresses attacked Vlissingen, 56 Fortresses turned to Poix and Amiens, 61 B–17s bombed Vitry-en-Artois, and 82 aircraft delivered their load on Merville and Lille. Two Fortresses were lost.

Medium bombers of the 8th continued their attacks on enemy-held airfields, flying a mission to Abbeville and Woensdrecht.

Early in the morning, Thunderbolts were ranging in the Calais-Ypres area, sent out on a fighter sweep.

Monday, 16 August

The 8th Air Force bombers set off again to the French airfields. 169 Fortresses went to Le Bourget and 66 Fortresses were to carry their load to Poix and Abbeville. Thunderbolts of the 56th, 78th, 353rd, and 4th Fighter Groups furnished escort.

The 4th Fighter Group Thunderbolts took off at 0805 and climbed on a south by southeasterly heading. At 24,000 feet, they winged high above formations of Spitfires, also taking part in the mission. The Thunderbolts crossed the French coast near Dieppe and proceeded in the direction of Rouen. From here, they would go to Le Bourget to escort the Fortresses of the 1st Division over the target.

Near Rouen, the group became embroiled in a savage battle with the Luftwaffe fighters. Major Don Blakeslee led the Thunderbolts into the attack. The battle became an outstanding victory for the group: 18 German fighters shot down for the loss of only one P–47. Blakeslee ran into serious trouble when his damaged plane was chased by three Focke Wulfs. Lt. Goodson spotted the tight situation his leader was in and he managed to close in on the Focke Wulfs. The first fighter he sent down had its wing cut off at the wingroot and it spun into the ground. Goodson's fire sent the second FW–190 diving straight down. Only the earth was to stop the dive. Watching the Thunderbolts of Goodson and his wingman drawing near and aware of the absence of his two comrades, the remaining German pilot gave up the chase and disappeared. Blakeslee was escorted back to England by Goodson and his wingman, Wehrman. All three were very low on fuel but they managed to reach Manston.

The 353rd Fighter Group, having taken off with 44 Thunderbolts at 0826, had its first combat with the German fighters. The group lost its commanding officer, Lt. Col. Joe Morris, in the fight. It was the only loss for the 353rd, yet it was a severe blow to start with. Four heavy bombers failed to return from the mission.

The 387th Bomb Group was the fourth medium bomb group to join in the assaults on enemy-held territory. The Marauders delivered their bombs on the airfields at St. Omer, Bernay, and Beaumont-le-Roger.

Tuesday, 17 August

Hitherto, the 8th Air Force had flown 83 missions at the cost of 411 heavy bombers and more than 4000 crewmen. However, before this day was to pass into history, these figures would have increased considerably.

Mission No. 84 called for two aerial task forces to fly to two highly strategic targets. The 4th Bombardment Wing, with its longer-ranging B–17s, was to attack the Messerschmitt factory at Regensburg with seven bomb groups, involving 146 Fortresses. After bombing, they were to continue on in southerly direction to fly over the Alps, Italy, and the Mediterranean to land in North Africa. The 1st Bombardment Wing was to undertake a mission to Schweinfurt, where 230 Fortresses were to unload on the ball-bearing plants. After bombing, this force was to return to England.

The first to take off was the Regensburg force. Ground mists had delayed the departure, but at 0930 hours, two hours after take-off, the combat wings were assembled and heading out in easterly direction across the North Sea towards the Dutch coast. Leading the bomberstream was the 96th Bomb Group, and one of its bombers carried the Wing commander, Colonel Curtis E. LeMay. The two other groups in this formation were the 388th, in the low position and the 390th, flying in the high position, the latter with no combat experience.

Trailing this wing was the combat wing, with the 94th Bomb Group in the lead position and the 385th in the low quarters. The last formation of this force was composed of the incendiaries-carrying 95th Bomb Group, and the 100th Bomb Group, flying the low position.

Only a few patches of clouds and unlimited visibility were the excellent conditions in which the Fortresses were heading toward their up-to-this-date most distant target.

Two Thunderbolt groups, involving eighty-seven fighters, should have rendezvoused with the Regensburg force over the Dutch Islands. Only the 353rd Fighter Group arrived to take its position at 26,000 feet to shepherd the bombers of the lead formation. This left the rearmost boxes unprotected, which gave the German fighters the chance they were always quick to exploit. To add to the unfortunate situation, these last groups were trailing too far behind the lead formations. Hence the escorting P–47s were totally unaware of the mauling the Fortresses got some fifteen miles behind them. It was only when they turned back over Eupen at 1032 that they witnessed some Fortresses tumbling down, knocked out by the Focke Wulfs flashing head-on through the formations.

The Germans concentrated again on the low group. One B–17 of the 100th Group exploded in the air and, before the bombers changed course near Eupen, four B–17s had been shot down. The next course change was about twenty miles west of Kaiserslautern, and another three B–17s went down before this point was reached. From here onwards, a more direct course was flown to the target, and on this stretch seven more Fortresses were lost. A Fortress dropped out of formation, its wheels down to signify surrender, and, under the watchful eyes of three Me–109s, the bomber started its way down. The Germans obviously hoped to get a B–17 intact.

With their fuel tanks nearly empty, the Thunderbolts could make only a single pass at the German fighters. The Group commander sent an Me–109 down, the first victory for the 353rd Group. But there was no jubilation, because the P–47 pilots could only witness the slaughter of the Fortresses while they had to continue on to England.

The Germans kept on coming all the way to the target. After exhausting their fuel and their ammunition, they quickly landed to refuel and rearm.

The bombers passed Mannheim when the single-engine fighters withdrew. However, there was to be no respite for the bomber gunners, for the place of the single-engine fighters was taken by the twin-engine Me–110s and Ju–88s, some of them lobbing rockets into the bomber formations. The path of the Fortresses was marked by flames, smoke, debris of aircraft, parachutes, men hurtling through the sky, and the smoking remains of Fortresses and German fighters on the ground.

After 1½ hours of the most persistent and vicious attacks, the Germans withdrew. The bombers were near their target now, and the Messerschmitt factories were clearly picked out. When the bombers turned away from their target, a pillar of smoke rose from the Messerschmitt plant. Bombing was highly accurate and the plant was severely damaged. Unknown at this time was the fact that most of the fuselage jigs of the secret jet fighter, the Me–262, were also destroyed.

The German fighters were waiting for the return flight, but they waited in vain. Via the snow-capped Alps, and flying over Italy and the Mediterranean, the bombers landed in North Africa. The first B–17 touched down at 1728, after more than eleven hours in the air. Total losses suffered by this force were 24 Fortresses, of which number fourteen were lost by the rear combat wing, and of these fourteen, the 100th Bomb Group alone lost ten aircraft. Two B–17s had landed in Switzerland.

The lead position in the first task force heading for Schweinfurt was taken by the veteran 91st Bomb Group. Brigadier General Robert B. Williams flew the mission in one of its bombers as task force commander. The lead Fortress was piloted by the group commander, Colonel Wurzbach. By 1100, the ground mist had lifted and 230 B–17s, including spares to replace abortives, of the 1st Bombardment Wing were in the air.

Four squadrons (331st, 332nd, 403rd, and 421st) of RAF Spitfire IX's met the lead combat wing of the first task force north of Walcheren at 1336. Three RAF squadrons (129th, 222nd, and 303rd) picked up the second combat wing of the leading task force over Walcheren. The second task force was left without fighter protection.

East of Antwerp and near Neuzen, Thunderbolts relieved the Spitfires, but, from the area of Aachen onwards, the B–17s had to cope with the Luftwaffe alone.

The Spitfires made contact with the German fighters near Antwerp. That was where the Germans started their attacks, and the hordes of fighters the Germans sent up to encounter the Schweinfurt force more than justified the most ominous predictions. They used any device they could think of: dropping time-bombs into the formations, time-fused rockets from astern, and further, their whole scale of familiar tricks. They came down in vertical attacks from above, diving straight down at the bombers with fire concentrated on the vicinity of the top-turrets with effective results.

Again the trajectory was marked with metal and parachutes, and this time not only all the way to the target, but also the whole long way back. And again the low group received the brunt of the hammering. Eleven Fortresses of the 381st Bomb Group were shot down, while the leading 91st Bomb Group had its rows depleted of ten B–17s. Near the target the bombers were greeted with a hail of flak. Yet the bombing was good and the factory was plastered with explosives. However, the price was high: 36 Fortresses were shot down, which meant that the 8th Air Force was short sixty heavy bombers from this combined mission.

Thunderbolts of the 56th Fighter Group took off at 1530. The 51 aircraft retained their belly tanks after crossing the enemy coast to add another ten minutes, and they picked up the bombers fifteen miles past Eupen, at 1621. After taking position above the bombers, they were not kept long in uncertainty about the intentions of the Luftwaffe. When the German fighters started their head-on attacks, Hubert Zemke led his group in the battle against an enemy who was completely surprised by the presence of the American fighters so far inland.

On this occasion the 56th Group in fact started its fame as one of the highest scoring fighter groups in the European theater, which fame would last for the duration of the war. Many German fighters went down in front of the guns of the Thunderbolts, losing three of their number. The battle raged all the way to Antwerp, where the Spitfires took over the escort. One of the German fighter pilots shot down was Major Wilhelm Galland, a brother of the well-known General Adolf Galland.

The senior officers who joined the mission all survived to give testimony of the hazardous enterprise of flying bombers unescorted deep into the heart of Germany. It would take nearly a month before the 8th Air Force had recovered from its wounds and before another massive attack could be mounted. Research after the war revealed that the German losses were only 25 aircraft.

RAF Spitfire IX's of the 485th (New Zealand) and 341st (Fighting French) squadrons took off at 1000 to escort B–26 Marauders out on a mission to attack enemy airfields at the limit of their range in France and the Low Countries. Among the targets were Bryas-Sud and Poix; however, 10/10 clouds at 17,000 feet caused the diversionary mission to be cancelled shortly after rendezvous.

At night, German raiders attacked the 8th Air Force medium-bomber base at Boxted, home of the 386th Bomb Group. The living quarters was hit by a 500-lb. bomb, killing two men and wounding 29.

One B–17, equipped with an H2S installation, dropped two tons of bombs on Frankfurt. It was a trial attack and the first time that an 8th Air Force bomber released its load with the aid of radar equipment.

This same night, 597 heavy bombers of RAF Bomber Command climbed into the late evening sky for a long run to the Baltic coast to deliver the first blow to the new threat: the V-weapon production at Peenemünde. Since November, 1939, the British government had had reliable and relatively full information on German long-range weapon activity. In April, Duncan Sandys of the War Cabinet advised, after a careful study, that the threat from German "secret weapons" should be taken seriously. From May 1, 1943, until March 31, 1944, more than 1,250,000 aerial photographs were taken. WAAF Flight Officer Babington-Smith first identified the V–1 on a photograph taken of Peenemünde. As a result of the continuous reconnaissance of the installations there, it was decided to send a force of bombers to eliminate the danger.

Shortly after midnight, the attack started. In bright moonlight, 571 bombers dropped nearly 2000 tons of high explosives and incendiaries on the target. The whole bombing attack was controlled and directed by a master bomber, Group Captain J. H. Searby, who remained over the target in the most hazardous conditions. More than 700 persons at the station were killed, among them a most prominent rocket expert, Professor Thiel.

Though many buildings in which experiments were going on were completely wrecked, the efforts of the bombing on the development of the V-weapons proved afterwards to be much less than expected. The Germans were anyhow fully alarmed that from then on massive attacks could be expected to prevent the use of their new weapon. Forty bombers failed to return from the raid.

August 17, 1943. Germany's second largest aircraft factory at Regensburg is nearly obscured by smoke when Fortresses carry out their attacks. (Official USAF Photo)

Wednesday, 18 August

In the morning, Thunderbolts ranged over western Holland, making a fighter sweep. Medium bombers of the 8th attacked airfields at Woensdrecht and Lille. The 322nd Bomb Group made an identification error and bombed the wrong airfield.

Thursday, 19 August

In late afternoon, the 8th Air Force mustered 170 bombers into the air to strike airfields in Holland. Heavy overcast was met and many bombers turned back. 93 Fortresses continued on their targets and dropped a load on Gilze-Rijen and Vlissingen.

Fortresses of the 1st Bombardment Wing were escorted by Thunderbolts. Luftwaffe fighters put in an appearance near Woensdrecht and immediately became embroiled in a fight with the Thunderbolts. The 56th Fighter Group claimed nine German fighters. One of its Thunderbolts failed to return because of mechanical failure. Five Fortresses were lost.

B–26 Marauders turned to airfields in France and dropped bombs on Amiens/Glisy and Bryas-Sud.

Sunday, 22 August

Medium bombers of the 8th Air Force crossed the French coast setting out on their usual mission to enemy airfields in France. This time the target was Beaumont le Roger and hardly had the Marauders completed the bomb run when the German fighters tore into their formation. Again, the 386th Bomb Group bore the brunt of the attack. One Marauder was hit in the bomb bay and in one engine. Fire spread quickly and threatened to engulf the fuel tanks. The pilot kept control of the aircraft and put it into a shallow dive to enable his crew to bail out. Only four crewmembers had time to jump before the Marauder exploded.

Monday, 23 August

Thunderbolts took off in the afternoon for a fighter sweep near Rotterdam.

Tuesday, 24 August

With airfields and aircraft factories still high on the priority list, the 8th Air Force dispatched its bombers to carry out a mission to these targets in France, attacks which would also serve Operation Starkey.

Under heavy escort, 86 Fortresses made for the Focke Wulf workshops at Villacoublay, while 22 bombers turned to the airfields at Conches and Evreux/Fauville. The airfield at Bordeaux/Merignac was attacked by 58 Fortresses of the 4th Bombardment Wing, returning from North Africa. The bombers were part of the force that bombed Regensburg on the 17th.

German fighters met the bombers with their escort, and in several engagements they destroyed four B–17s. One of the Fortresses returning from Conches was forced to ditch in the Channel. The crew was saved by Air-Sea Rescue.

Thunderbolts of the 56th Fighter Group, flying at 27,000 feet over Dieppe, caught sight of German fighters flying below. The Thunderbolts swooped down and caught three of them. One was shot down by Major Francis Gabreski, who would end the war as one of the top-ranking American aces.

Thirty-six heavy bombers flew a diversionary sweep.

Wednesday, 25 August

Medium bombers of the 8th Air Force went for several airfields in France. Flak took its toll and one Marauder of the 322nd Bomb Group was shot down.

Thunderbolts set out on a fighter sweep over northern France in the late afternoon.

Friday, 27 August

Late in the afternoon, 187 Fortresses flew a mission to the French coast. Under heavy fighter escort, involving 117 Spitfires and four Thunderbolt squadrons, in small units from a low altitude of 14,000 feet, the bombers attacked the large rocket-launching site at Watten. At briefing, the target was called "an aeronautical facilities station," but later on it was to be identified as a rocket-launching site.

The immense buildings at Watten were later described by General Brereton as "more extensive than any concrete construction we have in the United States, with the possible exception of Boulder Dam." However big the construction, considerable damage was done because the V-weapon site was still under construction and much of the concrete was still wet when the 368 bombs hailed down. This was the first of the many missions that would be flown to these targets. The Allied attacks against all installations involving V-weapons were code-named "Crossbow."

The Luftwaffe reacted in strength and violent air battles ranged all over the sky. One Spitfire that went down was of the French "Alsace" Squadron from Biggin Hill, taking the Commander René Mouchotte to his death.*

---

*A clear account of the battle that cost Mouchotte his life is given in Pierre Clostermann's *The Big Show*. Clostermann, flying with the "Alsace" Squadron, shot down one Focke Wulf in this battle.

Monday, 30 August

The bombers of the 8th Air Force again dropped a load on the V-weapon site at Watten.

Tuesday, 31 August

An attempted assault by the 8th Air Force bombers on air depots and factories around Paris in late afternoon had to be abandoned due to deteriorating weather conditions. Of the 319 heavies dispatched, only 106, all of the 1st Wing, were able to drop their loads on a secondary target, the airfield at Amiens.

The Fortresses of the 4th Wing returned with their bombs. Near Amiens, two escorting Thunderbolts of the 353rd Fighter Group collided at 29,000 feet. Both aircraft tumbled down. Three Fortresses were lost.

Mediums of the 8th paid their regular visit to airfields in France. One Marauder of the 387th Bomb Group was shot down by flak.

August 31, 1943. Bombs burst on the enemy fighter base at Amiens. (Official USAF Photo)

81

9

SEPTEMBER

Thursday, 2 September

More than 300 bombers of the 8th Air Force tried to find gaps in the clouds. However, only two small formations involving 34 bombers succeeded in dropping on the airfield of Mardijck. Escorting Thunderbolts became engaged in several battles with the Luftwaffe. The 56th Fighter Group lost two aircraft, one shot down over Brussels and the second Thunderbolt bellied in the water between the Dutch islands.

B–26 Marauders employed a new bombing technique when they attacked a power station and chemical plant. In order to obtain better results than achieved in the past, the bombs were dropped ''on the leader,'' a technique already successfully in use with the heavy bomber formations. It was used to good advantage by the 386th Bomb Group, and they achieved a concentrated bomb pattern, putting the power station and plant out of action. The system was later adopted by the other medium bomber groups.

Friday, 3 September

Weather had improved and it invited the 8th Air Force to dispatch 298 Fortresses to France in the early morning. 140 Fortresses of the 1st Wing made a successful attack on the airfield at Romilly-sur-Seine, while aircraft component factories in the Paris area received a bombload from 93 B–17s of the 4th Wing. At Romilly-sur-Seine, four Fortresses were shot down, and at Paris the 8th lost five B–17s.

A large force of German fighters intercepted Thunderbolts making a fighter sweep to Woensdrecht in the afternoon. In the ensuing melee, ranging all the way down to Paris, four German fighters were caught for the loss of one P–47 of the 56th Fighter Group.

82

Monday, 6 September

Because the three Liberator groups had in the meantime returned from North Africa, the 8th Air Force was capable of mustering a force of 407 heavy bombers into the sky. Led by Brigadier General Robert Travis, 338 heavy bombers were heading out over the Channel towards aircraft and bearing factories in and around Stuttgart.

Flying across France the bombers encountered cloud formations which became thicker and thicker all the way. Near Rheims, the Thunderbolts turned back to England. While the bombers droned on to their target through heavy cloud formations, only sporadic fighter attacks were experienced, until the bombers neared their objectives. A new kind of escort arrived and numerous Me–109s and FW–190s flew ahead of the bomberstream. Flying at the same level, they suddenly turned and rushed head-on at the bombers with their guns blazing. As usual, they concentrated on the low group and, before the target was reached, one Fortress of the 388th Bomb Group dived earthwards.

Arriving over the target after the extremely long route, the bomber crews found their objectives obscured by low overcast and smokescreens. General Travis circled the defenses for nearly half an hour in hopes of identifying the instrument factories he had flown 600 miles to destroy. After a very costly time of half an hour in the target area, only part of the bombers dropped their explosives on the target; most of them turned to targets of opportunity.

The 388th Bomb Group suffered the loss of another ten Fortresses. One squadron, the 563rd, was completely annihilated. Not all 45 bombers which failed to return were victims of the Luftwaffe. Some bomber groups overshot Stuttgart and were consequently faced with a rapidly diminishing fuel supply. The same happened to those groups which had to make several bomb runs. Also taking into consideration the many times the bombers had to take evasive action, it is easy to understand that the consumption of fuel highly exceeded the planned quantity, even to such an extent that twelve Fortresses could not make the English coast and ditched into the sea. One hundred eighteen men were rescued by Air-Sea Rescue.

Many scattered groups bombed targets of opportunity when they were on the way back home. German fighters were hunting these profitable targets, and southwest of Paris they ran into the 100th Bomb Group, preparing to bomb airfields. Three Fortresses of the group went down. All these bombers were lost with practically no benefit to the war effort.

Meanwhile, 69 B–24 Liberators were sent on a diversionary sweep over the North Sea. They had a new group in their midst, the 392nd Bomb Group, flying the new B–24H with its power-operated nose-turret.

83

The marshalling yards at Rouen were selected for a visit by the 3rd Wing Marauders. Just about to start the bomb run, one of the engines of *Incendiary Mary* quit, yet the pilot decided to continue the bomb run. After dropping its bombs, the B–26 turned for home, crossing the French coast at about 7000 feet. Flak opened up and the pilot took evasive action considered by most pilots to be impossible to execute with a Marauder on one engine. It only added to the faith the pilots were gaining in their Marauder.

One Thunderbolt of the 353rd Fighter Group failed to return for unknown reasons.

September 6, 1943. 1st Division Fortresses en route to Stuttgart. (Official USAF Photo)

Tuesday, 7 September

Excellent fighter cover was furnished to the 185 heavy bombers of the 8th when they set out to a variety of targets in France, Belgium, and Holland early in the morning. 58 Fortresses of the 4th Wing attacked the rocket site at Watten, by now one of seven large sites identified along the French coast from which it was supposed the Germans would fire their rocket missiles against London and other targets in Great Britain. However, cumulus clouds forced several bombers to bring back their 2000-pound bombs. 105

84

aircraft dropped on the airfield of Brussels/Evere, while 22 Fortresses turned to the airfield at Bergen.

B–24 Liberators of the 44th and 389th Bomb Groups made for the airfield at Leeuwarden. Heavy cumulus clouds forced the bombers to turn to another airfield which they also found partly obscured. Other Liberators attacked a convoy which was sighted off Texel.

September 8, 1943. B-26 Marauders leave the French coast behind. One of them is trailing smoke, yet this aircraft got home. (Photo Imperial War Museum, London)

Wednesday, 8 September

Five B–17 Fortresses of the 422nd Squadron, 305th Bomb Group, participated in a night raid with bombers of the RAF. It was the first time they made such a raid, and a few more of this kind were to follow before the experiment was discontinued. An attack was carried out on the coastal defenses near Boulogne.

Marauders of the 8th Air Support Command set out on a mission to France. On the way back, a Marauder was flying on one engine and trailing behind the main force. Spitfires escorted the bomber, but the plane lost altitude rapidly and, as the other engine also showed signs of malfunctioning, the pilot decided to ditch the aircraft. A Spitfire dropped a life raft

85

and all crew members but one were rescued by Air-Sea Rescue. One gunner could not free himself from the aircraft before the sea closed above *Margie*.

Thursday, 9 September

A large fighter force accompanied the heavies of the 8th Air Force on their penetration into France. They headed for nine different airfields and included in the targets that received their share of explosives were Beaumont-sur-Oise, Beauvais, Lille, St. Omer, and Abbeville. The Luftwaffe reacted vigorously, and two bombers were shot down. These operations were still in connection with "Starkey," but apparently the Germans were not fooled.

Two hundred nineteen B–26 Marauders were dispatched by the 322nd, 323rd, 386th, and 387th Bomb Groups to strike coastal defences near Boulogne. Take-off became a hazardous enterprise for the 387th Group because mist up to 400 feet limited runway visibility to 100 yards—the more so because most pilots had hardly any experience in instrument take-offs. One Marauder crashed off the end of the runway, killing all but the tail-gunner. Three different targets were attacked at the cost of three B–26s, while many others received damage.

Saturday, 11 September

Marauders of the 3rd Wing were out on a mission to France. Deteriorating weather conditions forced the bombers to leave their assigned targets unharmed and they diverted to a secondary target.

Wednesday, 15 September

Some changes to the command structure of the 8th Air Force resulted in renaming the 1st, 2nd, and 4th Bombardment Wings the 1st, 2nd, and 3rd Bombardment Divisions, respectively. Informally, these designations had been in use already for several months.

Airfields at Romilly-sur-Seine were visited by 87 Fortresses. In the meantime, another 186 Fortresses arrived over an airfield at Chartres and over the industrial areas around Paris. Flying through a heavy flak barrage, the Fortresses dropped from 22,000 feet on the Caudron-Renault plants, situated along the Seine. Some Fortresses of the 1st Division carried two 1000-lb. bombs slung under the wings between the inboard engines and fuselage, which was only possible on short range missions. Six bombers failed to return.

86

B–24 Liberators of the 2nd Division took off in late afternoon to carry out an attack on Chartres. Only eighteen B–24s of the 93rd Bomb Group managed to strike the assigned target, losing one bomber to intercepting nightfighters.

Meanwhile, more Liberators of the B–24H type had reached the various squadrons, but they were not greeted with much enthusiasm. Being heavier in weight made them less speedy and less responsive to the controls. Moreover, insufficient padding around the nose-turret caused an icy draught that added to the already not so comfortable situation in a bomber.

A new group identification mark was introduced for the 2nd Division Liberators composed of a group letter in a white disc on the tail fins.

Medium bombers of the 8th Air Support Command hit a variety of targets in France.

Thursday, 16 September

The 1st and 3rd Divisions of the 8th Air Force set off on a mission that would take them far out over the Atlantic. After rounding the Brest peninsula, the 1st Division B–17s continued on to Nantes, while the 3rd Division with its long-range Fortresses had the aircraft factories at Bordeaux as its destination. A small force of this division would head to Cognac airfield. FW–190s intercepted the 131 Fortresses bombing the port installations at Nantes.

A solid overcast protected Bordeaux from a treatment by 72 B–17s and the heavies looked for other targets. They finally dropped their load on the U-boat pens at La Pallice and other targets of opportunity. 21 Fortresses met with more success when they neared the airfield Cognac/Château Bernard and they plastered the field with their bombs.

The mission implied that the Fortresses had to make the longest round-trip so far undertaken, more than eleven hours flying time to cover 1600 miles. The bombers descended to 2000 feet to avoid detection by radar, and also to save fuel. Many bombers reached England in darkness and many pilots had to make their first operational nightlanding.

Several groups landed in southwest England and a few crashes occurred. Adverse weather forced several bombers to disperse and many found it difficult to locate airfields. At least three Fortresses crashed into the hills, while another B–17 landed at sea after thirteen hours in the air. In all, eleven Fortresses were lost.

Several airfields in France were again subjected to a harsh treatment by Marauders of the 8th.

Crew members of the 2nd Division 44th, 93rd, and 389th Bomb Groups again received orders to depart to North Africa.

Saturday, 18 September

One hundred sixty-two B–26 Marauders ranged over northwestern France. They turned to a variety of targets; however, the bombing was poor because of heavy clouds.

Sunday, 19 September

As on the previous day, clouds over France made successful attacks by the Marauders of the 8th Air Support Command not very likely.

Monday, 20 September

The Radiation Laboratory in the United States had built and installed H2X radar sets in twelve B–17 Fortresses. Twelve navigators had received some training in their operation. H2X was the American equivalent of the British H2S radar set.

Tuesday, 21 September

In spite of heavy clouds over northwestern France, Marauders of the 387th, together with some units of the 322nd Bomb Group, attacked the dispersal area of Beauvais/Tille. German fighters rose to challenge the American bombers. One B–26 of the 387th Group was lost, although flak was credited for bringing down this bomber and not the enemy fighters. One Focke Wulf was shot down by gunners of the 322nd.

Wednesday, 22 September

Forty Thunderbolts of the 353rd Fighter Group flew a fighter sweep over Holland in the morning. While crossing the coast at Zandvoort, they caught sight of eight enemy aircraft, flying in westerly direction at an altitude of 18,000 feet. Assuming that it was a decoy force, the Thunderbolts continued their flight.

Near Gilze-Rijen, the P–47s were jumped by six Me–109s. In the ensuing dogfights, two Messerschmitts were sent earthwards without loss for the Thunderbolts.

In the afternoon, 35 Thunderbolts of the same group flew another rodeo over the Belgian coastal area.

88

Thursday, 23 September

Fortresses of the 1st Division encountered heavy cloud conditions when they neared the port area of Nantes. As a result, only 46 bombers were able to drop on the harbor installations. 108 aircraft delivered their load on secondary targets.

A few hours later a second force, composed of Fortresses of the 3rd Division, arrived over Nantes. This time 80 B–17s unloaded on the target area which included the airfield at Vannes/Meuçon. All this didn't pass undisturbed, and soon the German fighters, both Me–109s and FW–190s, made frantic attacks against the bombers. Escorting fighters tore into their formations and one fighter group, the 353rd, destroyed three Focke Wulfs and one Messerschmitt for the loss of one Thunderbolt.

A pilot who scored his first victory was Captain Walter C. Beckham, who would later become the 8th leading fighter ace, until he was shot down himself and taken prisoner.

Three B–17s were lost.

A trial was carried out to drop bombs on the release of a B–17 equipped with H2S. Bombs were dropped on a smoke marker over the North Sea and the results were promising for the future.

Sunday, 26 September

Heavy clouds again spoiled the intentions of the bombers of the 8th. They were en route to the Paris region and they had to abandon the mission. Most bombers returned with their bombs. Only 40 Fortresses pressed on to the airfield at Rheims/Champagne. There were no Fortresses lost on account of enemy action. However, upon return over their bases in England, two Fortresses collided due to the very poor visibility. Both B–17s were of the 385th Bomb Group. 37 Bombers flew a diversionary sweep.

B–26 Marauders paid their regular visit to airfields in France.

Monday, 27 September

On this day the first H2S equipped bomber mission was flown against a German target. The selected objective was Emden, because, apart from being an important port, it was also small enough to test the accuracy of the equipment, and its location on the coast made it a suitable objective for not-too-experienced navigators, because H2S discriminated more sharply between land and water than between various land surfaces.

Early in the morning, 305 B–17 Fortresses of the 1st and 3rd Divisions set out on their mission. Both divisions operated as separate task forces with two Pathfinder planes of the special 813th Bomb Squadron with H2S equipment assigned to each force. It was not a superfluous measure, for by the time the target area was reached equipment failure left only one set operational in each formation. Each task force flew in three combat wings, with the Pathfinder in the lead wing. On signal of the Pathfinder, all bombers of that wing would release their charges. The Pathfinder also dropped marker bombs to guide the following wings.

For the first time, the Thunderbolts would accompany the bombers the entire way. Near the Frisian Islands, Thunderbolts of the 4th and 353rd Fighter Groups picked up the bombers of the first task force to escort them all the way to the target and back again. The second task force was to be escorted by the Thunderbolts of the 56th and 78th Fighter Groups, however, deteriorating weather prevented the 56th Group from rendezvousing on time and the P–47s could only provide withdrawal support.

Only the 4th Fighter Group carried the 108-gallon belly tanks; the other three groups used the new metal, pressurized, 75-gallon tanks, enabling the Thunderbolts to fly at higher altitudes.

The first engagement with the Luftwaffe took place south of Groningen, when the 353rd Fighter Group caught sight of twelve Me–109s flying at 30,000 feet. Four Messerschmitts were shot down before the Thunderbolts continued on to their rendezvous point with the bombers.

A mass of German fighters was waiting in the target area and they started their attacks on the bombers, unaware of the presence of the escort, which took them completely by surprise. As a result, the American fighter pilots claimed 21 German fighters shot down for the loss of only one Thunderbolt. This Thunderbolt was probably shot down by the German fighter pilot Heinz Knoke, who was shot down himself, in this battle. Knoke freed himself from his burning aircraft and parachuted to safety. Another Thunderbolt was abandoned by its pilot over England.

As it turned out, at 1000 hours the second wing of the first force succeeded in bombing on the smoke marker after the first wing had successfully dropped from 22,000 feet on indication of the Pathfinder. The second wing of the second force found a break in the 9/10 cloud and attempted to bomb visually. The third combat wing of each force was unable to locate the markers, and bombed targets of opportunity in the neighborhood. 246 bombers actually made an attack. Seven bombers were lost.

After photo-reconnaissance aircraft revealed the results of the radar bombing, it was shown that combat wings bombing on indication of an H2S aircraft achieved a reasonably small average circular error from one-half to one mile. Bad results were achieved by the wings dropping on the markers, with an error of about five miles.

Twenty-four B–24 Liberators of the 2nd Division made a diversionary sweep to the Brussels area. None of the B–24s was as yet equipped with H2S.

Overcast bombing was also considered safer from the fact that the enemy fighters had to intercept through the overcast, which meant a distinct disadvantage to the German fighters.

By this time the German fighter force facing the 8th Air Force in the west had a strength of about 800 aircraft, or 65 percent of the entire German fighter strength.

To support the bomber mission, the freshmen 352nd and 355th Fighter Groups flew a fighter sweep over Holland with their P–47 Thunderbolts.

10

OCTOBER

Saturday, 2 October

Three hundred forty-nine heavy bombers of the 8th Air Force took off for a renewed attack on Emden. Again the bombers were protected all the way by the Thunderbolts. German fighters approached the Fortresses and mounted frontal attacks, but their attacks were less massive than on the previous occasion.

Two H2S aircraft led the bombing. However, one of them released too early, with the result that many bombers dropped short of the target. And this is not the only reason for the poor bombing—the smoke was carried away by the wind, making good aiming impossible for following formations. The equipment still had much to be improved.

Enemy interest in H2S aircraft (recognizable by an external dome) was probably shown by two unidentified B–17s flying alongside the formation.

Two Fortresses were lost, whereas five German fighters were shot down by the Thunderbolts. One of these was finished off by the 56th Fighter Group leader Hubert Zemke, while one of his squadron leaders, David Schilling, took two for his account.

Sunday, 3 October

Good weather enabled the 8th Air Support Command to dispatch its B–26 Marauders for an assault on Amsterdam/Schiphol. Anti-aircraft guns opened up as soon as the bombers arrived and one Marauder was severely damaged. Possibly the name of the bomber attracted the flak. Yet, the pilot managed to bring his crippled *Flak Happy* home.

Thirty-nine Thunderbolts of the 353rd Fighter Group flew a fighter sweep in the area of Ghent.

Monday, 4 October

The 8th Air Force dispatched 323 heavy bombers on a mission to targets in the Reich. Droning on through heavy cloudbanks, it became apparent that an attack on the primary targets was not advisable. 130 Fortresses attacked targets in and around Frankfurt. They were opposed by strong enemy fighter forces and eight bombers went down. The gunners of one B–17, *Murder Incorporated*, of the 351st Bomb Group, claimed eleven enemy aircraft and, although this figure must be considered as highly exaggerated, it reflected the violence of the battle.

Undoubtedly the losses would have been much higher but for the excellent fighter cover. Thunderbolts penetrated deep into Germany and near Düren, the P–47s ran into a formation of some forty twin-engine Me–110s preparing to launch an attack on the last box of Fortresses. Despite the odds, Major David Schilling, deputy leader of the 56th Fighter Group, led his men in, and within the next few minutes, fifteen Zerstörer were shot down with no loss for the Thunderbolts. Mainly used for firing rockets into the bomber formations, these Zerstörer were too slow and too badly armed to be a match for single-engine fighters.

Other bomber formations attacked targets of opportunity, industrial areas near Saarlautern, marshalling yards at Saarbrücken, and various other objectives. These forces lost four bombers.

Another four bombers were lost by the Liberators of the 392nd Bomb Group, when 38 of its aircraft encountered more than thirty Luftwaffe fighters while making an unescorted diversionary sweep. This made the total bomber losses for the day sixteen aircraft.

Among the fighters that provided withdrawal support were 43 Thunderbolts of the 353rd Fighter Group. While guarding the stragglers, the Thunderbolts encountered several German fighters hunting after the bombers. One Me–109 was destroyed by Major Beckham.

Thunderbolts were credited with 19 victories for the day for a loss of one aircraft.

Thursday, 7 October

One of the means of waging warfare was to drop leaflets by aircraft, distributing information and propaganda to friend and foe in the occupied countries and Germany. For these so-called "nickling" operations, the 8th Air Force had transferred the 422nd Bombardment Squadron of the 305th Bomb Group into a Special Leaflet Squadron. (In addition, sometimes both medium and heavy bombers carried leaflets on regular missions as well.)

On this night, the first leaflet operation was carried out by four aircraft of the Special Leaflet Squadron. They would drop their paper-load on Paris.

Friday, 8 October

Heavy bombers of the 8th Air Force took to the air to fly a mission to northwestern Germany where Bremen and Vegesack were going to be visited by 357 aircraft.

While the 1st Division took a more easterly course across Holland, the Fortresses of the 3rd Division flew the North Sea route to attack Bremen from a northwesterly direction. This was undoubtedly meant to divert the German fighter forces. However, the Luftwaffe could muster sufficient numbers of fighters to meet both B-17 forces.

The submarine buildings and airframe factories at the other North Sea port, Vegesack, were selected for an attack by 55 Liberators of the 2nd Division.

A piece of new equipment was carried by forty aircraft in the lead combat wing of the 3rd Division, a kind of transmitter used to jam the German ground radar, called "Carpet." No evidence of the effectiveness of this equipment was shown.

Shortly after the escorting Thunderbolts had withdrawn, the FW-190s from Leeuwarden and the Me-109s from Schiphol arrived and their deadly attacks would last until the Thunderbolts again came to the rescue, about 30 minutes from the target.

Again the unlucky 381st Bomb Group, flying the low position, suffered the most severe losses, and seven of its eighteen bombers were shot out of the sky. The 3rd Division didn't fare much better, and the 100th Bomb Group shared the fate of the 381st Group in also losing seven aircraft. Flak over Bremen was very heavy and accurate, and both the leader and the deputy leader of the 100th Group were brought down. 27 Fortresses of both the 1st and 3rd Division went down.

Vegesack was bombed by 43 Liberators. Three B-24s were lost. And apart from the 30 bombers that failed to return, another 26 received major damage.

Many battles raged between the German fighters and the Thunderbolts. The 56th Fighter Group sent five earthwards. The German Air Force lost 33 fighters in the battle, of which number twelve were shot down by the 8th Air Force fighters. In a fight between Thunderbolts and FW-190s, one of the German fighters going down in flames killed the commander of JG 1, Oberst Hans Philipp.

Medium bombers of the 322nd and 386th Bomb Groups made a mission to the airfields Lille/Vendeville and Chièvres.

94

October 9, 1943. 94th Bomb Group Fortresses turn for home after bombing the Focke Wulf plant at Marienburg. (Official USAF Photo)

Saturday, 9 October

One hundred sixty-three heavy bombers headed out across the North Sea on a heading that took them via Denmark to the most distant target so far attacked by the 8th Air Force: the port facilities and naval units at Gdynia and the submarine installations at Danzig. The Danish coast was crossed at 1030.

At the same time, 100 bombers followed a similar route into East Prussia, to attack the Focke Wulf assembly plant at Marienburg, some 200 miles east of Berlin.

Meanwhile 115 bombers set out to bomb the Arado aircraft factory at Anklam. Acting as a diversionary force, they were supposed to attract the German fighters. And indeed they succeeded in keeping the Germans away from the bombers heading for the more distant targets, though at the terrible cost of 18 of their number.

The B–24s of the 44th and 392nd Bomb Groups going to Gdynia, and those of the 93rd and 389th Bomb Groups with destination Danzig, missed their targets completely because of very effective smokescreens. Some of the B–17s made two bomb runs in an attempt to locate the target and some hits were placed on ships in the harbor.

It was at Marienburg that the most accurate bombing was done. From a relatively low altitude, between 11,000 and 14,500 feet, 286 of the 598 500-pound GP-bombs fell within the factory area. At least 35 were direct hits on buildings. Major damage by fire was caused by a shower of incendiary bombs.

All told, 352 bombers made attacks for a loss of 28 aircraft.

Woensdrecht airfield was the target for the B–26 Marauders of the 323rd and 387th Bomb Groups, making their last mission under 8th Air Force Command before being transferred to the 9th Air Force which was to take place on the 16th of this month.

October 9, 1943. A Flying Fortress leaving the blazing target at Marienburg. (Official USAF Photo)

Sunday, 10 October

The target for the 8th Air Force bombers was Münster and, in the clear blue sky on this bright Sunday, 236 B–17 Fortresses winged high over the

Dutch countryside to carry out an attack for the third day in succession. The 117 bombers of the 1st Division and the 119 B–17s of the 3rd Division flew a direct course to be assured of fighter protection all the way. Directly after withdrawal of the penetrating escort, a fresh Thunderbolt escort was to take its place, flying a straight course to the pick up point. And that is where things went wrong, because the Thunderbolts of the 56th Fighter Group made a small navigational error and their rendezvous with the bombers was consequently delayed. And, as usual, the Germans were never slow in taking advantage of situations they were in fact waiting for.

The leading 13th Wing was composed of the 95th, 390th, and the 100th Bomb Groups, respectively in the lead, high, and low positions. Perhaps the men had already expected trouble. They certainly didn't expect the extent of the disaster that was laid in store for them, at least not until they spotted some 200 tiny specks, rapidly growing in size and rushing to the bombers.

At 1453, some nine minutes from Münster, the mass of German fighters started its attack, all concentrating on the lead wing. And their first victim was the ill-fated 100th Group, flying the low position at 23,000 feet. The Focke Wulfs closed in to 50–75 yards before breaking away. The lead bomber was hit by a rocket and caught fire. When it peeled off, five bombers followed its course, splitting the group in two. Within two minutes the group was broken up. Bombers tried to avoid the Fortresses tumbling down and within seven minutes the group was entirely dispersed, with most bombers shot down. Then the Germans directed their assault against the 390th Group.

FW–190s, Me–109s, Ju–88s, and Me–110s and 210s flew parallel to the bombers, out of range, in groups of twenty to forty, stacked in echelon down. Suddenly they peeled off, singly or in pairs, in quick succession. "The Germans were queuing up for us. You didn't have to aim; just stick your gun out the window and pull the trigger."—Comment after the mission from pilot Captain Robert D. Brown of the Fortress *Cabin in the Sky* of the 390th Bomb Group.

Near Gronau, twin-engine Ju–88s lobbed rockets into the 390th Group from 100 yards astern. One Fortress blew up; another received a hit amidships and broke in two. Part of this plane slammed into another B–17 and this one went down as well. In all, the group lost eight bombers. The remains of the 100th Group were further treated by other German formations. Even bombers of the Do–217 and Do–215 type flew parallel to the bombers, firing rockets from their sides at 1000–1500-yard ranges.

Heavy flak was met over the target. In spite of the mauling, the 95th kept good formation and unloaded well in the target area. Returning from the target, the Fortresses were again subjected to constant attacks from the Luftwaffe and the entire lead wing was threatened with annihilation. However, total disaster was prevented by the arrival of the Thunderbolts at 1530; but by this time, twelve of the thirteen Fortresses of the 100th Group were shot out of the sky. The sole survivor struggled home on two engines and with two badly wounded gunners on board. This Fortress, *Rosie's Riveters,* piloted by Lt. Robert Rosenthal, was in fact the only bomber of the group to reach the target. The 95th Bomb Group lost five Fortresses out of the 19 taking part in the mission.

All told, 29 Fortresses of the 3rd Division were destroyed, while the 1st Division had lost one bomber.

The German losses were 22 fighters shot down and five damaged. Three of these were sent down by Captain Walter C. Beckham of the 353rd Fighter Group. Two pilots of the 56th Fighter Group became aces: Major David Schilling and Lt. Robert S. Johnson.

The town of Enschede in Holland, near the German border, suffered 149 civilian casualties when bombs descended on the southern part of the city.

Thursday, 14 October

The 8th Air Force was still licking its wounds after the loss of 88 bombers in three days, not counting the number of aircraft that reached England in one way or another but could be written off after landing. However, for mission No. 115, the 8th was again capable of mustering 324 battleworthy Fortresses and 60 Liberators to make a deep penetration into Germany to visit the ball-bearing factories at Schweinfurt.

Briefing was at 0600. Outside it was cold and foggy, and at some bases a heavy rain splashed down, while at other bases a light drizzle persisted. Two hours later, the first B–17s started to thunder along the runway, followed by the other bombers from the many airfields in southeastern England. 149 bombers from the 1st Division and 142 Fortresses from the 3rd Division climbed through the overcast. From both divisions respectively 15 and 18 B–17s had aborted the mission.

Leading the bomber force was the 1st Division 40th Combat Wing with the 92nd Bomb Group in the lead position and the 306th and 305th Bomb Groups, respectively, in the high and low positions. However, at the final point of combat wing rendezvous, the 305th Group was not in evidence.

At the departure point on the Channel coast, the division commander, Colonel Budd J. Peaslee, ordered the 1st Combat Wing, which was next in line, to take the lead position, while both the 92nd and the 306th Groups joined the leading formations, thus grouping a mass of aircraft in a six-group combat wing. Unknown to Colonel Peaslee, the 305th Bomb Group had joined the 1st Combat Wing as low group, unable to find the 40th Combat Wing.

The 91st Bomb Group was now in the lead, the same position it held on the previous mission to Schweinfurt which had cost them so dearly. The 3rd Division, composed of the 4th, 13th, and 45th Combat Wings, was slightly behind the 1st Division and made its penetration thirty miles further south. The 2nd Division failed to make assembly because of the weather over Norfolk, and did not make the mission. Instead, the 29 Liberators that managed to assemble set out to fly a diversionary feint in the direction of Emden. Over the Frisian Islands, they turned back to England. 56 Thunderbolts of the 352nd Fighter Group, assigned to escort the Liberators, soon returned to their base.

When the bombers approached the Channel, the overcast disappeared with a sharp contrasting line between the white cloud deck and the bright, clean sky stretching to the east over Europe.

P–47 Thunderbolts flew peacefully along the flanks of the bomber formations. The 44 Thunderbolts of the 353rd Fighter Group had picked up the bombers midway across the Channel and, after they had taken their positions above and alongside the bomber formations, they accompanied the Fortresses of the 1st Division into hostile skies. Landfall was made over Walcheren, and here the first enemy reaction was encountered. 16 Me–109s and four FW–190s of JG 26 came in at an altitude of 34,000 feet to engage the penetrating forces with the obvious purpose of drawing the escorting fighters into combat so that they would have to drop their belly tanks. This would have left the bombers unescorted at an early stage. The Thunderbolts of the 352nd Squadron turned into them. At this altitude, the Thunderbolt was in its prime and the pilots used this advantage cleverly. The battle lasted for twenty minutes, and in those minutes, four German fighters were sent spinning to the ground.

The other two squadrons of the group continued with the bombers and in the area of Sittard-Düren they ran into some sixty Focke Wulfs and Messerschmitts. Six of them were knocked down for the loss of one P–47. Another Thunderbolt crashed upon return near Hornchurch, killing the pilot.   .

The Thunderbolts continued their escort until they were at the limit of their capability, which was a few minutes past Aachen. Then the last friendly planes flashed across the nose of the leading bombers waggling their wings, their way of wishing "Good luck."

The bombers pressed on to a point twenty miles west of Bonn where they arrived at 1340. From there, they flew in an ESE direction to pass north of Frankfurt, which city was skirted on the east side when the bombers turned in a SSE direction. The time was then 1410. Once the Thunderbolts withdrew it was only a matter of five minutes until the German fighters took over the escort, flying parallel to the bombers on both sides and at the rear of the formations.

Suddenly, the first Focke Wulfs approached the bombers head-on. In a six-abreast formation, they plunged through the center of the formation, immediately followed by other batches of Focke Wulfs and Messerschmitts. Soon the attacks came from all directions. Rocket-firing Ju–88s, and Me–110s and 210s approached the bombers, and this time varied their tactics with the use of single-engine fighters as a screen for the twin-engine aircraft. They fired 8-inch rockets from about 1000 yards, just out of accurate machinegun range. Even Ju 87 Stukas tried to break up the bomber formations.

The Germans attempted to repeat their tactics which destroyed the 100th Group in a few minutes during the 10th of October mission. But the leading 1st Combat Wing, the strength of which was boosted by the bombers of the 40th Combat Wing, could keep its formation. The attacks were launched from all around the clock, and the rockets took their toll. One B–17 was shattered into a hundred pieces; a B–17's wing was ripped off and fell to the rear, enveloped in flames, propellers still turning.

The air battle continued for hours, but the bomber formation never wavered and bore on to the heart of Germany at 25,000 feet of altitude. At the Initial Point, Berghemfeld, ten miles south of Schweinfurt, the lead formation made a left turn and, of the 40th Combat Wing, only sixteen planes were left to start the bomb run. They were the remnants of the 92nd and 306th Bomb Groups. Only three Fortresses of the 305th Bomb Group turned to the target and, by the time the target was reached, only two were left.

German fighters were aware of the target and attacked vigorously, with complete disregard for their own safety. Over the target, the bombers had to pass a concentrated barrage of anti-aircraft fire. At about 1440, the bombing started.

The Fortresses of the 3rd Division arrived over Schweinfurt six minutes after the last bombs from the 1st had been dropped. They crossed the Belgian coast near Knocke and over Sas van Gent contact was made with the Thunderbolts of the 56th Fighter Group. At 1330, the Thunderbolts turned back.

Flying a route that took them northeast of Luxembourg, the bombers met only slight resistance from enemy fighters. At 1405, they passed a point northwest of Trier and took a course due east towards Darmstadt.

A few miles from Schweinfurt, some bombers went down, but the heaviest beating came on the return flight when the Luftwaffe fighters pressed home their attacks all the way back. Relief was expected from the fighter escort, but instead of Thunderbolts and Spitfires, the Focke Wulfs were waiting near the coast. Fog over their bases kept the AAF and RAF fighters grounded.

Two hundred twenty-eight B–17s dropped 1113 high explosives, of

100

October 14, 1943. A B–17 over the burning Schweinfurt
works. (Official USAF Photo)

which number 143 bombs fell within the factory area, with 88 direct hits
on the buildings. 1751 incendiary bombs were unloaded.

On the return flight, the 1st Division took a course somewhat southerly
of the one followed on the penetration flight. But again the Germans were
waiting, and their force was composed of all types of aircraft, including
many twin-engine aircraft and nightfighters. One fighter collided with a
bomber and both went down.

Sixty Bombers were lost, five Fortresses crashed on return to England,
while twelve bombers that managed to land were too badly shot up to be
repaired. That meant a total loss for the day of 77 heavy bombers. The
German losses were 38 fighters shot down and 20 others damaged.

Although considerable damage had been done to plants supporting the
aircraft industry, which eventually would lead to the dispersal of the vital
industries causing a decline in aircraft production, if only for a short
period, there was no reason for the optimistic views shown by Generals
Eaker and Arnold, who were of the opinion that the German Air Force was
in its last final struggle ("the last final struggle of a monster in his death
throes"). Undoubtedly this opinion was fed by wishful thinking and also
by the claims of American bomber crews—of 186 enemy aircraft destroyed
on the Schweinfurt raid.

101

The fact was that the 8th Air Force for the time being had lost air superiority over Germany and that this superiority could not be regained unless sufficient long-range escort fighters became available.

No deep penetration of Germany took place for the rest of the year.

Friday, 15 October

The first fighter group of the 8th Air Force to be equipped with the P-38H Lightning became operational. 36 aircraft of the 55th Fighter Group flew a sweep along the Dutch coast.

With two 75-gallon wingtanks, the Lightnings could achieve a maximum escort range of 520 miles and, with two 108-gallon tanks, they would by February, 1944, go up to 585 miles, which meant a considerable improvement over the Thunderbolt. Even when using the 108-gallon belly tank, the P-47 had a radius of 375 miles at the most.

Also, a new P-47 group became operational. It was the 356th Fighter Group of the 8th Air Force.

Saturday, 16 October

A new tactical air force was established in England. General Brereton assumed command of the newly formed 9th Air Force. Headquarters was in Sunninghill Park-Berkshire. 9th Bomber Command was placed under the command of Brigadier General Samuel E. Anderson. The nucleus of the Command was formed by the four medium bombardment groups taken over from 8th Air Support Command: the 322nd, 323rd, 386th, and 387th Bomb Groups, divided between the 98th and 99th Combat Wings.

Brigadier General Elwood R. Quesada took command of 9th Fighter Command. Only one unit was attached to this command: the 67th Tactical Reconnaissance Group, equipped with photo-recon Spitfires and F-6 Mustangs.

Brigadier General Benjamin F. Giles assumed command of the 9th Troop Carrier Command.

The primary mission of the 9th Air Force was support of the continental invasion and cooperation with the ground armies in their subsequent move into the heart of Germany.

The 55th Fighter Group took its Lightnings up for a sweep. This second operational flight of the group was uneventful and the fighters returned to their base.

October 16, 1943. P–38 Lightnings are ready to take off
on their second mission. (Official USAF Photo)

Sunday, 17 October

The 55th Fighter Group set off again to carry out a fighter sweep.

Monday, 18 October

Thirty-six Marauders of the 322nd flew their first mission as a 9th Air Force Bomber Group when they headed out for the airfield at Evreux/Fauville. Heavy clouds were met and the bombers returned without bombing.

In the afternoon, 36 Marauders tried it once again. Escorted by Spitfires and 46 Thunderbolts of the 353rd Fighter Group, the bombers crossed the Channel on their way to St. Omer/Longuenesse airfield. Again heavy clouds barred the way to their target and, after receiving a recall sign from the Spitfires, the Marauders turned back home.

The Lightnings of the 55th Fighter Group made another fighter sweep.

Tuesday, 19 October

P–38 Lightnings of the 55th Fighter Group flew a fighter sweep for the fifth day in succession, and again it passed uneventfully.

Wednesday, 20 October

A mission to the non-ferrous industries at Düren was launched by the 8th Air Force, dispatching 212 heavy bombers. The formations, with their escorting Thunderbolts, encountered cirrus stratus up to 30,000 feet. The heavies released on pathfinder indications. The latter were of the 813th

103

Bomb Squadron, making their first OBOE attack. Unfortunately, the pathfinders unloaded prematurely, with one combat wing dropping likewise. Several bombers unloaded on airfields in Holland.

German fighters rose to meet the attacking force and were intercepted by the Thunderbolts. 114 bombers actually made attacks at the cost of nine Fortresses.

Seventy bombers flew a diversionary sweep.

Friday, 22 October

The first objective of the medium bombers of the 9th Air Force remained the reduction of the German Air Force by attacking its airfields and installations, and the second objective was to share in the struggle against the V-weapon sites.

The missions of the Marauders and the heavy bombers were mostly coordinated in a hope that this might draw the German fighters away from the heavy bombers. However, the Germans preferred to concentrate on the heavies, and withdrew their fighters from the advanced fields. Many times the mediums arrived over empty airfields.

During the morning, 36 Marauders made another attempt to bomb the airfield at Evreux/Fauville, and this time 32 mediums dropped on the airfield. Only meager flak was thrown up with no sign of German aircraft.

In late afternoon, the Marauders headed for the Cambrai/Epinoy airfield. Weather was deteriorating so thirty bombers of the 322nd Bomb Group decided to turn back with their bombs. The six remaining aircraft of the group continued with another group. Yet the target was not bombed because some 36 Me-109s interfered. From the ensuing air battle, the Marauders escaped without losses.

Two Thunderbolts of the 353rd Fighter Group were lost, though not by enemy action. The group climbed into heavy clouds and, even at 35,000 feet, the fighters still didn't come out. Two Thunderbolts spun out and the pilots were unable to recover.

Sunday, 24 October

Aerial reconnaissance revealed a new type of German construction on the French coast. They were concrete structures, the largest part made up of two buildings, strangely shaped, and resembling gigantic skis laid on edge.

By 12 November, 21 ski sites would be identified. Allied intelligence discovered very soon that all ski sites in the Pas de Calais area were pointing to London, designated to launch V-1s. The ski sites in the Cherbourg area all pointed to Bristol and Southampton.

104

Not everybody in the Allied camp was convinced that all this was a real threat and rather thought it a German feint to divert the attention and effort of the Allies from their forthcoming attempt to invade the continent.

Airfields remained the main concern of the medium bombers, and 36 Marauders of the 322nd Bomb Group turned to the airfield of Montdidier. Lightnings and Thunderbolts of the 8th Air Force accompanied the bombers. Some forty German fighters approached the bombers but, thanks to the escorting fighters, all bombers turned back, though many of them were damaged.

Thursday, 28 October

Marauders of the 9th Air Force ranged over France to visit several airfields.

Saturday, 30 October

General Arnold decided to stop the delivery of long-range P–51 Mustangs and P–38 Lightnings to tactical reconnaissance units or to any theater of operations other than the United Kingdom.

Marauders of the 9th Air Force struck airfields in France.

11

NOVEMBER

Wednesday, 3 November

In the United States, the Radiation Laboratory had undertaken to develop an improved version of the H2S-type radar set. Using a shorter microwave length than had ever been used before scientists had succeeded in building a radar set which gave a sharper and more faithful picture of the ground. The new device, called H2X, had been put into production in the summer of 1943. Time was short, however, and twenty sets were produced and twelve B–17Fs were equipped with the remaining sets as spares. These twelve planes, manned by partially trained crews, had arrived in England in early October.

After several training missions, the first "practice" mission took place with eleven B–17s (nine of them with the new H2X sets and two carrying H2S sets) acting as pathfinders for a force of 539 bombers, despatched by the 8th Air Force to attack Wilhelmshaven. The decision to strike Wilhelmshaven reflected the need to test the new radar device rather than as part of an effective bombing campaign before D-day. With the possibility of providing escort throughout the entire route, Wilhelmshaven was the ideal objective.

P–38 Lightnings of the 55th Fighter Group accompanied the bombers all the way, while Thunderbolts escorted on the way in. Other Thunderbolt groups escorted over the target and again shepherded the bombers on the way back.

The 1st Division, commanded by Brigadier General Robert B. Williams, and the 3rd Division, commanded by Brigadier General Curtis E. LeMay, despatched a task force of over 200 B–17s each. The 2nd Division under Brigadier General James P. Hodges sent out a force of 117 B–24 Liberators.

November 3, 1943. The Marauders drop their loads on
the airfield at Schiphol, Amsterdam. (Official USAF Photo)

The eleven pathfinder aircraft were distributed among the eleven combat
wings of both the 1st and 3rd Divisions. This left the B-24s without
pathfinders, but they were instructed to drop their bombs on the parachute
marker-flares, released by the preceding Fortress formations. Since the interval between the formations gave time for the flares to drift, it was clear
that from these bombers no accurate bombing could be expected.

On the way to their rendezvous point with the bombers, the 4th Fighter
Group was jumped by Me–109s at an early stage. One squadron separated
from the group to engage the enemy, while both other squadrons continued
to pick up the bombers. However, they failed to make contact and turned
back to base.

The Lightnings saw their first real combat in the ETO. They claimed
three German fighters shot down for no loss. The score might have been

107

even higher but, according to strict orders then governing the tactics, the P–38s stayed close to the bombers.

Me–110s and 210s were among the fighters attacking the bombers over the target, concentrating on the rear of the second box of bombers. Five of the Messerschmitts were claimed by the Thunderbolts of the 353rd Fighter Group, providing escort over the target. Another five Luftwaffe aircraft were claimed by the pilots of the 56th Fighter Group.

Five hundred thirty-nine bombers carried out their attack. Seven bombers were lost and of these, probably only three were shot down by German aircraft, undoubtedly a success for the excellent fighter escort furnished by eight groups of 8th Fighter Command. Damage through bombing was moderate, but the importance lay in the fact that the yards were hit through 10/10 cloud by inexperienced pathfinder crews.

In the morning, 72 Marauders of the 9th Air Force set out to attack the airfield of St. André-de-l'Eure. FW–190s arrived to intercept the bombers and, in persistent attacks lasting for some ten minutes, one B–26 of the 322nd Bomb Group went down.

The Marauders took off again in the afternoon. They crossed the Dutch coast as they headed for Amsterdam where the airfield at Schiphol was to be visited.

Luftwaffe fighter strength in the West had by now grown to 1660 aircraft.

Friday, 5 November

Led by B–17 pathfinders equipped with OBOE, two forces of heavy bombers flew across Holland to make small penetrations into the Reich. 379 Fortresses went to Gelsenkirchen, and 118 Liberators with B–17 pathfinders made for Münster. Both targets lay within reach of OBOE. This navigational aid depended on beams transmitted by ground stations and could only be used for short-range missions.

The attack on the marshalling yards and oil plants at Gelsenkirchen was carried out by 328 aircraft and, although pathfinders led the attack, the results were far from satisfying. The same could be said of the Liberators striking on the marshalling yards at Münster. A pathfinder was hit on the bomb run, and as a consequence some formations tried to bomb through gaps in the clouds.

Escorting fighters went along with the bombers and the Luftwaffe made their presence soon needed feel. The 353rd Fighter Group provided escort over the target, Gelsenkirchen. The Thunderbolts became engaged in a vicious fight with some 50 German fighters, of which five were shot down for the loss of three Thunderbolts.

Lightnings of the 55th Fighter Group set off to rendezvous with the

November 5, 1943. Canopy and pieces fly off the Me–410 and, with the right engine on fire, this aircraft is doomed before the guns of a 353rd Fighter Group Thunderbolt. (Photo Imperial War Museum, London)

Liberators on their way to Münster. Mechanical failure caused some P–38s to abort the mission, which left 47 Lightnings to continue on. Climbing for altitude, the Lightnings met extreme cold at 25,000 feet, resulting in further engine troubles and again some P–38s returned. Only one squadron of the group managed to make contact with the bombers. The others arrived at the rendezvous point but found no sign of the bombers. The one squadron that did was just in time to encounter a strong force of Me–109s and rocket-carrying Do–217s preparing to launch an attack.

Heavily outnumbered, the sixteen Lightnings attacked, breaking up the enemy formations. Realizing that their primary task was to protect the bombers, they didn't let themselves be drawn away from the heavies. Without losses, they survived the struggle, claiming the destruction of three German aircraft.

The 56th Fighter Group became the first group in the 8th Air Force to be ·credited with 100 enemy aircraft destroyed. Escorting the bombers to Münster, the group was soon embroiled in a battle with the Luftwaffe, and the 100th kill for the group was an Me–210, going down in flames after mixing it up with a Thunderbolt piloted by George Hall. This Me–210 was one of six aircraft shot down by the group on this mission.

Seven bombers of the Gelsenkirchen force failed to return, while the bombers with a Münster destination lost three aircraft.

B–26 Marauders of the 9th Air Force attacked "construction works" on the French coast near Mimoyecques. Flak was heavy and two Marauders were brought down. Only a few men were able to abandon one of the bombers before it disintegrated in mid-air.

Sunday, 7 November

OBOE-equipped pathfinders led a force of 57 heavy bombers in an attack on Düren. The pathfinders again encountered difficulties with their equipment, and the bombs were scattered over a hundred miles as they were dropped from an altitude of 28,000 feet. 53 heavy bombers visited Wesel. Thunderbolts shepherded the bombers.

P–38 Lightnings of the 55th Fighter Group, together with elements of the 20th Fighter Group, were suddenly jumped by FW–190s diving out of the clouds. The Lightnings were escorting the B–26 Marauders to Melun airfield. One P–38 of the 20th Fighter Group was severely hit and the pilot bailed out over the sea. Another Lightning of the same group failed to return, its fate unknown.

This one squadron of the 20th Group acted as a fourth squadron to the 55th Group until the 20th received its full strength.

Thursday, 11 November

In early afternoon, formations of Thunderbolts flew at 24,000 feet over and through heavy cumulus clouds under a misty cirro-stratus layer. The P–47s escorted 172 heavy bombers of the 8th Air Force on their way to the marshalling yards at Münster.

Near the target, the German fighters started their assault against the intruders and they kept on coming until the bombers crossed the Dutch coast again. Only 59 aircraft unloaded. Four bombers were shot down.

The 56th Fighter Group claimed five German aircraft, losing two of their number, while the 353rd Group sent three down for no losses.

One hundred sixty-two Marauders of the 9th Air Force returned to the construction works on the French coast.

The first 9th Air Force fighter group, the 354th, which had arrived at Greenham-Common on November 4th, received its first fighters today. The group would be equipped with the P–51B Mustang.

110

Saturday, 13 November

Shepherded by the P–47 Thunderbolts, a large bomberstream composed of 268 aircraft winged its way to Bremen. P–38 Lightnings arrived to escort the bombers over the target. Although a relatively small force of 47 aircraft and, finding themselves outnumbered possibly as much as five to one, the P–38s provided invaluable support when they encountered the onrushing German fighters.

The Germans tried all their tricks to draw off the escort. They brought their rocket-firing planes, mostly Ju–88s, into a position to lob their charges into the bomber formations. Five Lightnings were seen to be shot down, whereas two others also failed to return.

Sixteen heavy bombers were lost from the various missions. Yet the

November 13, 1943. The 8th Air Force bombers leave long trails on their way to Bremen. (Official USAF Photo)

Lightning had proved to be an effective fighter. A disadvantage was the fact that it was the easiest of all fighters for the Germans to identify, even by its condensation trails.

Nearing the target, one of the pathfinders met with H2X equipment failure. Presuming that the situation of Bremen was pointed out by a heavy concentration of flak, several bombers dropped their explosives. In all, 115

111

heavies bombed. This kind of fruitless bombing demanded much improvement of the equipment. 25 bombers turned to targets of opportunity. Of the sixteen bombers shot down, seven were lost by this small formation.

The 56th Fighter Group provided withdrawal support. The Thunderbolts met the bombers at 29,000 feet, just east of the Zuider Zee.

Tuesday, 16 November

One hundred eighty-nine Fortresses of the 1st Division droned over the North Sea in a northerly direction to visit Knaben in Norway, where the molybdenum mines were the objectives for a visual bombing attack. A generating plant at Rjukan, presumed to be involved with nuclear experiments, was the target for 199 Fortresses of the 3rd Division.

Most opposition came from the clouds over the target, forcing several formations to fly around in the hopes of finding an opening to start the bomb run. The absence of German fighters allowed this luxury.

A total of 306 B-17s delivered their bombs on the assigned targets. Mechanical trouble caused the loss of two Fortresses. One of them ditched near some fishing boats; the other went down over Norway after the crew had left the plane. One of the Fortresses that touched down after returning from the mission was *Knockout Dropper*, the first bomber in the 8th Air Force that had completed fifty missions.

November 16, 1943. Smoke rises from the target at Knaben. (Official USAF Photo)

112

Thursday, 18 November

One hundred two B-24 Liberators were dispatched to make the North Sea crossing for another visit to Norway where the Kjeller aircraft factories and other aircraft plants at Oslo were to be bombed. 82 Liberators accomplished a very accurate attack from an altitude of 12,000 feet.

No enemy aircraft interfered until the bombers were on the return flight and well out over the sea. Then Me-109s and some Ju-88s approached the bombers and six B-24s were sent into the dark waters below. Three others were so heavily damaged that they dared not risk the long over-water flight, and so landed in neutral Sweden. Another damaged Liberator returned to its base to make a landing after the pilot had ordered his crew to bail out over England. Having a badly wounded gunner on board, the pilot tried to land on the one main wheel he had left. He managed to put the aircraft on the ground and both pilot and gunner left the wreckage without further harm. An unexploded 20-mm. shell was found in the one good engine.

Friday, 19 November

The 8th Air Force sent 167 heavy bombers to Gelsenkirchen. Again all depended on the OBOE sets of the six pathfinder aircraft when they penetrated Germany above a solid overcast. And again the equipment failed to give the right position and 127 bombers dropped on targets of opportunity. One of the objectives that received a bombload shortly after noon was the airfield at Rheine.

The overcast also kept the German fighters grounded, and all bombers returned to base. Thunderbolts furnished support to and from the targets.

Wednesday, 24 November

Aerial reconnaissance revealed that the number of ski sites along the French coast had increased to thirty-eight.

Thursday, 25 November

With winter weather unsuitable for big bomber operations, the thought of fighter-bomber tactics was revived. The aircraft on hand was the Thunderbolt. The shackles that could carry the belly tank were also suitable to carry a 500- or 1000-lb. bombload.

It was the 353rd Fighter Group that undertook the task of experimenting. For nearly two and a half months the crew had been intensively trained.

113

The best method proved to be to start a 60-degree dive at 10,000 feet and to pull out at 4000 feet.

The value of this technique was put to a test and sixteen Thunderbolts, with 500-lb. bombs slung under their bellies set course to the St. Omer/Ft. Rouge airfield. The fighter-bombers were of the 351st Squadron and they were escorted by both other squadrons of the group, and also by the Thunderbolts of the 78th Fighter Group. Rendezvous with this group was made at Cap Griz Nez at 1102. Heavy flak was met near the target and the commander's aircraft was fatally hit. With his Thunderbolt engulfed in flames, the pilot managed to bail out.

Results of the bombing were poor and only very little damage was done.

Meanwhile, fifty Thunderbolts with 500-lb. bombs under their bellies, all of the 56th Fighter Group, and escorted by P–47s of the 356th Fighter Group, flew in tight formation with a B–24 Liberator. All headed for the St. Omer/Longuenesse airfield. This technique involves a level flight and a bomb drop on the leader. However, the B–24 had a delayed release due to mechanical trouble and most of the Thunderbolts dropped beyond the target.

Friday, 26 November

The largest bomber force to date took to the air as the 8th Air Force dispatched 633 bombers on a mission to Bremen and Paris. 128 Fortresses of the 3rd Division went to Paris. The mission was founded on a hopeful forecast for a visual attack, but when the bombers neared Paris they found the city completely hidden by a solid blanket of clouds. Without bombing, the Fortresses returned to their bases.

A strong force of 1st Division Fortresses and 2nd Division Liberators ascended to over 25,000 feet to proceed above the clouds in extreme cold to the assigned target, Bremen, where the bombers would arrive shortly after noon. Fourteen pathfinders led the formations, while following the main force came the 401st Bomb Group with its new B–17Gs (Fortresses equipped with a chin-turret for increased forward firing power).

German fighters swarmed up in strength. They included many twin-engine aircraft. When they unleashed their assault, they again used every trick they could think of. Some fifty to sixty Me–110s and Me–410s, with a whole bunch of single-engine fighters as escort, swooped down on the bombers. Shortly after the last box left the target, the Thunderbolts of the 56th Fighter Group plunged into the battle to deal a terrible blow to the Luftwaffe fighters. It was undoubtedly a big day for the 56th, sending 23 German fighters earthwards for the loss of one Thunderbolt—and this Thunderbolt was lost because of a tank leakage. Out of gas, the pilot bailed out over Holland.

114

November 26, 1943. B–17s of the 96th Bomb Group, 3rd Division, deliver their loads on the Focke Wulf factory at Bremen. (Official USAF Photo)

Many well-known pilots such as Ralph Johnson, David Schilling, Francis Gabreski, and others scored double kills, while Walker Mahurin sent three down. In all, 36 German aircraft were claimed by the American fighter pilots for the loss of four of their own.

Twenty-five bombers failed to return from the mission. One of them gave further consequences on both sides. Three members of a bomber crew taken prisoner, wore flight jackets under their furlined flying clothes carrying on the backs the name "Murder Incorporated." It was the name of their bomber, which, however, did not participate in the mission because it stayed on the base for repairs. Needless to say, the German propaganda fully exploited this incident, and pictures of one of the crew members appeared in all papers.

On the return flight to England, pilots of the 352nd Fighter Group spotted a straggling B–24 about to be attacked by a number of Me–109s. The Thunderbolts turned into the German fighters and knocked down two of them, driving off the rest.

One hundred ninety-eight B–26 Marauders headed into France to attack a variety of targets. The airfield at Cambrai/Epinoy was bombed by the

115

B–26s of the 387th and 323rd Bomb Groups (98th Wing). The Marauders of the 322nd and 386th Bomb Groups (99th Wing) mistook the landing ground at Roye Amy for Rosières-en-Santerre. In the afternoon, the Marauders turned again to the still secret construction works in the Pas de Calais area. Three groups unloaded with fair results.

Monday, 29 November

Only 154 bombers out of 360 dispatched managed to bomb the target area at Bremen, though with very poor results.

In the afternoon, Lightnings of the 55th Fighter Group, with elements of the 20th Group, crossed the Dutch coast at an altitude of 31,000 feet on their way to Bremen. They were intercepted by Me–109s in a surprise attack, and seven Lightnings were lost. Three German fighters were shot down in the engagement.

Thunderbolts also ran into enemy fighters and, in several battles, fifteen German fighters were claimed to be shot down, six of them by the 56th Fighter Group. In spite of tenacious action to ward off the Luftwaffe fighters, the Germans broke through the Thunderbolt defenses and knocked down thirteen bombers.

Sixteen Thunderbolts of various groups failed to return, of which several were believed to have become victims of deteriorating weather conditions.

B–26 Marauders of the 9th Air Force were greeted with murderous flak when they neared their target, the airfield at Chièvres. One bomber of the 386th Bomb Group was severely damaged and dropped out of formation. Six German fighters jumped their prey and did their utmost to blow the aircraft out of the sky. In spite of the severe punishment, with one engine shot out and the other damaged, with a disabled rudder and shattered instrument panel, the bomber returned to base, though not before a gunner shot down two of the attackers.

Tuesday, 30 November

Solingen came in for a turn to be visited by the heavies of the 8th. 381 bombers were despatched to this city but only 79 dropped their load, with discouraging results. Three bombers were lost. On this morning mission, the bombers were again escorted by the Thunderbolts. One of them encountered engine trouble and the pilot made his way back on the deck. A locomotive loomed up ahead of him and he poured his fire into it. The ensuing explosion fascinated the pilot so much that he never saw the steel tower looming ahead of him, and he smashed right into it. The disintegrating plane was thrown up, whereupon the pilot still managed to bail out.

116

Two additional fighter groups joined the 9th Fighter Command: the 357th, equipped with P–51B Mustangs, and the 362nd Fighter Group, flying P–47D Thunderbolts. Together with the 354th Fighter Group, they formed the 70th Fighter Wing.

12

DECEMBER

Wednesday, 1 December

General Eaker, commanding general of the USAAF in the United Kingdom, agreed with the proposal of Air Chief Marshal Leigh Mallory of the AEAF (Allied Expeditionary Air Force) that the Tactical Air Forces, assembled for use in "Overlord," should directly begin with the attacks on the ski sites (which were more than 50 percent completed). General Brereton was instructed to use the 9th Air Force for the same purpose. The sites were later code-named "Noballs," and the operations against targets connected with "Noballs" were codenamed "Crossbow."

The 8th Air Force dispatched 299 bombers to return to Solingen after the failure of the previous day. 281 heavies dropped their bombs, but again no damage of importance was inflicted.

Luftwaffe fighters opposed the bombers in force, and the Me–109s and FW–190s attacked in quick succession, while Me–110s and 210s, with Focke Wulfs flying top-cover, lobbed their rockets into the bomber formations.

Thunderbolts tore into the German formations wherever they saw them, yet in spite of their efforts to keep the Germans away from the bombers, twenty-four heavies went down. Several German fighters underwent the same fate. Three of them were shot down by the 56th Fighter Group, but the group lost an equal number.

Many bombers returned with damage, and one Liberator had its wing torn off while trying to land at Manston. The bomber exploded, killing all on board. A Fortress made an overshoot and plunged into the Channel. Only a few got out.

One hundred seventy-six Marauders of the 9th Air Force made successful attacks on the airfields at Cambrai/Niergies, Cambrai/Epinoy, and

Lille/Vendeville. Fighters escorted the bombers and only weak enemy resistance was met.

9th Air Force fighters made their first operational sortie as 24 P–51 Mustangs of the 354th Fighter Group carried out a sweep over Belgium and northwestern France. The group was led by Lt. Col. Blakeslee of the 4th Fighter Group, temporarily detached to this outfit for training the pilots on the new fighter.

Saturday, 4 December

Intensified aerial reconnaissance started this day (as ordered by the War Cabinet on November 29th). At the end of the first week, 64 ski sites had been identified.

Thunderbolts of the 353rd Fighter Group renewed their dive-bombing attacks. In the afternoon, sixteen aircraft delivered their 500-lb. bombs on the airfield at Gilze-Rijen. 27 P–47s of the two other squadrons, together with P–47s of the 56th Fighter Group, flew cover. This time the flak was weak and inaccurate.

Though the bombing was slightly better than on the first mission, there was still much experience needed and it still did not bring the Luftwaffe into the air, which was, after all, one of the main purposes of these attacks. The Germans seemed to preserve their fighters solely for encounters with the bombers.

Sunday, 5 December

Till recently, all AAF P–51 Mustang units in the ETO had been assigned to the 9th Air Force for the tactical support of "Overlord." However, late in October an agreement had been made that the primary role of all US fighter units in the United Kingdom was to support and protect the heavy bombers until further notice. Accordingly, the one P–51 unit (the 354th Fighter Group) operating in the theater prior to 1944 was to fly almost exclusively in support of the daylight bomber missions and under 8th Fighter Command Control, although assigned to 9th Fighter Command.

On this day, the P–51s of the 354th Fighter Group flew escort for the first time in a strategic mission to the Amiens area. Two squadrons of Mustangs escorted the B–17s from the French coast to Poix, southwest of Amiens, where the P–47s took over for the remainder of the mission.

The 546 heavy bombers were on a mission to airfields in France, but they found all targets obscured by clouds. Except for three bombers finding an opportunity to drop their load, the others returned with their bombs. Not all others, for nine heavies were shot down.

After preliminary attacks on the "construction works," the 9th Air

119

Force started its operations in support of "Crossbow," joining the 2nd Tactical Air Force (RAF) in an attack on those targets, which were by then on the top-priority list for tactical air forces. The results were, however, negligible.

Friday, 10 December

At 1920, the first bombs dropped by German raiders started to fall on an airfield occupied by the 9th Air Force. Some twenty German aircraft carried out attacks on the airfields of the 322nd, 323rd, and 386th Bomb Groups, and another 9th airbase. The attacks lasted until 2000, and most bombs struck living quarters, killing several men.

The Germans could carry out their attacks undisturbed, because there was practically no anti-aircraft protection.

Saturday, 11 December

Early in the morning, 583 heavy bombers climbed through the clouds to assemble over England. After sliding into pre-arranged formations, the bomber column wheeled on a heading toward northwestern Germany, where they were going to visit Emden. The bombers thundered over the North Sea. Up ahead, breaks in the cloud layer became larger revealing the northern coast of Germany, and soon the bombers proceeded in a clear winter sky.

Thunderbolts of the 56th Fighter Group were part of a force of some 200 American fighters assigned to protect the bombers. The P–47s had taken off from their base at 1100. They skirted Holland's northern coast at 22,000 feet. The pilots strained their eyes to pick out the bombers ahead. When they got sight of them, they rapidly closed the distance to take their positions near the first two boxes of the 3rd Division.

Over the Frisian Islands, and still at a considerable distance from the bombers, the first German fighters were sighted, rapidly coming in from the east at 35,000 feet. Twelve Thunderbolts turned into the onrushing eight to twelve Me–109s, while the 36 P–47s of the two other squadrons continued to the bombers. Their aid was badly needed for they observed a mass of at least forty twin-engine aircraft manoeuvring to launch a massive cannon and rocket assault. Meanwhile, German single-engine fighters tore into the bomber formations.

The Thunderbolts raced to the battle area. A change of course resulted in two Thunderbolts' colliding, exploding in a blinding flash. The P–47s arrived in the nick of time to reap a rich harvest of twin-engine fighters. Major Gabreski led the Thunderbolts into the attack and, swooping down on the Zerstörer, they destroyed fourteen of them.

120

After the battle, Major Gabreski found himself separated from the other pilots of his group and a glance at his fuel gauges made it clear to him that he had to take a straight course home. After erroneously nearly joining up with a formation of FW–190s, he headed for England. However, his course crossed the path of an Me–109 and the German pilot did not intend to let him go. The Messerschmitt made several passes at him. In the third attack, the German pilot managed to score a hit in the cockpit and in the engine, Gabreski's Thunderbolt plunged down in a left-handed spiral, seemingly out of control. But Gabreski had seen a cloud layer at 14,000 feet below him. At first, the trick worked, but then the German pilot realized Gabreski's intentions and he flung his aircraft down in hot pursuit. Gabreski made a run for it; he hurtled his Thunderbolt straight down, with the German fighter full throttle behind him, both at tremendous speed. But Gabreski reached the cloud tops before the German was in firing range. Apart from his fuel, his oil was also dangerously low, with oil streaming away from the damaged aircraft. Yet he managed to reach Halesworth.

Mustangs of the 354th Fighter Group escorted Fortresses of the 1st Division. Though they did see enemy fighters, no contact was made. One Mustang failed to return.

Thunderbolts of the 353rd Fighter Group were among the fighters that provided escort over the target. 523 heavy bombers arrived over Emden and dropped their bombs by radar. The results were again doubtful.

The 4th Fighter Group did not rendezvous with the bombers because the group ran into the Luftwaffe on their way to the pick-up point. In spite of excellent fighter cover, seventeen bombers were shot down.

Monday, 13 December

A maximum effort of the 8th Air Force brought the hitherto largest force of heavy bombers into the air: 710 Fortresses and Liberators set out to the North German ports. Conditions were perfect for radar bombing, with clouds not too high but opaque enough for enemy fighters to make their way through only with difficulty.

Three of the twelve combat wings went for Bremen, where they arrived around midday under escort of chiefly P–47 groups. The larger force comprised of the remaining nine wings, involving 478 bombers including twelve pathfinders, attacked Kiel. The force was supported in the target area by the two long-range units of P–38s from the 55th Fighter Group, and 48 P–51s from the 354th Fighter Group, the latter flying to the limit of their escort range, which at this time meant a record for fighter escort.

The Mustangs saw little action. One of the pilots, Lt. Glenn T. Eagleston, attacked an Me–110, but could only claim a probable after knocking out an engine. One Mustang failed to return, cause unknown.

121

Damage was done to town and dock areas, and the principal submarine building yard, "Deutsche Werke," received several hits from high explosives and incendiaries. One of the 2nd Division Liberators that arrived over the city was piloted by the famous filmstar James Stewart. Five bombers were lost.

The 9th Air Force also sent a record number of bombers to Amsterdam/Schiphol. Of the 208 Marauders dispatched, 109 dropped almost 400 tons of bombs on the airfield. Eight formations of Marauders arrived over Schiphol between 1415 and 1445, releasing 787 bombs; 65% fell in the target area. The hangar and repair shops on the south side of the field received many direct hits.

Flak was heavy and accurate, and two Marauders were brought down. Most of the Marauders returned with heavy damage. One of them, *The Flying Dutchman*, piloted by Lt. van Antwerp of the 323rd Bomb Group, received 150 holes.

The 359th Fighter Group, 8th A.F., flew its first operational mission with the P–47 Thunderbolt into northern France.

Wednesday, 15 December

Hitherto, the United States Army Air Force (USAAF) controlled both the 8th and 9th Air Forces. However, from this date onward the 9th Air Force came under the control of the Allied Expeditionary Air Force, under the command of Air Chief Marshal Sir Trafford Leigh Mallory. He now had under his control both American and British Tactical Air Forces, committed to operation "Overlord," the invasion of the continent, and thereafter the support of the ground armies in their battle for ultimate victory.

Thursday, 16 December

Six hundred thirty one Fortresses and Liberators set out on the by-now familiar route that took them to Bremen. Eleven pathfinders led the mission. Luftwaffe fighters took to the air to meet the bombers, and they soon became embroiled in frantic battles with the escort. Mustangs of the 354th Fighter Group engaged the Me–109s and Ju–88s a quarter of an hour after they rendezvoused with the bombers over Holland. Their first Me–109 was shot down.

Total cloud covered Bremen, causing pathfinder bombing. Although the results could not be observed, crews reported a heavy black smoke, towering through the cloud bank up to 10,000 feet.

In spite of the fighter protection, ten heavy bombers were lost. One Liberator, *Bomerang*, completed her 50th mission after she had nearly been confined to scrap after her first mission. It was a record for an 8th Air Force B–24.

Monday, 20 December

Five hundred forty-six heavy bombers were dispatched to renew the visits to Bremen. P–47 Thunderbolts furnished cover to and from the target, while 44 P–51 Mustangs and 35 P–38 Lightnings formed the umbrella over the target area.

Strong German fighter forces were up to meet the bombers. Under cover of single-engine fighters, the Germans tried to place their twin-engine rocket-carrying aircraft in a position to lob their explosives into the bombers. This, however, could successfully be prevented by the Mustangs and Lightnings.

Some bombers were thirty minutes late due to strong adverse winds. Because of this, they were off-course. This could easily have ended in disaster but for their fighter escort giving excellent protection. Yet 27 bombers were lost on this mission, one of them going down after a head-on collision with a German fighter. Four Me–110s were shot down by the Mustangs of the 354th Fighter Group for the loss of three P–51s.

Better weather conditions than on the 16th permitted the bombers to drop a concentrated pattern of explosives and incendiaries on docks and warehouses along the river. Smoke was seen for fifty miles.

All four Marauder groups of the 9th Air Force set out on a mission to the ski sites. Clouds concealed some of the assigned targets, but the 323rd and 386th Bomb Groups were able to pick out the site when they arrived over Agenviller. Results of the bombing were difficult to judge because most of the very small targets were located in woods, obscuring ground details in reconnaissance photos.

Tuesday, 21 December

Seventy-nine Marauders of the 9th Air Force continued their attacks on the ski sites. The assigned targets were now at Cocove and Vacqueriette. The latter target should have been bombed by the 323rd Group, but the Marauders dropped their load on St. Remy au Bois instead. For navigators it was very difficult to locate and identify these pinpoint targets with hardly any reference points to make up their position.

Wednesday, 22 December

A small penetration into Germany was made by a heavy force of 8th Air Force Fortresses and Liberators. 225 B–17s headed across Holland to the marshalling yards at Münster and 346 B–17s and B–24s, with an additional eight B–17s acting as pathfinders, droned over Holland to visit the marshalling yards at Osnabrück.

Thunderbolts of the 56th Fighter Group rendezvoused with the Osnabrück force over the Zuider Zee. Just beyond Zwolle, a B–17 dropped out of formation and aborted the mission. Two Me–109s spotted the lonely bomber and closed in to finish it off. Their intentions were realized by two Thunderbolt pilots watching the Messerschmitts sneak to the bomber. Each Thunderbolt came down in a screaming dive to end up behind the tail of one of the Messerschmitts. The German pilot banked slightly to the left and looked back. The last he saw in his life were the eight gunbarrels of Robert Johnson's Thunderbolt blazing away at him. The second Messerschmitt broke off the chase and dived for shelter in the clouds.

The German fighters offered strong opposition. Thunderbolts forced them into many combats, but they could not prevent the Germans from breaking through the defenses and 22 heavy bombers were shot down. Thirteen of them were Liberators of the 2nd Division. One of the Fortresses crashlanded near Delden in Holland. Three new Liberator groups, with the 448th Bomb Group making its first mission, lost two aircraft each.

Thunderbolts of the 4th Fighter Group escorted the bombers to Münster. One of the pilots, whose name would come to fame in the 8th Air Force,

December 22, 1943. The Flying Fortress *USS Aliquippa,* moments after coming down. After bombing the marshalling yards at Osnabrück, she was hit by flak, and two engines were on fire when the plane left formation to crashland near the city of Delden in Holland. (Photo from *Air Combat 1939–1945*)

December 22, 1943. USS Aliquippa with German guards.
(Photo from *Air Combat 1939–1945*)

scored his second kill. He was John Godfrey, flying in *Reggie's Reply* (named after his brother Reggie, who had been lost at sea when his ship was torpedoed by a German submarine). John Godfrey almost lost his life in this mission. After shooting down an Me–109, he was almost shot down himself by an Me–109 approaching him from behind. Nose over tail, his Thunderbolt tumbled down. The German could only assume his victim was lost when he saw the fighter tumbling into the clouds. Only by pushing throttle and stick forward did he manage to recover. With several instruments shot out, Godfrey ran for home. Flying through the murk, he again escaped death by only a few feet when his aircraft dropped down several times as he became a victim of vertigo.

A new fighter group was added to the strength of the 9th Air Force. It was the 365th Fighter Group, flying P–47 Thunderbolts.

Thursday, 23 December

Gilze-Rijen was again the target for the bomb-carrying Thunderbolts of the 353rd Fighter Group, and in the morning 44 aircraft arrived over the field to make their divebombing attack.

The 9th Air Force was strengthened with another fighter group: the 363rd, equipped with the P–51 Mustang.

Friday, 24 December

The 8th Air Force dispatched 722 heavy bombers to fly a mission to the Pas de Calais area. Escorted by Thunderbolts, Mustangs, and Lightnings, together more than 1300 aircraft, 670 bombers dropped 1700 tons of bombs on 23 ski sites, or "special military installations" as was briefed to the crews.

It had been agreed that the 8th Air Force should carry out a mass attack on the chain of ski sites with their heavies because the efforts of the tactical air forces to damage the sites significantly had been very ineffective so far. Yet the attacks by the mediums on these targets continued, and the Marauders appeared over several sites to add their share to the heavy bombload that descended on the "Noballs" today.

To find the right way of attack against those sites, a replica was built at Eglin Field in the United States and all kinds of attacks were tested. It was found out that medium-and high-altitude bombings were the least effective and most wasteful. The answer lay in minimum altitude attacks by fighters. All the results were laid down in a final report, which would be issued on 1 March 1944.

The British were very sceptical about the results and doubted the value of the Eglin probings. Indeed, no significant results had been achieved by the American minimum-altitude attacks, so the British would stick to their tactics of medium- and heavy-bomber attacks.

A trial minimum altitude attack was to be carried out on 6 May 1944.

Tuesday, 28 December

The 20th Fighter Group flew its first operational mission with P–38J Lightnings.

Thursday, 30 December

Long-range P–51s escorted the 658 heavy bombers of the 8th over the target, Ludwigshafen. Eleven pathfinders led the bombing, but again the results were discouraging. The I. G. Farben plant suffered only minor damage. At the end of the year, it had become clear that the importance of radar bombing lay rather on continuous bombing with a presumed pressure on the enemy than on accuracy.

Flak was heavy over the target and the bombers ran occasionally into attacks from German fighters. On the route back, a wave of twenty yellow-nosed Focke Wulfs made a concentrated attack near Rheims during a ten-minute period. 23 bombers failed to return.

Thunderbolts of the 56th Fighter Group, giving withdrawal support, stayed longer with the bombers than planned because the relieving fighter group appeared late. As a result, many P–47s were very low on fuel and had to make emergency landings along the English south coast. Two Thunderbolts of the group mixed it up with two long-nosed FW–190s near Nancy.

Another fighter group that became engaged with the Luftwaffe was the 353rd Group, escorting the bombers over France on their way to the target. Three German Me–109s were shot down for the loss of two P–47s.

Marauders of the 9th Air Force attacked the sites on the French coast.

December 30, 1943. A fighter pilot brings his Thunderbolt in close formation with a Liberator during the bomb-run-in to Ludwigshafen. (Official USAF Photo)

Friday, 31 December

Improved weather conditions were expected over the southern part of France, so part of the 572 heavy bombers dispatched by the 8th Air Force went to many airfields along the French coastal area, even as far as Bordeaux.

Other forces were on a route that took them to the C. A. M. ball-bearing works at Paris. These works were adjacent to the Hispano-Suiza plant, which was also on the receiving end of a bombload. Heavy cloud formations were met, with tops mounting to 25,000 feet. Yet this was only a small part of the inconvenience, for the Luftwaffe intended to let its existence count heavily. Many encounters took place with the bombers, of which 464 actually attacked. The cost was 25 aircraft.

Mustangs and Lightnings escorted the heavies on the farthest leg of the

December 31, 1943. Cognac/Châteaubernard Airfield re-
ceives attention from 8th Air Force bombers. (Official USAF
Photo)

mission, with the Mustangs of the 354th Fighter Group going to Bordeaux,
thus covering a distance of more than 500 miles. During one of the many
combats with the German fighters, Lt. Robert Johnson of the 56th Fighter
Group sent two Focke Wulfs into the ground as his ninth and tenth victories in the air.

After eight hours in the air, the returning bombers reached the English
coast in darkness and heavy clouds. And another eighteen bombers were
written off. Some bombers crashed because their fuel tanks ran empty
while searching for a landing place. Others crashed because the aircraft
was too heavily damaged to execute a normal landing. Others, which did
land, were in such bad shape that they were confined to scrap.

Not only the bombers, but also the fighters were very short on fuel on
the return flight. Several Lightnings force-landed, others managed to reach
airfields along the south coast, and one Lightning ditched near a rescue
launch.

Marauders of the 9th Air Force turned to France again to bomb the ski sites.

By this time, the 8th Fighter Command was composed of ten Thunderbolt groups: 4th, 56th, 78th, 352nd, 353rd, 355th, 356th, 358th, 359th, and 361st; and two Lightning groups: 20th and 55th. Still the 8th Fighter Command was three groups short of its planned strength.

9th Fighter Command would start January with only one operational fighter group, the 354th.

(Date approximate.) B–24 Liberators of the 392nd Bomb Group. (Official USAF Photo)

Part III

1944

1

JANUARY

Tuesday, 4 January

Five hundred fifty-five heavy bombers of the 8th Air Force took off in the morning on their first mission in the new year: a radar-bombing attack on the port installations and shipbuilding plants at Kiel, with Münster as a secondary target. Fighters escorted the bombers all the way to the target and back. Another mission was carried out against Tours.

A special outfit in the 8th Air Force was formed by the "Carpetbaggers." Carpetbagger was the codename for the delivery of supplies to underground movements, dropping agents, etc. Charged with these missions were two squadrons, forming a subgroup of the 482nd Bomb Group. (From 28 March onward they formed a special group, the 801st Bomb Group, until August when it became the 492nd Bomb Group with four squadrons—the 856th, 857th, 858th, and 859th Squadrons.)

The planes were B–24 Liberators with special modifications: removed ball-turrets, a cargo hatch called a "Joe-hole" (because parachutists had to drop through it), blisters for the pilot's and co-pilot's window, and several other changes.

To direct the navigator to a ground operator, a special device was installed called "Rebecca," recording radar impulses on a grid. The ground operator's set was called "Eureka." To the equipment belonged a two-way radio to provide contact with a ground phone called an "S-phone." The B–24s were all painted a shiny black.

Tonight the first "Carpetbagger" mission was flown to France. Until May, 1945, the Carpetbaggers would complete 1860 sorties out of 2857 attempted. They would drop 20,495 containers and 11,174 packages of supplies to patriots in western and northwestern Europe. 1043 agents would jump through the "Joe-hole." During these missions, twenty-five B–24s were lost.

Wednesday, 5 January

A clear sky offered good prospects of visual bombing, and when the 215 bombers reached their target at Kiel, they inflicted severe damage to three of the buildings of the German Werft. The Luftwaffe rose and among the fighters harassing the bombers were several rocket-firing Me–110s.

Mustangs provided target support, and in encounters with the German fighters the 354th Fighter Group claimed eighteen shot down for no losses. One of their P–51s was hit by a rocket after it had shot down two Me—110s and, although the pilot was hurt and his aircraft severely damaged, with its guns no longer firing, he continued to attack the Me–110s. He then turned for home and managed to land his plane safely.

A new practice of fighter escort was introduced, with Thunderbolts, patrolling assigned areas along the bomber route, while longer-ranging P–38s and P–51s escorted along the target leg.

Other bomber formations went to the Jaeger ball-bearing works at Elberfeld. However, cloud conditions and the failure of pathfinder equipment forced the bombers to turn to targets of opportunity. Bombs were dropped on a small town near Elberfeld.

Thursday, 6 January

A new organization, the "United States Strategic Air Forces in Europe," was established, embracing the 8th Air Force and 15th Air Force. Its purpose was to coordinate the operations of the 8th Air Force from England and the 15th Air Force from Italy.

General Carl Spaatz assumed command of USSTAF, with Lt. Gen. James H. Doolittle in command of the 8th Air Force and General Ira C. Eaker in command of the 15th Air Force.

Near Coblenz, the 56th Fighter Group Thunderbolts encountered fifteen FW–190s and in the ensuing air battle at least one Focke Wulf was shot down.

Friday, 7 January

Guided by pathfinder aircraft, 500 heavy bombers of the 8th Air Force set out for Ludwigshafen. The ten groups of Fortresses and Liberators first headed for Frankfurt before they suddenly changed course to the target: the huge chemical works of the I. G. Farben industry at Ludwigshafen. Thun-

134

derbolts and Mustangs escorted the bombers. Over Belgium, the German fighters made several attacks. After that the sky was filled with flak bursts.

Clouds made visual bombing impossible and 279.5 tons of high explosives were dropped on radar indication. After this bombing, no methanol or isobutyl oil was produced for the remainder of the month. In proportion to the attack, however, the results were small, only 127 bombs, or 36 tons, hitting the target.

After the bombing, the lead Liberator group, the 389th, took a course that brought the group too far south and out of the protective bomber formations. The leader of the trailing Liberator group, Captain James Stewart (better known as a famous filmstar), decided to join the wandering 389th group to add the firepower of his group to that of the other formation.

Forty-eight Thunderbolts of the 353rd Group rendezvoused with the Liberators near Metz at 1225 hours at an altitude of 24,000 feet. They escorted the bombers out, flying over a solid overcast. In the vicinity of Orleans, the fighters withdrew, but they had not gone far when they heard the calls for help. Fully aware of the fact that their fuel supply was nearly depleted, they returned to the aid of the bombers. They managed to disperse the German fighters, but not before eight Liberators had been shot down, all of the 389th Group, including the leader. Three Focke Wulfs were shot down, all three by one pilot, Lt. Jesse W. Gonnam. After crossing the English coast, the Thunderbolts landed at various airfields in the south, and one made a crashlanding.

9th Air Force Marauders visited the Cherbourg/Maupertuis Airfield. The bombers were heavily escorted but, although one of their main purposes was to draw the German fighters into combat, the Luftwaffe did not show much interest in countering them.

Tuesday, 11 January

The weather over central Germany had cleared and though it was only for a brief period, it was sufficient to allow the 8th Air Force to dispatch a large force of 663 heavy bombers to high-priority targets in the German aircraft industry.

Heading the bomberstream was the 1st Division with three combat wings going to Oschersleben to bomb the AGO Flugzeugwerke AG, principal center of Focke Wulf production. Two other combat wings of the same division headed for Halberstadt to strike the Junkers Flugzeug und Motorenwerke.

Next in the stream were the Fortresses of the 3rd Division, while the Liberators of the 2nd Division brought up the rear of the column. These two divisions, involving seven combat wings, also went to the Brunswick

135

area to attack three separate plants operated by Mühlenbau und Industrie AG (Me–110 aircraft and assembly plants).

All targets were situated on the route to Berlin, so very heavy opposition from the German fighter force was expected. Therefore, eleven groups of P–47 Thunderbolts and two groups of P–38 Lightnings were allocated to cover the three bomber formations from the Dutch coast to about 70 miles from the target. Only the first formation Fortresses would have fighter escort in the target area provided by the one available P–51 group, the 354th Fighter Group.

Forecasters had predicted a clear sky over the targets. Over the various bases in England, it was quite a different story, however, and trouble was met on take-off and assembly. Once the large force was in the air, weather conditions en route grew worse and worse with very high cloud formations extending all the way across the Channel and Holland. Some of the Lightnings, not breaking out of the clouds at 24,000 feet, returned to base.

With no favorable prospects for successful bombing, the B–24s of the 2nd Division and the B–17s of the 3rd Division were recalled. The 1st Division droned on because, at the moment that the recall message was received, the Fortresses had already neared their target to within 100 miles.

The leading combat wing of the 3rd Division was also far in enemy territory, and its commander decided to proceed to the primary target flying at 17,000 feet under an overcast at 25,000 feet. The remaining three combat wings of the 3rd Division and the entire 2nd Division turned back. On their way home, they bombed targets of opportunity.

The Mustangs of the 354th Fighter Group rendezvoused ahead of schedule and could do little more than escort the bombers to the target. They had to split their force of 49 P–51s into two sections, one to protect the 174 bombers on their way to Oschersleben and one to accompany the B–17s to Halberstadt.

Perhaps fearing that Berlin was the target, the Germans were up in such a force that many American pilots got the idea that Germany had sent its entire air force into the sky. Using bellytanks, the German fighter formations flew parallel and out of range of the bombers and their escort, waiting for the moment the American fighters had to withdraw because of reaching the limit of their range. At that moment, they dropped their bellytanks and pressed home their savagely coordinated attacks, concentrating on the Oschersleben and Halberstadt forces.

Where the defensive boxes of the bomber formations were tight, the Germans placed their twin-engine rocket-firing planes in position beyond normal gun range, and they poured their rockets into the mass of Fortresses with devastating results. Where the defensive boxes were not so tight, their elements were attacked by a mass of single-engine fighters.

And, as usual, the leading formations bore the brunt of the mauling. 34

Fortresses of the 174 sent to Oschersleben were shot down. The 303rd Group in the lead position lost ten. *The Eight Ball,* carrying the task commander, Brig. General Robert Travis, survived the slaughter.

The few Mustang pilots fought with great bravery against overwhelming odds, destroying eleven German fighters for no loss. One of their pilots, Major James H. Howard, commanding the 356th Squadron, earned the highest US award for bravery, the Medal of Honor. Major Howard was a former Flying Tiger pilot with 6½ victories over Japanese planes. He was the only AAF fighter pilot flying from England to be awarded this decoration.

In the fighting, Major Howard became separated from his squadron and wingman. He returned to the bombers just as they came under attack by thirty enemy fighters. Realizing that he was their entire fighter cover, he unhesitatingly attacked the Germans and, in an unequaled display of tactical skill and aggressiveness, he managed in the next thirty minutes to break up all enemy attacks. After the first two encounters, two of his four machineguns stopped firing and after half an hour, only one of the guns of his Mustang, *Ding Hao* (AJ-A), was operating, but by that time the German fighters withdrew.

January 11, 1944. A Fortress of the Oschersleben force goes down under the fire of an FW-190. (Official USAF Photo)

137

Howard's award was primarily due to the enthusiastic reports of the B–17 crews of the 401st Bomb Group he protected.

With the 94th Group in the lead position, the solitary combat wing of the 3rd Division droned on to its target, the Me–110 assembly plant at Waggum. Despite heavy fighter attacks, the commander wheeled the lead box around to start a second bomb run when he found the target difficult to identify on the initial approach. Coming in after the two other boxes, he placed 73 percent of his bombs within 1000 feet of the aiming point and, with the other boxes also bombing very accurately, considerable damage was caused and all major installations were hit.

Severe damage was also done to the factory buildings at Oschersleben. Considering the size.of the attacking forces, the results were encouraging.

Sixty bombers failed to return. The Luftwaffe losses seemed to amount to 39 from the 207 participating in the battle; 28 of these were claimed by the 8th fighters.

January 11, 1944. Flying Bison of the 303rd Bomb Group passes a cloud of smoke left by a disintegrating B–17. (Photo from *Air Combat 1939–1945*)

Friday, 14 January

Fifty-seven Thunderbolts of the 353rd Fighter Group, 8th Air Force, flew an afternoon patrol in an area north of Amiens. They formed part of a large fighter force that ranged over France. Led by Col. Don Blakeslee, the 4th Fighter Group set off on a fighter sweep to Marigny. They became entangled in a dogfight with Luftwaffe fighters and claimed ten enemy aircraft shot down.

9th Air Force B–26 Marauders paid one of their regular visits to the "Noballs" sites. Heavy flak was thrown up, and one of the Marauders was severely hit. With a shattered nose, the hydraulic system punctured, the right engine knocked out, and the propeller damaged so it could not be feathered, the pilot managed to keep his aircraft on course over the target. After delivering his load, he brought the plane back to England, crossing the coast at minimum altitude. Only with the greatest effort could the plane be kept in the air, slowly descending with open bomb-bay doors, until it touched the ground in a well-executed crashlanding.

Also, heavy bombers of the 8th returned to the V–1 installations, and in perfect visibility bombs were dropped on the rocket site at Quoeux, while others dropped on Croisetter.

January 14, 1944. B–17G, *Pistol Packin Mama* of the 1st Division, 91st Bomb Group, flying at 12,100 feet toward France. (Official USAF Photo)

Thursday, 20 January

In a dogfight between Focke Wulfs and Thunderbolts over Rouen, one Thunderbolt was shot down, for at least one German fighter.

Friday, 21 January

While paying their frequent visit to the V-weapon sites along the French coast, B–24 Liberators of the 44th Bomb Group were bounced by Focke Wulfs in a surprise attack. The Liberators were trying to find a gap in the

139

clouds to locate their target. Five B–24s were shot down, and a sixth, the lead bomber, was so heavily damaged by anti-aircraft fire that it crashed at the English coast. Also, one Fortress failed to return after a similar operation.

Escorting Thunderbolts had several encounters with the Luftwaffe. P–47s of the 353rd Group, out on an area support mission in the Pas de Calais area, came across four Me–109s. The Thunderbolts dived down behind the Messerschmitts and sent three earthwards. A few moments later, Thunderbolts of the same group were in hot pursuit of two enemy planes, chasing them through the clouds. When the Thunderbolts broke out below the clouds, they had lost the sight of their two Luftwaffe fighters. However, down below an airfield was clearly visible with a Do–217 bomber on it. Three Thunderbolts swooped down and, in a strafing pass, they destroyed the German bomber.

While making their bomb runs on the V–1 installation at Heuringhem, the Fortresses met heavy flak from the batteries at St. Omer, and one B–17 was shot down. Other Fortresses dropped bombs on La Glacerie.

Sunday, 23 January

Gilze-Ryen airfield was the target for P–47 Thunderbolts of the 356th Fighter Group making their first divebombing mission. In the afternoon, the P–47s of the 353rd Group were also out on a divebombing mission; however, cloud conditions under way forced the Thunderbolts to return without bombing.

Monday, 24 January

British and American commanders came to an agreement that placed the majority of the P–51 units under 8th Air Force command. This Air Force would eventually be almost exclusively equipped with the Mustang fighter in the near future. It was obvious that the 8th Air Force was most urgently in need of these long-range fighters. The P–47 Thunderbolts and the P–38 Lightnings were to be transferred to the 9th Air Force.

Heavy bombers of the 8th Air Force were recalled due to poor weather conditions. After receiving the recall message, some of the bombers dropped on targets of opportunity. A small town east of Aachen received a bombload from seventeen bombers which formed part of the force that had the Deutsche Metall Werke at Frankfurt as their assigned target.

The P–47s returned from their area support assignment, and it was near Tirlemont that the Thunderbolts of the 353rd Group spotted five Me–110s with radar equipment flying at 5000 feet. In a swift action, all five were shot down. Near Brussels, they dived on an Me–109 landing on Gosson-

140

court Airfield. A Mustang of the 354th Fighter Group was shot down over Brussels.

Tuesday, 25 January

All three squadrons of the 353rd Fighter Group were bombed up, and 46 Thunderbolts crossed the Dutch coast and headed for the airfield at Leeuwarden. Diving from about 15,000 feet, the fighters dropped 44 500-lb. bombs. They met no flak, and the group managed to score some hits.

Mustangs of the 354th Fighter Group, along with five Mustangs of the new 357th Fighter Group, were crossing Antwerp when suddenly FW–190s tore into their formation and two Mustangs went down.

Saturday, 29 January

Eight hundred three heavy bombers of the 8th Air Force were out on a mission in the morning to strike the industrial area and marshalling yards at Frankfurt-am-Main. The bombers were guided by pathfinder aircraft, and flew with a heavy fighter escort. It soon became clear that the escort would be badly needed.

The Luftwaffe appeared to intercept the bombers, but the escort encountered the German fighters before they were able to press home their attack. In the ensuing battle, the American fighters claimed 45 enemy aircraft shot down for the loss of fourteen.

P–38 Lightnings of the 20th Fighter Group scored a success when their contribution in the fight led to the destruction of ten enemy fighters. Four Lightnings failed to return; two of them had collided in the battle. Returning from the combat in the German skies, two P–47s of the 352nd Fighter Group passed over Belgium when one of them was hit by flak. The pilot was Captain George Preddy, one of the most successful American fighter pilots. He bailed out over the Channel and was picked up by Air-Sea Rescue.

4th Group Thunderbolts roamed the area near Koblenz and destroyed nine Luftwaffe aircraft.

Sunday, 30 January

Led by pathfinder aircraft, 778 heavy bombers of the 8th set off to attack Brunswick. One combat wing of the 2nd Division, composed of the 44th and 392nd Group Liberators, became separated from the main bomber force. Near Hannover, a break in the clouds revealed a large synthetic rubber plant. Taking advantage of a visual bombing possibility, the forty

141

B–24s started their bomb run on this target of opportunity and unloaded their bombs on the factory installations.

A heavy fighter escort accompanied the bombers, and they didn't have to wait long to justify their presence. Many Lightnings were forced to withdraw prematurely because extreme cold at high altitudes resulted in engine failures, a common feature with this type of aircraft. About 200 German fighters arrived on the scene, and the next moment the sky was filled with whirling and twisting fighters. The American fighter pilots claimed 45 Luftwaffe fighters, losing four of their number.

Escorting the bombers with destination Bremen, both the 56th and the 353rd Fighter Groups (the latter on the way out) also mixed it up with the Luftwaffe fighters. The 56th Group destroyed sixteen and the 353rd three enemy aircraft.

Monday, 31 January

A Gee–H-equipped B–24 was the lead aircraft for each of the four groups of Liberators going to "Noball" targets in the Pas de Calais area.

Gilze-Rijen was again the favorite target for a divebombing attack. This time the Thunderbolts of the 4th and 78th Fighter Groups made their debut with this technique.

2

FEBRUARY

Thursday, 3 February

Heretofore, fighters escorting the bombers of the 8th Air Force had been under control of 8th Fighter Command. However, today two P–38 Lightning groups of the 70th Fighter Wing 9th Tactical Air Command escorted the heavy bombers to Wilhelmshaven. Escort was also provided by 46 Thunderbolts of the 353rd Fighter Group and, in encouters with the Luftwaffe, they sent two Me–109s and an FW–190 down. One of the three Thunderbolts lost by this group had its tail completely sawn off when it flew into the prop of another P–47. Clouds up to 27,000 feet forced many bombers to fly at an altitude above 28,000 feet. Bombs were dropped through the undercast at 5,000 feet higher than the briefed bombing altitude.

Friday, 4 February

Extreme cold caused nearly half of the 20th and 55th Fighter Group Lightnings to abort their mission when they escorted the heavy bombers of the 8th to Frankfurt.

It was obvious that the Lightnings were difficult to operate in very cold conditions. Therefore, they preferred to stay below 30,000 feet to avoid engine failure, but this brought them also in a very disadvantageous and hazardous position with the German fighters operating at altitudes up to 35,000 feet.

Returning from the marshalling yards at Frankfurt, some bomber formations met Focke Wulfs over Belgium. Thunderbolts escorted the bombers back to England.

Saturday, 5 February

More than one thousand British and American fighters escorted the heavy bombers of the 8th Air Force when they were out on a mission to targets in the Paris area. A single Me–109 dived out of the clouds through a formation of Thunderbolts of the 56th Fighter Group. In this flashing attack, two Thunderbolts were shot down.

Many German fighters were encountered, and one FW–190 was sent down to crash in the woods near Paris. The Focke Wulf was shot down by a P–47 of the 353rd Group, which group also lost one aircraft.

Hampered by bad weather during the opening days of the month, the mediums of the 9th Air Force took to the air again and 226 Marauders struck on seven "Noball" targets in the area of St. Omer. Flak near these targets was becoming increasingly heavy, and six bombers fell victim to their fire.

Sunday, 6 February

Enemy-held airfields in France were visited by B–26 Marauders of the 9th Air Force. Many targets were hidden by clouds as heavy bombers of the 8th also turned to airfields in France and, because of the covered areas and the scattered attacks by enemy fighters, many bombers brought their loads back home.

Tuesday, 8 February

The 8th Air Force dispatched its heavy bombers on a mission to Frankfurt. Over France, a number of small groups of German fighters were met, resulting in several dogfights with the escorting fighters.

Captain Walter Beckham of the 353rd Fighter Group destroyed an FW–190 and an Me–109 and became the top-ranking ace in the 8th Air Force, with 18 victories. Thunderbolts of this group downed seven Luftwaffe fighters without loss to themselves.

Mustangs of the 354th Group provided support over the target and on the way back. Returning from their mission, the P–51s went down on the deck and strafed targets of opportunity. But this experiment cost the group four aircraft, three of them shot down by a large formation of Luftwaffe fighters bouncing the Mustangs in a surprise attack. Escorting the bombers out, one of the Lightnings of the 20th Fighter Group got supercharger trouble at high altitude and it descended with its flight to 12,000 feet. Flying at this low altitude over the German countryside, one of the pilots had the fortune three times to send down a totally surprised enemy fighter pilot.

144

The same pilot came across a locomotive near Saarburg and he shot it up. He became separated from his flight and took a straight course home. But then a fourth German fighter loomed ahead and in a surprise attack, he destroyed it, his fourth aerial victory for the day. The pilot was Lt. James M. Morris, and he undoubtedly had given the Lightning pilots more faith in their aircraft by his action.

Two missions to the V-weapon sites in the Pas de Calais area were flown by Marauders of the 9th Air Force.

Wednesday, 9 February

9th Air Force B–26 Marauders were heading for Tergnier in northern France. They would carry out the first of what was to become a long series of attacks against marshalling yards.

It had been learned that a complete Panzer Division was on the move and was likely to pass through Tergnier. 54 Marauders of the 322nd and 386th Bomb Group dropped their loads on the target and several hits were scored.

Thursday, 10 February

In these early days, the Mustang pilots were not only troubled by enemy fighters, flak, and bad weather, but also by identification problems. Especially in the heat of battle, friend or foe were often only identified by a quick glance and as the silhouette of the Mustang had some resemblance to that of the Me–109, it had happened on a number of occasions that the Mustangs were jumped by the Thunderbolts or Lightnings.

One of these occasions took place today when Captain Glenn Eagleston of the 354th Fighter Group lined his Mustang up behind a German fighter and was suddenly shot at by a Thunderbolt. He managed to get his plane back over England where he bailed out. The group lost three P-51s in their battle with the Luftwaffe fighters, launching attack after attack on the 169 B–17 Fortresses returning from a bombardment on Brunswick. The bad weather that upset the accuracy of the bombing also caused rendezvous troubles with the escort.

An estimated 310 German fighters had approached the bombers, making use of the thick and persistent contrails for cover. In spite of all efforts of the escorting fighters to ward off the attacks on the bombers, during which the 354th Group sent eight German fighters earthwards, 29 Fortresses went down. The 353rd Fighter Group, escorting the bombers out, claimed the destruction of three enemy aircraft, while another group, the 4th, counted up eight victories in a struggle with the Luftwaffe near Hannover. Eight

145

February 10, 1944. The end of the war for the 452nd
Bomb Group's *Dinah Might*, at rest in the Ijsselmeer Pol-
der. (Photo from *Air Combat 1939–1945*)

escorting fighters failed to return, and a Fortress of the 100th Bomb Group
landed in Sweden.

Friday, 11 February

The production of methanol or isobutyl had just resumed after it had
been stopped as a result of the bombing on the 7th, when the 8th Air Force
heavies appeared again over the chemical works at Ludwigshafen to bring
it again to a halt. Their other target was Frankfurt.

Thunderbolts escorted the bombers flying under a high overcast. Soon
after the Mustangs of the 354th Fighter Group had crossed the French coast
on their way to the rendezvous point with the bombers, they were jumped
by Luftwaffe fighters in an attempt to stop them from joining the bombers.
Again when the Mustangs were close to the bombers, the German fighers
repeated their attacks. In the ensuing melee, the group commander, Colonel Martin, collided with an Me–109 when both aircraft came rushing on
toward each other, both firing in the head-on pass. Miraculously, both
pilots managed to bail out of their wrecked aircraft. Two Mustangs were
lost, but the group claimed fourteen enemy aircraft.

146

After a battle with Me–109s, two squadrons of the 56th Group caught sight of an enemy airfield near Rheims when they returned from their escort mission. Hubert Zemke led his fighters down and, in a single strafing pass, they set several aircraft ablaze. Eight P–38 Lightnings of the 20th Group were shot down on their escort mission to Frankfurt.

Major James Howard from the 354th Fighter Group took the first operational 8th Air Force P–51 group, the 357th Fighter Group, up on a mission. 41 Mustangs flew a support mission for B–24 Liberators bombing the V-weapon sites in the Pas de Calais area.

Saturday, 12 February

P–47 Thunderbolts and P–51 Mustangs escorted the bombers to targets in the Pas de Calais area where they visited the "Noball" targets.

Sunday, 13 February

Both the 8th and 9th Air Force dispatched its bombers to the rocket installations along the French coast. From 12,000 feet, the heavies dropped their loads on the ski sites, notably at Crequi and Ruisseauville. 207 Marauders of the 9th unloaded on the V–1 installations.

Thunderbolts and Mustangs escorted the bombers over France. Although no enemy fighters were seen, one bomber exploded near Abbeville. On the way back to base, flying over the North Sea, the engine of a Mustang of the 357th Fighter Group suddenly quit. Descending from 20,000 feet, the pilot tried in vain to start the engine again. At 6,000 feet he bailed out. An Air-Sea Rescue launch picked him up after he had stayed for thirty minutes in the icy cold waters.

Monday, 14 February

Gilze-Rijen Airfield was again the target for a divebombing mission carried out in the morning by 48 Thunderbolts of the 353rd Fighter Group. They dropped 48 500-lb. GP bombs, along with fragmentation bomb clusters.

Tuesday, 15 February

During the morning, 247 B–26 Marauders struck several airfields in France, and in the afternoon, 141 Marauders dropped their loads on "Noball" targets.

A new Marauder group became operational in the 9th Air Force. It was the 391st Bomb Group.

Saturday, 19 February

The 8th Air Force had now 19¾ B–17 groups, 8½ B–24 groups, eight P–47 groups, two P–38 groups, and two P–51 groups.

Sunday, 20 February

During January and the first half of February, weather made all precision bombing impossible and it was not until the 19th that forecasters were able to predict fair weather over the continent for the next day.

It also meant that plan "Argument" came into operation: coordinated precision-bombing attacks by the 8th and 15th Air Forces against aircraft manufacturing targets, principally airframe and final assembly plants deep in the Reich, in order to gain air superiority over Western Europe before the invasion date, which had been set for May under the codename "Overlord." The bombing job was to be completed by March 1st. The RAF agreed to make its night attacks coincide with the daylight missions, both in time and place.

With icy cloud decks at 500 feet and snow showers sprinkling the fields, 1003 heavy bombers of the 8th Air Force thundered along the runways and climbed into the clouds. A force of 16 combat wings, the largest in the history of the American strategic forces, assembled in the clear sky above the clouds, and set out for twelve vital targets.

Six combat wings took a course that led them across the southern part of Denmark in the direction of Poland, where they would attack targets in the Posen area and at Tutow. The remaining ten combat wings of the 1st and 2nd Division were going to targets in central Germany, in the Brunswick-Leipzig area. This force was spearheaded by the 401st Bomb Group.

All available fighter escort was given to this force. They entered the German radar screen in time to prevent large numbers of enemy fighters from concentrating on the unprotected northern force. 835 American fighters raced through the clouds to protect the bombers: thirteen groups of P–47 Thunderbolts carrying 150-gallon metal drop-tanks, two groups of P–38 Lightnings, and two groups of P–51 Mustangs. An additional sixteen fighter squadrons of Spitfires and Mustangs of the RAF were taking part in the escort duties. The so-called Big Week had begun.

The sky over Germany was not as clear as had been predicted by the forecasters, yet excellent bombing results were achieved in several cases. Severe damage was done to the Junkers airframe factory and assembly plant at Leipzig. The Erla Machinewerke at Heiterblick and the assembly plant at Mockau were badly mauled. Both were involved in the production of Me–109s. It was this raid that made the plant authorities decide to begin a serious policy of dispersal.

148

Luftwaffe fighters tried to break up the leading formations but, thanks to excellent fighter escort, the bombers suffered relatively little, undoubtedly also due to the fact that the RAF had worn out the nightfighter force during their heavy attack against Leipzig the night before.

The Mustangs rendezvoused with the bombers near Brunswick at about 1230 hours to escort the heavies to Leipzig. Thunderbolts of the 56th Group intercepted thirteen Me–110s cruising near Minden in preparation for an attack on the bombers. In a few seconds, nearly all of them were shot down. Total claims for the group amounted to fourteen.

Total claims for the day by the American fighters were 61 shot down for the loss of eleven. Although the American airmen feared losing some 200 planes, the actual losses were 21 heavy bombers out of the 941 that actually made the mission.

Monday, 21 February

Again some 950 heavy bombers of the 8th Air Force were dispatched to strike on aircraft targets in Germany. Half a dozen important airfields and storage plants in western Germany such as at Gutersloh, Lippstadt, Achmer, and Stuttgart, and also two M.I.A.G. factories producing component parts for the twin-engine rocket-firing Me–110s at Brunswick, were the assigned targets for the day's mission.

Mustangs of the 357th Fighter Group crossed the Dutch coast on their way to the rendezvous point near Osnabrück. From there they would escort the bombers to Stuttgart. Southeast of the Zuider Zee, they had their only encounter with the Luftwaffe and two Me–109s were shot down. The group lost one Mustang.

Bombing at Stuttgart was done by radar. Many bombers found the weather conditions less favorable than predicted by the forecasters, and so they attacked targets of opportunity. Although a large airpark at Diepholz was severely and accurately bombed, as were several of the other airfields attacked, the strategic result was not encouraging.

The principal targets at Brunswick were covered by clouds. The bombardiers switched from visual to pathfinder tactics and dropped a heavy tonnage of bombs on the city without damaging the aircraft factories directly. Some bomber formations, hampered by heavy clouds, dropped their bombs on Hannover.

German fighters intercepted the bombers near Steinhuder Lake. One squadron of the 354th Fighter Group turned into them; the other two squadrons of the group supported the bombers to the target and back. Near Osnabrück, they left the bombers at 1445 hours. The group had destroyed ten Luftwaffe fighters for the loss of two Mustangs.

Thunderbolts of the 56th Group sent twelve single-engine German fighters down over Holland. After the many dogfights, the American fighter pilots claimed the destruction of 33 German aircraft for a loss of five of their own.

After returning from their mission, two B–17 Fortresses of the 385th Bomb Group descended through a thick overcast to land at their base. Emerging from a cloudbase at 3,000 feet, one of the Fortresses, which was brought in in a side-slip, smashed its tail into the wing of the other B–17 and both aircraft tumbled down. There were no survivors. One of the crews was returning from its 25th, and last, mission.

Seventeen B–26 Marauders of the 322nd Bomb Group, 9th Air Force, attacked Veurne/Koksijde Airfield in Belgium. The bombers were led for the first time by a pathfinder aircraft. It was a B–26 of the First Pathfinder Squadron, equipped with GEE.

A new group was added to the 9th Air Force: the 10th Photographic Group (Reconnaissance), with only one squadron, the 30th Photo Reconnaissance Squadron.

February 21, 1944. 400 holes were counted in this damaged Liberator that came to rest off the runway. (Official USAF Photo)

Tuesday, 22 February

The 8th Air Force dispatched 466 heavy bombers to strike the enemy's aircraft industry for the third day running. This time difficulties came directly after take-off. In an attempt to break out of the clouds to assemble, the 3rd Division ran into extreme trouble and several collisions occurred. The commander, General LeMay, decided to abandon this part of the mission, which was destined to attack Schweinfurt.

The B–24s of the 2nd Division also ran into trouble. Crossing the Dutch coast on their way to Gotha, they became badly strung out. Finding it impossible to organize their formations, the decision was made to recall. Scattered groups of Liberators returned to England. Some of these groups bombed targets of opportunity. Taking them for German towns, Liberators erroneously bombed the Dutch towns of Nijmegen, Arnhem, and Enschede. Nijmegen suffered the largest number of civilian casualties, about 200, while at Enschede a Liberator group distributed its incendiaries over the city.

This left only five combat wings of the 1st Bomb Division, with 289 Fortresses, heading for their assigned targets. They were scheduled to attack Oschersleben, Halberstadt, Bernburg, and Aschersleben. Oschersleben, the most important of these, was obscured by clouds and was passed over. The Halberstadt force encountered the same trouble and bombed as an alternative, targets of opportunity.

Out of the large force that took the air this morning, only 255 planes bombed different targets, and of these, only 99 succeeded in bombing their primary targets. Most damage was done at Aschersleben where the 303rd Group Fortresses, aided by a few B–17s from the 384th Group, delivered their bombs on the mark and production at the Junkers works was cut by half for two months. The B–17 Fortresses from the 306th Bomb Group dropped their bombs on the aircraft factory at Bernburg engaged in Ju–88 production, and caused severe damage to installations. Of this group, seven bombers went down during the return trip when they were intermittently intercepted by Luftwaffe fighters.

The German fighter defenses tried a new tactic successfully. Instead of concentrating their efforts in the target area where fighter escort was usually provided, they attacked early in the penetration, at a time when fighter escort was either thin or entirely lacking. For the two groups of escorting P–51s, it was very difficult to give cover to the spread formations.

Thirty Mustangs of the 357th Group accompanied part of the 1st Division Fortresses to Bernburg and, in an encounter with the Luftwaffe, they sent seven Me–109s down for the loss of two P–51s. Mustangs of the 354th Fighter Group fared even better and destroyed thirteen for the loss of one.

Thunderbolts of the 353rd Group cruised in the designated area to pick up the B–24s. When the Liberators didn't appear, they escorted three groups of Fortresses into Germany. A direct flak hit over Antwerp sent one Thunderbolt straight down. Over Cologne, the Thunderbolts became engaged with the German fighters and in quick succession two Me–109s were shot down. One Thunderbolt was sent spinning down.

Returning from their escort, the Thunderbolts passed over Ostheim Airfield. A closer look revealed many twin-engine aircraft on it. Colonel Duncan took his group down on the deck and, coming in over the treetops,

151

they lined up on the Ju–88s. After his strafing pass, one of the pilots pulled his Thunderbolt up, but at that moment his aircraft was hit by antiaircraft fire and, with the engine of his P–47 on fire, the pilot, Major Walter Beckham, leading ace of the 8th fighter force, bailed out to spend the rest of the war in a POW camp.

The 8th Air Force had lost 41 heavy bombers, 38 from the 1st Division, and eleven fighters. The American fighter pilots claimed sixty German aircraft destroyed.

A diversionary force of B–17 Fortresses of the 92nd Group, equipped with radar-jamming devices, made a mission to Denmark to bomb the airfield at Aalborg. The 15th Air Force from Italy bombed Regensburg.

Wednesday, 23 February

Due to poor prospects for visual bombing, no missions were planned by the 8th Air Force today. This also gave an opportunity to catch up on repairs to the many damaged aircraft.

Only the 15th Air Force from Italy was able to launch an attack against the Steyr Walzlagerwerke at Steyr, Austria. 102 bombers took part in the mission.

Thursday, 24 February

The weather over central Germany had opened up and again a full-scale mission was undertaken against the German aircraft industry and the industries connected to it. 238 B–17 Fortresses of the 1st Division headed for the anti-friction bearing plants at Schweinfurt. 239 B–24 Liberators of the 2nd Division, assembled in three large combat wing formations, flew ahead and below the 1st Division. They took a course to Gotha to deliver a blow to the Gothaer Waggonfabrik AG, producing Me–110s.

The third force, comprised of B–17s of the 3rd Division assembled in five combat wings, took a course to targets in northern Germany and Poland to bomb the aircraft factories at Tutow, Kreising, and Posen. In case the initial targets were not open to visual bombing, the city of Rostock was to be visited. The extreme length of the flight left this force without fighter escort since even the P–51 did not at this time have sufficient range to cover the distance.

Finding their objectives obscured, the Fortresses turned to Rostock where they unloaded by radar. After bombing, they turned for home, without encountering much opposition.

However, it was the Schweinfurt force, and more specifically the 2nd Division on the way to Gotha, that ran into plenty of trouble. Soon after

152

crossing the Dutch coast, the German fighters started their concentrated and coordinated attacks, pulling every trick out of the bag: air-to-air bombing, towing cable-bombs, firing rockets, and many more devices invented to annihilate the bomber formations. Many B–24s went down in spite of escorting fighters. Soon after 1230 hours, the P–51 Mustangs of the 357th Fighter Group rendezvoused with the Liberators and they stayed with the bombers for two hours, all the way to the target and for a while on the return flight.

The leading 389th Bomb Group went off course when the lead aircraft suffered oxygen trouble. The bombardier collapsed over his bombsight and against the bomb release switch, with the result that the bombs were dropped. At his release, the other bombers in the group also unloaded. The 445th Bomb Group continued to the target and after the bombing, the Luftwaffe fighters concentrated on this lone formation for about one hour. Of the 25 bombers, thirteen were shot down.

With the losses of the 389th Bomb Group, which also ran into the German fighters, the total loss for the lead wing was nineteen bombers. Two FW–190s, an Me–109, an Me–110, and a Ju–88 were shot down by the 357th Group Mustangs, losing two aircraft. In spite of being under constant attack, considerable damage was inflicted. Over 400 bombs, both high explosives and incendiaries, fell in the target area, and the Gothaer Waggonfabrik was to lose about six to seven weeks production, or an equivalent of 140 planes.

The B–17s of the Schweinfurt force were also continuously attacked, and eleven Fortresses went down. The damage inflicted on the Schweinfurt plant was not as heavy as after the October 14th bombing chiefly because many machines had been removed to other places, leaving only 73 percent in the Schweinfurt plant.

At the end of the day, 49 heavy bombers were missing. The 2nd Division's Liberators' contribution to this figure was 33. Ten fighters also failed to return.

Heavy losses were also suffered by the 15th Air Force from Italy, bombing Steyr at the same time with 87 B–17s and an oil refinery at Fiume with 27 B–17s. Seventeen Fortresses did not return from the mission.

A diversionary mission was flown across the North Sea by the newly operational 458th Liberator Group.

In coordination with the mission of the heavy bombers, 226 B–26 Marauders attacked airfields in Holland. They dropped their bombs with good results on Leeuwarden, Gilze-Rijen, and Deelen.

In the afternoon, 146 Marauders set out to pay their frequent visit to the "Noballs" in France.

The 4th Fighter Group of the 8th Air Force received a large batch of P–51 Mustangs and it would soon convert to the type, replacing the Thunderbolts.

153

February 24, 1944. B–26 Marauders of the 9th Air Force blasting the airfield at Leeuwarden, Holland. (Official USAF Photo)

Friday, 25 February

A large force of 830 heavy bombers of the 8th Air Force climbed into a clear, blue winter sky to carry out a mission that promised to be a dangerous one: a deep penetration into Germany to the Messerschmitt factories at Regensburg and Augsburg, the anti-friction bearing plant of V.K.F. at Stuttgart, and the factory of Bachmann–von Blumenthal at Fürth involved in Me–110 production.

The 1st Division had to divide its Fortresses between Augsburg and Stuttgart, the 2nd Division went to Fürth, and the 3rd Division was going to pay another visit to the Messerschmitt plants at Regensburg. The latter force would have a Mustang escort to the target. Regensburg was also the

154

February 24, 1944. B–24 Liberators of the 448th Bomb Group in tight formation heading for the large Me–110 plant at Gotha. (Official USAF Photo)

target for the 15th Air Force, attacking one hour before the arrival of the 8th. It was hoped that this coordinated attack against the same objective would confuse the German fighters.

This time the Germans concentrated on the 15th Air Force, being the smaller one and unprotected during the most distant phase of the penetration. 33 bombers were shot down out of a force of 176 B–17s, giving another proof of the fact that deep penetrations into enemy territory without sufficient fighter cover could not be completed without excessively high losses.

But the 8th Air Force also met the German fighters. Mustangs of the 354th Fighter Group encountered some twenty Me–109s and FW–190s, most of them west of Kitzingen. The group destroyed seven fighters, including one over the target. Another five were shot down over the target by the Mustangs of the 357th Group, losing two of their number. All told, 26 German fighters were claimed by the AAf fighter pilots on this mission. Thirty-one heavy bombers were lost. All primary targets were bombed by the 738 heavies actually making the mission.

The destruction caused at the Regensburg factories by this combined attack and by the assault on the 22nd by the 15th Air Force would bring aircraft production from 435 planes per month in January, 1944, to 135 per month in March. The main Messerschmitt plant at Augsburg received a similar treatment. Production had been reduced by about 35 percent; however, it would be back in full production again in little over one month. Since the bombing of August 15th, the Messerschmitt Company had dispersed the activity of all major plants, reducing the effect of the bombing attacks.

Besides underestimating the recuperability of the plants, the Americans failed in many instances to plan a scheduled return raid in time to keep the plant out of full production. Undoubtedly, the bombing did deny many hundreds of aircraft to the Germans at a time when they badly needed them, but it was also beyond doubt that Air Intelligence overestimated the results grossly. The average monthly production of German single-engine aircraft during the last half of 1943 was 851. Allied Intelligence estimated 645. Actual production of single-engine fighters in the first half of 1944 had mounted to a monthly average of 1581, whereas Allied Intelligence estimated 655. However, according to the US Strategic Bombing Survey, the February campaign would have paid off even if its only effect had been to force the enemy into an intensive program of dispersal.

It was also true that the German fighter losses in the air battles were high, and that they lost many irreplaceable skilled fighter pilots. A sign of Allied air superiority in the skies above Germany would manifest itself during the months to come in that the Germans did not commit themselves to a policy of full-scale opposition to the daylight campaign. Instead, they would go into a policy of conservation of strength.

From now on, the bomber missions were no longer scheduled or plotted along routes with the best chances of avoiding enemy fighters, but it became a deliberate policy to force the Luftwaffe into combat. Fighter escort, hitherto always in close support of the bombers, was now increasingly cut loose from strictly defensive assignements to "seek out and destroy the foe." From a defensive role, it became an offensive role.

9th Air Force B–26 Marauders attacked the airfields at Venlo and St, Trond. They also paid a visit to the "Noball" sites in France.

The nine P–38 Lightnings of the new 10th Photographic Group (see 21 February) flew their first mission through 9/10 cloud over Cherbourg.

After this day, the weather turned bad again, and that meant the end of "Big Week," during which over 3300 bombers from the 8th and 500 from the 15th Air Forces dropped almost 10,000 tons of bombs. The 8th Air Force lost 137 heavy bombers and the 15th 89. Fighter sorties amounted to approximately 2548 for the 8th, 712 for the 9th, and 413 for the 15th Air Forces. 28 fighters were lost.

During the same period, the RAF made five heavy raids against Leipzig, Stuttgart, Schweinfurt, Steyr, and Augsburg. 2351 heavy bombers dropped 9198 tons of bombs. Bomber Command lost 157 heavy bombers. The American losses being 6 percent and the British 6.6 percent, it gave an interesting picture in view of the controversial opinions about day and night bombing.

B–26 Marauders of the 9th Air Force made 2328 sorties this month for a loss of twenty aircraft.

156

Monday, 28 February

Thunderbolts of the 56th Fighter Group flew a mission to the Ruhr Valley. One Me–109 was shot down.

The 4th Fighter Group took off from Debden at 1310 hours to fly its first operational mission with the P–51 Mustang in an offensive patrol to Compiègne. Under the inspiring leadership of Colonel Don Blakeslee, the group had become operational in the shortest time possible due to badly needed long-range escort for the bombers.

Heavy overcast prevented many bombers of the 8th Air Force from bombing V–1 installations along the French coast.

Tuesday, 29 February

A solid overcast covered western Germany when the 8th Air Force heavy bombers were en route to Brunswick. Over 500 fighters joined the mission, but this time the Luftwaffe did not show up. One Mustang of the 354th Fighter Group encountered engine trouble and the pilot was captured.

Lt. Col. Grambo flew with the 20th Group Lightnings to gain experience before taking command of the newly formed 364th Fighter Group flying the P–38 Lightning. On the return flight, first one engine quit and then the other one, and the P–38 crashed near Zwolle, killing Gambo. Another aircraft that crashed in Holland was a P–47 Thunderbolt of the 56th Fighter Group.

The 4th Fighter Group flew its first bomber escort mission with the P–51 Mustang, accompanying the bombers to Brunswick.

3

MARCH

Thursday, 2 March

Thunderbolts and Mustangs escorted the heavy bombers on their journey to the marshalling yards at Frankfurt. Several fighter groups became involved in dogfights with the German Air Force fighters. One of them was the 56th Fighter Group. On the way home, flying at 10,000 feet, far below normal escort altitude, they spotted an airfield south of Aachen. Colonel Gabreski led the 61st Squadron down and, in a strafing pass through heavy ground fire, they destroyed a hangar. The 4th Group lost one Mustang in the battle, but the pilots of the group claimed the destruction of two German fighters. In all, seventeen German fighters were brought down, including one shot down by a Thunderbolt taking one of the most experienced German fighter leaders, kommodore of JG 2, Egon Mayer, to his death.

Other 8th Fighter Groups flew patrols over Luftwaffe bases in France.

B–26 Marauders of the 322nd and 387th Bomb Group 9th Air Force, led by B–26s of the 1st Pathfinder Squadron, struck targets in France. 126 B–26s delivered 224 tons of bombs on the marshalling yards at Amiens/Longeau, inflicting severe damage. Other Marauders turned to the sites along the French coast.

Luftwaffe bases in France were also the target for formations of heavy bombers of the 8th, but a dense overcast forced most bombers to bring their loads back home. A Fortress was shot down over Abbeville by intense and accurate flak.

Friday, 3 March

An attack on Berlin was attractive for the Allies for a multiple of reasons. There were indeed important industries in the area, it also would

158

shake German morale when both RAF Bomber Command and the Army Air Force struck at their capital. On the other hand, for the people in Britain and America, it represented the ultimate in German targets, but at this stage of the war the most important factor was that the German Air Force would react in strength to any threat to their capital city, with the chance for the Allies to deal with the Luftwaffe in the anticipated battles.

Over the North Sea, the bombers of the 8th Air Force ran into steadily deteriorating weather. Over Jutland, cloud tops even reached to 28,000 feet. Therefore, the decision was made to abandon the mission. A few units bombed Wilhelmshaven and targets of opportunity. Two B–17 Fortresses collided on the way out and exploded.

Fighters of both the 8th and 9th Air Forces escorted the bombers, with Thunderbolts carrying 165-gallon belly tanks for the first time. Mustangs of the new 363rd Group, 9th Air Force, had their first encounter with the Luftwaffe and claimed their first two victories. The 4th Fighter Group spearheaded the bomber formations but the squadrons became separated in the clouds over Germany. Suddenly, nine Mustangs found themselves amid some fifty to sixty German fighters. Fighting against the odds, the Mustangs succeeded in shooting down six enemy aircraft for the loss of four. One pilot, Captain Don Gentile, sent two down and his wingman, John Godfrey, one. After the short melee, the Mustangs managed to escape.

One Messerschmitt, pursued by a Mustang, suddenly found its path crossed by a P–51 from the 354th Fighter Group, and it slammed right into it. Both aircraft exploded.

Although the 354th Fighter Group Mustangs ranged near Berlin, it was actually a P–38 Lightning that made its first appearance over Berlin. It was the *Texas Ranger IV* piloted by Lt. Col. Jack Jenkins, commander of the 55th Fighter Group, to be the first USAAF combat aircraft to accomplish this feat. Jenkins' group was unaware of the fact that the bombers had returned and half of the group (the others had dropped out with engine trouble) had proceeded to Berlin. For fifteen minutes, they circled in the surroundings, waiting in vain for the bombers.

The 9th Air Force 416th Group, the first to be equipped with the A–20 Havocs light bombers, flew its first mission, a diversionary flight.

Saturday, 4 March

Weather conditions were poor, with snow showers over the English bases. The target for the 8th heavy bombers was again Berlin. If visual bombing was possible, the VKF anti-friction bearing plant at Erkner and the Robert Bosch AG in Berlin were the targets; if not, the Friedrichstrasse section of Berlin, with its large railway facilities, was to be the target for radar bombing.

These attacks would also mean a milestone in the development of the long-range fighter. Since January the range of the P–51 Mustang had been extended to 475 miles from base without external tanks. With two 75-gallon wing tanks, the escort range was 650 miles from base, and now with two 108-gallon tanks, it could even reach an escort range of 850 miles.

Fourteen combat wings had been planned to bomb Berlin, but as on the previous day, the weather was the German's ally and the bombers were recalled. However, this signal was not received by a combat wing composed of two squadrons from the 95th Bomb Group and one from the 100th Group. Together with a Fortress of the 457th Bomb Group and a radar aircraft of the 482nd Group, they formed the only formation that continued toward the heart of the enemy.

They managed to get through or around the huge cloud formations, and they were only fourteen minutes from the capital when thirty Luftwaffe fighters intercepted the 31 Fortresses with their escort of only one P–51 group, composed of fighters from the 357th Group with some units from the 4th. One Me–109 was shot down by a Fortress gunner from the 100th Bomb Group. Lt. Col. Donald Blakeslee was the first Mustang pilot to accompany the bombers with his fighters over Berlin.

The Klein Machnow suburb was the target and the bombs were released on signal from the radar aircraft. The bombing was significant chiefly because it was the first time in the history of the 8th Air Force that its bombers were over the city. The return trip went through the clouds as the bombers had to descend because of diminishing oxygen supplies.

Again the German fighters harassed the bombers, yet losses today were rather inflicted by weather conditions than by enemy action. The 95th Bomb Group lost four B–17s, and the 100th one. The fighters claimed eight German aircraft shot down, whereas twenty-three of their own failed to return, not counting the many that crashed while trying to land in the foul weather.

Not all losses, however, were on account of the weather. A well-executed surprise attack by Me–109s destroyed eight Mustangs of the 363rd Fighter Group, 9th Air Force (temporarily under 8th Air Force control). Three more Mustangs of the same group did not return either.

Sunday, 5 March

Forty-six P–51 Mustangs of the 357th Fighter Group accompanied the heavy bombers of the 8th Air Force on their long journey to Bordeaux on the Bay of Biscay. The Mustangs rendezvoused with the bombers soon after making landfall and stayed with them for over two hours.

160

Three four-engine FW–200s were taking off from Cholet Airfield at the same moment the Mustangs appeared over the airfield. Unaware of the P–51s closing in on their tails, the Focke Wulfs started their climb but they didn't get far before all three were shot down.

Near the target the Mustangs became engaged in fights with the Luftwaffe and one of the P–51s was hit in the engine. The pilot, F/O Charles Yeager, wounded in both feet, bailed out. He was picked up by the French underground and, after spending three weeks in several French homes, he made his way back to England via Spain.

On the way back, the Mustangs crossed the Loire at 10,000 feet. They then came down on the deck only to pull up again when they had to pass over Caen. Flak was thrown up and the plane of the commanding officer, Colonel Spicer, was hit. He had to bail out, and landed in the sea. RAF Typhoons made a search for him but didn't find any trace. It was learned afterwards that he had been picked up by the Germans, to spend the rest of the war in a POW camp.

9th Air Force Marauders paid their regular visit to the "Noball" targets in France.

Monday, 6 March

The target was Berlin. This time, weather conditions were more hopeful and 730 heavy bombers of the 8th Air Force set out on a mission to the Erkner and Boschplant at Berlin, and the Daimler Benz Motorenplant at Genshagen, twenty miles south of Berlin.

One of the principal intentions of USSTAF, to force the German Air Force into battle, would be fully realized, and the bombers would run into very heavy and effective opposition from single-engine and twin-engine aircraft, and even from nightfighters. The appearance of the latter can be explained by the absence of the RAF over Germany for several nights. 169 Luftwaffe fighters were waiting for the enormous bomberstream on the way in, 202 Luftwaffe fighters were waiting over the target, and 244 fighters were ready to meet the bombers on the way out.

The bombers were escorted by fifteen fighter groups of the 8th Air Force, four fighter groups of the 9th Air Force, and even by two squadrons Mustangs of the RAF. Involved were 615 Thunderbolts, 86 Lightnings, and 102 Mustangs.

The fighter force was spearheaded by the 4th Fighter Group. Led by Col. Don Blakeslee, the Mustangs accounted for fifteen Luftwaffe fighters. A P–51 chased an Me–109, both racing toward Berlin. Tempelhof Airfield lay ahead and, while German fighters were in the circuit and others were taking off, the two fighters came roaring in at 500 feet above the ground.

161

After the Mustang poured in another burst, the Messerschmitt flicked on its back and went in at one end of the field, exploding on impact.

The 4th Group lost four P–51s, but it was the new 357th Group that sent the highest number of enemy fighters down. The group had taken off and formed up shortly after 1030 hours. The Mustangs crossed The Hague at 23,000 feet and headed for the rendezvous point in the target area.

Upon arrival, they found their big friends of the 3rd Division in a most precarious situation and at the edge of being annihilated by a hundred single- and twin-engine aircraft. The Mustangs plunged immediately into the battle and notwithstanding being heavily outnumbered, the Mustangs achieved the near impossible by shooting down twenty German fighters without suffering one loss. Hereafter, they escorted Liberators on their last leg and then headed for home. On the return flight, they strafed an airfield at Ulzen.

Also at 1032 hours, Thunderbolts of the 56th Fighter Group started to thunder along the two runways at Halesworth. The group was divided into two forces, one led by Hubert Zemke and the other by Robert Johnson. The Thunderbolts crossed the Dutch coast at Walcheren, at altitude 27,000 feet. They picked up the bomber armada just across the Zuider Zee. Heavy flak was thrown up near Zwolle. The procession droned on inland and approached the German border. At this moment, eight Thunderbolts separated and tore down on some thirty Me–109s flying far below and preparing to attack the bombers.

Near Dümmer Lake, about 150 German fighters rushed in to the bomberstream. Johnson's group was the first to encounter them. The Thunderbolts dropped their tanks and turned in on the enemy fighters as they came through. A ferocious battle developed, with fighters chasing each other through the bomber formations and bomber gunners shot at friend and foe because there was no time to make out who was who.

When 31 Thunderbolts of the 353rd Fighter Group joined the bomberstream near Dümmer Lake to accompany the bombers to Berlin, they ran into some twelve FW–190s attacking the B–17s. Two bombers went down before they could interfere.

The Erkner bearing plant was the target for the Fortresses from five combat wings of the 1st Division. Though this force was heavily escorted, overwhelming numbers of enemy fighters took their toll and many B–17s went down. One attacking Me–109 held its head-on pass too long and crashed into a Fortress. The wreckage fell upon a second Fortress and all three aircraft tumbled down.

The 3rd Division, however, heading for the Bosch electrical factory, sustained the heaviest losses. The German ground controller became aware that the middle combat wing of the 60-mile-long column was without escort. While the German fighters kept the escort of the first and last combat

162

wings busy, about one hundred bore down on the formations of the middle wing and 23 Fortresses were blown out of the sky, making the total loss for this division 35 aircraft. The ill-fated 100th Group, with the loss of fifteen bombers, was on top of the list for losses sustained by one group.

Overcast conditions caused a split-up in the bomber formations, confusing the aimings, and as a result the bombs were scattered within the Berlin area, few near any of the targets. Actually 660 bombers dropped 1626.2 tons of bombs, both high explosives and incendiaries.

The rear of the bomberstream had been brought up by the B–24 Liberators of the 2nd Division, and though they met less opposition than the Fortress formations, sixteen B–24s failed to return. When the final score was made up, this mission proved to be the most costly so far undertaken: 69 heavy bombers and eleven fighters were lost. Most of the losses were due to enemy fighter action, though more than usual had fallen victim to anti-aircraft fire. American fighter pilots claimed the destruction of 82 German aircraft.

9th Air Force B–26 Marauders of the 323rd and 391st Bomb Groups set off on a mission to rail communications at Hirson. Heavy clouds impeded the bombing of the rail center at Creil.

March 6, 1944. Flying Fortresses flying through flak-filled sky as they attack Berlin. (Official USAF Photo)

163

March 6, 1944. With engine No. 3 afire, this Fortress goes down over Berlin. (Official USAF Photo)

March 6, 1944. This B–24 Liberator of the 392nd Bomb Group made an emergency landing near Amerongen in Holland. (Photo from *Air Combat 1939–1945*)

Tuesday, 7 March

A new attempt to strike at the rail center at Creil was prevented by bad weather conditions. The medium bombers of the 9th turned to the "Noball" sites.

Wednesday, 8 March

It must have been difficult for the German newspapers to explain to the Berliners the sight of large formations of American bombers in the blue sky above their city, and even more embarrassing must have been the sight of large formations of single-engine fighters escorting the bomberstream.

On this clear day, the 8th Air Force dispatched 590 heavies and 1015 fighters to take the familiar route to the capital of the Reich. 174 Mustangs from four fighter groups stayed with the bombers on their last leg to the target and also for a considerable time on the return flight.

Before the P–51s took over the escort of the 3rd Division, which was heading the bomberstream, there was a lapse of time during which the bombers were without escort and the Germans, never slow in taking advantage of such a situation, hit the leading wing in a sharp encounter. Several Fortresses went down, including the leaders. In the confusion, the leading wing took an incorrect course. The next wing took over and the 100th Group, recognizing the error, was the first of the whole bomber force to arrive over Berlin. In spite of its forward position, this group suffered this time only one bomber lost, supposed to have encountered engine trouble.

Four hundred sixty-two bombers were left to drop 300.4 tons of high explosives and 762.8 tons of incendiaries on the city. The bearing plant at Erkner got a severe mauling with 75 direct hits of high explosives and a considerable amount of incendiaries, putting the plant entirely out of operation for some time.

Fighter opposition was much weaker than on the previous occasion. Especially the twin-engine aircraft were kept on the ground. Undoubtedly losses and strain imposed on the overburdened German pilots kept many fighters grounded.

Yet the American fighters claimed 79 German aircraft destroyed. The 4th Fighter Group coming to the aid of the heavies sent fifteen aircraft down. Captain Don Gentile destroyed four, and his wingman, John Godfrey, two. The pilots caught the sight of some twenty German fighters making head-on passes at a box of bombers over the outskirts of Berlin. They turned into the enemy fighters and by working as a perfect team, they scored their victories. While on the way back home and practically out of ammunition, the two pilots spotted a straggling B–17 with German fighters lining up overhead. Both Mustangs joined up with the Fortress and luck was with the Americans, for the German fighters withdrew.

The 56th "Wolfpack" Group was credited with 27 German fighters, but the group also suffered the highest losses after being caught in a surprise attack which cost them five Thunderbolts. One Polish pilot serving with the group, Lt. Gladych, had an engagement with three Focke Wulfs over Dümmer Lake. Turning into them, he exploded one of them. With his fuel at a critical minimum he dived for the deck to escape his two pursuers. But then his emergency coolant cut out and he had to slow down.

The two Focke Wulfs lined up to the side and behind his Thunderbolt to escort him to an airfield that loomed up ahead of them. One of the Focke Wulfs had a large "13" painted on the fuselage and Gladych knew instantly that he was accompanied by *Lucky 13*. Rather than the name of the pilot, his aircraft number was well-known by RAF and USAAF pilots because many of them owed their lives to his mercy.

Both Gladych and *Lucky 13* had met twice before. The first time was near Rheims in 1940 and the second time it was over Lille on June 5, 1942, when the German ace crippled Gladych's Spitfire. Instead of shooting the Spitfire down, the German pilot brought his aircraft (No. 13) alongside his victim, waved, and disappeared. He would not kill a man who had no chance to defend himself. In this manner, he spared several Allied pilots.

Nearing Vechta Airfield, Gladych eased his plane into a glide with both

March 8, 1944. Chow-hound, a B-17G of the 91st Bomb Group ("The Ragged Irregulars") with companions on the way to Berlin. (Official USAF Photo)

166

March 8, 1944. A Flying Fortress above the heart of the Reich capital. (Official USAF Photo)

Germans falling behind him. Coming down over the edge of the field, many parked aircraft were lined up ahead of him and Gladych knew what he had to do. His gunsight was lighted and suddenly he pressed the gunbutton, pouring a long burst of fire into the German aircraft. And it happened as he had expected: the flak started blazing away and both Focke Wulfs behind him were shot down. Gladych made it back home, though he had to swim the last two hundred yards to shore. The pilot of *Lucky 13*, Major Georg-Peter Eder, survived. He would spend five weeks in a hospital recovering from his wounds. (After the war, Gladych and Eder met each other in Frankfurt.)

After the confusion over Berlin, 68 bombers attacked targets of opportunity. Losses for the day were 37 bombers and 17 fighters.

To confuse the German defenders, strong forces of B–26 Marauders, escorted by RAF Spitfires, bombed airfields in Holland.

167

Thursday, 9 March

Berlin was covered by 10/10 cloud when the 330 bombers of the 8th Air
Force arrived over the city to bomb the Heinkel Aero Plant at Oranienburg.
There were no German fighters to meet the bombers, but as in previous
cases, the flak over the city was heavy and took its toll. Nine bombers
were shot down.

Bombing was done by radar and caused mainly piles of rubble in the
Berlin streets.

Thunderbolts and Mustangs escorted the bombers, but the mission passed uneventfully for the fighters.

March 9, 1944. A solid cloud cover lays ahead when the B-17s proceed to Berlin. (Photo Imperial War Museum, London)

March 9, 1944. With its tail completely knocked off, this Flying Fortress of the 384th Bomb Group goes down over Berlin. (Photo Imperial War Museum, London)

Friday, 10 March

Hitherto, the medium bombers of the 9th Air Force had mainly been employed in assistance of the heavy bombing operations. From now on, they would concentrate more on targets in direct connection with the coming invasion. Part of this was the transportation plan with the purpose of sealing off Normandy by extensive bombing of vital rail centers and repair facilities in northern France and Belgium. Thirty targets in France and Belgium were assigned to be visited by the 9th Air Force.

Saturday, 11 March

Heavy bombers of the 8th Air Force set out on a mission to the marshalling yards at Münster. Many fighters escorted the bombers while simultaneously numerous fighter attacks were carried out against ground targets in France.

Flak towers, airfields, gun emplacements, and a large variety of other ground targets were worked over by the Thunderbolts of the 352nd Fighter Group, taking part in the operation with 36 aircraft. Led by Col. Joe Mason, the Thunderbolts ran into very intense anti-aircraft fire and two P–47s were brought down.

B–26 Marauders of the 9th Air Force crossed the French coast to drop their loads on the ski sites.

Monday, 13 March

Medium bombers of the 9th Air Force turned again to the "Noball" sites in France. This time the sites were also visited by the bombers of the 8th Air Force.

Twenty-one Fortresses of the 457th Bomb Group flew for the first time as an all "silver group" (distinguished by their lack of olive drab camouflage paint). Their targets were near Amiens, but en route they encountered very heavy weather and the B–17s took their loads back home.

Forty-seven Thunderbolts of the 353rd Fighter Group flew a morning patrol in the area of St. Quentin.

Wednesday, 15 March

A large bomberstream of the 8th Air Force was heading for Brunswick. The escorting fighters flew well ahead and at a considerable distance at either side of the bomber formations. Part of the long caravan was made up of 86 fighters of the 9th Air Force. Over Dümmer Lake, the first Focke

170

Wulfs rushed toward the lead bomber formations. A few moments later, the sky was filled with the battle of hundreds of fighter planes. The escort was very effective and only three bombers went down.

Thirty-five Luftwaffe aircraft were claimed by the American fighter pilots, of which number the 56th Fighter Group claimed 24. One of their pilots, 1st Lt. Robert S. Johnson, became the leading ace of the 8th with twenty-three victories. He shot down four German aircraft in this battle.

The 9th Air Force practiced fighter-bomber tactics for the first time when seven Thunderbolts of the 366th Fighter Group attacked the St. Valery airfield, each of them dropping one 250-lb. bomb.

The 353rd Fighter Group of the 8th was also still experimenting with this kind of technique, and two Thunderbolts with two 1000-lb. bombs under each wing-shackle carried out trial attacks from different heights on an unfortunate barge in the Zuider Zee. The barge survived, although by near misses.

Thursday, 16 March

Some 500 B–17 Fortresses and 200 B–24 Liberators of the 8th Air Force crossed the English coastline when they headed toward the aircraft factories in southern Germany, and more specifically at Augsburg, Friedrichshafen, and Lechfeld. Clear skies were predicted, but again the forecasters had been too optimistic and when the bombers found secondary targets in the clear, they didn't hesitate and unloaded.

The Luftwaffe was up in strength again and the Fortresses of the 3rd Division, leading the bomberstream, bore the brunt of an assault chiefly carried out by twin-engine rocket-firing Me–110s and Me–410s.

Mustangs of the 357th Fighter Group rendezvoused with the bombers near Stuttgart and almost immediately they became entangled in a ferocious dogfight with the German fighters. Mustangs of the 4th Group sent down thirteen Luftwaffe fighters. Just outside Augsburg, some 35 Me–109s, Fw–190s, and Me–110s carried out a simultaneous attack against the bombers. Mustangs of the 354th Fighter Group tore into their formations, broke up the attack, and knocked down ten of them.

Eighteen B–17s were lost, but seven managed to reach Switzerland. The 2nd Division fared better, and all its B–24s returned to base, though several sustained flak damage. Escorting fighters (237 were of the 9th Air Force) claimed 75 German fighters.

One German destroyer Geschwader, ZG 76, lost 26 out of 43 aircraft. The Mustangs attacked at the moment that the Zerstörer prepared to start a mass assault against the bombers. Another ten crashlanded which left only seven to struggle home.

Friday, 17 March

The airdrome at Chartres was strafed by P–47 Thunderbolts of the 361st Fighter Group, 8th Air Force, when they carried out low-level attacks in northern France.

In the afternoon, 29 Thunderbolts of the 353rd Fighter Group dive-bombed Soesterberg Airfield.

Seventy B–26 Marauders of the 9th Air Force made another effort to deliver their loads on the rail center at Creil, and this time the 322nd and 323rd Bomb Groups dropped their bombs with fair results.

Saturday, 18 March

After weather interfered with the bombing of primary targets on the 16th, the 8th Air Force bombers set out again to strike aircraft factories in southern Germany. This time the weather enabled many bombers to drop on their primary targets such as Augsburg, Friedrichshafen, München, and various others. In fact, six primary targets and two secondary targets were bombed, while five targets of opportunity received their share of the total load carried by some 500 Fortresses and 200 Liberators.

At Friedrichshafen, the Germans had apparently anticipated the objective and the target was found obscured by a very effective smokescreen, forcing the bombers to drop by radar.

A murderous flak barrage greeted the bombers. It was so intense that the Liberators broke up their formation. They even wandered into Swiss air space where another reception committee was waiting with its flak batteries. Out of the bomber column and in poor formation, the bombers were left for some time without fighter escort due to an error in timing, a situation the Germans were always quick to exploit to full advantage.

The Germans hit hard and most of the 43 heavies lost fell to their guns. The unlucky 44th and 392nd Bomb Groups took 22 of this number for their account, mauled by the persistent attacks from some 75 FW–190s and Me–109s. For over a hundred miles the bombers were subjected to mass attacks, most from the rear, which even continued when P–38 Lightnings arrived on the scene. Sixteen bombers sought sanctuary in Switzerland. Escorting fighters, which included 261 from the 9th Air Force, had many engagements with enemy fighters, the 4th Group knocking twelve out of the sky.

A special group, composed of volunteers from four different groups, was formed to train and to gain experience in low-level attacks. They carried out their missions as the 353rd "C" Group. They were nicknamed "Bill's Buzz Boys."

172

Sunday, 19 March

9th Air Force Marauders crossed the French coastline again to attack the "Noball" targets. Heavy bombers of the 8th turned to the same kind of targets, and one of these targets was the renowned site at Watten. Ground defenses sent up accurate flak when the bombers dropped on the site at Mimoyecques.

Monday, 20 March

Heavy bombers of the 8th Air Force bombed the marshalling yards at Frankfurt. They were escorted by 8th fighters and also by 79 fighters of the 9th Air Force.

Thirty-six B–26 Marauders turned to the "Noball" target at Zudausques. Heavy flak was met and one of the two Marauders shot down made a couple of loops before crashing into the ground. Both Marauders were of the 322nd Bomb Group.

One hundred twenty-four Marauders composed of aircraft from the 344th, 386th, 387th, and 391st Bomb Groups dropped 199 tons of bombs on the rail center at Creil, plastering lines, locomotive works, a railway bridge, and a nearby factory.

Tuesday, 21 March

Weather hampered extensive air operations and the bombers turned to targets near the French coast. The "Noballs" were visited by the 9th Marauders, while the Liberators of the 8th struck targets in the Pas de Calais area. Only a small escort was provided.

173

Forty-eight P–51s of the 4th Fighter Group took off to carry out a fighter sweep in the Bordeaux area. A number of airfields were strafed, and several German aircraft were destroyed. Groundfire, however, took its toll, and seven Mustangs failed to return.

Wednesday, 22 March

On this day, the Heinkel plants at Oranienburg and the Bayerische Motorenwerke at Basdorf were on the target list of the 8th Air Force. However, weather conditions made a visual bomb run very doubtful and therefore, 669 heavy bombers out of the approximately 800 which made sorties, were sent to the Friedrichstrasse section of Berlin where the load was chiefly delivered by means of radar. Pathfinders of the 482nd Group led the mission, their last mission in this capacity because sufficient H2X bombers were available to establish a pathfinder squadron in each division. 221 of the escorting fighters were from the 9th Air Force.

One flight of escorting Thunderbolts of the 56th Fighter Group flew into heavy clouds, and in a storm three Thunderbolts dived out of control into the North Sea.

Twelve bombers went down, for the greater part by accident and anti-aircraft guns, for the resistance of the Luftwaffe was again very limited. They were obviously instructed to avoid contact with the escorting fighters. The American pilots could claim not a single enemy fighter.

It was the last attack on Berlin for the month of March. Because of very poor weather conditions, the 8th Air Force was forced to limit its activities to pathfinder attacks on targets like Frankfurt, Brunswick, Wilhelmshaven, and Münster. When activity over Germany was out of the question, the French coast was visited.

From March onward, it became clear that the threat from enemy aircraft tended to decrease; on the other hand the threat from anti-aircraft guns was going to increase as the ground defenses had been considerably reinforced since January and the bombers would not only have to face an increase in quantity but also in accuracy. By late spring, more Army Air Force bombers would be shot down by flak than by German fighters.

Also important at this stage was the decrease in quality of the German pilots. Due to a shortage in oil, the German High Command was forced to shorten the training of pilots to be able to produce the required number of pilots. As a consequence, the demand for replacements rose rapidly. From this point on, the German Air Force would have to face an enemy superior both in numbers and in quality.

B–26 Marauders of the 9th visited the "Noball" targets in France.

Heretofore the Spitfires of 11th Group, RAF, had provided cover for the

March 22, 1944. Fortresses drop their bombs through the clouds by radar. (Official USAF Photo)

medium bombers, but by the end of March they had been replaced by 9th Air Force fighters.

Thursday, 23 March

The 8th Air Force dispatched its heavy bombers on a mission to Brunswick and to various other aircraft targets in Germany. Through a miscalculation, the 3rd Division penetrated ahead of schedule and was consequently left without fighter escort for a considerable time. The Luftwaffe appeared to take advantage of this error.

Many fighter groups accompanied the other formations. Thunderbolts of the 56th Fighter Group escorted the bombers to Osnabrück, where the Mustangs took over. The 4th Group had several encounters with the Luftwaffe fighters and they emerged from these fights with claims of fourteen enemy aircraft shot down. One of the German pilots shot down by a Mustang was the commander of JG 3, Oberst Wilcke, one of Germany's most experienced fighter pilots.

Near Osterburg, two Liberators of the 466th Bomb Group, out on their second mission, collided, and both tumbled down. Thunderbolts picked up the bombers near Münster for withdrawal support.

Two hundred nine B–26 Marauders from six bomber groups of the 9th headed for Creil again to unload 381.5 tons of bombs on the rail center.

175

Again, much damage was caused. The 394th Bomb Group Marauders flew their first mission to the Beaumont-le-Roger Airfield. The mediums also dropped bombs on the "Noballs."

Friday, 24 March

The name Schweinfurt brought fearful associations and the worst was expected when the bombers of the 8th Air Force set out for this city. But the city did not live up to its reputation, and only a few fighters were seen making for some stragglers. Three bombers failed to return after the mission, two of which had been involved in a mid-air collision.

Sunday, 26 March

8th Air Force heavy bombers set out to the French coast to bomb the V-weapon sites such as the ones at Watten and La Glacerie.

240 fighters of the 9th Air Force carried out divebombing attacks on "Crossbow" targets and marshalling yards.

Three hundred forty-four B–26 Marauders of the 9th set course to Ijmuiden, a target notorious to Marauder crews. The Operational Research Section of 9th Bomber Command had stated that the bombs carried by Marauders could not penetrate the heavily reinforced structures of the E- and R-boat pens; instead they had proposed to hit the cofferdam. This would flood the pens, while at the same time the bombs that missed the target would cause a lot of damage to equipment around the pens.

Strangely enough, however, the crews had not been informed that the cofferdam was their aiming point. So 1120 1000-lb. semi-armor-piercing bombs descended on the E- and R-boat pens. Much stronger winds than predicted at briefing resulted after all in many bombs falling off their target, causing considerable damage to equipment, stores, and some births, while several "E" boats and gun boats were sunk. In fact, even the cofferdam was hit four times, but it didn't breach. One Marauder of the 394th Group failed to return.

"Bill's Buzz Boys" were on their way to France with twelve P–47s to attack airfields near Châteaudun, in the afternoon. Four Thunderbolts carried each two M–4 frag-clusters. At 1440, they crossed the French coast and raced to their targets. The airfields at Chartres, Châteaudun, Anet, St. André de l'Eure, and Beauvais/Tille received the special treatment of the "Buzz Boys."

At some distance from the target, they dived to gain speed, then leveled out on the deck to come in with speeds in excess of 400 m.p.h. in line-abreast formation, shooting up anything that loomed in front of their guns.

176

At Chartres' Airfield, the Thunderbolts delivered their frag-clusters. One P–47 was shot down.

Monday, 27 March

The 8th Air Force heavies struck with strong forces against airfields in France. Bombs were also dropped on an aircraft factory at Tours. Other forces of the 8th turned to targets in western Germany.

Flying a mission to Bordeaux, the 4th Fighter Group had some encounters with the Luftwaffe, and claimed two destroyed in the air and another 24 in strafing attacks on the ground. One Mustang was shot down.

A Thunderbolt of the 56th Fighter Group bounced a Dornier Do–217, which was running for safety over the treetops. Screaming in at 200 feet, the Thunderbolt poured a long burst from the eight heavy guns into the Dornier. But at the same time, the bomber's rear gunner sent a stream of shells into the Thunderbolt's engine. With his engine on fire, the P–47 pilot waited until the Dornier exploded and then he bailed out. The pilot was one of the most successful fighter pilots of the AAF, Walker H. Mahurin. Mahurin managed to evade capture and, aided by the French underground movement, he returned to England on May 7, 1944.

March 27, 1944. Fortresses of the 452nd Bomb Group heading for Bordeaux, France. (Official USAF Photo)

177

Tuesday, 28 March

Both in the morning and in the afternoon, the bombers of the 8th Air Force struck airfields in France. Intense flak was met when the bombers attacked Châteaudun from an altitude of 18,000 feet. Another airfield on the receiving end of a heavy bombload was Dijon.

Fighters supported these attacks by strafing the airfields. On an airfield ten miles south of Paris, five Ju–88s were destroyed in a strafing attack, while a hangar was left burning. Two Mustangs were shot down by the guns surrounding the airfield.

One of the most bombed railway yards in France, Creil, was visited again by the medium bombers of the 9th Bombardment Division. The attack started at noon and after sixteen minutes when the last of three waves of Marauders had passed, 300 tons of bombs had been delivered on this important junction.

March 28, 1944. Buildings on Dijon Airfield are left burning. (Photo Imperial War Museum, London)

March 28, 1944. Bombs from Marauders burst on the railroad junction at Creil. (Official USAF Photo)

Wednesday, 29 March

Another mission by the heavies of the 8th Air Force to Brunswick met with sharp resistance from German fighters. However, the bombers were well protected by their little friends, and the 4th Fighter Group achieved marked success with the destruction of 24 enemy aircraft. Another seven were sent to earth by the P–47s of the 353rd Fighter Group.

On the way in, climbing through the overcast, two Mustangs collided and crashed into the Channel.

Led by Colonel Duncan of the 353rd Fighter Group, "Bill's Buzz Boys" carried out attacks against airfields in northwestern Germany and Holland. Twelve P–47s strafed the airfields at Quackenbrück, Vechta, Bohmte, Hesepe, Rheine, Enschede/Twente, and Bramsche. Duncan himself took one flight to the airfields of Bramsche, Vechta, and Twente. Many aircraft were strafed, one of them a B–17, sitting on its belly in an open field near Vechta. The Fortress was set afire.

One of the Thunderbolts was hit in the fuel tank and ran out of gas some forty miles off the English coast. The pilot was picked up by Air-Sea Rescue. Total claims included the destruction of seven enemy planes on the ground.

179

4

APRIL

Saturday, 1 April

The 8th Air Force heavy bombers tried a "third time best" when they took off in the morning for a mission to Ludwigshafen, already planned and afterwards abandoned due to weather on the last two days of March. And for the third time the bombers cancelled the mission when they ran into cloud formations up to 21,000 feet. Only the Liberators of the 2nd Division droned on, but they got badly off-course and 38 B–24s from the 44th and 392nd Bomb Groups dropped their loads on Schaffhausen in Switzerland, taking it for a German town. Only the German propaganda could appreciate this incident. One Liberator failed to return.

A flight of the 56th Group Thunderbolts went down to strafe an airfield at Lille. The moment the P–47s started their dives, a murderous flak was thrown up and one P–47 was set afire. While strafing the field, the flight leader was so close to the ground that he sheared a telephone pole in two and, with a piece stuck in his wing, he landed the plane at his base.

Nine Thunderbolts of "Bill's Buzz Boys" carried out strafing attacks on airfields in northwestern Germany.

By April, the strength of the two tactical air forces in England was as follows:

9th Air Force	496	medium bombers
	96	light bombers
	670	fighters
2nd Tactical Air Force	70	medium bombers
	38	light bombers
	1764	fighters

180

The 9th Air Force had primarily been occupied with escorting the 8th Air Force bombers, but from now onward preparations for the invasion became the paramount effort.

For the American pilots, a milestone had been reached. Not only had Captain Don Gentile become the leading ace in the 8th Air Force with 27 confirmed kills, but with this number of victories he had passed the legendary 26 kills of World War I pilot Eddy Rickenbacker.

Wednesday, 5 April

With most of the 8th Air Force bombers grounded because of a complete and thick overcast, 456 fighters of the 8th set out on a strafing mission to France and Germany. Eleven fighter groups took to the air but only three succeeded in reaching their assigned targets. The others found their objectives hidden by groundhaze or low clouds.

The 4th and 355th Fighter Groups, however, encountered improving weather conditions when they ranged in the areas of Berlin and Munich. The 4th Group Mustangs strafed five airfields in the Brandenburg area near Berlin, destroying 43 aircraft on the ground, including five Ju–88s, shot up by Captain Don Gentile. The Germans were taken completely by surprise. Two Luftwaffe aircraft were picked off in the air.

The 355th Fighter Group scored the most successes at Oberpfaffenhofen Airfield, shooting up more than forty aircraft on the ground and destroying another eight in the air.

Groundfire always made strafing of airfields a hazardous venture, and four Mustangs of the 4th and three of the 355th Group were shot down. The 4th Group lost one of its most successful pilots, Major Duane Beeson, who managed to bail out to become a prisoner.

Thunderbolts of the 9th Air Force attacked airfields in France. They destroyed two aircraft on the ground at Friqueville and they left six aircraft wrecked at Orleans and Châteaudun. Among the airfields harassed by the Mustangs of the 354th Fighter Group are Châteauroux, Conches, Chartres, and Bourges. Six German aircraft were shot up for one Mustang lost to flak.

Saturday, 8 April

Six hundred forty-four heavy bombers from the three divisions of the 8th Air Force set out on a mission to strike aircraft targets in western Germany. 712 Fighters, both from the 8th and 9th Air Forces, escorted the bombers and soon one of the decisive battles between the American fighters and the German Air Force was to be fought.

181

Soon after rendezvousing with the B–24 Liberators of the 2nd Division heading for Brunswick, the Mustangs of the 4th Fighter Group became engaged with a large force of German fighters attacking the lead box of B–24s proceeding to Oldenburg. Six Liberators were shot down, all from the still-fresh 466th Bomb Group. 31 Me–109s were blown out of the sky, including three shot down in quick succession by Captain Don Gentile. Four Mustangs were lost by the group.

The Mustangs of the 354th Group also became embroiled in the raging air battle. Near Wittingen, they intercepted some sixty FW–190s and fifteen Me–109s attacking the bombers. The Germans were already heavily engaged with the 4th Group when the 354th joined the melee, and in the ensuing battle they knocked down another 21 German fighters for the loss of four P–51s.

Thunderbolts of the 56th Fighter Group escorted the bombers to Hesepe, which place received a heavy bombload. This group met no fighters, only plenty of flak. The 78th Group P–47s sent three German fighters down.

The German Air Force lost 88 fighters in the air and another forty on the ground. The 1st and 3rd Division Fortresses suffered no losses and all returned safely to their bases.

Forty-eight P–38 Lightnings of the 20th Fighter Group took off from their base at Kings Cliffe at 1402 for a fighter sweep deep into Germany. With their base shrouded in fog until noon, they had been unable to take off for their planned escort mission in the morning.

After nearly two hours, they arrived near Salzwedel, 80 miles west of Berlin. Here the three squadrons separated, each going for a number of airfields in a planned area. One squadron attacked an airfield north of the town and destroyed thirteen aircraft in four strafing passes. Groundfire became intense and they looked for other targets. Army barracks were strafed and two locomotives were shot up. Then, all of a sudden, seven Me–109s swooped down on the squadron and one Lightning crashed into the ground. An Me–109 received a burst from a P–38 and the German fighter slammed into another Lightning. Both aircraft went down in flames. Two more Messerschmitts fell victim to the P–38s of this squadron.

One of the other two squadrons strafed an airfield southwest of Salzwedel, shooting up eight aircraft on the ground and, in an encounter with the Luftwaffe fighters in the air, they picked off two of the enemy. One Lightning of this squadron was lost.

The third squadron didn't find an airfield, but they did find plenty of targets to work over with their guns. One Lightning received a direct hit and crashed. For this kind of work, the Lightning was much more suited than for high-altitude escort work. "Bill's Buzz Boys" ranged with eleven Thunderbolts over northwestern Germany, strafing airfields, flak towers, locomotives, and a large variety of other targets. One Thunderbolt was shot down.

182

In the afternoon, 163 B–26 Marauders and 101 P–47 Thunderbolts of the 9th Air Force set out on a mission to the rail center at Hasselt in Belgium. After the mediums had dropped their loads, the Thunderbolts started their divebombing attacks, delivering their 250-lb. bombs on the yard and surrounding repair shops, which were still smoking after a couple of days.

Sunday, 9 April

Five hundred forty-two heavies of the 8th Air Force took off and climbed on a course that would take the Fortresses of the 3rd and the Liberators of the 2nd Divisions via Denmark to Poznan and Tutow, and the Fortresses of the 1st Division to Gdynia and Marienburg, where the aircraft factories were to receive another beating. Heavy escort was provided by 8th and 9th Air Force fighters.

Assembly had been difficult and many aircraft had abandoned the mission after flying for a considerable time blindly through the dense clouds near the assembly point. And again when the bombers crossed the Danish coast, they were confronted with heavy clouds. One complete group and some boxes of the leading wing cancelled the mission and flew back home.

The reduced force continued on and suddenly the clouds broke and the primary target could be clearly outlined. Bombing was good in spite of heavy flak, and many buildings were wrecked.

Over Denmark, some sixteen FW–190s tore into a Liberator formation. At this moment only two P–47s covered this bomber box. Both Thunderbolts turned head-on into the Focke Wulfs to break up their formation. One of the Thunderbolts could not jettison its frozen belly tank, yet the pilot, Robert Johnson of the 56th, sent a Focke Wulf down after a sharp dogfight. Two more Focke Wulfs went down, destroyed by the other P–47 pilot.

Leading his formation to the Schleswig area, Lt. Col. David Schilling also became separated from his men. Only his wingman was with him when he ran into some thirty Luftwaffe fighters. One Focke Wulf exploded, the pieces of it damaging Schilling's aircraft. He destroyed a second Focke Wulf, whereafter he brought his Thunderbolt down to zero feet to run for home on the deck. Sweeping across Schleswig, he destroyed an Arado Ar–196 on the sea.

After bombing, the reduced leading wing of the 3rd Division received radio orders to join the Fortresses of the 1st Division coming back from Marienburg. Their small formation of 33 Fortresses without fighter escort was noticed by a ground controller, and the German fighters were vectored to their position. Before the bombers could contact the Fortresses of the 1st Division, two of them were shot down.

Meanwhile the 1st Division had met enemy resistance when they were near their target. The Focke Wulf plant had been successfully hit. On the way home, a running battle with Luftwaffe fighters developed and several Fortresses went down before the P–51s arrived.

Forty-eight P–47 Thunderbolts of the 9th Air Force ranged over the French countryside, looking for goods trains.

Monday, 10 April

Seven hundred thirty heavy bombers of the 8th Air Force with heavy fighter escort were out to visit aircraft targets in France and the Low Countries, and to bomb the marshalling yards at Brussels. With clouds obscuring the target at Brussels, several bombers dropped on Maldegem Airfield.

Many 8th Air Force fighters were out on "Jackpot" (airfield strafing) missions, and on one of these missions to southern France, the 4th Fighter Group scored 28 "kills" (bringing their total to over 400 enemy aircraft destroyed).

9th Air Force medium bombers were also on their way to attack rail targets, and 148 Marauders delivered a load on the railyard at Namur in Belgium, while at Charleroi forty B–26s of the 9th and B–25s of the 2nd Tactical Air Force tried to impede the movement of goods trains to Normandy.

Gun emplacements near Le Havre and "Crossbow" targets were visited by 580 bombers of the 9th Air Force.

Fifty-six P–51 Mustangs headed for the rail center at Hasselt in Belgium to divebomb the target, which was left blazing two days before after a visit by Marauders and Thunderbolts.

After the failure of November 25th, when Thunderbolts used a B–24 as sighting aircraft for their bombing attack, another and more promising variety of this kind of bombing was practiced by Lightnings of the 55th Fighter Group in an attack on Coulommiers Airfield (St. Dizier being the primary objective but found covered by clouds). Bombs were dropped from 20,000 feet by two squadrons on signal from a Droop Snoot, a modified P–38J, stripped of gun and ammunition compartment and equipped with a cabin for a bombardier, operating a Norden bombsight through a plexiglass nose.

The third squadron acted as top-cover, while target support was provided by seven Thunderbolts of "Bill's Buzz Boys." After bombing, the Lightnings came down on the deck to strafe the airfield. The gunners of the airfield were alert when the Lightnings made a second pass, and both the leader and his wingman were shot down; the former managed to make a belly-landing.

After a mission to Florennes airfield in the morning had been foiled by

184

clouds, the 20th Fighter Group took off again in the afternoon on a Droop Snoot mission. The target was Gutersloh in Germany, and 27 Lightnings dropped two 500-lb. and 25 1000-lb. bombs on Droop Snoot indication. Again a very good concentration was achieved and continuance of these tactics seemed to be fully motivated.

One Lightning crashlanded near Leiden in Holland, forced down through mechanical failure.

April 10, 1944. A P-38J Lightning of the 20th Fighter Group came to rest in a meadow near Leiden in Holland. (Photo from Air Combat 1939–1945)

Tuesday, 11 April

Thunderbolts escorted more than 900 heavy bombers of the 8th Air Force on the first leg of a deep penetration into eastern Germany where they were going to bomb six aircraft plants involved with Focke Wulf and Junkers production. After the Thunderbolts, six Mustang and four Lightning groups shepherded the enormous bomberstream.

The 3rd Division had Poznan again as its assigned target, but this time they found it completely covered by clouds, so they turned to their secondary objective, Rostock. With so many forces, the fighters had to divide their strength, and unfortunately the Rostock force was deprived of the luxury of escort.

185

And the Luftwaffe was alert. First, the rocket-firing Ju–88s and Me–410s arrived, and then the Focke Wulfs came head-on in line-abreast formation. 25 B–17s were lost, ten of them from the 96th Group. Nine Fortresses dropped down in Sweden for a permanent stay.

The Fortresses of the 1st Division headed for different targets: 88 B–17s went to Cottbus and Sorau, where they delivered 131 tons of HE and incendiaries on the Sorau Focke Wulf plant. It would cut production in half. Three other groups of the 1st Division turned to Stettin, also without fighter escort, but with full attention of the Luftwaffe, pouring rockets and cannonshells into their formation.

The escorting fighters lost sixteen aircraft, whereas the American pilots claimed the destruction of 51 German aircraft; 25 of them were claimed by the 357th Fighter Group, escorting the Fortresses to Sorau. The Mustangs of this group started the battle with the Luftwaffe fighters when the Germans came swarming in at the bombers approaching Hannover.

P–38 Lightnings joined in the melee and the Mustang pilots were left in no doubt that the Lightnings shot on anything that had one engine. A P–51 chasing an Me–109, which had just fired on a bomber crew in their parachutes, was suddenly attacked by a Lightning. It was one of the many examples that took place this day, and what would occur many times again, more than once with tragic results. After the battle, the Mustangs came down to strafe ground targets near Hannover.

The B–24s of the 2nd Division also had their formations diminished by many aircraft, and when the bombers returned to their bases and the total losses were made up, 52 Fortresses and 12 Liberators were missing.

Charleroi was again the target for the bombers of the 9th Air Force. 347 1000-pound bombs and 1160 250-pound bombs hailed down on the rail center, dropped by 193 Marauders. To improve accuracy, the groups of bombers were broken up into sections of four to six planes.

General Eisenhower visited Debden, where he presented the successful fighter pilots Donald Blakeslee, Don Gentile, and Robert Johnson a DSC. He took the opportunity to make a flight in a Droop Snoot Lightning.

Wednesday, 12 April

A pathfinder B–17, landing at an English base prior to a morning mission, was suddenly jumped by a Ju–88 intruder and shot down.

The 8th heavy bombers headed their way into Germany to attack aircraft targets in the Leipzig area. They were heavily escorted by Thunderbolts and Mustangs. However, weather conditions forced the mission to be abandoned.

Near Saalfeld, six Me–109s bounced a formation of Mustangs of the

357th Group. After the attack, they continued their dive into the cloud cover. One P–51 was shot down. The pilot managed to bail out.

Thunderbolts of the 56th Fighter Group carried out a strafing sweep near Oldenburg. They were greeted with a dense flak barrage.

Today the 353rd "C" Group, nicknamed "Bill's Buzz Boys," flew its final mission, with eleven Thunderbolts. They carried out strafing attacks in northwestern Germany in the afternoon. After the unit was dissolved, the pilots and planes returned to their assigned groups. The group had developed the methods for low-level strafing attacks which meant that in the future, the German Air Force would not only be hunted in the air, but also on the ground.

Thursday, 13 April

A large bomberstream of the 8th Air Force made a deep penetration into Germany in the afternoon on a course to targets in southern Germany. The 1st Division went to Schweinfurt, the 3rd Division to Augsburg, and the 2nd Division to Oberpfaffenhofen and Lechfeld. Escorting fighters were both from the 8th and 9th Air Forces.

The Luftwaffe rose in force to intercept the Schweinfurt force and, in savage frontal mass attacks concentrating on the high group, eight B–17s of the 384th Bomb Group were shot out of the sky. Mustangs of the 354th Group claimed 14 for the loss of two in a battle that raged all over the sky.

Nearing the Messerschmitt factories at Augsburg, the Fortresses of the 3rd Division ran into heavy and accurate anti-aircraft fire and several B–17s went down. The plant was severely hit. Many Fortresses were damaged and ten took refuge in Switzerland.

The Dornier factory at Oberpfaffenhofen received a severe battering from sixty B–24 Liberators. Repair and storage buildings were demolished. Other B–24s plastered the airfield at Lechfeld.

Near Mannheim, escorting Mustangs tangled with Luftwaffe fighters. The Mustangs had picked up the B–24s near Brussels. They swept ahead of the bombers to Karlsruhe and then turned back to run into the Luftwaffe fighters. The P–51s sent down three FW–190s and four Me–109s.

Don Gentile had made his last mission before returning to the USA for a bond-selling tour. Seeing all the cameramen waiting for him, he decided to make very low passes over the field. Unfortunately, he hit the grass and the plane came to rest with a broken back after a successful belly-landing.

Of the utmost importance for a successful invasion was the neutralization of the coastal batteries of the Atlantic Wall, an exceedingly difficult task in view of the way they were located, camouflaged, and casemated. However, it was deemed necessary to determine whether they could be destroyed before D–Day at all.

A good opportunity arose when it was discovered that eight of the major batteries were under construction and thus temporarily vulnerable. To conceal from the Germans the intended landing zone, for each battery along the Normandy coast two batteries outside the area had to be chosen. The first of the bombing missions in this campaign by the 9th Air Force medium bombers was carried out today, and before the month was out another 23 missions against the batteries would be flown.

April 13, 1944. Wreckage of Don Gentile's *Shangri La.*
(Official USAF Photo)

Friday, 14 April

P–47 Thunderbolts of the 9th Air Force crossed the French coastline and made for enemy-held airfields. At Thionville, they destroyed at least eleven German aircraft on the ground.

Saturday, 15 April

An ambitious plan for large-scale strafing assaults on Luftwaffe airfields had been drawn up by the 8th Fighter Command after the experiments of "Bill's Buzz Boys" (see 18 March). Each fighter group was to have assigned a specific area in Germany and German-held territory in which several airfields were located. Each group would be responsible for the attacks on targets in its own area. The pilots were to become familiarized with their assigned area. They would come to know the defenses and the best

188

way of attack. Moreover, it would also prevent the chance of receiving a very hot welcome from alarmed ground defenses in case another group had visited the place previously.

For this purpose, Germany had been divided into a northern and southern sector, each subdivided in areas of several hundred square miles. When a field order used the code "Jackpot A," the group knew it had to strafe airfields in one or more areas in the northern sector, and when "Jackpot B" was used, the group had to turn to the southern sector.

Today this plan was going to be realized as 616 fighters took off and headed for France and the Low Countries in appalling weather with heavy clouds extending to 24,000 feet. Many airfields were strafed and at least forty aircraft were destroyed on the ground, and in several skirmishes with the Luftwaffe, another eighteen were shot out of the sky. But the price was high and 32 fighters of the 8th failed to return. Half of this number was supposed to have fallen victim to the weather.

Monday, 17 April

"Crossbow" targets received a bombload in the afternoon. Thunderbolts provided escort.

April 17, 1944. B-26 Marauders over cloud-covered France (date approximate). (Photo from *Air Combat* 1939—1945)

189

Tuesday, 18 April

Seven hundred forty-five Fortresses and Liberators of the 8th Air Force crossed the North Sea and headed for targets in the area of Berlin. Heavy fighter escort rode along with the bomberstream. Most bombers reached their targets undisturbed by enemy fighters. There was reason to believe that the Luftwaffe was conserving its strength for sudden advantageous circumstances.

And such an opportunity arose when the 3rd Division neared cloudbanks towering up to 30,000 feet. The leading wing decided to go through it, but trailing wings considered it too dangerous and turned to go for targets of opportunity.

Emerging from the clouds, the lead wing found its group separated and on the wrong course. Moreover, the escort had become confused. It stayed with the trailing wings leaving the leading wing without escort.

Luftwaffe fighters roared down the runways and raced towards the three boxes of Fortresses, making efficient use of on the spot information from the ground controller. Leading the Focke Wulfs was Major Friedrich Müller, a very experienced veteran with many victories. Contact was made at Havel, northwest of Berlin, at 1300 hours, and in the battle that raged for half an hour, eight Fortresses of the 94th Bomb Group went down while two pathfinder aircraft followed their fate.

April 18, 1944. B–17 *Short Stuff* at the end of her career on Swedish soil. (Photo courtesy Swedish government)

Nine other bombers also failed to return, making the total bomber loss for the day nineteen. *Short Stuff* of the 390th Bomb Group landed at Bulltofta in Sweden.

190

Bombs were dropped on the Heinkel complex at Oranienburg and the airfield next to the assembly factory was also covered.

Hitherto, 9th Fighter Command controlled IX Air Support Command and XIX Air Support Command. Both support commands were now redesignated IX and XIX Tactical Air Commands, respectively, A much more fitting title for the kind of operations they were soon to carry out.

Wednesday, 19 April

The 8th Air Force bombers set out again to continue the campaign against aircraft targets. Many airfields such as Eschwege and Werl were plastered by the heavies. Heavy flak was thrown up in many places and one Fortress of the 1st Division, carrying the air commander, went down.

Fighters of both the 8th and 9th Air Force accompanied the bombers. About twenty single-engine German fighters came rushing in on a box of B–17s, straggling east of Kassel. However, the P–51s interfered and five Luftwaffe fighters were picked off.

Fighters of both air forces carried out divebombing attacks in France and Belgium. One of the fighter groups, the 354th, struck rail installations at Namur. One of their Mustangs, *Short Fuse Sallee,* piloted by Captain Richard E. Turner, made a solo attack on Abbeville Airfield. The marshalling yards at Hasselt received a treatment as well.

One hundred eighty-two B–26 Marauders caused much damage in a concentrated attack on the marshalling yards at Malines.

Thursday, 20 April

With clouds and haze preventing clear visibility at many places, heavy bombers of the 8th struck V–1 installations such as at Heuringhem, La Glacerie, and Marguenville.

P–47 Thunderbolts divebombed the rail centers at Mantes, while Creil-Cambrai was worked over by divebombing Mustangs.

Creil was also the target for the B–26 Marauders of the 9th Air Force, but the results were poor.

In the afternoon, a new B–26 outfit, the 397th Bomb Group, flew its first mission. Escorted by Thunderbolts, the Marauders dropped their bombs on a "Crossbow" target.

Friday, 21 April

RAF Typhoons carried out experimental attacks on bridges in France and Belgium. It was believed that knocking bridges out of use could contribute

191

to the transportation program in a considerable, if not decisive, way. Results in Italy confirmed this thesis.

B–26 Marauders of the 9th turned again to the French coast and this time the site at Bois d'Esquerdes was the objective. One B–26, leading a box, was hit by flak and, with one propeller feathered, it continued its bomb run. After leading the bombers over the target, the B–26 slid out of formation and returned to base on one engine.

Railway targets in France and Belgium were attacked by divebombing Mustangs and Thunderbolts.

Saturday, 22 April

In coordination with the nightly RAF assault on Düsseldorf, 8th Air Force heavy bombers dropped 1350 tons of explosives and incendiaries on the marshalling yards at Hamm, one of the greatest traffic centers in western Germany. One formation was off-course and made an ineffective attack on Soest. 40 FW–190s jumped this formation which wandered out of the bomberstream, and one bomber was downed.

Weather had hampered take-off and it was scheduled that the return to base would take place in falling darkness. And this time the Germans intended to make their profits. Some fifteen Me–410s followed the 2nd Division Liberators when they returned to base. At about 2130 hours, when the Liberators were in their landing patterns, the Germans struck and the burning aircraft that dived into the ground caused enormous confusion.

One B–24 was shot down by anti-aircraft fire near Norwich. Nine Liberators were either shot down or destroyed in crashlandings. After the shooting in the air, the Messerschmitts came down to bomb and strafe the airfields, wrecking two more B–24s. One Me–410 was shot down by the gunners of a Liberator.

A formation of 4th Group Mustangs was intercepted by a batch of Me–109s; however, it turned out to be a resounding defeat for the German fighters. Seventeen Messerschmitts were shot down. Donald Blakeslee took two and John Godfrey took three for his account. The encounter took place near Kassel. North of Osnabrück, a squadron Mustangs of the 357th Fighter Group attacked thirty FW–190s, sending two down. Thunderbolts arrived on the scene and took over the fight.

B–26 Marauders of the 9th Air Force received a hot welcome when they neared their target at Heuringhem. The aircraft of the 394th Bomb Group commander was hit by the accurate anti-aircraft fire. One engine was cut, and part of the horizontal stabilizer was torn off, while instruments and part of the hydraulic and electrical system were destroyed. Unable to use his bombsight, the bombardier scattered his bombs in the vicinity of the target, yet the following Marauders dropped right on the target. The disabled bomber returned to England, leaving the formation in order to land as quickly as possible to get medical aid for the wounded co-pilot. After the bomber had landed, they counted 264 holes in the aircraft.

Thunderbolts and Mustangs continued their attacks on railway targets in France and Belgium.

Sunday, 23 April

An overall plan for "Overlord" (the invasion of the Continent) was issued: the primary mission was to attain and to maintain a situation in which it was impossible for the German Air Force to interfere with the landings. The priorities were given in different phases.

Returning from an escort mission, 8th Air Force fighter pilots spotted an abnormally large concentration of rolling stock at Namur. Immediately after receiving the message, 100 P–51 Mustangs and P–47 Thunderbolts of the 9th Air Force took off and raced to the city. Arriving on the spot, the fighters went down in screaming dive attacks and plastered the yard with their bombs and gunfire. At 1944 hours, four groups of B–26 Marauders continued the work and completed the destruction.

Laon/Couvron Airfield received 93 500-lb. bombs from 55th Group Lightnings, again out on a Droop Snoot mission. Lightnings of the 20th Fighter Group achieved only doubtful results when they attacked the Focke Wulf plants at Tours.

Thirty-seven Thunderbolts of the 353rd Fighter Group took off from Raydon in the afternoon to carry out a fighter sweep in northwestern Germany. Airfields were strafed and one German aircraft was damaged on the ground, whereas two Thunderbolts were shot down.

Meanwhile, 46 Mustangs delivered their bombs on Löningen Airfield. Other formations of P–51s flew a fighter sweep in the Hannover area.

Monday, 24 April

Some 750 heavy bombers were dispatched by the 8th Air Force to strike on aircraft industries and airfields in the Munich area. When the bombers arrived over Friedrichshafen, they found their target obscured by effective smokescreens. Yet some direct hits were placed on hangars of the Dornier aircraft plant. Heavy flak added to the discomforts of the 3rd Division Fortresses, and just before reaching the target, one B–17 was hit and after a wing had torn off, the bomber exploded.

But the worst situation was encountered by the Fortresses of the 1st Division when part of this division headed to Oberpfaffenhofen and was left without escort for more than an hour. An estimated 200 German fighters took to the air to deal with the Forts. The 384th Bomb Group bore the brunt of the onslaught and seven B–17s were shot down by wave after wave of German fighters flashing through the formations in their head-on passes.

Heavy flak over the target was responsible for part of the grievous losses suffered by the leading wing. Fifteen B–17s of this wing went down. Another wing in the same force also suffered heavy losses. One Fortress was hit by two 500-lb. bombs from a Fortress flying overhead as it took evasive action to avoid flak bursts. Part of the tailplane was knocked off, while the other bomb hit the wingroot, glanced off, and buried itself in No. 3 engine.

The pilot tried desperately for one nerve-wrecking hour to shake off the bomb by jiggling the aircraft. At last he succeeded but as would appear after an emergency landing in England, the fuse of the bomb was still embedded in the engine.

Bombs also descended on Erding Airfield. Fighters of the 8th and 9th Air Forces claimed 66 German aircraft in the air and another 58 on the ground.

Switzerland lived to see another Fortress invasion, and thirteen diverted to this neutral country.

April 24. 1944. *Shoo Shoo Baby* after landing in Switzerland. (Photo from *Air Combat 1939–1945*)

Tuesday, 25 April

8th Air Force heavies headed towards airfields in France. Thunderbolts and Mustangs accompanied the bombers.

When the bombers arrived over Nancy/Essey Airfield, the target was cov-

194

ered by clouds and the bombers assigned to bomb this objective turned for home with their loads. Crossing the coast, the lead aircraft caught fire and after releasing its bombs in the Channel, the bomber headed back into France where the crew bailed out.

The Fortresses with destination at the airfield at Dijon had more luck, and they found the field in the clear. Bombs were dropped successfully. Only a few enemy fighters were met.

The first group in the 9th Air Force to be equipped with the P–38 Lightning, the 474th Fighter Group, mounted its first fighter sweep.

A sweep in the Mannheim area brought the 354th Group in contact with the Luftwaffe and in the engagement, two Mustangs were lost. However, the Americans claimed the destruction of eighteen enemy aircraft.

Wednesday, 26 April

In the morning, heavy bombers of the 8th Air Force paid a visit to Brunswick and Hannover. Fighters of the 8th and 9th Air Forces escorted the bomberstream. The Luftwaffe made no appearance, and even the flak was not what it used to be and all bombers returned safely, a remarkable event since especially these targets were notorious for their effective defenses. Thunderbolts picked up the bombers near Osnabrück and escorted them home.

Thursday, 27 April

It was a busy day so far as the transportation program was concerned. This time the heavy bombers of the 8th joined the mediums of the 9th in fulfilling this program. 342 tons of bombs hailed down on the rail center at Blainville, and 230 tons from 190 B–24s descended on Châlons-sur-Marne. Other heavy bomber formations struck airfields and V-weapon targets. The airfield at Nancy/Essey received the portion that the bombers had taken home on the 25th. Fortresses also dropped bombs on Le Culot airfield in Belgium.

A new face in the rows of the 9th Air Force bombers attacking transportation targets appeared over Arras when 71 A–20 Havocs dropped their loads. After the weather had kept the Marauders on the ground for some days, 100 B–26s bore on to Cambrai. Air support was provided by Thunderbolts and Mustangs.

Lightnings of the 20th and 55th Fighter Groups were out on Droop Snoot missions, the former group going to Péronne but the Lightnings found their target obscured by cloud and they turned to Albert/Méaulté. Some P–38s dropped their bombs prematurely when they mistook an approaching batch of Thunderbolts for Focke Wulfs. The 55th Fighter Group was more successful when it dropped its bombs from 17,000 feet on Roye/Amy Airfield.

Friday, 28 April

Twelve heavy bombers of the 8th were shot down by ever-increasing numbers of anti-aircraft guns while paying visits to the "Noballs" and to enemy airfields.

P-38 Lightnings of the 55th Fighter Group dropped forty-nine 1000-lb. bombs on the airfield of Châteaudun from an altitude of 18,000 feet. After this Droop Snoot bombing, the Lightnings served as top-cover for Thunderbolts from the 353rd and 56th Fighter Groups attacking the same airfield. The latter group made its first divebombing attack. Lightnings of the 20th Group bombed the airfield at Tours.

Many fighter groups were in the air to attack a large variety of targets such as Charleroi and Creil.

The rail center at Creil was also attacked by the bombers of the 9th Air Force, whereby all lines were blocked.

Saturday, 29 April

Hitler's capital was again visited by the 8th Air Force heavies. A solid carpet of clouds stretched out all the way to Berlin when over 700 bombers droned along to their destination in a large column with their heavy fighter escort from the 8th and 9th Air Forces.

The 3rd Division, leading the mission, had encountered difficulties upon assembling and when enemy territory was penetrated, the division was so badly strung out that effective fighter cover was impossible. One combat wing was fifteen minutes ahead of schedule, whereas another was twenty-five minutes behind. Faulty navigation placed one wing forty miles south of the main bomber force and it was this force that presented the Luftwaffe with the most attractive target. Near Magdeburg, the Focke Wulfs approached the bombers. The first group to become confronted with the on-rushing Luftwaffe fighters was the 385th Bomb Group, and seven of its Fortresses were shot out of the sky. In twenty minutes time, seventeen B-17s went down. Another Fortress that did not make it back to England ditched in the sea (crew saved).

The other wings of the 3rd Division and the entire 1st Division had a solid fighter screen and the Germans made no attempt to interfere.

There was, however, a second victim, and that was the 2nd Division, trailing the other formations and behind schedule. Only one P-51 Mustang

196

group escorted the Liberators. They reached their target unmolested and they added their share to the 1402 tons which were unloaded through clouds. After turning on a homeward course, the escort had to withdraw. The P–47s were planned to meet the bombers at Dümmer Lake. But that was still far off. And, as usual, the unescorted bombers were noticed by the German controller. It didn't take long before the Luftwaffe fighters tore along the runways and assembled in a mass force of a hundred fighters. They rushed toward the bombers, making contact near Hannover. In savage attacks, the Germans knocked down 25 Liberators.

Sunday, 30 April

Heavy bombers of the 8th Air Force struck airfields in France. One of the targets that received a severe blow was Lyon. Fighters escorted the bombers.

One hundred forty-three medium bombers of the 9th Air Force visited Béthune and Somain, and 71 Havocs dropped their bombs on Busigny. Thirty freight cars were destroyed on the marshalling yards at Béthune.

The Allies had not counted on the fact that repairs could be executed in such a short time to have at least the main rail lines operative again. Many times repairs were done in a few hours. This made a frequent return necessary, while also a careful planning had to be done to keep the centers out of use.

Leigh Mallory issued a paper in which he urged the air forces to use every effort to step up the prosecution of the campaign, and he made a special call upon the 8th Air Force for full participation.

Many fighter sweeps were carried out over France. Mustangs of the 4th Fighter Group destroyed a German aircraft they encountered on their way to the Lyon area. Another four were shot up while strafing an airfield. Tours' airfield was attacked by Lightnings of the 20th Group.

The 8th Air Force's total heavy bomber losses for the month were 371 aircraft. The four Mustang groups of the 8th lost 67 aircraft, while the Thunderbolts suffered a loss of 42 aircraft. This was partly due to the fact that the Mustang was more vulnerable and could not sustain the amount of damage that a Thunderbolt could take and still bring its pilot home.

Four new fighter groups and two new bomber groups had been added to the strength of the 9th Air Force this month.

5

MAY

Monday, 1 May

The month of May was marked by a great increase in the intensity of attacks on transportation targets in an all-out effort of all air forces to wreck the German railway system.

And they made no exception on the first day of the month. 328 heavy bombers of the 8th Air Force and 16 fighter groups delivered a load of 1000 tons of explosives on the marshalling yards at Troyes, Rheims, Brussels, Liège, Sarreguemines, and Metz. Northwest of Saarbrücken, German fighters put in an appearance, but they were attacked by the escorting Mustangs. Additional bombloads were dropped on the "Crossbow" targets along the French coast.

Eleven different forces of B–26 Marauders of the 9th Air Force attacked the rail centers at Mantes, Montignies-sur-Sambre, Douai, Monceaux, and Valenciennes. 37 A–20 Havocs went to Charleroi. Haine–St. Pierre, St. Ghislain, Amiens, Arras, and Valenciennes were subjected to divebombing attacks from P–47 Thunderbolts.

Tuesday, 2 May

Ten different forces of 9th Air Force fighters, each force composed of some 28 aircraft loaded with 250- and 500-lb. bombs went to the marshalling yards and repair shops at Le Mans, Aulnay, Tergnier, Hasselt, Mantes, Tourcoing, Charleroi, Somain, and Péronne. Meanwhile, six forces of light and medium bombers dropped their loads on the yards at Valenciennes, Busigny, and Blanc Misseron.

The heavy bombers of the 8th Air Force turned to the same kind of targets. Two new groups made their combat debut with an attack on the

198

railyards at Liège. They were the 486th and the 487th Bomb Groups, both equipped with the B–24H/J, forming a new wing in the 3rd Division. The 3rd Division was now a mixed Fortress-Liberator unit.

Thurdsay, 4 May

The 8th Air Force heavies were dispatched to fly another mission to Berlin. However, weather intervened and the bombers turned to other targets.

Six groups of B–26 Marauders and A–20 Havocs crossed the Channel for a bombardment on the coastal batteries.

8th Air Force fighters attacked enemy airfields. One of the groups, the 359th, made its last claims with the Thunderbolt before converting to the Mustang.

Saturday, 6 May

In the morning, an F–5 Lightning skimmed the wavetops as it crossed the Channel at a height of fifteen feet. The French coast was crossed at Berq-sur-Mer. Then the Lightning made a sharp turn around a large dune in order to lessen the chance of being hit while turning. Afterwards, it was learned that this dune was in fact an enemy gun position.

Racing just above the beach, the cameras clicked all the way. The Lightning encountered five groups of men working on the beach defenses and, steering his plane in their directions, the pilot was already overhead when the men scattered and fell in all directions. At the end of the run, the Lightning missed the edge of a cliff by six feet and turned for home. The first "dicing mission" was completed by the 10th Photo Reconnaissance Group of the XIX Tactical Air Command.

In February, a new kind of V-weapon site had alarmed the Allies. These were very simple installations which could be easily camouflaged and were intended to launch pilotless aircraft. These "Modified Sites" were very difficult to detect and offered poor targets because of their size.

By now one could recognize a more or less fixed pattern in the "Crossbow" operations. Massive 8th Air Force heavy bomber formations (mostly B–17s) attacked from altitudes varying from 12,000 to 20,000 feet. There were almost continuous attacks (depending on the weather) by medium bombers from the 9th and 2nd Tactical Air Forces, and by fighters and fighter-bombers.

A trial minimum-altitude attack on the ski sites was carried out by four P–47 Thunderbolts from the 365th Fighter Group, 9th Air Force. Each Thunderbolt, carrying two 1000-lb. delayed-fuse bombs, attacked a ski site. Although they were greeted with very heavy machinegun fire, three

May 6, 1944. Men working on the beach defenses scatter and fall in all directions. (Official USAF Photo)

sites received major damage and all four P–47s returned to base. The four pilots had received an intensive training and briefing by Eglin Field officers (see 24 December 1943).

Sunday, 7 May

The 8th Air Force heavy bombers were again en route to Berlin. A milestone was reached because the bomber force comprised 1000 bombers. Swarms of fighters accompanied the aerial armada. Flying above a solid overcast, the main force arrived over Berlin, while smaller forces headed for two other targets in central Germany. Only nine enemy fighters were spotted, but they made no passes at the bombers. Bombs were also dropped on the marshalling yards at Münster. Target support was provided there by Thunderbolts of the 353rd Fighter Group.

All doubts about the possibility of demolishing a bridge without too many wasted bombs were removed by eight 9th Air Force Thunderbolts. The target was a 650-foot steel railway bridge over the Seine near Vernon. Each Thunderbolt carried two 1000-lb. bombs as they came flashing in. And when the last Thunderbolt pulled out of its dive, a smashed railroad crossing was left behind. Other formations of Thunderbolts and Marauders badly damaged the bridges at Oissel, Orival, and Mantes-Gassicourt. The

200

May 7, 1944. A Thunderbolt of the 361st Fighter Group on escort duty during the attack on Berlin. This photo was taken from one of the Fortresses. (Official USAF Photo)

bridges over the Loire had to wait until D-Day to achieve maximum surprise.

Monday, 8 May

Berlin was the target for some 800 bombers of the 8th Air Force, taking off early in the morning.

One wing from the 3rd Division became separated too far from the main force and joined the Liberators on their mission to Brunswick. There were no fighters to escort this wing and as usual such a situation did not pass without being noticed by the German ground controller.

Immediately, the Luftwaffe took to the air and near Nienburg the Focke Wulfs commenced their head-on passes. Following their customary tactics, they came in with flashing guns only to break away at the very last moment. One Focke Wulf misjudged that moment and collided with a Fortress, both tumbling down. Another Fortress was destroyed by a parachute-bomb dropped by a German fighter. Thirteen Fortresses were lost, a very high price for their course alteration.

The Liberators were escorted by the blue-nosed Mustangs of the 352nd Fighter Group. Climbing through a solid overcast, the Mustangs emerged over Holland where contact was made with the last elements of the bomberstream at 20,000 feet. Flying above the column, they overtook the successive boxes and took station in front of the leading group, at that moment flying near Nienburg.

It was here that they met the mass of the Me–109s and FW–190s already engaged in beating up the lone 3rd Division wing. Pursuing the German fighters right through the bomber formation, they knocked 27 Luftwaffe fighters out of the sky for the loss of but one Mustang. One returning Liberator was abandoned by its crew over England. The bomber crashed and from its remains stepped the uninjured ball-turret gunner who had not

201

heard the bail-out order and hadn't the slightest idea that he was alone in the aircraft.

The Germans brought up some 200 fighters to meet the bombers, most of them encountered in the Hannover area. Major Robert S. Johnson of the 56th Fighter Group scored his 27th and 28th victory.

In the afternoon, heavy bombers of the 8th turned to the "Noballs" and a final attempt was made to knock out the site at La Glacerie before the invasion was to start. One lead bomber was shot down by intense flak.

9th Air Force mediums and fighter-bombers flew several missions to airfields and bridges in France. One Marauder group attacked the airfield at Evreux/Fauville, while other medium bombers attacked the Seine bridge at Oissel. Thunderbolts knocked out three of the eleven spans of the railway viaduct at Hirson. P–47s also attacked bridges over the Meuse, and the bridge at Mézières was destroyed. The railway bridge at Namur was covered by bombs dropped by Marauders, which also bombed the bridges at Illus and Sédan.

Tuesday, 9 May

The 8th Air Force dispatched its bombers on a large-scale bombing mission to airfields and transportation targets in France. In a clear morning sky, 772 heavy bombers headed across the Channel and approached the French coast. Gunners always checked their guns at this point and by doing so, one directed his fire too carelessly and a Fortress was hit. The aircraft had to make a crashlanding on the French coast.

Over Laon, a Fortress had to take evasive action and one of its bombs smashed into the tailgunner's compartment of the bomber below, fatally wounding the gunner. The bomb didn't explode and the pilot brought the aircraft back.

The airfield at Laon-Athies was successfully attacked by 113 Fortresses of the 3rd Division. Many planes were damaged by flak. Heavy escort was provided all the way.

Returning from escorting the bombers to St. Dizier, a squadron of Mustangs of the 4th Fighter Group spotted some flying boats on a lake. The Mustangs came down and gave them a harsh treatment.

P–47 Thunderbolts of the 404th Fighter Group, 9th Air Force, took off for a visit to three different V-weapon sites. Two squadrons found their target, but the third searched in vain due to a briefing error, and it dive-bombed the heavily defended railyard at Serqueux, twenty miles northeast of Rouen. One Thunderbolt was shot down.

Two squadrons of the same group were out again in the afternoon to attack the ski site at Vacqueriette and a number of other targets. This group was one of the many that ranged over France during the day. Five groups of B–26 Marauders headed for the coastal batteries along the French coast while the mediums of the 9th also dropped a load on the railway bridge at Mahon. One Marauder of the 322nd Bomb Group, *Mild and Bitter*, completed its 100th combat mission. The aircraft was flown by Captain Paul Shannon.

Wednesday, 10 May

An attack was carried out on the so-called Hoarding long-range aircraft reporting system, part of the extensive radar defense system of the Germans along the coast (with an efficient network inland) covering a distance from Norway to the border of Spain.

The 9th Air Force continued its attacks in accordance with the interdiction program, sealing off the intended landing area from reinforcements. 39 B–26 Marauders of the 394th Bomb Group delivered sixty-eight tons of bombs on the marshalling yards at Creil. A flight commander's B–26 was hit by flak and went down. Marauders also struck railway bridges over the Meuse.

Thursday, 11 May

The 8th Air Force sent 973 heavy bombers to a large number of rail targets. B–17 Fortresses set out in a clear sky to drop 600 tons of bombs on the marshalling yards at Saarbrücken, Lüxembourg, Ehrang, Konz-Karthaus, Bettembourg, Thionville, Völklingen, and Liège in Belgium. B–24 Liberators headed for Mulhouse, Belfort, Épinal, and Chaumont, and threw 440 tons of explosives on the rail centers.

Unfortunately, the 96th Bomb Group heading for the yards at Épinal made a bad approach and dropped part of its load on the town, hitting among other things a prisoner of war camp, killing 300 men.

The two Liberator groups from the 3rd Division had Troyes as their assigned target, however they would not reach it. A heavy flak barrage near Châteaudun fatally hit both the leader and his deputy and both B–24s tumbled to earth. The ensuing confusion caused the mission to be abandoned.

Today the first 9th Air Force attack was made in a campaign to neutralize enemy airfields from which the Germans might operate against the Allied invasion forces. It was hoped that the Germans would be forced to withdraw to airfields from which they would have no advantage in distance over Allied fighters operating from bases in England. Approximately 100 airfields existed within a radius of 350 miles from the Normandy shore. Many were deserted but could easily be put into operation again. Meanwhile, heavy bomber attacks deep into the heart of Germany would continue to prevent the removal of fighters to France.

The 9th Air Force started the campaign in spite of the bad weather, and 37 Marauders attacked the airfield at Beaumont-le-Roger while at the same time eighteen A–20 Havocs visited Cormeilles-en-Vexin, where good results were obtained.

Coastal batteries along the French coast were attacked by two groups of Marauders, each group concentrating on one battery.

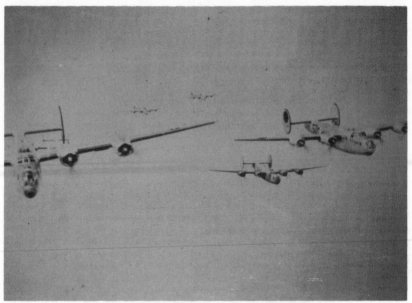

May 11, 1944. 492nd Bomb Group Liberators set out on
their first mission. (Official USAF Photo)

Friday, 12 May

Not until now did the Allies open a serious campaign against German oil facilities. One of the reasons was that they did not have sufficient heavy bombers available to attack the widely scattered eighty-one oil targets: twenty-three synthetic plants and fifty-eight crude oil refineries. But now huge forces of the 8th Air Force, RAF Bomber Command, and the 15th Air Force from Italy made out that the time was opportune to undertake the campaign.

General Spaatz expressed, in his Combined Bomber Offensive Plan of 4

204

March, the possibility of depriving the Germans of a large part of their gasoline supply by a combined effort. Besides, he believed that the German Air Force would react in force when the oil plants were at stake and this would not only cost the Germans dearly in aircraft, but also in consumption of gasoline. This would never be achieved in the transportation campaign. Most probably the Germans were confident that the efforts were used against rail centers instead of against more important targets. And the General was right.

The campaign opened with the 8th Air Force's dispatching 935 heavy bombers to attack the plants at Merseburg-Leuna, Brüx, Lützkendorf, Böhlen, Zeitz, Zwickau, and other cities. The two leading wings were to bomb the FW–190 repair depot at Zwickau, more to conceal the true objective of the mission than anything else. Escorted by the fighters of the 8th, 9th, and Royal Air Force, the bombers set course to a point south of the Ruhr, skirting the highly defended sites in this area, and continuing on around the cities of Hannover and Brunswick. They proceeded on an easterly and northeasterly course, which was maintained toward the target area.

Near Frankfurt the bomber crews spotted some 150 to 200 tiny specks, growing rapidly in size as they rushed to the bombers. They attacked mostly en masse, concentrating on the leading combat wings of the 3rd Division. About thirty German fighters came in abreast, blasting away with everything they had, even ramming the bombers. The 4th Wing lost half of its bombers: eleven Fortresses went down, seven from the 447th Bomb Group. The escorting Mustangs and Thunderbolts came to the rescue. The P–47s of Zemke's 56th Fighter Group claimed eighteen German fighters for the loss of three P–47s.

The bombers continued to their targets and 886 heavies dropped 1718 tons with great accuracy on the oil plants. The oil plant at Brüx was left burning by the load from two wings of the 3rd Division. Liberators of the 2nd Division struck Zeitz and Böhlen, while Fortresses of the 1st Division dropped their bombs from 18,000 feet, to achieve maximum results, on several oil targets including the plant at Lützkendorf.

On the return flight fifty German twin-engine fighters made desperate attacks against the bombers for half an hour while small groups of single-engine fighters attempted interception. In all, the 8th Air Force lost 46 heavy bombers; ten Allied fighters also failed to return to their bases. But the German Air Force had received a blow: of the estimated 300 fighters involved in the air battle, 66 were shot down by the AAF fighters.

The damage inflicted to the targets was considerable. Brüx, Böhlen, and Zeitz were temporarily out of action. Accidentally a building at Merseburg-Leuna was destroyed in which experiments were being conducted with heavy water for the atomic bomb project.

May 12, 1944. A direct flak hit in the fuel tanks while attacking military installations in France means the end for this A–20 Havoc of the 416th Bomb Group. (Photo Imperial War Museum, London)

Coastal batteries on the French coast were bombed by three groups of Marauders and Havocs of the 9th Air Force.

Saturday, 13 May

The 8th Air Force bombers crossed the North Sea as they proceeded to oil targets and aircraft plants in Poland and Germany. However, the weather in the eastern part of Germany was not as good as in the western part of the country, and the Fortresses of the 1st Division, on their way to the oil targets in Poland and the Focke Wulf plants at Kreising and Posen, had to turn to targets of opportunity.

The 2nd and 3rd Divisions, however, could fully realize their intended attacks on their primary targets. The Liberators of the 2nd Division achieved excellent results when they dropped their loads on the FW–190 assembly plant at Tutow and the same good visibility that made it possible for the Liberators to destroy part of the Focke Wulf plant enabled the Fortresses of the 3rd Division to bring destruction to the marshalling yards at Osnabrück, one of the biggest marshalling yards in Germany.

Fifteen fighter groups of the 8th Air Force, eight 9th Air Force groups, and two RAF Mustang groups took part in the bomber support. When the bombers neared Jutland, they found some 120 German fighters waiting for

206

May 13, 1944. A German soldier sitting on the nose of a B–24 Liberator that made a belly-landing near Voorst in Holland. (Photo from *Air Combat 1939–1945*)

them. The strong escort made the Germans change their mind and they turned to make for the Liberators of the 2nd Division. Before the Germans could start their assault, the Thunderbolts of the 356th Fighter Group, returning from escorting the 1st Division Fortresses, turned into them. Only a few enemy planes managed to reach the bombers and one B–24 was shot down.

But the Thunderbolts could not stay with the bombers because a fuel shortage forced the fighters to turn back to England. And that was what the Germans had been waiting for. More than 150 fighters assembled ahead of the 1st Division, only accompanied by the Mustangs of the 352nd and 354th Fighter Groups. Within ten minutes, six Fortresses were shot down.

The 3rd Division with its fighter escort had no encounters with the Luftwaffe on their journey to Osnabrück and back.

Forty-two A-20 Havocs of the 9th Air Force attacked Beauvais Airfield and three groups of B-26 Marauders delivered a load on Beaumont-sur-Oise, Chièvres, and Abbeville. Eight aircraft were damaged by flak but none was lost. Three Marauder groups bombed three coastal batteries.

Monday, 15 May

A small force of heavy bombers of the 8th visited the French coast. 58 Fortresses of the 1st and 108 Liberators of the 2nd Division unloaded 484 tons of bombs on the V-installations Marquise-Mimoyecques and Siracourt. Only light flak was thrown up.

Thursday, 18 May

Bombs were dropped on enemy radar installations along the French coast. Thunderbolts of the 404th Fighter Group, 9th Air Force, set out to strike the Beaumont-sur-Oise Airfield. Arriving over their target, they were confronted with heavy clouds that made a divebombing attack not possible and the P-47s turned for home. Suddenly six Me-109s jumped the Thunderbolts. In the brief engagement, one Messerschmitt went down.

Friday, 19 May

Berlin and Brunswick were the targets selected for the day's mission and 1000 heavy bombers of the 8th Air Force crossed the North Sea, flying in close formations, with 331 Liberators going to the marshalling yards at Brunswick and the Fortresses on their way to Berlin. Leading the bomberstream was the 1st Division.

The Liberators of the 2nd Division crossed the Zuider Zee at 1207 hours. The force of 331 Liberators had meanwhile been reduced to 291 aircraft. Fifteen B-24s were unable to assemble because of heavy clouds; other B-24s had turned back for other reasons, most of them with mechanical failures.

The Luftwaffe rose as expected, though they mainly concentrated on the 2nd Division. West of Dümmer Lake, the Germans approached the bombers with some 150 single-engine fighters and about ten twin-engine fighters. They bore into the Thunderbolt escort composed of two fighter groups. With the escort kept busy, a second German fighter force started the assault on the Liberators now only protected by Thunderbolts of the 56th Fighter Group. The newest operational bomb group, the 492nd, bore the brunt of the assault and eight Liberators went down, one of them crash-landing near Warmenhuizen in Holland.

Only when the P–38 Lightnings from the 370th Fighter Group arrived on the scene were the Luftwaffe fighters dispersed. Three Mustang groups, the 352nd, 357th, and 359th encountered the Germans near Brandenburg, and in the fierce battle the groups claimed respectively eleven, ten, and eleven enemy fighters shot down.

Two hundred P–47 Thunderbolts flew in an early-evening sky a fighter-bomber mission to the airfields at Beauvais, Monchy, Breton, Abbeville, and Cambrai.

Six groups of 9th Air Force medium bombers concentrated on the coastal batteries along the French coast.

Saturday, 20 May

8th Air Force heavy bombers took off early in the spring morning to carry out an attack on various targets in the occupied countries, all connected with the forthcoming invasion.

Today most victims were not caused by enemy action but by early morning ground mists. Five Fortresses and three Liberators were destroyed in take-off crashes. At Podington one bomber broke off its take-off run and started taxiing back up the misty runway at the same moment the next Fortress pushed the throttles forward and thundered down the runway. The head-on collision cost 21 lives.

Among the many targets bombed were the airfields at Orly and Villacoublay. Two Fortresses of the 3rd Division failed to return, shot down over Belgium.

Seven groups of B–26 Marauders turned to Denain, Evreux, Beaumont-sur-Oise, and Cormeilles-en-Vexin. One group of A–20 Havocs dropped its bombs on the airfield at Montdidier.

The coastal batteries in France were also not overlooked, and two groups of B–26 Marauders gave them a treatment.

Sunday, 21 May

"Crossbow" targets on the French coast were attacked by 150 8th Air Force bombers. All of them returned to base.

For some time, fighters had already been strafing trains and, although the fear existed that this might have caused a considerable loss of civilian lives, it was believed that after the 20th most civilian rail traffic had ceased and a large-scale operation was ordered.

And the first of the large-scale missions, the so-called "Chattanooga

209

Choo Choo'' missions would take place today: 763 fighters of the 9th Air Force and 2nd Tactical Air Force swept over northern France; 552 fighters of the 8th Air Force ranged over Germany to shoot up or to bomb trains, rail installations, bridges, barges, and numerous other targets.

In addition to these transportation targets the fighters claimed the largest number of enemy aircraft destroyed on the ground: 102, with another 76 damaged.

One 353rd Group Thunderbolt returned to its base at Raydon with part of the engine of a locomotive embedded in its fuselage. It had exploded at the moment the Thunderbolt passed overhead.

The 353rd Group ranged with 44 P–47s in a square area 60 miles wide and deep south and west of Hamburg. Each aircraft carried two 500-lb. GP bombs. Very heavy flak was met and two Thunderbolts were lost.

The 357th Fighter Group, one of the many on a wild ride across Germany, sent its three squadrons in different directions: one going to the Wismar area, one to Anklam, and the other heading to the Neubrandenburg area. One section of the latter squadron had the most profitable hunting of the day when they spotted an airfield crowded with aircraft. The Mustangs accepted the invitation and came down and, as it turned out, the flak was surprisingly light. The Mustangs made eight passes over the field, blazing twelve Me–109s, two other aircraft, and a hangar.

A P–38 pilot, hedge-hopping home, suddenly found a high-tension wire in his way. Too low to pass over it, he decided to fly under the wire, but the cable cut off part of the left port fin and wound around the other fin, blocking the rudder. Yet he managed to bring his aircraft with his souvenir home.

Two groups of Marauders bombed Abbeville Airfield.

Monday, 22 May

A Ju–88 paid an early morning visit to Great Ashfield, the base of the 8th Air Force 385th Bomb Group, and delivered seven bombs. One B–17 was destroyed.

8th Air Force heavies flew a northeasterly course, crossing the North Sea to bring another visit to Kiel. The U-boat bases and harbor installations were bombed. Mustangs rode along with the bombers all the way.

The airfield of Beaumont-le-Roger was attacked by two groups of Marauders. Two other B–26 groups headed for the airfield at Beauvais. Three groups of A–20 Havocs bombed Evreux and Cormeilles-en-Vexin. Strafing and dive-bombing of the airfields by fighters had become a common practice after the mediums had bombed. Three groups of B–26s dropped their charges on gun positions along the French coast.

210

P–38 Lightnings of the 9th Air Force set course to Orly Airfield. While one squadron of the 474th Fighter Group flew top-cover, the two other squadrons dropped their bombs and strafed the airfield. Hereafter, the Lightnings strafed locomotives, railway cars, a flak tower, and many other targets of opportunity. Running into flak, one P–38 took wild evasive action and flew through a tree, leaving its nosewheel behind. The pilot made a successful belly-landing at his base.

In the afternoon, 46 Thunderbolts of the 353rd Fighter Group bombed the bridges near Liège. One P–47 received a direct hit by flak and the pilot bellied-in south of Brussels. Thunderbolts of the 356th Group attacked the rail bridge at Hasselt in Belgium.

At night, one group of sixteen B–26s was dispatched on their first night mission. The target for the 322nd Bomb Group ("Nye's Annihilators") was Beaumont-le-Roger, already bombed by the group the same day. The target was illuminated by indicators dropped by pathfinders, and the bombs were well placed. A German nightfighter made a single pass at the bombers, but all returned safely to base.

Tuesday, 23 May

One thousand forty-four heavy bombers were unleashed by the 8th Air Force to attack airfields and marshalling yards at Épinal, Metz, Saarbrücken, Bayon, Chaumont, and Étampes. Much damage was committed.

The airfield at Beaumont-le-Roger was the target for one group of the 9th Marauders.

An intended attack on the airfield at Melun-Villaroche had to be abandoned because of cirrus clouds at bombing altitude, and the heavies took their loads back.

Wednesday, 24 May

More than 400 B–24 Liberators of the 8th Air Force took care that the airfields around Paris were treated according to the directions in Leigh Mallory's airfield plan. They were part of a force of 1100 bombers.

B–17 Fortresses of the 1st and 3rd Divisions droned on an easterly heading, high above scattered clouds, to visit the capital of the Reich. The Germans rose in strength to meet the bombers, and this time the escorting fighters were too late to intercept them, their view being curtailed by the heavy condensation trails of the leading wings. Shortly after the bombers left the Berlin area, the German fighters started their assault. Heavy flak over Berlin had already shot five bombers out of the sky, but more bombers were going to fall under the tenacious head-on attacks of the

Luftwaffe fighters. And, as usual, there was one group taking the brunt of the punishment and this time the 381st Bomb Group was the unlucky one: eight Fortresses went down.

Eight of the German fighters shot down were claimed by the Mustangs of the 4th Fighter Group. In all, 33 Fortresses failed to return from the mission.

Two squadrons of the 9th Air Force, 363rd Group, made no contact with the bombers because of the weather, and returned to base. One squadron went down to strafe and the Mustangs reaped a rich harvest of locomotives at Nordhorn, Hannover, and other places.

Thunderbolts of the 78th Fighter Group, led by a Droop Snoot Lightning, tried to bomb the Creil rail bridge. The bridge escaped unscathed.

Five groups of Marauders and Havocs carried out an attack on the coastal batteries. The airfield of Beaumont-le-Roger again received a bombload from three groups of Marauders of the 9th Air Force.

Thirty P–51 Mustangs of the 357th Fighter Group took off in the evening and climbed on a heading to France. They were out on a strafing mission and when the fighters headed out over the French coast again, they had destroyed six locomotives, a number of flak towers, tanks, trucks, hangars, and many other targets with their 500-lb. GP bombs or with their guns. Two Mustangs were shot down.

Thursday, 25 May

A heavy bombload was delivered by the 8th heavies on the marshalling yards at Mulhouse, Belfort, Tonnerre, Thionville, Sarrequemines, Metz, Blainville, Liège, Brussels, Charleroi, and Aalst. Fourteen combat wings were involved in this operation in connection with the transportation program. Heavy bombers also visited the important Luftwaffe airfields at Belfort, Nancy, and Brussels. They contributed in the coastal battery campaign as a force of 54 B–17s and B–24s turned to the French shoreline and attacked Fécamp and St. Valéry. With an eye on the possibility that the targets on D-Day might be obscured, the bombing was done by H2X, but the results were discouraging.

After escorting the bombers, 736 American fighters went down on the deck; some 600 8th Air Force fighters ranged over Belgium and France searching for trains and three 9th Air Force fighter groups shot up trains in northern France and the Rhineland.

After these missions, most movements by rail were carried out by night.

Friday, 26 May

In order not to give too much indication in advance about a possible invasion area, the bridges over the Seine had not been on the target list until shortly before D-Day. However, today a low-level attack was carried out by P–47s and B–26 Marauder bombers on the bridges at Le Manoir and Poissy. The latter was completely destroyed by the Marauders.

Saturday, 27 May

Rail centers and marshalling yards at Ludwigshafen, Mannheim, Karlsruhe, Strasbourg, Konz-Karthaus, Neunkirchen, and Saarbrücken were attacked by the heavy bombers of the 8th Air Force with devastating results. Hitherto, the German Air Force had not shown much ambition in interfering with the transportation attacks. However, today they were up in force. Mustangs had just rendezvoused with the bombers north of Strasbourg when an estimated sixty Me–109s and FW–190s arrived on the scene and launched an attack on the lead box of Fortresses. The first bombers went down, but claims mounted to twenty German aircraft shot down. Nine bombers were lost. One Liberator made a landing in Switzerland, while one Mustang pilot also bailed out over this country.

After fulfilling their escort mission, the fighters again went on the deck and strafed targets of opportunity with a special eye on airfields and locomotives.

P–47s and B–26s of the 9th Air Force made a low-level attack on the bridges at Juvisy, Le Manoir, Maisons-Laffitte, and Le Mesnil Ande.

Thirty-eight A–20 Havocs flew in two boxes of nineteen planes to the marshalling yards at Amiens. Near Formière, at 11,500 feet, some 27 miles from the target, the bombers ran into a heavy and accurate flak barrage. One Havoc in the leading element received a direct hit and spun into the ground with no one getting out. Then the second aircraft took a steep dive downwards with the pilot slumped over the wheel. At about 5000 feet above the ground, one wing broke off and the bomber spun into the ground. The other Havoc in the lead element received a hit that knocked its engine out. The pilot immediately turned back to England, but he was rapidly losing altitude. Still over France, he ordered his crew to bail out. One crew member was strapped in his compartment and by the time he had freed himself, they were over the Channel. There both jumped and they were picked up by Air-Sea Rescue.

Two more squadrons were added to the strength of the "Carpetbaggers" (see 4/5 January): the 788th and the 850th Bomb Squadrons.

213

Sunday, 28 May

A record force of 1282 heavy bombers of the 8th Air Force, involving nine B–17 wings and six B–24 wings, formed a tremendous bomberstream proceeding, in the afternoon, to the synthetic oil plants and aircraft factories at Reihland, Magdeburg, Zeitz, Merseburg-Leuna, Dessau, and Lützken-dorf. 610 Fortresses of the 1st Division were heading the column; then followed 255 Fortresses of the 3rd Division with the 106 Liberators of the same division following in their wake. Trailing the bomberstream were 311 Liberators of the 2nd Division.

A heavy fighter escort accompanied the bombers and the first task of the Luftwaffe was to try to keep the escort fully occupied before a mass attack on the bombers was launched. For the Germans did not intend to let this mass of aircraft pass without making a try to diminish their rows.

The leading wing of the 1st Division took the first blow and the low 401st Group saw its formation dwindled by six B–17s. A seventh would ditch in the sea on the return flight. Twelve bombers out of the lead wing were shot down, making the loss for the Dessau force seventeen aircraft.

And the lead wing of the 3rd Division heading for Magdeburg did not fare much better. Nine Fortresses and 3 of the division's Liberators went down, finished off by some eighty fighters and flak. In the air battle with the escorting fighters, many Luftwaffe aircraft went down, the 354th Fighter Group claiming the destruction of nineteen for the loss of two of their number.

The 2nd Division met only scattered enemy opposition when they carried on to Merseburg/Zeitz at an altitude of 20,000 feet with five escorting fighter groups. Bombing was good and Zeitz was put out of operation again.

Fifty-nine Fortresses headed for Cologne, each B–17 carrying two glider bombs, normal 2000-lb. HE bombs strapped in a kind of glider frame with a 12-ft. wingspan incorporating a simple automatic pilot to compensate for induced roll after release. The large marshalling yards were the target for the reception of 109 of these bombs, but even this target was not large enough. Inaccuracy proved to be such that continuance of such experiments was considered useless.

P–47 Thunderbolts and B–26 Marauders of the 9th Air Force attacked the Seine bridges at Mantes, Orival, Rouen, and Maisons-Laffitte. Flak around the latter bridge was extremely heavy when the Marauders of the 397th Bomb Group arrived, and although no bombers were lost, 21 returned with battle damage.

May 28, 1944. B–24s of the 486th Bomb Group flying over the burning oil plant at Lützkendorf. (Photo Imperial War Museum, London)

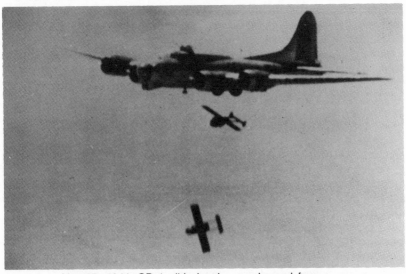

May 28, 1944. GB–1 glide bombs are dropped from a 303rd Bomb Group Fortress. (Photo from *Air Combat 1939–1945*)

Monday, 29 May

Two hundred twenty-four B–24s of both the 2nd and 3rd Divisions headed the bombertrain when they set out again on a mission to deprive the Germans of their precious oil. And this time the targets were the distant synthetic oil plants at Pölitz, northeast of Berlin. The Liberators flew across the North Sea to a point north of Heligoland; they then followed a southeasterly course to pass north of Hamburg. From here they proceeded on an easterly heading to Parchim where part of the force took a heading to aircraft plants at Tutow with the majority going to the oil plants at Pölitz.

Following the Liberators out, the Fortresses of the 1st and 3rd Divisions took a heading that brought them via the Zuider Zee to a point north of Magdeburg. Here they turned southeast to the vicinity of Dessau where both divisions split to go to several targets connected with aircraft production.

Fifty-eight B–17s of the 1st Division delivered a load on the Focke Wulf plant at Poznan that stopped the production until August, while at Strau a blow was dealt depriving the Germans of some 50 percent of the production facilities. 48 Fortresses blasted the Focke Wulf factory at Cottbus. Fifteen 8th Air Force and twelve 9th Air Force fighter groups escorted the bombers.

German fighter opposition was again heavy. They concentrated their attacks on the four Liberator wings with destination Pölitz. Some forty Luftwaffe fighters drew the sole Mustang group away from the bombers and then another sixty fighters launched their assault on the B–24s flying at an altitude of about 22,000 feet. Heavy flak over the target added to the perilous situation. The German fighters kept on coming with many twin-engine fighters pouring their rockets into the formation. The fight lasted until the bombers were far out over the Baltic. Twenty Liberators would not return to their bases.

Yet the Luftwaffe had missed a chance to deal a blow to the 3rd Division approaching Leipzig when this force was left without escort for thirty minutes, though several single-engine fighters did make attacks. For once the Germans missed such an opportunity; instead they shadowed the 1st Division all the way to Sorau. Out of fuel, the Germans had to land at this base but unlucky for them, one wing of the Fortresses was just on the bomb run to plaster the field.

It was clear that the Allies were now working over the Achilles' heel of Germany. Indeed the Germans were appalled at the vulnerability of their oil plants and were quite aware of the possibility that all German forces might become hampered by lack of fuel and lubricants if the Allied bomb-

216

ing of oil plants continued. And that was exactly what the Allies intended to

Another Chattanooga mission found 571 fighters of the 8th Air Force sweeping over eastern Germany and Poland.

The Seine bridges were looked over by the Thunderbolts and Marauders of the 9th Air Force making a heavy attack on the bridges at Conflans, Orival, Juvisy, and Athis. The damage inflicted was greater than the Germans, even by superhuman effort, were able to reconstruct. Repair work was difficult because of constant strafing by Thunderbolts, Lightnings, and Typhoons. Everything that moved along the line was attacked, while bridges were bombed as soon as they were repaired.

Tuesday, 30 May

The 8th Air Force dispatched 978 heavy bombers to a large variety of targets-aircraft factories at Dessau, Halberstadt, and Oschersleben; marshalling yards at Troyes, Reims, and Brussels; a rail bridge at Hasselt; an oil refinery at Merseburg; V-weapon sites on the Pas de Calais; and a large number of airfields. B–24 Liberators flew a mission to Rotenburg.

Two new Liberator groups flew their maiden missions, one from the 2nd and one from the 3rd Division. The group from the 3rd Division became dispersed in the heavy clouds and abandoned the mission, leaving one Liberator to proceed alone above the clouds because the crew had not heard the recall sign. After orbiting for some time but failing to see the other bombers, it dropped its bombs on an airfield near Rotterdam and turned back to base. The other novice group crossed the Dutch coast ten miles south of the planned checkpoint and ran into an accurate flak barrage. On return from the target, one aircraft ditched in the North Sea due to fuel shortage.

The fighter escort had several encounters with the Luftwaffe. Near Leipzig, the 357th Fighter Group mixed it up with some 75 German fighters. Four Mustangs of this group were on their way back home when they were jumped by four Me–109s, diving out of the sun. One Mustang was shot down, but the other three Mustangs destroyed the four Messerschmitts. Returning from their escort mission, the fighters ranged over the countryside to strafe their favorite targets.

P–47 Thunderbolts of the 56th Fighter Group tried to destroy the bridge at Creil in a renewed attack led by a 20th Group Droop Snoot Lightning. Flak was too heavy and they turned to the rail bridge at Chantilly. From 12,000 feet, the Thunderbolts destroyed the bridge.

9th Air Force Thunderbolts and Marauders carried out attacks to finish off the bridges at Mantes, Rouen, Meulan, Bennecourt, and Conflans.

Marauders destroyed the road bridge at Elbeuf. The common procedure was first a bombardment by the Marauders, then the Thunderbolts came down to deliver their 500-lb. bombs, while the finishing touch came from the rocket-firing Typhoons of the RAF. The road bridge at St. Pierre du Vauvray was divebombed by Thunderbolts.

Wednesday, 31 May

Heavy bombers of the 8th Air Force attacked airfields in France and Belgium. The bombers were heavily escorted by a large fighter force. Other formations dropped on the marshalling yards at Osnabrück. The 8th lost only one bomber during the day.

Four special B–24 Liberators carrying special 1000-lb. radio-controlled bombs, so-called AZON bombs, flew a trial mission to the Beaumont-sur-Oise bridge, and to the bridges at Melun and Meulan. At 10,000 feet, heavily escorted, the bombers released fourteen without achieving more than a few near misses.

1204 American fighters made sorties. 596 of them were from the 9th Air Force. In late afternoon, 36 Thunderbolts of the 353rd Fighter Group bombed Gutersloh Airfield. The road bridges at Meulan and the east bridge at Rouan were knocked out by Marauders of the 9th Air Force.

Starting in February, a steady flow of fighter groups began to arrive in England, the majority going to the 9th Air Force. Planned strength for both air forces for mid-June was as follows:

8th Air Force

Fighters:
7 P-51 Mustang groups: 4th, 339th, 352nd, 355th, 357th, 359th, 361st.
4 P-38 Lightning groups: 20th, 55th, 364th, 479th.
4 P-47 Thunderbolt groups: 56th, 78th, 353rd, 356th.

Heavy Bombers:
24 B–17 Fortress groups
16 B–24 Liberator groups

From May to September, 21 B–17 and 19 B–24 groups:

1st Division

Boeing B–17 Fortresses

218

1st Combat Wing:	91st Bomb Group
	381st
	398th
40th Combat Wing:	92nd
	305th
	306th
41st Combat Wing:	303rd
	379th
	384th
94th Combat Wing:	351st
	401st
	457th

3rd Division

Boeing B–17 Fortresses

4th Combat Wing:	94th Bomb Group
	385th
	447th
13th Combat Wing:	95th
	100th
	390th
45th Combat Wing:	96th
	388th
	452nd
92nd Combat Wing:	486th
	487th
93rd Combat Wing:	34th
	490th
	493rd

The 92nd and 93rd Combat Wings of the 3rd Division were equipped with the B–24 Liberator from the beginning of May until August/September for the 92nd Wing and from the end of May until August/September for the 93rd Wing. From September onward, these combat wings would be equipped with the B–17 again.

2nd Division

Consolidated B-24 Liberators

219

2nd Combat Wing:	389th Bomb Group
	445th
	453rd
14th Combat Wing:	44th
	392nd
	492nd
20th Combat Wing:	93rd
	446th
	448th
95th Combat Wing:	489th
	491st
96th Combat Wing:	458th
	466th
	467th

9th Air Force

Fighters:

13 P–47 Thunderbolt groups: 36th, 48th, 50th, 358th, 362nd, 365th, 366th, 368th, 371st, 373rd, 404th, 405th, 406th.
3 P–38 Lightning groups: 367th, 370th, 474th.
2 P–51 Mustang groups: 354th, 363rd.

Medium Bombers (98th and 99th Bombardment Wings):
8 B–26 Marauder groups: 322nd, 323rd, 344th, 386th, 387th, 391st, 394th, 397th.

Light Bombers (97th Bombardment Wing):
3 A–20 Havoc groups: 409th, 410th, 416th.

Due to the outstanding performance of the P–51 as a long-range escort fighter, the majority of these aircraft went to the 8th Air Force. The Thunderbolt could take much more punishment than the Mustang and in many cases where other aircraft would have failed, the Thunderbolt was still able to carry its pilot home. Therefore, the rugged P–47 was much more suited to the tactical role than the P–51.

6

JUNE

Friday, 2 June

A massive raid of 8th Air Force bombers was carried out against the coastal batteries on the French shoreline and against transportation targets in France and Belgium. A deviation from the briefed route brought two Liberator groups of the 2nd Division, flying at 16,000 feet, from one flak battery to the other. One B-24 was hit over Chartres and turned back. Four P-51s escorted the bomber, but it would never reach England. Near Paris, three others were shot down and of the 77 B-24s involved, five were brought down and three crashed in England.

9th Air Force fighters were fully employed in practicing their skill in attacking ground targets when they shot up trains in France. Among the many fighter groups of both air forces that ranged over France were 37 Thunderbolts of the 353rd Fighter Group flying a morning patrol in the Pas de Calais area.

Investigations after the war in order to come to a final conclusion about the results of the various methods employed in the transportation program about which the opinions in the higher circles were very controversial, indicated that the bombing of bridges and strafing of trains had a far more decisive result than the rail center bombings. An AAF report based largely on French railway records even stated that it had been a waste of effort and that the 70,000 tons involved could have been used to bomb more important targets.

Today one of the marshalling yards to be severely hit was Achères near Paris, bombed from an altitude of 22,000 feet. Other bombers dropped bombs on Boulogne.

221

Saturday, 3 June

8th Air Force heavies dumped their loads in a heavy attack on the German batteries along the French coast.

9th Air Force fighters did their utmost to disrupt enemy rail traffic in France and to shatter the nerves of the railroad personnel. The fighters came in on the deck, dropped their belly tanks on the trains, and wheeled around to make another run over the trains, setting them ablaze with their gunfire.

B–26 Marauders destroyed the bridges at Conflans, Bennecourt, and Courcelles. All bombing missions were heavily escorted.

Sunday, 4 June

Airfields and several transportation targets in the suburbs of Paris were attacked by the 8th Air Force bombers. The heavies appeared in force over the coastal batteries where they unloaded their portion of the 4700 tons dropped on these targets during the last three days. Many fighters accompanied the 1000-bomber force.

June 4, 1944. The airfield near St. Dizier under attack. (Official USAF Photo)

9th Air Force fighters set out again on their Chattanooga mission. Morale of the railroad personnel was dwindling and French train crews deserted in large numbers.

Thunderbolts of the 9th Air Force destroyed the west bridge at Rouen in a fighter-bomber attack.

At a tensely dramatic meeting in the early morning hours, the date for the great assault on "Fortress Europe" had been irrevocably fixed as 6 June. First scheduled for June 5, very unfavorable weather forecasts made a postponement of 24 hours inevitable.

All tactical aircraft taking part in the invasion were painted with Invasion Stripes of alternating white and black bands around fuselage and wings.

Monday, 5 June

8th Air Force bombers again went to the coastal defenses between the Cherbourg peninsula and the Pas de Calais.

An enemy coastal defense near Wimereux was the target for B–24s of the 2nd Division. A Liberator from the 489th Bomb Group in which the air commander, Lt. Col. R. Vance, was riding received a direct hit from flak, killing the pilot instantly and seriously wounding the co-pilot. Vance, standing behind the pilots' seats, had one foot practically severed, yet he managed to nurse the badly damaged plane, on which three engines were hit, back to the English coast where he ordered his crew to bail out. One man was too badly injured to jump, so Vance decided to ditch the airplane. However, it exploded on impact and Vance was thrown clear of the wreckage. After fifty minutes, he was picked up by A.S.R. and was to survive this episode. (In July he was evacuated to the USA, but the C–54 in which he made the crossing disappeared between Iceland and Newfoundland. In his honor, an air force base in the USA was named after him.)

Fighter sweeps were carried out to Abbeville and many other places in France.

A huge Allied armada was ready on numerous airfields in Great Britain to start one of the most critical struggles in the Second World War:

Heavy bombers:	3467
Light and Medium bombers:	1645
Fighters:	5409
Transport & Troop-carrier Aircraft:	2316

The German Air Force in the West was in a neglected state, in spite of being well aware of the forthcoming invasion. An additional ten wings of fighters were promised by the Oberkommando der Luftwaffe to be used against the invasion forces, but these reinforcements for Luftflotte 3 did not arrive until two days after D–Day and thereafter. And not by far in the numbers requested. At the moment the Allied Air Force was confronted with some 290 fighter aircraft of the German 3rd Air Fleet, 156 of which were serviceable. The majority of the fighter force was used for the defense of the Reich. Of these 1180 fighters, 656 were on operational status.

The entire Luftwaffe on all fronts was composed of 2367 aircraft, of which some 1300 were serviceable.

General Eisenhower and General Brereton visited units of the 101st Airborne Division during the evening and they witnessed their take-off.

In the darkness in the last hours before midnight, great sky trains of troop carriers and gliders left the British Isles to start the biggest military operation in history. The 82nd and 101st Airborne Divisions of the US Army were on their way to the drop targets behind Utah beach near St. Mère Église. More than 900 aircraft and 104 gliders of IX Troop Carrier Command assembled in darkness, a very complicated task that, thanks to thorough training, was accomplished without accidents.

RAF nightfighters and intruders escorted the procession, attacking searchlights and gun positions. Meanwhile, RAF Short Stirlings dropped Window to simulate large airborne movements well south of the intended landing zone. At 2354, the German radio gave warning of large formations of aircraft northwest of Cherbourg. . .

June 5, 1944. The black and white invasion stripes are clearly demonstrated by the P–47 Thunderbolt, *Arkansas Traveler,* of the 353rd Fighter Group. The date is approximate as the photo was actually taken after D–Day. (Official USAF Photo)

Tuesday, 6 June–D-Day

The troop-carrying airfleet met heavy anti-aircraft fire when they flew inland into the Cherbourg peninsula. Difficulties arose rapidly. Ground ob-

224

servation was hampered by fog and clouds, and even the pathfinders found it very difficult to identify the drop targets. Some planes circled around and dropped accurately, but most of them unloaded too soon or overshot their targets.

The main drops were carried out between 0016 and 0404 hours and were generally scattered. (At the end of the day, 2500 of the 6600 men of the 101st Airborne Division would be under unified control.) Twenty-one troop carriers and two tugs were lost.

Meanwhile, RAF Bomber Command concentrated on coastal batteries between the Cherbourg peninsula and Houlgate in characteristic area bombing executed during the early hours preceding H–Hour. B–17s of the 422nd Special Leaflet Squadron flew unescorted over the landing areas to drop warnings to the people of seventeen French cities and villages.

At 0155 hours, the first heavy bombers of the 8th Air Force thundered along the runways in England and the last bomber lifted into the air at 0529 hours. This stretch of time was necessary because the bombers were to attack in waves. Flying in formations of six squadrons abreast with H2X Pathfinders in the lead, 1083 of the 1361 B–17s and B–24s dispatched in this first mission set out to attack coastal batteries and shore defenses. They came in at right angles to the beaches. As bombing had to be done by instruments through overcast, it had been arranged, for safety, that the last bombs would be dropped ten minutes before the invasion armies were to go ashore and, as a further precaution, bombardiers would drop ten seconds after the release point had shown on their scopes. 2944 tons of bombs with instantaneous fuses to avoid cratering were dropped. One bomber, a B–24 from the 487th Bomb Group, was lost, while two other Liberators from the 493rd Bomb Group collided and tumbled down.

Between 0343 and 0500 hours, 278 A–20 Havocs, B–26 Marauders, and 2nd TAF B–25 Mitchells took off from their bases in England and, after forming up in boxes of 18 planes, each box set course to the French coast. Because of the overcast, attacks were made at altitudes ranging from 3500 to 7000 feet.

At the same time, the coastal batteries were attacked by 33 fighter-bombers of the 9th Air Force, while transportation targets, mainly in the Cherbourg peninsula, were worked over by 129 fighter-bombers.

H–Hour for the seaborne landings was set for 0630 hours on the American beaches, Utah and Omaha, and from 0700 to 0730 hours on the British beaches, Juno, Sword, and Gold. Continuous cover of the seaborne armada was deemed essential and it was executed as planned.

With their black and white invasion stripes around wings and twin-booms, four groups of P–38 Lightnings of the 8th Air Force and two groups of P–38 Lightnings of the 9th Air Force formed the umbrella for the invasion fleet involving 4483 Allied ships. (The P–38 had been chosen for this task because it was easily recognizable.)

As soon as the assault forces went ashore, RAF Fighter Command provided the low cover with five Spitfire squadrons, and five P–47 Thunderbolt groups of the 9th Air Force furnished high cover. Another five groups acted as a striking force.

Two groups of P–38s and four groups of P–47s of the 9th Air Force bombed gun batteries and provided support for ground forces. Six heavy gun batteries in a position to fire on the assault forces in the Channel were attacked by eleven groups of A–20s and B–26s. Hereafter, the bombers flew to defended localities behind Utah beach to drop their bombs just five minutes before the assaulting forces went ashore.

At 0300 hours, the first P–51 units of the 8th Air Force had taken off in darkness and at many places in light rain that restricted visibility; yet assembly had been accomplished according to plan. Only one Mustang took off on the wrong heading and crashed into the control tower at Bodney.

Flying at altitudes above 8000 feet, the Mustangs and Thunderbolts provided high cover for the bombers and troop carriers and kept watch that no enemy aircraft sneaked into the assault area. Nine groups of the 8th flew patrols from Dungeness across Dieppe and Rouen through Avranches and Jersey to Torquay with P–47s in the eastern area and P–51s in the western area. Two other Mustang groups, the experienced 4th and 355th Fighter Groups, flew patrols northwest and west of Paris.

In a second phase, the fighters carried out bombing and strafing attacks against rail and road transport, fuel and ammunition dumps, airfields, and troop concentrations.

Everybody had expected an all-out effort by the German Air Force to oppose the landings, but only three Luftwaffe aircraft showed up to take a closer look at the convoys. They were chased off by the P–38s and, until nightfall, these three Focke Wulfs were the only enemy aircraft seen over the battlefield during the day.

The 8th fighters flew 1813 sorties in 73 patrols and 34 fighter-bomber missions. The fighters claimed 24 German aircraft destroyed in the air and four on the ground. According to German statements, only twelve fighter-bomber missions were started, of which ten were forced to jettison their bombs and fight for their lives before even nearing the battle area. Another German statement gave the total of attempted sorties as 250 for the day.

After nightfall, twenty-two German aircraft arrived on the scene and started an attack on shipping without inflicting more than slight damage to one ship. The 355th Fighter Group intercepted a formation of Ju–88s and claimed the destruction of fifteen of these aircraft trying to reach the Channel.

From this point on, IX Fighter Command had started its career of close support to the ground forces. At first, all requests of support from ground commanders went via the control center at Uxbridge. However, it was soon discovered that it took too much time before air support could be provided. Therefore, air alert squadrons were put under the supervision of an air representative, stationed on board the ANCON headquarters ship, anchored off Omaha beach.

Chokepoints at Thury Harcourt, St. Lô, and Caen in the immediate vicinity of the battlefield were the targets for 528 heavies of the 8th Air Force out on their next mission. First leaflets were dropped to warn the population. When the bombers arrived, the targets were obscured by clouds. Only three groups unloaded; the others took their bombs back home. 56 B–24 Liberators carried out an attack on Caen on their third mission. Falaise was heavily bombed by the Fortresses. The last mission of the day was flown by more than 550 B–17s and B–24s heading for transportation targets near the assault area.

The medium bombers of the 9th Air Force also had a very busy day, with many crews flying two missions. Their main targets were coastal batteries, strongpoints, chokepoints in several towns as Falaise, Valognes, and Carentan, and also four freight yards east of the Seine. At 2015 hours, the Havocs crossed the Channel again in appalling weather. Flying at 3000 feet, the 416th Bomb Group made landfall near Cayeux and soon their route was marked by exploding shells. But the Havocs bore on to their target, the marshalling yard southeast of Dieppe. The bombs were delivered on the target but not without cost. The heaviest concentration of anti-aircraft fire the crews had ever met knocked three Havocs out of the sky, one over the target. Another two crashlanded in England.

9th Air Force fighters also made two divebombing attacks on the Seine bridge under repair at Oissel. The bridge was heavily damaged.

Between 2053 and 2250 hours, reinforcements for the airborne troops arrived by 188 gliders.

At night, twelve B–17s of the special 422nd Squadron dropped leaflets over thirty-four targets in France and the Low Countries.

Total losses for the day suffered by the 8th and 9th Air Forces were 71 aircraft, attributed to flak as well as air combat. Exclusive of flights to determine weather, to drop leaflets, or out on reconnaissance missions, both air forces dispatched 8722 aircraft.

June 6, 1944. The first 8th Air Force heavy bomber mission is led by *Red Ass*, a Liberator of the 446th Bomb Group. (Official USAF Photo)

June 6, 1944. A Marauder wings over the invasion coast. (Official USAF Photo)

June 6, 1944. A B–26 of the 386th Bomb Group leaves the invasion coast behind. (Photo from *Air Combat 1939–1945)*

Wednesday, 7 June

While RAF Bomber Command attacked the freight yards at Dreux, Evreux, and other places, 500 heavies of the 8th Air Force set course to the same sort of targets and their bombs came down on bridges and freight yards. One B–24 was shot down by flak and a B–17 ditched in the Channel. (The crew was picked up by A.S.R.)

When the bombers came back from their last mission at dusk, a few Me–410s were trailing the bombers, and as the Liberators peeled off to set in for the landing, the Messerschmitts struck. Within a couple of minutes, four B–24s were shot down. One of the intruders was picked off by a nightfighter.

Thunderbolts of the 56th and 353rd Fighter Groups out on a mission to destroy parts of four main rail routes in an area northwest of Paris ran into German fighters, and in the ensuing melee the Americans claimed twenty-three enemy aircraft shot down. Total Allied claims amounted to 58 German aircraft. 31 of them were shot down by the fighters of the 8th Air Force in 1445 sorties, with another 21 destroyed on the ground in strafing attacks. Losses of 8th Fighter Command were also considerable: 27, most of them shot down by flak. One Thunderbolt was destroyed by the explosion of its own bombs dropped on a marshalling yard.

From 0600 until 2230 hours, the 9th Air Force provided continuous armed reconnaissance with 467 fighter-bomber sorties in thirty-five missions by the 365th, 366th, and 368th Fighter Groups. In search for artillery firing on the Omaha beachhead, most of the Thunderbolt squadrons flew four missions in the course of a day in which the success of the Omaha beach landing hung in the balance. Thirteen aircraft were lost.

Many individual squadrons were over the battle area attacking artillery, troop concentrations, armor, and trucks. When a battery held up the Rangers, the forward controller directed a squadron overhead to the enemy position and the battery was hit. Fighter-bombers put an emergency one-track bridge near Oissel out of service. 9th Air Force medium bombers attacked bridges and road chokepoints in the vicinity of the front line in towns like Caen, Isigny, and Aunay-sûr-Odon.

Ten marshalling yards were visited and in the Folligny freight yards, two troop trains received a full load from the mediums, wrecking the trains, killing approximately 500 soldiers, and wounding more than that number.

The Luftwaffe started the transfer of its units hitherto employed in the defense of the Reich to airfields in France. Most airfields were hastily improvised. A chaotic situation arose when many fields were just rendered inactive after a treatment by Allied bombers, while others were overcrowded. Many times, destinations were changed in flight.

June 7, 1944. A–20 Havocs of the 410th Bomb Group roaring low over southern England after returning from Normandy. The date is approximate, although the photo was taken shortly after the invasion. (Photo from *Air Combat 1939–1945)*

230

Half of the units became involved in dogfights on the way to their new landing grounds. They became dispersed and in several cases they didn't find an airfield at all, also due to insufficient training. It all resulted in many crashes. (In mid-1944, the German pilot had only 150 training hours before being placed in an operational unit, whereas an American pilot had 450 training hours.)

Early in the morning, between 0700 and 0855 hours, reinforcements had arrived by 220 Horsa gliders. Further reinforcements were carried by some 320 C–47s and C–53s. Of the 1606 troop carriers involved in the airborne operation, 41 were lost. 503 gliders were released at their landing zone. In fact, all gliders were considered lost after landing.

Thursday, 8 June

Weather hampered air operations but close support actions were carried out whenever possible. Formations of 8th Air Force heavy bombers struck targets near the beachhead. Fortresses bombed the important marshalling yard at Tours.

Twelve Me–109s "jumped" Liberators of the 446th Bomb Group in a surprise attack near Jersey. One B–24 was shot down. The Luftwaffe showed an increasing activity and some 130 FW–190s and Me–109s were sighted. Allied fighters destroyed 46 of them, the highest score going to the 8th fighters, claiming 31. The 56th Fighter Group caught seven Luftwaffe fighters when they took off from Illiers.

The 8th Fighter Command lost 24 aircraft, again most of them to ground fire while attacking road convoys, bridges, marshalling yards, locomotives, wagons, a radio tower, trucks, and many more targets.

The crossroads near Port-en-Bessin were bombed by the fighters of the 9th Air Force shortly after a request from a forward controller. The fighter-bombers chased every movement they spotted on rail or road.

An attack by medium bombers of the 9th on the bridges at Caen, ordered by Montgomery, wrecked many houses and filled the streets with rubble, but it hardly impeded the Germans in their movements. The railway bridge at Tours-la-Riche was bombed out of use. The Marauders also attacked a large dump in the Forêt de Grimbosq.

Contact was made between American and British ground forces.

Friday, 9 June

Poor weather conditions permitted only a few missions in support of the ground forces. Photo Reconnaissance missions were flown with an escort of fighters of the 8th Air Force. Two Mustangs of the 67th Tactical Reconnaissance Group were shot down by intense anti-aircraft fire from US

231

ground forces, twenty-five minutes later followed by another two Mustangs brought down by Allied navy guns. Only 28 Lightnings managed to maintain their shipping patrols.

Saturday, 10 June

A plan defining the objectives of a renewed strategic campaign by 8th Bomber Command was drawn by USSTAF recommending priorities in the order of oil production, ball-bearing industry, tank production, and ordnance depots, V-weapons, and motor transport industry, with visits to the German aircraft industry as frequent as seemed necessary.

At all times, when ground battles urged assistance, both 8th Air Force and RAF had to respond to every call whenever vital support was needed.

Today the bombers of the 8th visited airfields in France and also dropped a considerable load on marshalling yards in several cities such as Chartres.

By now Luftwaffe Command had stationed about ten extra Jagdgruppen at bases some distance from the landing area, and an increase in air activity was noticeable. Some forty bomb-laden Me–109s made for the beachhead at an altitude of 300 feet. They were intercepted by a Mustang squadron from the 352nd Fighter Group, causing them to jettison their loads and, after a short engagement, the Messerschmitts headed for home.

In the opposite case, Thunderbolts of the 78th Fighter Group made ready for a bombing attack on a marshalling yard when Me–109s and FW–190s tore into their formation and sent five P–47s down to earth. In the combat that ensued, an equal number of German fighters was shot down. The 78th Group lost four more Thunderbolts in various operations, plus two P–47s that collided in a cloud near London. Five Thunderbolts of the 353rd Fighter Group failed to return from three missions flown during the day when they attacked targets of opportunity in the Seine area and Brittany.

Mustangs of the 359th Fighter Group escorted four F–5 photo-recon aircraft. Anti-aircraft fire made photographing the target impossible and one of the escorting Mustangs dived deliberately to 100 feet, heading straight to the main gun positions to draw the fire so the F–5s could take their pictures. The photographs were made, but the Mustang was shot down and the pilot was killed.

During an early beach patrol, Thunderbolts of the 371st Fighter Group, 9th Air Force, were attacked by Me–109s coming in from behind and one Thunderbolt went down, its pilot bailing out.

One of the many fighter groups ranging over France was the 404th Group. In the morning, 48 of its aircraft pounded on German artillery positions and in the early afternoon, the Thunderbolts went after bridges.

And now, late in the day another mission was flown by the three squadrons. Rail lines near Chartres were cut in many places, railcars and locomotives were destroyed, and station buildings were attacked, while one squadron set fifteen tank cars ablaze. Another squadron suddenly spotted two trains approaching each other. The Thunderbolts bombed the rail tracks in two places so both trains came to a halt side by side. They then worked them over, making several passes.

Flying at 5000 feet near Le Havre on the last patrol of the day, two Thunderbolts of the 371st Fighter Group encountered seven FW–190s firing rockets at ships in the Channel. One of the P–47 pilots picked off two Focke Wulfs and, after bringing a third into his gunsight, he found himself chased by an FW–190. Taking wild evasive action after diving his Thunderbolt on the deck, the pilot barely missed some trees. But the Focke Wulf was still on his heels. He threw his fighter in a sudden sharp turn; the Focke Wulf pilot lost control of his aircraft and it hit the ground with the debris of the wreckage spreading over several hundred feet.

Other flights of the same group also had encounters with the Luftwaffe and sent two Focke Wulfs down. One formation was jumped by Me–109s and two Thunderbolts were lost while a third, with flak damage, had to ditch in the Channel.

Mustangs escorted C–47s with their gliders on a mission to drop reinforcements behind Utah beach,

Sunday, 11 June

Weather conditions in the St. Lô region were so abominable that early in the day all strikes in this area were cancelled. When an urgent request mission arrived over the target marked with red smoke, the results were of such danger to the friendly troops that no further request was made.

A heavy counterattack by the Panzer Lehr Division brought the 366th Fighter Group Thunderbolts under a 1000-foot ceiling on three subsequent missions on the scene, and when they left the spot, twenty-two smokepiles marked the doom of an equal number of tanks (a figure afterwards substantiated by the army.)

Heavy bombers of the 8th Air Force maintained their pressure on airfields and other tactical targets in France.

8th Air Force Lightnings were relieved from their task of shipping patrols. This task was now passed to RAF and 9th Air Force fighters.

55th Fighter Group Lightnings out on a Droop Snoot mission encountered a Staffel of FW–190s near Tours. Three Focke Wulfs were destroyed, but two Lightnings were also shot down.

June 11, 1944. A "Droop Snoot" Lightning with a glass nose for the bombardier. (Official USAF Photo)

Monday, 12 June

Heavy bombers of the 8th Air Force struck airfields in France. Luftwaffe fighters appeared and near Rennes a Liberator of the 446th Bomb Group was shot down. Before further harm could be done, fighters of the 352nd Fighter Group came to the rescue of the Liberators and three Me–109s were shot down for no loss to the American fighters.

The first four-engine aircraft landed on an Allied airstrip in France when the pilots of a Liberator of the 467th Bomb Group decided to try a landing on the short strip after the rest of the crew had bailed out. The bomber had been hit by flak, which was by now a far greater danger to Allied aircraft than the Luftwaffe.

Yet the Luftwaffe again gave signs of increased activity and over 200 aircraft were reported today. Over Paris, fighters of the 359th Group had an encounter with eight Focke Wulfs. The Americans left the area without loss, whereas the Germans returned with one less.

Forty-four Thunderbolts of the 353rd Fighter Group took off at 0434 hours for a bombing-strafing mission against communications targets near Evreux-Dreux. While strafing a truck convoy, one squadron was bounced by a Gruppe of more than thirty Me–109s, and in the battle that ensued, six P–47s were shot down. Another squadron of the group ran into some fifty enemy aircraft and had two Thunderbolts shot out of their formation.

Later in the day, the 353rd Group set out again to Dreux/Evreux Airfield where the Messerschmitts encountered earlier in the day were supposed to be based. While the 353rd circled the area to draw the Messerschmitts into combat, the 56th Group rushed to the spot to arrive there half an hour later as was planned. It worked well, and the Thunderbolts of the 353rd were attacked by twenty Me–109s, and in the vicinity of Paris another forty

234

joined the melee. Nine Messerschmitts were claimed by the P–47s.

Meanwhile the 56th Fighter Group met twelve Me–109s, which were immediately assisted by another dozen. In the violent battle, five Messerschmitt fighters were sent down for no loss, though one Thunderbolt of "Zemke's Wolfpack" was damaged and the pilot had to make a belly-landing on a beachhead airstrip.

The 354th Group Mustangs divebombed targets in northern France, one of the squadrons knocking out the railroad bridge near Rouen. In a strafing attack, they destroyed some twenty enemy aircraft. A Ju–88 was caught in the take-off and blew up. One P–51 pilot turned into an oncoming FW–190 and without dropping his two 500-lb. bombs the Mustang sent the Focke Wulf down in flames. The P–51 continued to its target to deliver its bombs.

The bridge at Conflans, where reconstruction had started only a few days before, was totally destroyed by fighters of the 9th Air Force. They also divebombed radar installations at Cap Fréhel and Pointe de Grouin.

9th Air Force B–26 Marauders with an escort of 43 P–51s of the 357th Group, 8th Air Force, attacked the railroad bridge at Dreux.

Tuesday, 13 June

Shortly before dawn, the first German secret weapon, the V–1, left the continent and with a bundle of flames pouring backwards, the pilotless aircraft, with its short square wings, headed towards London through the dark skies. Above London, the engine suddenly cut out with a muttering sound and without further noise, the flying bomb dived straight into the center of London. This night eleven V–1s were fired. Four of them exploded in the British capital.

In 1931, Capt. Walter Dornberger had already been given the task of developing a military rocket program. Hampered by the Treaty of Versailles which forbade the Germans to develop military aircraft, far-sighted militarists in Germany got the idea of considering the creation of long-range missiles powered by rocket or jet propulsion.

In 1932, the construction of rockets was underway. Hitler visited the rocket station at Kummersdorf in 1933, but he was unimpressed and didn't see much in the development of rockets as a military weapon for the next ten years. However, the German High Command was very impressed after the prototype of a V–2 was demonstrated in 1934, and firmly supported the program.

The V–1 program was pushed by Goering, considering the development of the V–2 as an army matter and although the V–2 was a more spectacular mechanism, the V–1 was more efficient for its special purpose. The

V–1 was in full production less than two years after the initial experiment began.

The "V" of V-weapon stood for "Versuchmuster" ("Experimental type"), and the interpretation "Vergeltungswaffe" came much later from the German propaganda.

Since the beginning of December, 1943, the continuous Anglo-American attacks on the sites had been a costly affair. In 25,150 bombing sorties, in which 36,200 tons of bombs were dropped, 154 aircraft with 771 airmen had been shot down. The American bomber losses were: 8th Air Force heavy bombers—49 with 462 men; 9th Air Force medium bombers—30 with 148 men.

On the other hand the Germans launched only one V–1 from the ski sites. All other V–1s were fired from the modified sites, although it would always remain difficult to determine how much the Allied bombing was responsible for the development of the modified sites and a presumed consequent delay in starting the launching of the V–1.

The heavy bomber attacks on tactical targets in France continued. The 8th fighters had several encounters with Luftwaffe fighters, claiming the destruction of six aircraft. At 0659 hours, Thunderbolts of the 353rd Fighter Group divebombed the rail bridge at Tours which received considerable damage. In the evening, the fighters returned to bomb the nearby Loire bridge. One P–47 of the group was lost.

The first combat squadrons of the 9th Air Force began using the landing strips in France on a regularly scheduled basis. Fighter-bombers ranged over the battle area and beyond. They attacked a dump in the Cherbourg area and a powerhouse at Vire. Medium bombers turned to a large fuel and ammunition dump near Domfront and Forêt d'Andaine.

Wednesday, 14 June

Heavy bombers of the 8th turned to airfields in France and Belgium. In an attack against the airfields Le Bourget and Melun near Paris, five Fortresses were shot down by flak. B–17s also went to the airfield Le Culot in Belgium, where hits were scored on the main runways. Clouds over the target forced some formations to turn to the secondary target, the airfield at Chièvres. Bombs were scattered throughout the dispersal areas.

In the afternoon, the heavies set out on a mission to Germany to attack a number of targets, including the oil installations at Emmerich.

Many fighter groups ranged over France. One of them was the 353rd Group. The Thunderbolts flew an early morning patrol which brought them south of Brussels. The 36 fighters strafed several targets there. In the evening, the group sent out 25 P–47s to bomb airfields and marshalling yards north of Paris.

236

The bridge at Le Manoir was totally destroyed by fighter-bombers of the 9th Air Force. Medium bombers delivered their loads on the bridges at Chartres.

Thursday, 15 June

Heavy bombers of the 8th Air Force carried out a limited mission to oil refineries in northern Germany. The oil refinery at Misburg, near Hannover, was bombed through 9/10th's cloud.

Early in the morning, other formations set course to bridges and marshalling yards and various other targets in support of the ground armies. The airfield at Bordeaux was "worked over" by Fortresses.

Nearing the railroad bridge at La Frillière, a formation Liberators encountered some 25 FW-190s, some of them carrying black and white invasion stripes. The Focke Wulfs made only one head-on pass, but one B-24 was hit. After completing its bomb run, it struggled back to the coast where the bomber was abandoned by its crew, all but one coming down within the beachhead. The man who jumped too early was the navigator who miscalculated his position. He was captured by the Germans. Both heavy bomber missions were flown with heavy fighter escort.

Medium bombers of the 9th attacked the fuel and ammunition dumps near Domfront, Forêt d'Aindaine, and Forêt d'Écoures. All three targets were "worked over" once more by the fighter-bombers which also dive-bombed a radar installation near St. Pierre-Eglise. Marauders bombed a dump at Valognes close to the battlefront while another dump at Vire was attacked by the fighter-bombers. These were also present to help the infantry along the Martinville Ridge in their final stage of the drive.

Friday, 16 June

After the dream of many Allied authorities—that the V-weapon threat was only a hoax to mislead the Allies and was even meant to dissuade them from launching the invasion—had been cruelly disturbed by the explosion in the night of 12/13 June, there had been a silence for a few days. But this night, the real "Flying Bomb Battle" started, and within 24 hours about 300 V-1s were fired against England. Seventy-three exploded in London, causing a considerable damage and many civilian casualties.

The 8th Air Force bombers carried out four small missions against V-1 launching sites in the Pas de Calais area.

The primary objective for the 8th fighters, flying fourteen ground-attack missions, was the railway system through which reinforcements reached the front. A marked success was achieved by Mustangs of the 357th Fighter Group when they attacked rail yards at St. Pierre and Poitiers. Attacking the goods trains in flights of four, the first dropped their auxiliary tanks 2/3 filled with gasoline, and the second flight, following close behind, fired into the burst tanks, setting the train cars afire. One of the trains was an ammunition train and exploded. Enormous fires raged when the Mustangs left the scene. The attack was led by Lt. Col. Hayes, who used this kind of attack against the Japanese in New Guinea. Four fighters failed to return from the various missions.

Deteriorating weather left only two planes out of two groups of medium bombers of the 9th Air Force to attack strongpoints near St. Lô. At 2000 hours, signs were received of another German counterattack and P–47 Thunderbolts of the 404th Fighter Group were briefed in the air by the air support party. From the air, the pilots saw the lines of their own troops marked with panels and even with undershirts. At 2105 hours, they went down for a close-in attack right on the target. Other fighter-bombers attacked the bridges over the Vire near to the battle line.

Saturday, 17 June

Fighters of the 8th Air Force escorted the heavy bombers to airfields in France. They flew patrols and carried out fighter sweeps. A lone FW–190 was met by Thunderbolts of the 353rd Fighter Group out on a support patrol, and the German fighter was sent spinning into the ground.

Two groups of 9th Air Force medium bombers set out again to bomb the strong points near St. Lô, and this time they achieved better results. The mediums also turned to a large dump near La Loupe.

Fighter-bombers carried out repeated attacks on the bridges over the Vire to cut off the German 352nd Infantry Division. By now eight of nineteen bridges over the Loire between Tours and Nantes were demolished.

Sunday, 18 June

Not only had the 8th Air Force been occupied with operations in connection with "Overlord" and "Crossbow," but also the weather above Germany had prevented visual bombing in connection with the oil campaign. Although weather forecasts were far from promising for today, the 8th Air Force had dispatched its B–17s and B–24s against eleven oil installations in northwestern Germany.

No German fighters were met when nine combat wings approached Hamburg, but the flak was the heaviest the flyers had ever experienced. As had happened so many times in the past, an unidentified Liberator flew with the bomberstream, some 2000 yards out. At such moments, flak was very heavy and accurate. This was undoubtedly a captured B–24 the Ger-

238

mans used for transmitting all information about altitude, position, speed, and course of the bomber formation to the flak batteries.

Pathfinders marked the dropping zone and 1150 tons of bombs were unloaded. Much damage was done to the installations. However, worse results were obtained by the other wings running into very poor weather over Bremen and Hannover, and their blind bombing had little effect. Other formations dropped on Brunsbüttel instead. Several bombers were shot down and one B–24 landed in Sweden.

Medium bombers of the 9th Air Force, led by pathfinder aircraft, attacked three "Noball" targets. After the Marauders had bombed the marshalling yards at Rennes, their fighter-bomber escort came down and with their bombs and guns they added to the devastation, leaving behind the passenger station three-quarters destroyed, and many locomotives and rail cars either destroyed or damaged.

Since the invasion, more than twenty marshalling yards were bombed by the mediums of the 9th, while the fighter-bombers accounted for another fifteen during the same period. All rolling stock within the line of interdiction was harassed continuously, and fighters of both the 8th and 9th Air Forces were collecting a high score of locomotives, rail cars, and railcuts. In fact, sending reinforcements by rail had been made virtually impossible.

Large dumps at Forêt d'Andaine and Bois du Hommet were bombed by Marauders, while the fighters attacked a dump in the Cherbourg area.

Monday, 19 June

The 8th Air Force started an offensive against "Crossbow" targets, meanwhile continuing its attacks on airfields. The V-weapon site at Corbronne was one of the targets to receive a considerable load in subsequent missions. Large-scale operations were out of the question because of the stormy weather.

The first fighter-bomber squadron became operational from a Normandy airfield. Thunderbolts of the 395th Squadron, 368th Fighter Group, started their operations from Cordonville.

Tuesday, 20 June

The oil targets at Hamburg, Harburg, Ostermoor, Misburg, Pölitz, and Magdeburg were the objectives for the largest bomber force ever sent out by the 8th Air Force. 1361 heavy bombers flew in close-knit formations when they proceeded to their targets, escorted by 729 fighters. Arriving at a point 50 miles west of Jutland, the 3rd Division turned to the southeast to head for the targets at Konigsborn, Magdeburg, Misburg, and Fallersleben.

The 1st and 2nd Divisions continued their flight across Jutland to the Baltic Sea. Here the 1st Division, plus the 96th Wing of the 2nd Division, turned to Hamburg and Ostermoor. The 2nd Division, minus one wing, continued to Rügen Island before peeling off in southerly direction to bomb the targets at Pölitz.

A dense and often too-accurate anti-aircraft barrage was thrown up by the Germans when the bombers neared their targets. When the Liberators of the 2nd Division approached Pölitz, they found 120 Luftwaffe fighters waiting for them. Most were of the twin-engine type. The single-engine fighters distracted the only escorting Mustang group, the 339th, forcing them into combat. As soon as the B–24s turned in from the Baltic, the Me–110s and Me–410s attacked, pouring their rockets into the rear and flanks of a formation and fourteen Liberators of the trailing low group, the 492nd, were lost. All told, 34 B–24s of the 2nd Division failed to return to England, however, it was soon learned that no less than 16 had landed in Sweden. And they were not the only ones, for another three B–24s and one B–17 put down in this neutral country.

Seven Me–109s turned to a B–24 still flying but in very bad shape. The Liberator belonged to a formation heading for targets in Ostermoor. But the Messerschmitts had bad luck—they ran into fifty Mustangs. Four Messerschmitts were sent into the ground.

The heavies of the 3rd division were attacked by single-engine fighters when they arrived at Magdeburg, and three Fortresses were shot down. Bombing results were very good, and the synthetic oil plants at Magdeburg and Pölitz had to shut down for extensive repairs.

Other formations of heavy bombers of the 8th Air Force attacked the V–1 sites in France, and ever-increasing flak near these targets took its toll of the bombers.

From all operations today, 49 heavy bombers were lost and 468 were damaged to some degree. The Germans lost 28 fighters.

Escorting fighters went down on the deck when no contact was made with the Luftwaffe and while strafing Neubrandenburg Airfield, the 4th Fighter Group lost one of its distinguished pilots, Major James Goodson. He made a belly-landing in a field and as his plane was a new P–51D, Goodson's wingman made several passes over the brand-new fighter while Goodson sat on a fence to watch the aircraft burn.

In a strafing attack, six He–111s, three Ju–88s and a Me–110 were destroyed on the ground by the 353rd Group returning from escort duties. In the afternoon, P–47s of the same group destroyed five enemy aircraft on the airfield at Plantlünne.

240

Wednesday, 21 June

The mission of the 8th Air Force today was preceded by a conflict of views between the AAf and RAF. A British proposal to send 3000 bombers to Berlin (1000 British and 2000 American heavies) was not cheerfully greeted by General Spaatz who didn't like to see his Air Force participate in area bombing. Only when a target plan singled out aircraft factories, railroad centers, etc., did he agree, although it was clear that also in this case part of the town would vanish. But then the British withdrew because it was evident that no sufficient fighters would be available to give adequate protection to the lighter-defended British nightbombers, since so many fighters were on the French battlefields.

And so it turned out to be an all-American force that took off and climbed into the sky. After forming over the North Sea, course was set to Jutland. There the twenty combat wings involving 1311 heavy bombers with their escort of twenty-three fighter groups composed of 1190 fighters (including five 9th Air Force groups) turned on a course southeast to Berlin. The enormous bomberstream was led by two combat wings of the 3rd Division. Next in line were the Fortresses of the 1st Division, and the rest of the Forts of the 3rd Division formed the rear of the column.

At 0728 hours, 70 P–51s of the 4th Fighter Group and a squadron of the 352nd Group took off, crossed the coast north of Over Flakkee at 20,000 feet, and proceeded to fly across Germany to rendezvous with the bombers at Leszno, Poland, where the Mustangs jettisoned their empty fuel tanks. When the bombers neared Berlin, they were greeted with a murderous flak barrage surrounding the city.

As soon as the bombers penetrated the area, the German fighters arrived on the scene. The first Me–410s came in on the tails of the 1st Wing Fortresses. But by far the heaviest assault was launched against the B–24s, taking the heaviest losses for the second day running. 44 Liberators and six Fortresses were lost, downed by flak and by the guns of the German fighters, of which 22 were shot down.

Two thousand tons of bombs were unloaded from 25,000 feet. Many primary targets received direct hits, notably the aircraft engine factories at Genshagen, while railroad centers and the oil plant at Ruhland were also severely damaged.

In the fall of 1943, the Americans were already urging upon the Russians the use of Russian bases for shuttle-bombing missions, since it was well known that the Germans relocated many of their plants in the east. From Russian bases, these targets could easily have been reached by the American bombers, which was not possible from British or Italian bases. Besides, at about the time of the invasion, the Germans should have been

241

exposed from all directions; but as it later turned out, the Germans did not redeploy their fighters. They were not fooled, and considered it as a mere propaganda stunt.

The Americans also hoped to attain more appreciation for their contribution to the war effort. And in case these shuttle missions turned out to be effective, the American High Command hoped to obtain Russian approval for the use of bases in Siberia in a later stage of the war from which Japan could be attacked.

After long, troublesome negotiations and persistent efforts from the side of American officials, things at last got underway and three airfields became available: Poltava, Mirgorod, and Piryatin, all three near Kiev and much farther to the east than the Americans had desired. Much reconstruction was required and the supplies had to come in by Murmansk convoys and the Persian Gulf Command. Further difficulties arose between the Russians and the Americans about the choice of the targets.

But after all was solved in the best possible way, the first mission was undertaken on 2 June by the 15th Air Force, taking-off from Italy at sunrise with General Eaker flying in the van of 130 B–17s. Subsequent missions were also flown by the 15th Air Force, the 8th being too much occupied with operation "Overlord."

However, today the first shuttle mission by the 8th Air Force was a reality and a task force composed of 114 B–17 Fortresses with an escort of 70 P–51 Mustangs proceeded to Russia. The bombers were part of the force that attacked the synthetic oil plant at Ruhland. Rendezvous with the fighters had been made at Leszno and approximately an hour and a half later, some twenty Me–109s were encountered near Diedlice, Poland. Five Messerschmitts were shot down, but one of the Mustangs, along with one of the bombers, was lost.

After the engagement, the bombers flew to their bases at Poltava and Mirgorod, and for the Mustangs, the 1600-mile journey came to an end when they touched down at their base, Piryatin, after having been aloft for seven and a half hours. At night, a great banquet was given, with the vodka flowing freely in toast after toast with the Russians. But unknown to the feasting airmen, a German Heinkel had trailed the American formation and had pinpointed the Russian bases on which the B–17s and P–51s had landed. . .

The 489th Bomb Group visited the "Noball" targets and in the co-pilot's seat of Lt. Rumler's Liberator rode Prince Bernhard of the Netherlands, unbeknownst to his mother-in-law, Queen Wilhelmina. They flew at 21,000 feet and only light flak was met.

After returning from their escort missions, the 8th Air Force fighters flew patrols over northwestern France.

Fighter-bombers of the 9th Air Force attacked an airfield at Chartres.

June 21, 1944. Mustangs of the 352nd Fighter Group lined up at the 4th Fighter Group base at Debden before taking off on the first shuttle mission to Russia. (Photo from *Air Combat 1939–1945)*

June 21, 1944. An unexpected visitor is this Fortress of the 351st Bomb Group after force-landing at Bultofta, Sweden. (Photo courtesy Swedish government)

243

Thursday, 22 June

The 8th Air Force continued its attacks on marshalling yards and airfields in France. Bombs were also dropped on oil storage sites near Paris.

In view of the planned final assault on the Cherbourg peninsula and on Cherbourg in particular, a major air support attack was requested by the army. Involved were the 2nd Tactical Air Force and the 9th Air Force, the former with 118 aircraft, the latter with 557 fighter-bombers and 396 medium bombers.

At noon four squadrons of rocket-firing Typhoons started the attack. In their wake followed twelve groups of the 9th Air Force; 557 fighters came in wave after wave, flying at 200 feet from west to east, especially aiming at six pinpointed targets. They bombed and strafed and disappeared in clouds of dust and smoke. The attacks lasted from 1240 until 1355 hours in which 520.5 tons of bombs were dropped. Fourteen British and twenty-four American aircraft were shot down.

At 1400 hours, the ground attack started. The attack was immediately followed by the appearance of eleven bomber groups of the 9th Air Force. Although the bombing line had been marked with white smoke and the ground forces had withdrawn 1200 feet from that line, some friendly units were hit, possibly by the misleading effect of the firing of smokeshells over the American lines by the Germans. One bomber was shot down.

The tactical results were, however, disappointing, and at the start of the new day only a small part of the bombed area was overrun, although it included some high ground in the vicinity of Chièvres.

The airfields at Creil and Péronne were attacked by the fighters of the 9th.

The historical mission of the 8th Air Force to the Russian bases on the previous day became historical in a respect neither the Americans nor the Russians had dreamt of. Large forces of German bombers and fighters crossing the frontline were announced by the Russian warning system and shortly after midnight the whole airfield at Poltava was illuminated by flares. The next moment, 110 tons of demolition, incendiary, and fragmentation bombs hailed down. The German aircraft came in low over the field, thoroughly strafing and bombing the American aircraft and ammunition dumps, and 450,000 gallons of gasoline which had been brought into Russia half around the world were ignited. Without a single loss, the Germans disappeared into the night sky and left the airfield at Poltava behind totally wrecked and littered with the remains of 43 B–17s totally destroyed, 26 B–17s damaged, while also 15 Mustangs, two C–47s and a photo-plane were destroyed.

June 22, 1944. Flares dropped by the German raiders and anti-aircraft fire illuminate the airfield at Poltava. (Official USAF Photo)

June 22, 1944. Wrecked B–17s litter the field of Poltava. (Official USAF Photo)

Friday, 23 June

Heavy bombers of the 8th Air Force visited airfields in France and Belgium. They also turned to the "Crossbow" targets. Fighters of the 8th flew escort and area support missions.

A renewed attack was launched against the railway bridge at Tours-la-Riche after it had been put out of service on the 8th. The Germans had repaired the bridge so far that only single cars without locomotive could pass. Fighter-bombers tried to make an end to the "pushing operations," as it was called by the exasperated Germans, and after a few repeated attacks, the Germans could save their muscles for other work. Trains loaded with tanks near Mantes were attacked by the fighters with devastating effect.

"Crossbow" targets were not only attacked by the heavies, but also by the medium bombers of the 9th Air Force.

Saturday, 24 June

Six combat wings of B–17 Fortresses of the 1st Division headed for the oil refinery at Bremen. Weather was bad but the target was considered favorably situated for an H2X attack. Again the bombing by radar of a target obscured by weather and smokepots gave no reason for optimism. The oil refinery escaped unscathed, though docks, railways, and an aircraft factory received hits. Other 8th Air Force bomber formations struck targets in France.

Escorting fighters of the 353rd Fighter Group destroyed an He–111 and a Ju–52 on the ground when they strafed the airfield at Deelen.

Thunderbolts of the 368th Fighter Group scored eighteen direct hits when they bombed the defenses at La Mare et Canards, a target left unharmed after the attacks on the 22nd. In supporting the army, the P–47s achieved another success when 23 of the 24 bombs hit the bull's-eye at La Glacerie, one of many targets attacked. The railway bridge at Tours-la-Riche was visited again. The fighter-bombers also found rewarding targets when they visited Mantes again and dived on the trains loaded with tanks.

Bombing or strafing of rails, bridges, trains, and traffic centers forced the German armor in many cases from the rails to the roads at points far from the battlefield. This caused not only delay in reaching their destination, but also wear of treads and engines and consumption of precious fuel.

June 24, 1944. Marauders attack road and rail junctions in Normandy. (Official USAF Photo)

Sunday, 25 June

Because of the enormous extension of the activities of the French Maquis and their lack of supplies to enable them to play an important role in the battle of France, it was decided to divert B–17s from the strategic bombing role to mass drops. Today the first of these drops was undertaken, and 180 B–17s of the 3rd Division took off at about 0400 hours. Escorted by many fighters, the Fortresses headed for four destinations.

One bomber was shot down by flak and another by an enemy fighter. Two other B–17s failed to complete the mission. 176 Fortresses dropped 2077 containers from an altitude as low as 2000 feet on areas marked by the Maquis.

To conceal the purpose and destination of these units, Fortresses and Liberators turned to "Crossbow" targets and airfields in France, notably the airfield near Toulouse. Again, an unidentified Liberator without markings flew parallel to the bombers.

By now, five fighter groups of the 9th Air Force were operating from bases in Normandy: the 50th, 354th, 366th, 368th, and 371st Fighter Groups.

Two tunnels were divebombed by the 9th fighters. Apart from their daily ground support missions, the fighter-bombers attacked three enemy airfields, destroying four aircraft. Four German aircraft were also destroyed on Bourges Airfield when fighters of the 353rd Group returned from escorting the bombers.

Again the fighter-bombers swooped down in determined dive attacks to put the Tours-la-Riche bridge out of service, and this time they hit the mark. The Germans started immediately with their attempts to make the bridge ready again with a single track to carry light locomotives.

Monday, 26 June

Surviving 8th Air Force bombers and fighters after the Poltava disaster on the 22nd left Russia. 71 Fortresses and 55 Mustangs, some of which had been patched up, attacked a synthetic oil plant at Drohobycz, Poland, before setting course to Italy. At dusk, the aircraft landed at Foggia and satellite fields. The Mustangs used auxiliary tanks which the bombers had brought with them from England to Russia. In Italy, they would fly one mission with the 15th Air Force on 2 July before returning to England on 5 July.

Tuesday, 27 June

Heavy bombers of the 8th Air Force attacked marshalling yards at Creil and many other places in France. The Liberators were again accompanied all the way by an unidentified B-24.

Fighters escorted the bombers, and flew patrols and many area support missions. Flying a patrol south of Rheims, the 353rd Fighter Group destroyed two German aircraft in the air and one on the ground.

The main efforts of the 9th Air Force were again concentrated in support of VII Corps, moving west to take Cherbourg and the Cherbourg peninsula.

Wednesday, 28 June

8th Air Force heavy bombers attacked the industrial area of Saarbrücken. Other formations headed for airfields in France. All operations were carried out under substantial fighter protection.

Flying a patrol over the beachhead Mustangs of the 354th Fighter Group spotted an Me–109 pursued by Spitfires. The Mustangs turned into the procession and before the Messerschmitt could reach a protective cloudbase, one of the Mustangs poured its fire into the German plane. The next moment the Messerschmitt disappeared into the clouds, but after a while the pilot tumbled out of the clouds, soon followed by his aircraft, diving into the woods near Caen.

Thursday, 29 June

1150 B–17 Fortresses and B–24 Liberators were dispatched by the 8th Air Force to attack the synthetic oil plant at Böhlen, the V–1 works at Fallersleben, and eleven small targets involved in aircraft production at Magdeburg and in the area of Leipzig. The bombers became widely scattered and for a certain period they formed a stream 200 miles long. But luck was with the bomber crews, and only limited German fighter action was encountered.

In the Leipzig area, the Me–109s and Me–410s rose to intercept the leading Fortress wing, but efficient fighter escort spoiled their intentions. Twenty-one German fighters were claimed by the Mustangs of the 357th Fighter Group: nine FW–190s, eight Me–109s, and four Me–410s. Fighters of the 361st Group chased the Me–109s.

After this short engagement, the fighters went on the deck and at Oschersleben they reaped a rich harvest when the airfields proved to be only weakly defended. After six passes over the field, they left sixteen aircraft behind destroyed, and many more damaged. Twenty bombers failed to return. The plant at Böhlen was severely hit by 81 aircraft. One of the Fortresses had to ditch in the North Sea.

Fighter-bombers of the 9th Air Force flew six missions on request of the ground forces.

A–20 Havocs attacked enemy positions facing the frontline troops and on one of these missions the Havocs of the 416th Bomb Group were forced to descend to 1500 feet to stay under the cloud cover. Met by intense light and medium flak, one Havoc went down in flames while others received severe damage.

June 29, 1944. A B–24 over Germany approaching Magdeburg. Its group letter has not yet been applied on the black disc on the wing. (Official USAF Photo)

June 29, 1944. B–24 Liberator, *Little Warrior,* wrapped in flame by a direct flak hit over Quakenbrück, moments before the big bomber exploded with no chance of survival for the hapless crew. (Official USAF Photo)

Friday, 30 June

The 8th Air Force possessed, at this point, 2100 heavy bombers on operational strength in combat units, and the RAF 1100. This month, the 8th had made a record number of sorties: 28,791. British and American Air Forces together had carried out 8310 bomber sorties against V-sites during the second half of the month, dropping 23,431.2 tons of bombs.

Obviously, the Germans had succeeded in dispersing much air potential during a critical period where the demands upon Allied air power were so varied and so many. No proof was obtained that these attacks were successful.

The German losses since the start of the invasion were 1000 aircraft. These included the losses the Germans suffered during the transfer from German to French bases.

Seven fighter-bomber groups of the 9th Air Force were now operating from an equal number of advanced landing grounds in France.

Heavy bombers of the 8th attacked airfields and other tactical targets in France. Apart from their escort duties, the fighters ranged over northern France bombing and strafing airfields, rolling stock, and various other targets of opportunity.

Fighters of the 9th flew close support missions for the ground forces, while the medium bombers attacked enemy strongpoints. Mustangs of the 354th Fighter Group set out on a patrol in the Vire-Caen area. They spotted a formation of aircraft which they didn't identify at first. Only when they had reached an altitude of 30,000 feet after climbing for ten to fifteen minutes did they become aware that they were pursuing a flight of Me–109s. Sneaking in on their tails, the Mustangs picked off several Messerschmitts.

June, 1944—date approximate. The first Lightning to land on an advance airstrip on the beachhead. Part of the invasion fleet is visible in the background. (Photo Imperial War Museum, London)

251

June, 1944—date approximate. A B–26 of the 386th
Bomb Group, 9th Air Force, about to release its bombs.
(Photo from *Air Combat 1939–1945*)

June, 1944—date approximate. A–20 Havocs over Le
Havre. (Official USAF Photo)

252

June, 1944—date approximate. Lt. Col. Francis Gabreski of the 61st Fighter Squadron, 56th Fighter Group, taxis his P–47D Thunderbolt out prior to take-off on an escort mission. At this time, Lt. Col. Gabreski had 28 confirmed victories, which would be increased to 31 before being captured by the Germans on July 20th. (Official USAF Photo)

7

JULY

Saturday, 1 July

Fighters of the 8th Air Force roamed the French countryside. They were out on area patrols, and bombing and strafing missions to keep a constant pressure on the harassed Germans. An evening patrol in the area around St. Quentin brought 52 P–51s of the 357th Fighter Group on the tail of eight Me–109s. Four Messerschmitts were shot down. The Mustangs destroyed another four German aircraft when they strafed an airfield. One P–51 failed to return. Other 8th Air Force fighters were out in the evening on a bombing and strafing mission in the area of Montdidier.

Sunday, 2 July

Mustangs of the 4th Fighter Group escorted 15th Air Force bombers to Budapest, operating from Italy. The Luftwaffe took to the air, and in the engagement seven German fighters were shot down for the loss of six Mustangs.

Fighter-bombers of the 9th Air Force kept on pounding enemy strongpoints in support of the army.

Beginning at dusk, the Germans succeeded in firing 161 V–1s against England in the next 24 hours.

Monday, 3 July

8th Air Force B–17 Fortresses, which were temporarily based in Italy after a shuttle mission to Russia, joined the 15 Air Force in a raid of almost one thousand bombers to the Balkans. Mustangs escorted the bombers.

254

Fighters of 9th Tactical Air Command (IX TAC) destroyed a church tower which served as an observation post. The fighters were on their usual support mission.

Tuesday, 4 July

8th Air Force Fortresses and Liberators attacked airfields, marshalling yards, and various other tactical targets. An intended attack on the railroad bridge at Saumur had to be abandoned. When the Fortresses arrived weather had become so bad that the target could not be identified. Beaumont-le-Roger Airfield received a load causing much damage.

P–51s and P–47s flew escort missions and further patrols, fighter sweeps, and bombing and strafing missions. It was a big day for the 56th Fighter Group. Out on a divebombing mission, the Thunderbolts arrived over their target, Conches Airfield. They had hardly dropped their bombs when all of a sudden a large number of Me–109s was spotted. The Thunderbolts chased the enemy fighters and in the dogfights ranging from 10,000 feet down to the deck, twenty Me–109s were shot down for no losses to the 56th (proof was given by gun camera).

Fighter-bombers of the 9th flew twenty missions today in the interdiction zone and made thirty rail cuts. Five locomotives and 113 cars were shot up.

General Eisenhower made a reconnaissance flight in the St. Lô area in the backseat of a twin-seated Mustang. The pilot was General Quesada. Escort was furnished by fighters of the 354th Fighter Group, all of them taking off from a landing strip on the beachhead. This twin-seated Mustang was an old war-weary fighter from which the fuselage fuel tank behind the cockpit seat had been removed. In its place, a second seat was installed.

Wednesday, 5 July

The 8th Fighter Command sent 139 Mustangs and 89 Thunderbolts to pick up the Fortresses returning from Italy after their shuttle mission that started on the 21st of June to Russia. En route, the Fortresses bombed Beziers in South France.

Near Evreux, Me–109s appeared but the escorting fighters took care of them. Lt. Col. Gabreski scored his twenty-eighth confirmed victory. Extensive damage was inflicted to the Beziers marshalling yards. Other 8th fighters ranged over Normandy on their daily strafing missions.

Fighter-bombers of IX TAC attacked command posts in the Periers area while flying their missions in support of the First Army.

Thursday, 6 July

8th Air Force bombers with escorting Mustangs headed out on a northerly course to pay another visit to Kiel. One B–24, *Boulder Buff,* was hit by flak and set course to Malmö Airfield. When crossing the town of Malmö, Swedish fighters attacked the bomber, but it managed to land at the airfield.

Other Fortress formations turned to "Crossbow" targets. Especially the sites supplying the V-bombs to the lauching sites were the objectives for missions both in the morning and in the afternoon.

8th Fighters carried out their usual missions. Four Mustangs set out on a search for a dinghy north of Borkum. They encountered a Ju–88 flying at 100 feet and sent it into the sea.

A counterattack by the 2nd SS Panzer Division was foiled by heavy attacks of the fighter-bombers. The P–38 Lightnings of the 367th and 474th Fighter Groups delivered such a blow to an enemy strongpoint that it was no longer capable of putting up a defense against the American infantry.

Fighter-bombers of the 9th flew fifteen interdiction missions. They flew even beyond the interdiction zone and roamed the French countryside south of the Loire, looking for possible enemy reinforcements moving north. 23 railcuts were made, and thirteen locomotives and 51 rail cars were destroyed. Troop concentrations southwest of Carentan and near Periers received their share of the fighter-bomber assaults.

B–26 Marauders of the 391st Bomb Group were heading for the long viaduct at Maintenon. When the mediums turned to base, the viaduct was out of use for the next couple of weeks. Medium bombers carried out large-scale missions against rail lines, however, with little effect.

Friday, 7 July

756 B–17 Fortresses and 373 B–24 Liberators headed for the synthetic oil plants at Böhlen, Merseburg, Lützkendorf, and the aircraft factories at Leipzig and Bernburg. The 1st and 3rd Division flew a converging course to a point 100 miles west of Berlin; they then flew a feint towards the city and arriving at a point forty miles southwest of Berlin, they sharply turned to the west and south to their respective targets in the Böhlen-Merseburg-Leipzig areas. They were supposed to draw most of the Luftwaffe fighters and therefore the bulk of the escorting fighters were assigned to those two forces. (Two Fortresses of the 3rd Division collided and were lost.)

However, it was the 2nd Division that received the most deadly opposition from swarms of German fighters that rose to challenge the bombers and an entire "clay pigeon" squadron was shot out of the sky. 23

Liberators were cut down by the fighters of JG 3; most of these bombers were from the 492nd Bomb Group attacking Bernburg. The force attacking Halle lost three aircraft, while one Liberator was shot down over Aschersleben.

Me–410s and FW–190s with a top-cover of Me–109s, in all some 175 single-engine and 125 twin-engine aircraft, tore into the unlucky Liberator formations of which the 492nd Group was without fighter protection. One group of P–38 Lightnings moved in to break up the attacks of the German fighters while another P–38 group dived on a formation of Focke Wulfs and Messerschmitts. Both Lightning groups claimed 25 German aircraft, a real success for the P–38 considering the total claim of 77 by the 8th fighters, of which six were lost. The total loss for the bomber force was 37 aircraft.

In the confusion and by a deviation in timing, two Liberator formations were placed on a collision course. Both formations were under heavy fighter attack and so it occurred that two B–24s collided, both going down in flames.

Two Thunderbolts of the 56th Fighter Group, returning from an escort to Leipzig, suddenly spotted a group of three-engine Ju–52s flying the landing pattern at Gardelegen Airfield. The Thunderbolts joined in the pattern, and in quick succession six transport aircraft were picked off.

Returning from a B–17 escort as far as Dümmer Lake, pilots of the 353rd Fighter Group spotted a number of aircraft on Wesendorf Airfield. Colonel Glenn Duncan led one squadron down into a strafing attack, but ground fire hit his *Dove of Peace*. He tried to make it as far west as possible, but near Nienburg he had to belly-in. Colonel Duncan was never captured; he managed to make his way out of Germany on foot and he would spend the rest of the war in the Dutch underground movement.

Thirty-two B–26 Marauders of the 322nd Bomb Group were dispatched to carry out a night mission to the "Noball" headquarters at Chateau de Ribeaucourt. Three pathfinders led the mission. The German defenses were alarmed and in the Oisemont area the nightfighters appeared. Me–109s, FW–190s, Me–110s, and Ju–88s worked in very well-executed cooperation with flak and searchlights. Even flares were reported to be used to illuminate the bombers. Some 23 Marauders managed to drop their bombs, but it had to be done individually. A single-engine fighter and a Ju–88 were shot down in flames, but nine Marauders went down and two were damaged beyond repair. It meant a new blow to "Nye's Annihilators."

The British and Canadian armies were pinned down in the outskirts of Caen by a heavy concentration of German armor, artillery, and other defenses to such an extent that the fear existed (as General Arnold expressed it) that Caen might turn into another Cassino. A major attempt to break through the defenses had been planned for the next day, and in preparation for the attack, Montgomery called for the assistance of the air force. At 2150 hours, RAF Bomber Command started to lay a carpet on Caen.

Saturday, 8 July

Early in the morning, five groups from 9th Bomber Command were dispatched to continue the attack of the RAF on the previous night. Only two groups and parts of two others were able to bomb.

Heavy cratering by air and naval bombardment added to the strength of the German resistance. The only result was the occupation of a larger part of Caen.

Large forces of the 8th Air Force were operating over northern France attacking interdiction targets. A mission to the "Noballs" by Fortresses was recalled. Bombs were dropped on the railroad center at Brussels. 8th Air Force fighters flew escort and strafing missions.

Troop concentrations near Carentan were again submitted to divebombing and strafing attacks, while buildings housing command posts in the Periers area were also hit.

Sunday, 9 July

Small forces of the 8th Air Force were operating over northern France. Fighters flew area patrols.

Medium bombers of the 9th Air Force turned to the oil storage depot at Rennes where they inflicted much damage.

Tuesday, 11 July

Weather forecasters had predicted a break in the overcast over Munich and as the large marshalling yards and aircraft engine factories were always worthwhile targets, more than a thousand heavy bombers of the 8th Air Force were on their way to the city. Munich was in fact a center for the development of jet aircraft and contained many experimental stations, assembly factories, and flying fields in the surrounding area.

Heavy anti-aircraft defenses north of Paris forced the bombers to take a more northerly course via the North Sea to the Schelde, and then in a southerly direction west of Brussels to the French border where the bombers turned to their destination. It was expected that the German Air Force would react in force. But the Luftwaffe was not at all in evidence. Another, though smaller, surprise was the predicted break in the clouds. A solid overcast covered the targets and made bombing by H2X necessary.

258

1048 heavy bombers unloaded 2353 tons of bombs on the targets at Munich, Augsburg, and Friedrichshafen. One Fortress was making its 200th mission. This record in the 8th Air Force was achieved by "Hell's Angels" of the 303rd Bomb Group. Again, some bombers damaged by flak sought sanctuary in Switzerland. Fighters escorted the bombers all the way. After the escort, the fighters carried out sweeps.

The 366th Fighter Group of the 9th Air Force was out on an early morning mission to attack pillboxes near St. Lô when the weather became worse and worse, with a ceiling down to 1000 feet. Unable to locate their targets, the group turned back. Still near St. Lô, one of the squadron leaders spotted a moving tank. No one else could see it, so the Thunderbolt peeled off to point it out with its guns. Coming down, the Thunderbolt opened up with its eight guns and suddenly the sky was filled with tracers and light flak, and the group overhead realized that they had bounced on a force of some fifty to sixty tanks.

After delivering their bombs, the P–47s went down to 100 feet, each of them blasting away with its guns. Within twenty minutes, one-third of the tank column was destroyed. The group landed at its advanced landing ground only to rearm and took off again in heavy rain to deliver a second blow. When they left the area, 35 tanks were destroyed. For a third time, the 366th Group set off, notwithstanding the appalling weather, and another tank column was found and worked over.

Wednesday, 12 July

Munich was again the target for the bombers of the 8th, although it had been the intention to attack Berlin. However, weather conditions made such an operation impossible. So it turned out that Munich received the blow from 2708 tons of bombs dropped by 1117 heavy bombers. There was again no sign of the Luftwaffe, but also no sign of a break in the clouds and the bombing had to be done by H2X.

The bridge at Saumur was knocked out after a second attack by the medium bombers of the 9th Air Force.

Fighter-bombers were now flying interdiction missions as far as Châlons, east of Paris.

Thursday, 13 July

For the third day running, a stream of more than one thousand bombers of the 8th Air Force was going to Munich, and both here and on the marshalling yards at Saarbrücken the bombs were dropped by radar. This time the German Air Force showed up, but only forty fighters made reluctant and ineffective passes at the bombers.

From the Munich missions of the last three days, fifty heavy bombers failed to return, either shot down by anti-aircraft guns or by mechanical failure.

The second Fortress to complete its 200th mission made a safe landing after the mission at its base. It was the bomber *Travelling Circus*, from the 93rd Bomb Group.

Friday, 14 July

Another supply mission for the Maquis was scheduled for today. Drops had to be done at seven points in three principal regions: in the Rhône and Saône valleys, southwest of Chalon-sur-Saône, and in the area of Limoges. Fighting was heavy in these regions as the Germans tried to eliminate the threat to their communications.

The bombers took off at 0400 hours. 324 B–17s, escorted by 524 P–51s and P–47s, winged over France on their way to their assigned areas. Southwest of Paris, some fifteen Me–109s were encountered. Nine of them were shot down. Two Fortresses were forced to land in Normandy. Two wings of 72 B–17s dropped 860 containers in the Rhône and Saône area, 36 B–17s dropped 429 containers southwest of Chalon-sur-Saône, and 214 B–17s dropped 2491 containers in the Limoges area on five different targets.

Sunday, 16 July

Weather forecasts gave suitable conditions for visual bombing over parts of Germany. As the marshalling yards at Saarbrücken were of great importance for the supply of German forces in France, approximately 450 B–24 Liberators headed for that city as part of a large force of more than 1000 heavy bombers going to targets in southern and western Germany, notably Munich and Augsburg. It was to these cities that for the first time scouts were used.

Operating as an auxiliary unit to the 1st Division, the Mustangs flew ahead of the bomber formation to investigate the weather conditions and to keep the bomber leader informed by radio. There had always been weather reconnaissance in advance of a bomber raid, but many times the weather deteriorated when the bombers were underway, hence the need was felt for a scouting aircraft preceding the bombers by only a few minutes and transmitting on-the-spot reports to the bomber leader. The pilot of the scouting Mustang was an experienced bomber pilot with a regular fighter pilot flying as his wingman in a two-plane element.

Nearing Munich, the 1st Division followed a few minutes behind the 3rd

Division when they encountered cloud conditions building up to altitudes of 30,000 feet. Reaching the target, the 3rd Division was on the edge of the clouds and made a turn as planned. In doing so, the bombers flew right into the clouds. Eleven B–17s were never seen again.

The 1st Division, however, was coached by the scouts and made the right turn off the target and didn't lose an aircraft on the mission. In spite of these unpredicted circumstances, the bombing was fairly accurate.

The bombing of the marshalling yards at Saarbrücken had to be done by H2X. Some Liberators came into a strange situation when they got mixed up with a force of B–17 Fortresses and followed this force almost to Munich before they became fully aware of their mistake.

Some of the fighter escorts didn't make the rendezvous with the bombers at the set time because fog at the bases had delayed the take-off. But the bombers had luck and the German fighters didn't show much interest.

Fighter-bombers of the 9th Air Force carried out heavy attacks in their strong ground-support role in the Vire valley near St. Lô. The attacks were executed in eight-squadron strength.

July 16, 1944. A B–24 Liberator of the 492nd Bomb Group winging its way toward Saarbrücken. (Official USAF Photo)

Monday, 17 July

The 8th Air Force concentrated on bridges and other tactical targets in France. Twelve P–47 Thunderbolts of the 9th Air Force set off on a mission to the railyard at Tiger-Quail. The Thunderbolts carried rockets for the first time (four each) which they poured into locomotives, rail cars, repair shops, and other targets.

Another novelty was carried by fourteen P–38 Lightnings of the 370th Fighter Group flying a mission to Coutances. The P–38s carried Napalm bombs: highly inflammable jellied-gasoline–filled drop-tanks. The mission, led by Droop Snoot Lightnings, was considered very successful.

Fighters of the 9th were out in great strength to attack seventeen bridges over the Vire. When the fighters assembled again for the return flight, they left seventeen destroyed bridges behind.

Medium bombers delivered a heavy blow against a fuel storage depot at Rennes. Along with the attack on 9 July, it deprived the Germans of 2,000,000 liters of gasoline. Warehouses and offices were wrecked.

Tuesday, 18 July

At first light, nearly 1000 heavy bombers of RAF Bomber Command appeared over Caen in preparation for a new attempt to break out. With the drone of the Merlins still in their ears, the Germans watched a new horde of bombers appear at the horizon. 571 B–24 Liberators of the 8th Air Force headed for three areas near Caen where they unloaded 1425.4 tons of HE and fragmentation bombs. After the Liberators, came the medium bombers of the 9th Bomber Command, arriving with eleven groups over five gun positions which were concealed by clouds of smoke and dust. When the first prisoners were taken by the ground forces, they proved to be stone-deaf for the first twenty-four hours.

The Allied armor, however, soon ran into a heavy anti-tank screen not reported by Intelligence and the offensive would soon be doomed to stick in the mud caused by the heavy rain that would start on the 20th.

750 B–17 Flying Fortresses flew in close formations across the North Sea en route to Jutland. Here the formations separated, one force going to Peenemünde and Zinnowitz where the secret scientific establishments were to be attacked, while the other force headed for the port area of Kiel, where 107 bombers dropped from above the clouds through intense flak. 379 Fortresses with their full fighter escort arrived over Peenemünde where eight separate aiming points within the concentrated target area received 920.6 tons of bombs, damaging the plant seriously. The German fighters didn't show any intention of disturbing the operations.

262

Bombers of the 9th Air Force set course to Laval where the high viaduct was bombed out of use when five spans were destroyed.

Wednesday, 19 July

The 15th Air Force from Italy directed its efforts against the aircraft factories at Munich. The 222 heavy bombers ran into very heavy anti-aircraft fire as the Germans had considerably increased their number of flak batteries after the attacks of the 8th Air Force on the 11th, 12th, and 13th. Many bombers suffered damage.

This mission of the 15th Air Force was only part of a gigantic operation in which the 8th Air Force took part with 1250 heavy bombers escorted by the total strength of the fighter force. Targets were spread over western and southern Germany and a heavy load was dropped on aircraft plants, notably at Augsburg and Lechfeld, ball-bearing industries, marshalling yards at Koblenz, chemical establishments, and many others. Bombing at Schweinfurt was hindered by an effective smokescreen. This time the German fighters were up to challenge the invaders and in the ensuing air combats, seventeen Luftwaffe fighters were shot down. Twenty-nine bombers failed to return.

July 19, 1944. Liberator of the 492nd Bomb Group nearing target at Koblenz. (Official USAF Photo)

July 19, 1944. Bombs explode on the jet airfield at Lechfeld. (Official USAF Photo)

The 55th Fighter Group of the 8th Air Force had by now replaced part of its Lightnings with Mustangs, and the group made its first operational flight with the new type today.

This time the 9th Air Force went after four bridges over the Loire. In the evening between 1920 and 2002 hours, the mediums dropped their bombs on the bridges at Nantes, Chalonnes, Les Ponts de Cé, and Tours-la-Riche. ". . . The bridges were eliminated because of the lack of anti-aircraft guns. . ." according to the German Seventh Army War Diary.

Fighter-bombers of the 9th ranged as far as western Belgium where several targets were attacked.

B–26 Marauders and A–20 Havocs attacked with a strong force gun positions in the Demouville-Guiberville area.

Thursday, 20 July

The 8th Air Force was up again in great strength for a wide-scale attack, in coordination with the 15th Air Force which went to Friedrichshafen, against various targets in Germany. One force was heading for aircraft factories in Saxony (Leipzig being one of the targets); a second force was on its way to the key synthetic oil plants at Merseburg, Leuna, and Lützkendorf; a third force went to south-central Germany where it would attack a variety of railway and aircraft installations; and the fourth force was going to strike at an important motor vehicle works at Rüsselsheim.

The German defense system was obviously confused by the various attacks by more than 2000 bombers, and fighter opposition was limited. Yet in many encounters, the Americans claimed the destruction of thirty German fighters, whereas ten bombers didn't make it back to their base either.

One B–17 was shot down by a long-nosed FW–190D, but in its turn the Focke Wulf was jumped by a Mustang and, after a wild chase, the German fighter was shot down. Shortly thereafter the same Mustang destroyed a second Focke Wulf heading for an airfield. The P–51 pilot let his aircraft down and made several strafing passes over the airfield. When he left he had destroyed a Do–217, a He–111, and a Ju–88. The 91st Bomb Group directed its activities against an airfield suspected of jet activity.

While strafing He–111s and Me–110s on Bassinheim airfield east of Koblenz, Colonel Gabreski of the 56th Fighter Group flew too low in order to avoid the ground fire. The propeller of his Thunderbolt hit the ground when the aircraft roared over a small hill at the end of the field. The Thunderbolt bellied-in and Gabreski escaped without a scratch in spite of his plane's touching the ground at a 250-miles-per-hour speed. After five days of hiding, he was captured and had to spend the rest of the war in a POW camp.

The 20th Fighter Group was also converting its Lightnings to Mustangs and today it flew the first operational mission with the type in a mixed formation.

Twelve interdiction missions were flown by fighter-bombers of the 9th Air Force.

Friday, 21 July

A planned carpet-bombing at St. Lô prior to the assault of the US First Army had to be put off because of the weather conditions. These conditions prevailed over a large part of the continent; however, no overcast was expected over central and southern Germany. Aircraft factories and airfields in southern Germany, together with the well-known ball-bearing factories at Regensburg and Schweinfurt, were the targets selected to be visited by 1068 heavy bombers of the 8th Air Force.

Arriving at their objectives after the long journey, only 414 bombers were able to bomb the primary targets. Some formations dropped on Stuttgart. One bomber force encountered eighty German fighters, but losses were not heavy and the plants at Regensburg and Schweinfurt received a severe mauling.

A scouting force proved its value when they ran into high cloud formations towering to 28,000 feet. Skirting the front, they found a route through the cloud formations and they transmitted their finding to the 1st Division. Unfortunately, this message was not received by the 2nd Division, and while the 1st Division Fortresses were able to avoid the clouds, the 2nd Division Liberators flew right through them and when they emerged they were in disarray.

When the Liberators came off their target, the assembly plants at Oberpfaffenhofen, they came under attack from Me–109s and especially the 2nd wing received the blow. Most bombers lost were from the 2nd Division: 23, while the 1st lost only three bombers. Again some B–24s wound up in Switzerland.

A flight of P–51 Mustangs of the 352nd Fighter Group disappeared into a thundercloud over the North Sea and the Mustangs were never seen again.

After five spans of the huge viaduct at Laval had been demolished by the mediums of the 9th Air Force, the Germans had started their reconstruction work at once. Although the repair work was not yet finished, the mediums renewed their visit and the Germans could start all over again.

Sunday, 23 July

On the eve of the great break-through at St. Lô, German airfields in France were plastered with bombs by the heavies of the 8th Air Force.

All eleven bomber groups of the 9th Air Force set off to attack nine bridges and one fuel dump. The groups were led by pathfinder aircraft.

Fighters of the 9th ranged over France. Over Cherbourg, a Mustang of the 354th Fighter Group was hit and the pilot bailed out. A tremendous blow from a collision with the tail section made him lose consciousness. When he recovered, he found himself hanging over the horizontal stabilizer of the plunging aircraft with the leading edge in his lap. He managed to free himself and looked for the ripcord, but he could not find it. After a few anxious seconds, he discovered it on his back and could just pull it in time to have his chute open before touching the ground.

P–47 Thunderbolts of the 406th Fighter Group, 9th Air Force, strafed an ammunition train in France. After a few passes, the train blew up.

Monday, 24 July

The assault on the beaches of Normandy had been the first stage. The second stage was the breakout, and this had been planned to be executed under overwhelming air power on the 21st. Adverse weather, however, had forced a postponement of the operation until the 24th.

Early in the morning, 10/10 cloud in the St. Lô area made Leigh Mallory decide to launch the air attack at 1200 instead of 1000 hours. Meteorologists had predicted that the sky would lift by that time. The decision was made possible by the willingness of the First Army to postpone

266

their attack until 1500 hours. Weathermen in the 8th Air Force doubted the solution of the AEAF meteorologists, and it did not take long before their doubts were proved to be well founded.

The first to take off were the fighter-bombers of the 9th Air Force. Six groups climbed into the sky and headed for their assigned targets: a rectangular area near St. Lô 250 yards deep and 7000 yards long, where they had to carry out their divebombing and strafing attacks. Weather over the target proved to be so abominable that three groups were recalled, and the other groups bombed on good luck. One pilot picked up the wrong landmark and hit an American ammunition dump which partly blew up, causing several casualties.

Meanwhile, the 1st, 2nd, and 3rd Divisions of the 8th Air Force, totalling 1586 heavy bombers, were airborne and on a course to their target; the area they had to attack was just south of the fighter-bomber area, one mile deep and five miles long.

While the observers on the French beaches heard the thunder of the engines above the overcast, Leigh Mallory at Bradley's field headquarters, decided to cancel the operation. However, this decision reached the bombers only a few minutes before the bombing was to commence, and only a few planes in the last three formations received the recall message.

But when the bombers arrived over the target area, visibility was so poor that the lead formations decided not to attack their primaries. The second formations found the same heavy overcast, and only thirty-five bombers tried to fulfill their task. Three times they tried to identify their targets, and on the third run they dropped their bombs. When the third formation arrived over the target, the weather had slightly improved and 317 bombers dropped their loads. Several units tried to make a second bomb run, and at that moment they received the recall message.

The bombardier of a Liberator struck the toggle-switch in a reflex when a packet of chaff hit the nose-turret. The bombs fell away and descended exactly on a 9th Air Force fighterfield at Chippelle where two Thunderbolts manned and bombed up were destroyed. The lead bombardier of another heavy bomber had trouble with his bombsight. Inadvertently, part of the load left the bomb-bay with the unfortunate consequence that the other fifteen bombers released on their lead ship. The bombs came down 2200 yards north of the northern boundary of their area where sixteen GI's of the 30th Infantry Division were killed and about 90 wounded. Three heavy bombers failed to return from this mission.

Medium bombers of the 9th Air Force had received the cancellation message in time. They were scheduled to attack directly after the heavy bombers had left the spot. The medium bombers turned to other objectives, and one of the groups that was on its way to a special tactical target was the 344th Group. It despatched 39 Marauders to bomb the Loire bridge near Tours. A heavy flak barrage was thrown up when the aircraft started their bomb runs. The leading element was dispersed, but the remainder of the group stuck together and unloaded above the bridge, destroying vital parts. 31 Marauders were damaged.

The operation was a failure. Besides, the enemy had now more or less been informed about the place and approximate time of the impending attack. Late at night that attack was set for the very next day.

Tuesday, 25 July

There was no alternative to a repetition of yesterday's mass attack in assistance of the outbreak at St. Lô which had been planned for 1100 hours. With the previous day fresh in mind, a weather reconnaissance aircraft was flown into the assault area at 0800 hours to keep the 8th Air Force informed with exact weather data.

The first of the 559 fighter-bombers of the 9th Air Force started their attack in the area closest to the American lines at 0938 hours. Eight groups, flying in column of groups, with all squadrons flying in column of flights, came in glide-bombing and strafing an area south of the St. Lô–Periers route. One group swept the eastern area, the next the western area, and so on.

Immediately after the fighter-bombers followed 1507 Fortresses and Liberators, dropping more than 3300 tons of bombs. Their attack started at 1000 hours. A precarious situation arose when it proved to be necessary to descend to a lower altitude and thus recompute hurriedly their bombing data as bombing from the predetermined height of 15,000 to 16,000 feet meant bombing through overcast. To drop to a lower level meant a perilous undertaking in view of the overcrowded skies. Some even dropped to an altitude of 12,000 feet.

Smoke markers to mark the target area proved to be of little value. The withdrawal of the army from the bombing zone had been 1500 yards. Yet bombing errors, though less than had been anticipated, occurred. A command pilot forgot that bombing had to be done by groups. When a wingleader failed to observe a landmark and ordered "Bombs Away," the command pilot also gave the order and his whole unit followed, 35 bombers dropping their load within the American lines. Another lead bombardier released visually because he had trouble with his bombsight. The results were tragic.

It was doubtless a huge performance to have more than 1500 bombers deliver an attack on such a small area in successive waves within the timespace of sixty minutes.

The big army offensive started at 1100 hours, directly after the attack of the heavy bombers and at the same moment that seven groups of fighter-bombers of the IX TAC came roaring in, flying low in their assigned eastern and western areas, bombing and strafing, using napalm bombs.

Next came 380 B–26 Marauders and A–20 Havocs of the 9th Air Force, flying in thirty formations and concentrating on strongpoints and areas beyond reach of artillery fire. The bombing was generally accurate; however, a tragic misidentification of the target caused 42 aircraft to drop their bombs within the American lines. Again the casualties were concentrated in the 30th Infantry Division: 102 army personnel were killed, including Lt. Gen. Lesley J. McNair. 380 men were wounded.

During the main attack, two groups of 9th Fighter Command flew an offensive mission against rail lines well beyond the battle zone. The remaining fighter group of the 9th had been assigned to care for special air support requests. Eight groups of fighters of the 8th Air Force flew cover for the heavies and the mediums.

Other groups flew fighter sweeps. One of these was carried out in the morning by P–51s of the 357th Fighter Group. Near Paris, they spotted a lone P–38 under attack from some 25 FW–190s and Me–109s. The Mus-

July 25, 1944. B–24, *Queen of Hearts,* after a crashlanding at New Romney, Kent. (Official USAF Photo)

269

tangs bore into the German fighters, the latter diving for the deck. The next moment a fight raged from between the roofs of the Paris houses up to 8000 feet, with fighters twisting and diving. Two Me–109s and three FW–190s were shot down.

Armed-reconnaissance missions were flown all day, starting in the morning before the attack by fighters of the 2nd Tactical Air Force. Between 1135 and 2104 hours, thirteen armed-reconnaissance missions were flown by 9th Air Force fighters. The pilots selected a large variety of targets. They demolished a bridge near Gavray, ammunition and fuel dumps in the vicinity of the battle field, towers used as observation posts, and many others. At the end of the day, their work was accomplished with four missions to important crossroads where delayed-fuse bombs were delivered, intended to surprise the Germans in their nightly traffic congestion near Coutances.

Thunderbolts of the 9th 406th Fighter Group bounced fifteen German fighters over Lisieux. In the ensuing fight, the Americans claimed four shot down for the loss of one P–47.

The viaduct at Maintenon, already bombed out of use on the 6th, was again visited by the medium bombers and the wrecked condition was prolonged.

From all bombers taking part in the assault in support of the First Army, eight heavies and one medium were lost.

Wednesday, 26 July

The big drive south had started in three columns which soon would fan out to drive against Coutances, Granville, and Avranches. And for the first time, a new form of close support was put into operation, the so-called armored column cover.

Each tank column carried an air-support party equipped with an air force–type VHF for two-way communication: tank-escorting plane. Each advancing tank column would be covered by four escorting planes armed with bombs or rockets on a 30-minute shift schedule. They formed the eyes of the column. Their task was to attack any enemy obstacle ahead, to inform the commanders about the obstacles that lay ahead, and in retrospect the commanders of the armored columns could ask the flight to attack anything they thought necessary to clear the way. If those obstacles were too much for the flight of four, reinforcements by fighter-bombers on ground alert could be required via the air-support channels. This procedure was to become standard for the duration of the war.

Seventy-two squadron missions were flown today as column cover by four fighter-bomber groups of IX TAC.

270

Fighters of the same command flew sixteen eight-plane armed-reconnaissance missions. In all, its fighter-bombers flew 1561 sorties, attacking road and rail transport, and bombing and strafing strongpoints, airfields, troops, and many other targets. They claimed the destruction of seventeen enemy aircraft.

B–26 Marauders of the 344th Bomb Group attacked a supply depot, inflicting considerable damage.

Thursday, 27 July

Armed column cover was provided throughout the day with IX TAC units flying 100 missions. During these missions, the fighters constantly harassed the enemy. Reports of the day mentioned a command post southwest of St. Lô left in flames, attacks on convoys, tanks, all kinds of vehicles, buildings, strongpoints, strafing a town crowded with troops and guns, etc. Fighters of IX TAC flew a total of 1451 sorties. Claims of the day included eleven enemy aircraft destroyed. Seventeen fighter-bombers were shot down.

Eighteen armed-reconnaissance missions were flown during which a rich harvest of enemy tanks, vehicles, and other materiel was reaped.

At night, delayed-action bombs were dropped on road junctions.

Friday, 28 July

Five hundred sixty-nine Fortresses of the 8th Air Force delivered a hammering blow to the synthetic oil plant at Merseburg-Leuna. About sixty German aircraft were airborne near Merseburg, but they didn't cause the bombers much trouble.

A much more alarming feature struck the crews of the B–17s when five Me–163 jets made their long-feared introduction into the air war. They made no attacks at the bombers, but confined their activity in showing their tricks obviously to demonstrate their superiority to any aircraft the Allies could bring into the skies. It was indeed a warning to air force commanders that their own supremacy in the air might possibly vanish before the guns and rockets of the new jets.

Colonel Avelin Tacon was leading his green-nosed Mustangs of the 359th Fighter Group, flying parallel to the bombers at 25,000 feet, when one of the pilots called out two contrails at 6 o'clock high. Looking back, Tacon saw the contrails at 32,000 feet. He put his flight into a 180-degree turn to meet the interceptors head-on. First the Me–163s made a slight turn to the bombers, keeping a tight formation; then suddenly, they split up, one pulling up into the sun and the other diving away.

271

The scores of the IX TAC fighter-bombers was mounting while they flew their column cover missions. Fighters of the command made 1250 sorties today, and included in the many claims were twelve German aircraft destroyed.

At night, delayed-action bombs were dropped on road junctions.

Saturday, 29 July

The 8th Air Force was back over the synthetic oil plants at Merseburg-Leuna with a force of 647 B–17 Fortresses, and this time the bombing caused the plant to close for several weeks. Only one jet was seen on this occasion; however, plenty of conventional fighters gave the American fliers worries enough. Eight bombers went down while the gunners accounted for at least nineteen enemies.

Four hundred forty-four B–24 Liberators arrived over Bremen, but they found the crude oil refineries hidden by smoke and clouds. Bombing had to be done blindly, with doubtful results.

The one Me–163 encountered in fact opened the battle between the jets and the conventional fighters. Escorting a straggling Fortress of the 100th Bomb Group returning from Merseburg, the Lightnings of the 479th Group watched an Me–163 making for the Fortress. The jet approached from the rear, but it pulled away under the B–17 without attacking it. The Lightnings tried to turn into the fighter and one of them managed to place some hits, but the jet started a dive and kept diving until it disappeared into the clouds.

Both the VII and VIII Corps of the First US Army were now in hot pursuit along the Normandy roads in southerly direction without a halt. The Germans flung all caution to the winds and retreated with all they had in daylight, crowding the roads with all kinds of vehicles. These profitable circumstances for fighter-bombers were fully exploited, and armed-reconnaissance flights were constantly made in increasing numbers.

Although bad weather prevented operations in the morning, the Thunderbolts of the 405th Fighter Group took off in mid-afternoon and set course to the area of Villedieu. Arriving over the area, they found only a few targets, but it was on their way back to Coutances that they saw a mass of traffic on the roads, with vehicles in some places driving bumper to bumper. The first flight immediately called the home controller for reinforcements. Then the Thunderbolts started to work it over.

The practice was to start with the head and tail of the column and then systematically to destroy all that was in between. Throughout the afternoon, the squadrons of the group rotated: as soon as the planes were back at their base, they were rearmed and refuelled and they took off again.

272

From 1510 until 2140 hours, the Thunderbolts came roaring down, blasting away with everything they had, thundering over the more than three-mile-long column, and when the last P–47s returned to their base, they left more than 400 motor transports, twelve tanks, and many other vehicles behind as blazing wrecks.

The fighter-bombers of IX TAC flew 1038 sorties, including constant column-cover patrols and armed-reconnaissance flights.

Sunday, 30 July

Fighters of the 8th Air Force flew patrols over northern France.

9th Air Force Mustangs, out on a patrol in the Vire area, spotted a lone Me–109 flying at 30,000 feet. The Messerschmitt was sent down as a flaming torch.

IX TAC fighter-bombers attacked bridges in the battle area. Fifteen enemy aircraft were claimed during the 1320 sorties flown today.

Monday, 31 July

Forecasts gave hope of good visibility over southern Germany and therefore the 8th Air Force had despatched 1169 bombers to attack various targets in this part of Germany especially Munich. But as had happened so many times before, when the formations neared their target, they found a solid overcast obscuring their objectives, forcing them to resort to blind bombing. About 2500 tons of bombs were dropped on Munich and Ludwigshafen on pathfinder indication.

During this month, RAF Bomber Command flew on all but two days against the "Crossbow" sites in the Pas de Calais area. In 102 missions, in which 5832 heavy bomber sorties were involved, 24,292.2 tons of bombs were dropped, being 30.7 percent of the sorties undertaken by Bomber Command and 42 percent of the tonnage of bombs expended. The 8th Air Force made 75 attacks against V-weapon targets this month.

RAF, 8th, and 9th Air Forces made over 16,000 sorties since D-Day in which more than 24,500 tons of bombs were dropped on bridge targets alone.

The bridge at Les Ponts de Cé was demolished today by 9th Bomber Command. This bridge had been out of service since 1940, but in July it had been repaired twice by the Germans after a bombing attack earlier this month. The bridge at Nantes was destroyed after a fifth attack; however, one attack by the Marauders was sufficient to knock out the bridges at Cinq Mars and La Frillière.

Dive bombers took care that no traffic could pass the bridge at Tours-la-Riche, and that the race between construction and destruction remained in favor of the latter.

By now sixteen fighter-bomber airfields were available in Normandy. 9th Air Force claimed from the 26th, 67 enemy aircraft. Its own losses during this period were 78 aircraft, including ten in air combat. During the last week of the month, IX TAC fighter-bombers claimed a large number of tactical targets, including 384 tanks, 2287 motor transports, fourteen locomotives, and 194 rail cars.

July, 1944—date approximate. Thunderbolts of the 78th Fighter Group lined up at Boxted, Colchester. (Official USAF Photo)

274

8

AUGUST

Tuesday, 1 August

The 8th Air Force bombers left England on their way to many targets in France and Germany, including the V-weapon targets and airfields in France and Germany, such as the important airfields at Tours and Chartres. The Fortresses also carried out a third mass drop on four targets: the Chalon-sur-Saône area, west of Geneva, Savoie in the Alps, and Haute Savoie.

In Savoie in the Alps, 5500 Maquis were waiting for arms and ammunition. In January, 5000 Maquis had fought here against an equal number of enemies, but they had been forced to disperse by lack of supplies. 39 B–17s delivered 463 containers to this group. 75 Fortresses dropped 899 containers at Haute Savoie, while 451 containers were dropped west of Geneva. In all, 192 Fortresses of the 195 dispatched dropped 2281 containers. Only six planes received slight damage.

Today the US Third Army under Lt. Gen. George S. Patton, Jr., became operational. Direct air support would be provided by the XIX Tactical Air Command of the 9th Air Force. IX TAC stayed in support of the First Army. Patton's Third Army operated on the right of Hodges' First Army. Both armies were under command of the 12th Army Group of General Bradley.

A repeated visit by the medium bombers of the 9th to the bridges at Les Ponts de Cé made sure that no trains would pass for the time being. They also attacked the approaches to the bridge at Cinq Mars.

Thunderbolts of IX TAC flew their usual pattern. In the Tessy area, P–47s of the 362nd Fighter Group, XIX TAC, destroyed seven tanks and several gun positions.

Wednesday, 2 August

Although the 8th Air Force devoted most of its efforts to attack tactical targets in support of the American Armies now racing across France, a substantial number of heavy bombers was now heading for Peenemünde to bomb the experimental station and V-weapon factory. Only one German fighter was sighted, and it was shot down by a 353rd Group Thunderbolt.

Mustangs of the 4th Fighter Group spotted a locomotive in a siding at Remy. When they came down, the pilots became aware that they dived on a complete train with camouflaged wagons. Strafing lengthways had little effect, and another four Mustangs came in at right angles. When number four opened fire, an enormous explosion threw the three other Mustangs on their back at 50 feet above the ground, but the pilots managed to recover. Nothing was ever found of the Mustang that caused the explosion. Roofs were torn off buildings in a village a mile distant. Probably the train carried warheads for flying bombs.

The Third Army's speedy drive south created a perilous situation because of the vulnerable spots in such a long, narrow corridor. This was especially the case at Avranches, and although the fighters of XIX TAC guarded the corridor, the army requested special protection for the bridges at Avranches, and five missions were flown for this purpose. Mustangs of the 363rd Fighter Group flew cover. Medium bombers of the 9th bombed two bridges over the Loire out of service. At army's request, no bridges and fuel dumps were to be bombed in the Brittany Peninsula any longer.

XIX TAC was very active all day. Near Mortain, an armored column was held up twice by enemy gun positions in buildings. The P–47s arrived on request and the column could proceed. Other fighter-bomber groups destroyed gun batteries and tanks with rockets. Two Me–109s attacked the rear of a column. A call for help reached a formation of Thunderbolts which chased the Messerschmitts. It was one of the first attempts of the Luftwaffe to interfere with the advance. At Noyon, an ammunition train was blown up.

The daily active strength of the German Air Force had increased to some 400 fighters, while the second reserve had been built up to a strength of 700 fighters. By cover of darkness, the Luftwaffe started a number of small raids in the area of Avranches and Pontaubault. Patton's headquarters received some near misses, and an ammunition dump was blown up. This new activity suggested a German counter-offensive, this time with the aid of a reinforced German Air Force.

A constant night patrol south of Avranches and in the area of Pontorson was flown by two P–61 Black Widows.

Thursday, 3 August

Early in the morning, 1138 heavy bombers of the 8th Air Force fanned out over the continent to attack many targets, such as the ones connected with V-weapons, the marshalling yards at Strasbourg, and many tactical targets in France. Mulhouse and Toul were among the bombed places.

Mustangs of the 354th Fighter Group escorted a Marauder group to a target northwest of Paris. Flying through huge clouds, the bombers arrived over their target and were greeted with intense anti-aircraft fire. One Marauder received a direct hit after releasing its bombs, and went down in a spin. However, the pilot recovered at low altitude and the Marauder flew a straight course again. All instruments were shot out and all crew members except the pilot were wounded. The bombardier had disappeared with the nose of the aircraft. The Mustangs led the blind bomber to an emergency field near Bayeux, and one Mustang actually led the bomber down by flying alongside until touchdown.

It was found necessary to plan a new line of targets in view of the quick advance of allied troops, an advance which was not to be impeded by demolished bridges and rails just in front of them. Medium bombers now struck bridges listed in the new schedule.

XIX TAC destroyed several tanks, motor transports, and many other targets near places at St. Malo and Rennes.

IX TAC operated in much the same way in its own area of responsibility.

Friday, 4 August

Four separate forces, totalling 1246 bombers of the 8th Air Force, escorted by all fifteen fighters groups, were out on a mission to oil refineries at Bremen, Hamburg, and Harburg, aircraft plants at Rostock, Anklam, and other places in northern Germany, the V-weapon experimental works at Peenemünde, and a torpedo plant at Kiel where jet parts were supposed to be manufactured. Excepting Peenemünde and Kiel, all bombing had to be done by means of H2X, with generally poor results.

While picking up the bombers at Hamburg at 1300 hours, the Thunderbolts of the 353rd Fighter Group encountered some 70 to 100 Me–109s attacking the bombers. The German fighters came in from 24,000 to 35,000 feet in line-abreast formation of three to five aircraft. Before they could do any harm, the Thunderbolts intercepted and dispersed them, and in the combat that ranged from 27,000 feet to the deck, fourteen Messerschmitts were shot down for the loss of one P–47. The Thunderbolts had already destroyed three He–111s on the ground at Plantlünne Airfield on their way to the rendezvous point.

They revisited the same airfield in the evening with 34 Thunderbolts along with the P–47s of the 56th Fighter Group. One Thunderbolt was shot down, whereas they left 24 twin-engine aircraft behind on the airfield as blazing wrecks.

In the afternoon, the heavies of the 8th turned to the "Crossbow" targets in France.

August 4, 1944. The Heinkel Flugzeugwerke in Rostock, burning. (Official USAF Photo)

Saturday, 5 August

The thunder of almost 4600 engines made the houses along its path some 25,000 feet below tremble as 1146 heavy bombers droned on to Germany. The sound was increased and made more sinister by the higher whine of the Merlins of the Mustangs riding alongside the bomberstream when they proceeded to their destinations in the Magdeburg-Brunswick-Hannover region.

The weather was favorable for visual bombing, and a heavy load was dropped on aircraft and armament plants and on oil refineries. Some 100

278

German fighters tried to interfere; 29 of them went down. Fourteen bombers were lost and six American fighters were also shot down. It was the first time that the German jets scored their first real success.

Returning from Magdeburg, the B–17s spotted contrails at about 35,000 feet. To the left and about 3000 feet above the bombers flew three escorting Mustangs of the 352nd Fighter Group. They formed the targets for the Me–163s diving down on them. They neared the Mustangs to point-blank range before they opened fire. After their flashing attack, the jets zoomed up into the clear sky. All three Mustangs caught fire and dived earthwards.

FUSA (First US Army) troops took Mortain. Seven bridges in the interdiction zone between the Seine and the Loire were bombed by the mediums of the 9th Air Force.

Headquarters of the 9th Air Force at Uxbridge in England, along with advanced headquarters in Normandy, were closed at 2400 hours.

Sunday, 6 August

A new headquarters of the 9th Air Force was opened at St. Sauveur-Lindelin at 0001 hours.

Favorable weather conditions over Germany had unfavorable consequences for a diesel works and aircraft engine plant in the suburbs of Berlin, oil refineries at Hamburg and Harburg, and the torpedo plant at Kiel. Ten major targets received a severe mauling from 999 heavy bombers of the 8th Air Force. Twelve fighter groups supported the mission. The Adam Opel works near Berlin received great damage. These kinds of attacks were carried out in a campaign against ordnance and motor-vehicles industries. Among the Fortress groups were the 486th and 487th Bomb Groups, only recently converted from Liberators to Fortresses, and they now flew their first mission with the type.

Seventy-six B–17s of the 95th and 390th Bomb Groups, along with 64 escorting P–51s of the 357th Fighter Group, landed at Russian bases after attacking a Focke Wulf factory at Rahmel, Poland. The fighters had taken off at 0930 hours and landed in Russia at 1700 hours. To ensure that the fighters would not be involved in combat before the rendezvous point at Gdynia, the 55th Fighter Group escorted the bombers on the first leg to this city. In doing so, the fighters made a round-trip of 1595 miles. Over Poland, some fifteen German fighters were met, but all bombers landed safely late in the afternoon in a storm. Southeast of Hamburg where a rendezvous with the bombers had to be made, the 352nd Fighter Group met some thirty Me–109s also heading to the bombers, but with a different intention. The Messerschmitts flew in tight formation at 28,000 feet.

Closing in from behind, Major Preddy, leader of the 352nd, knocked down five Messerschmitts in quick succession, and after a chase, a sixth

279

was sent down. Even when under attack, the Germans doggedly held their tight formation. They demonstrated clearly their inadequate training. Flying in large formations (or "gaggles" as the Americans called them), they stuck to their leader, mostly one of the few veterans.

Major Godfrey, leading a squadron of the 4th Fighter Group, destroyed an Me–410 in the air. He then led his squadron down to strafe an airfield. His aircraft received a hit from flak but by pumping the fuel primer manually for 2½ hours to prevent overheating of the engine, he managed to land his fighter back in England.

Meanwhile, tank columns of Patton's Third Army raced eastwards leaving the protection of his flanks to XIX TAC constantly flying armed-reconnaissance missions and regular tactical flights south of the Loire. As soon as they spotted a movement, the fighter-bombers softened up the threat. Laval was taken.

After an abortive mission in the morning due to weather, the A–20 Havocs of the 416th Bomb Group took off again at 1800 hours to make for the only bridge over the Seine still in use: the bridge at Oissel. Of course, the Germans were well aware of the importance of this bridge and they had it, therefore, surrounded by anti-aircraft guns for miles along the river. And all these guns were in action when the Havocs started their bomb run. In spite of the murderous fire, they placed their bombs right on the target and the bridge was knocked out. One flight even made two passes to make sure that the bombs would not miss. One of these Havocs, carrying the deputy group commander, was shot down. Two other A–20s also went down over the target while six others would never return to their base. Twenty were damaged by flak.

The gun emplacements at Île de Cézembre impeded the advance of VIII Corps to the citadel of St. Malo, while it also commanded the sea approaches to that town. This night, 9th Bomber Command joined in the bombardment by naval and ground artillery. With the aid of flares, the bombs hailed down on the heavily built emplacements and deep-dug shelters.

Monday, 7 August

V-weapon targets were again visited by the heavies of the 8th Air Force along with many targets, including a railroad bridge at Nanteuil.

Shortly after midnight, the Germans launched their counter-offensive as ordered by Hitler, notwithstanding warnings of his generals that this operation invited disaster. As Von Kluge stated: "To the best of my knowledge and conscience the execution of this order means the collapse of the whole Normandy front." Five Panzer divisions were massed under command of

280

SS General Sepp Dietrich of the Fifth Panzer Army, and the plan was to drive west via Mortain to the sea.

The fate of the German offensive was sealed in the first twenty-four hours although the struggle was to last for more than a week. Weather had limited flying the previous days but unfortunately for the Germans, it had now cleared and the protecting mist had vanished. 429 sorties were flown by the 9th Air Force, assisted by the rocket-firing Typhoons of the 2nd Tactical Air Force making 300 sorties. The German progress was halted.

Patton's Army planned to sweep north in the direction of Argentan, while Montgomery ordered an attack in the direction of Falaise. To pave the way, 1000 heavy bombers of the RAF were requested to give a nocturnal hammering on areas flanking the projected assault. Target markers were difficult to see because of weather and smoke, with the result that only 637 bombers attacked.

In the area of Chartres–Le Mans–Mayenne, four formations of American fighters became mixed up in a fight with the Luftwaffe. Two squadrons of the 373rd Fighter Group encountered more than 25 German fighters near Chartres. Five German fighters were shot down while a sixth was shot down by the third squadron of the group. An eight-plane formation of the 362nd Group ran into some sixteen German fighters and the Thunderbolts destroyed three of them. Near Mayenne, twelve 354th Mustangs were engaged with twelve Luftwaffe fighters. The Mustangs claimed five enemy fighters for the loss of two.

Three Mustangs were shot down in attacks on enemy airfields near Chartres. One of them was from the 354th Fighter Group attacking an airfield with twelve other Mustangs in which attack thirteen aircraft were destroyed on the ground. 85–100 freight cars were set afire in an attack on the marshalling yards at Chartres.

In support of the 2nd Armored Division, Thunderbolts of the 366th Group bombed woods in the neighborhood of Brécy, resulting in heavy explosions. Smoke towered to a height of 2000 feet.

Over the Brest Peninsula, XIX TAC, 363rd Group, flew fifteen armored-column cover missions.

The bombers of the 9th Air Force attacked bridges east of Paris. A single group struck the bridges at Corbie, inflicting heavy damage. A bridge at Neuvy-sur-Loire was put out of service. 36 Marauders headed for the bridge at Nogent-sur-Seine. Shortly after crossing the coast, heavy and accurate flak blew three Marauders out of the sky. The rest of the 394th Bomb Group carried on and wrecked the bridge completely. An ammunition dump south of Nantes was attacked by 34 Marauders in the afternoon. They left it blazing.

General Brereton, commander of the 9th Air Force was relieved of his command to form and command the First Airborne Army, a new organization comprising both AAF and RAF airborne and troop carrier units. Major General Hoyt S. Vandenberg was to succeed General Brereton the next day.

Part of the 8th Air Force that landed the day before at Russian bases bombed oil refineries at Trzebinia in Poland and then returned to Russian territory without sustaining losses. The bombing resulted in many explosions and fires. Only a few German fighters made attacks.

Tuesday, 8 August

After the RAF had done its work at night, the 8th Air Force arrived at 1300 hours to continue the bombardment. This time, many precautions had been made for the safety of our troops: smokemarkers fired by the artillery, flares, special aircraft to check the markers and so on.

Only a small formation of Luftwaffe fighters was met near the coast. 678 heavy bombers flew straight and level through very heavy flak on a course parallel to the frontline. Three areas received a concentrated bombing; the fourth assigned area could not be identified. In fact, 492 bombers dropped their loads. The murderous flak took its toll and nine bombers went down and more than 200 were damaged.

Errors occurred again, especially by two twelve-plane groups dropping their bombs within friendly lines. In another case, a formation dropped its bombs automatically when their lead bombardier released his bombs after his plane had been hit by flak. Twenty-five Canadians were killed on the ground and 131 were wounded; moreover, many troops became disorganized.

The enemy may well have had time to recover from the shock after the time interval from the end of the bombing to the start of the assault and the withdrawal of nearly one mile from the bombed zone by the Canadians. Anyhow, the progress was very slow after the ground attack started.

Heavy bombers of the 8th also turn to "Crossbow" targets.

All 8th Air Force planes stationed at Russian bases took off and after bombing Rumanian airfields, they landed in Italy before returning to England on the 12th. Thirty-five enemy planes were sighted, but only one Me–109 came close enough to be shot down.

P–51 Mustangs of the 4th Fighter Group escorted RAF Beaufighters on a shipping reconnaissance mission to Norway. Near the coast, the Mustangs strafed an airfield, but this time they had to pay dearly for their action and three Mustangs were shot down.

Thirty-six medium bombers of the 9th 394th Bomb Group destroyed a railway bridge at Nanteuil. Flak was heavy and every bomber was damaged.

IX TAC made some 532 sorties in the battle area, destroying 47 tanks, 122 M/T, and many other targets including dumps.

By now, all eighteen fighter-bomber groups, the 67th Tactical Reconnaissance Group, and the 10th Photo Reconnaissance Group of the 9th Air Force were operating from bases in Normandy.

Wednesday, 9 August

Three forces involving 824 heavy bombers of the 8th Air Force proceeded to southwestern Germany to maintain their pressure on aircraft and tank plants and oil depots. One force encountered a cloud front towering 28,000 feet high and turned back. The other forces bombed secondary targets with poor results. Elsenborn was one of the towns to receive a load from the 8th.

Medium bombers of the 9th Air Force carried out attacks on railroad bridges. Again, they met very heavy flak.

Thunderbolts flying their column-cover missions were directed to two strafing Luftwaffe fighters. The anti-aircraft guns held their fire when the Thunderbolts came roaring in at 700 feet. One of the German attackers was sent into the ground. A squadron Thunderbolts of the 362nd Fighter Group was operating near Le Mans when it was bounced by twenty-five German fighters. Before the Germans could even break their formation, two of their aircraft were shot down.

The Third Army (TUSA) had started its drive in a northerly direction toward Alençon with the intention of maintaining the northerly plunge to seal off the German forces employed in the counterattack.

Fighters of the 9th, flying in the region Flers-Argentan-LaFerté Macé, discovered a mass of enemy transport on the roads. The 2nd TAC was called on the scene and immediately rocket-firing Typhoons of 83 Group arrived and played havoc among the transport on the crowded roads.

Sixteen Mustangs of the 354th Fighter Group were out on an armed reconnaissance mission in the area of Rheims and Epernay. When they caught sight of an airfield some three miles north of Rheims, the Mustangs dropped down to attack. Their leader, Major Don M. Beerbower, flew a diversion to draw the flak. In this he succeeded, but it cost him his life. Pulling his stricken plane up, he went over the side, but he hit the ground before his chute had a chance to open.

Later in the afternoon, twelve Mustangs of the same group led by Captain Wallace Emmer flew a recon mission near Rouen. Some five miles north of the city and flying at 11,000 feet, Emmer's P–51 received a direct hit and went down in flames. Emmer managed to abandon the aircraft, but he was to die a few days later from his burns.

Thursday, 10 August

8th Air Force heavy bombers attacked "Crossbow" targets. Two escorting Mustangs collided and both went down. One of the pilots survived, but he was killed by the German troops.

Near Mortain, ground asked a formation Thunderbolts to attack fourteen mortar positions north of the town. The Thunderbolts came in and dropped fourteen 500-lb. bombs on the positions, whereafter no more fire was met from these positions. 405th Fighter Group Thunderbolts bombed a thirty-car train near Montargis and strafed twenty-five cars on a siding, causing heavy fires and explosions. A loaded troop train was strafed twice. Scores for the day of this single group included eleven locos and 146 cars.

Artillery and mortar positions near Argentan were silenced by fighter-bombers in support of Patton's drive to that city. Also, a number of tanks was destroyed. Thunderbolts of the 50th Fighter Group wiped out three anti-tank guns and six light guns near Sourdeval while other formations dealt with six smoke-marked positions held by the Germans.

August 10, 1944. Another target of the heavies today was the Gennevilliers oil plant in Paris. After this bombardment and that of June 22, the place was left in ruins. (Official USAF Photo)

Friday, 11 August

Again, the V-weapon targets were hit by the heavy bombers of the 8th, which also turned to Brest. Other formations of heavies headed for targets

284

in western Germany.

German fighters bounced a squadron Thunderbolts of the 406th Fighter Group, but they were scattered in all directions when the Thunderbolts suddenly fired their rockets at them. The same squadron observed a train loaded with sixty tanks east of Montrichard. In a dive-attack, they delivered their bombs on the train. A fuel train was totally destroyed and another damaged.

Fighter-bombers of XIX TAC flew all-day missions in support of TUSA, attacking troop concentrations, trains, motor convoys, trucks, pontoons, and even a railway gun, the latter holding up the 5th Infantry Division, but after the visit of the P–47s, the column could move on.

The advance on Alençon was halted by German armored units. Thunderbolts arrived on the spot and after bombing targets at St. Remy du Plain, during which four tanks were destroyed and the town was strafed, XV Corps was able to move again. Another enemy convoy near Alençon was also bombed and strafed, and many tanks were put out of action.

XV Corps moved through Alençon and continued its drive toward Argentan with the Canadian First Army beginning to close the gap north of Falaise.

August 11, 1944. P–47D Thunderbolt of the 373rd Fighter Group, 9th Air Force, passes Mont St. Michel, Brittany. (Official USAF Photo)

Saturday, 12 August

One of the places in France that received a bombload from the 8th Air Force was Buc, near Paris.

285

The B–17 Fortresses of the 8th which left England on the 6th on their shuttle mission to Russia and afterwards to Italy were now on the way home, delivering a bombload on Toulouse/Francazal Airfield en route. No losses were suffered by this force. One Ju–88 was met underway and shot down.

In a strafing attack, Colonel Thomas Christian, pilot of the 361st Fighter Group Mustang *Lou IV,* was shot down and killed. Three other Mustangs of the same group also failed to return.

9th Air Force aircraft continued their persistent attacks against the Germans in Normandy with fighter-bombers pounding on every tactical objective that came into their sight, while medium bombers made a last assault on the railroad bridge at Oissel. Many vehicles were on the bridge when it was hit and the block thus created caused a traffic jam extending for five miles back. Before the day was out, it would be transformed into a row of blazing wrecks. Six groups of 9th bombers carried out their tasks of blocking the roads west of Falaise and Argentan. 158 bombers were over their target from 1931 until 2051 hours, dropping 237.55 tons of bombs.

August 12, 1944. Col. Christian in his Mustang, *Lou IV,* during an escort mission in July. (Official USAF Photo)

Sunday, 13 August

8th Air Force heavy bombers attacked targets in close support of the advancing Allied ground forces. FUSA took over the responsibility of TUSA to proceed to Falaise and close the gap. 9th TAC and 2nd TAC were now fully occupied with blasting German concentrations.

Thunderbolts of the 366th Fighter Group flying near Carrouges suddenly noticed a suspicious-looking, long row of trees in the middle of a road. They didn't hesitate long and buzzed the column of tank trucks causing explosions and fires for a length of one and a half miles. Near Falaise the German congestion on the roads was only matched by Allied congestion in the skies overhead. At times formations were queued up and had to wait for their turn to come in for the attack. Enemy columns were halted by bombing head and tail, and then the fighter-bombers came in and worked it over systematically and at leisure. American and British planes relieved each other. Massed Allied ground artillery added to the slaughter.

Three squadrons of the 36th Fighter Group flew near Argentan when they spotted a congestion of 800 to 1000 vehicles on the roads. When the Thunderbolts left the scene, some 400 to 500 vehicles were destroyed. They even dropped their belly tanks on the convoys. Several trains were hit.

649 Sorties were flown by the fighters of IX TAC. XIX TAC Aircraft ranged over their assigned area all day, harassing enemy troops. 281 bombers of the 9th dropped 430 tons on the roads in the area of Lisieux, north of Falaise.

Near Le Mans, eight Mustangs of the 363rd Fighter Group attacked 25 German aircraft, eight of which were picked from the sky. Another formation attacked the fleeing aircraft and sent four down for the loss of one Mustang.

Bombers of the 9th Air Force scored a marked success when the first bombs of 397th Group Marauders descended on the marshalling yards at Corbeil. A gigantic explosion was the result when the first flight hit three cars filled with 100 tons of high explosives. A crater was created 360 × 120 feet with a depth of 30 feet. Near these cars stood three trains containing military equipment, two trains with tank cars and seven other trains. Cars of the trains close to the explosion were thrown in an arc 50 to 100 feet beyond the crater. Even nearby factories were completely demolished.

XV Corps reached Argentan, but before it could close the gap the corps was halted by orders from General Omar Bradley. For inexplicable reasons, it was left to the Canadians to close the pocket, notwithstanding the fact that they were still faced with a strong and determined German defense.

Monday, 14 August

The 8th Air Force dispatched its Fortresses on a mission to the synthetic oil plants at Ludwigshafen and the aero-engine and jet plants at Stuttgart and Mannheim. 730 B-17s delivered their loads on the targets with good results. Meanwhile, B-24 Liberators concentrated their efforts on tactical targets in France.

Medium bombers of the 9th Air Force carried out missions to targets in the gap Paris-Orleans, and strong forces attacked the bridges over the Touques and Risle rivers.

Aircraft of IX TAC flew 614 sorties. It was a memorable day for the 405th Fighter Group, XIX TAC. One of its squadrons was strafing a road while covering the 7th Armored Division north of Le Mans when the pilots noticed Germans on the road waving white flags. The squadron buzzed them several times and many hundreds of Germans formed in column and marched to the American lines to surrender with the Thunderbolts flying overhead as escort. Four Thunderbolts of the same group flew cover when they were suddenly bounced by sixteen German fighters coming in under the fighters flying top-cover for the fighter-bombers. In the ensuing battle, four Thunderbolts were shot down, whereas the Germans lost three aircraft.

Both the 9th Air Force and the 2nd Tactical Air Force continued their destruction of the Germans in the Falaise pocket.

Tuesday, 15 August

A large-scale offensive against German airfields in northern France, Belgium, Holland, and western Germany was carried out in a simultaneous attack by the heavies of the 8th Air Force, some 1000 bombers of the RAF, 500 medium bombers, and hundreds of fighter-bombers and fighters. 104 heavy bombers of the 8th, as part of this force, attacked the airfield at Venlo in Holland. A heavy concentration of bombs descended on runways, landing strips, and workshops.

Other formations of the 8th proceeded to Wiesbaden and it was near Trier that this force was jumped by some 24 FW–190s bearing down from the clouds. In this swift action, nine B–17s of the low 303rd Bomb Group were shot down. Near Meppel, four Liberators of a high formation were sent earthwards by cannonfire of a staffel of Me–109s. The Liberator gunners claimed nine Messerschmitts.

Three groups of Thunderbolts and Mustangs escorted 200 Lancasters and Halifaxes of the RAF.

The enemy airbase at Bretigny was the target for the fighters of the 373rd Group. Just as one of its formations started the attack, it was bounced by an equal number of German fighters. But the aggressive spirit of the Germans was not at the same degree as their skill and five of them were shot down.

The task of close support and bombing the enemy close to the front lines became more and more difficult because of the very deep and narrow penetrations into enemy territory with enemy pockets of resistance in many cases left behind. The attacking of their own troops had become a hazard with which the pilots had to cope. And today they made a special error as Thunderbolts of the 356th Fighter Group, 8th Air Force, strafed the headquarters of the 9th Air Force near Laval. One of the Thunderbolts was shot down.

On request of the 3rd Armored Division, the town of Ranes was twice bombed by P–47s of the 404th Group after elements of the 1st SS Panzer Division had reached the area.

When medium bombers were out to attack the bridges over the Risle they were recalled. The Marauders bombed the bridge at Avers-sur-Oise and they also delivered a load on the marshalling yards at Compiègne.

Chartres was taken by TUSA. American troops of the Seventh Army landed in southern France. '

Wednesday, 16 August

Oil refineries at Zeitz, Rositz, Böhlen, and Magdeburg, and aircraft plants at Halle, Schkeuditz, Dessau, Köthen, and Magdeburg were the objectives for 1090 heavy bombers of the 8th with their full fighter escort. The sky was blue and clear which enabled the bombers to blast their targets with good results. After the bombardments of 28 May, photoreconnaissance had revealed that the power station was once more in use so that a renewed visit to Zeitz was fully justified.

However, the Stars and Stripes were not the only colors in the sky, and 200 German fighters were ready to intercept the bomberstream. In the fierce air battles, twenty-four heavy bombers went down, though the German losses were very heavy, too.

South of Hannover, P–51s of the 355th Fighter Group ran into a batch of Me–109s and in the engagement twelve Messerschmitts were shot down for the loss of only one Mustang. Six Me–163 rocket-propelled fighters appeared in the vicinity of Leipzig, and this time they were intended not only to show their superiority as on July 18th, but to use it to full advantage as well. Passes were made both at the Fortresses and at the Mustangs of the 359th Fighter Group. One of the Me–163s overshot a crippled B–17 and was caught by a Mustang which could place several hits. The Messerschmitt dived to safety with the Mustang in hot pursuit. But then the Mustang pilot spotted another Me–163 some 5000 feet below. This Messerschmitt had probably consumed its fuel, and the Mustang caught it inside a turn. A long burst sent the Me–163 into the ground, the first Me—163 to be shot down by the AAF.

Again a clear demonstration was given that many German pilots lacked sufficient training. This time the veteran 354th Fighter Group of the 9th Air Force opened the melee as a squadron of eight Mustangs encountered

289

seventy bombed-up FW–190s. Without hesitation, the P–51s attacked. Two Mustangs went down, but they picked off an equal number of Focke Wulfs and they dispersed the formation.

In another encounter, a squadron of like size of the same group took on twenty German fighters over Maintenon. They did not notice some sixty German fighters flying high cover until they dived on the German formation below. That moment, the German fighters swooped down from the clouds and for the next fifteen minutes a wild fight raged from 11,000 feet to the deck. But numbers coupled with the element of surprise were not sufficient to compensate for lack of experience, and eleven Luftwaffe fighters were shot down for two P–51s.

B–26 Marauders made a concentrated attack on the bridges over the rivers Touques and Risle.

Thursday, 17 August

A gap still remained in the Falaise pocket through which a German army desperately tried to escape. As a fighter pilot reported upon return from the battlefield: "The whole goddam German army is moving through the gap."

Using main roads proved to be fatal to the Germans, and secondary roads were littered with the debris of all kinds of vehicles. General Bayerlein, who organized the Kampfgruppe Panzer Lehr from remnants of his division, got a special taste of the precarious situation when he looked out of a slit trench in which he had sought safety and, as he told afterwards, he was certain that a low-swooping pilot stared straight at him through the plexiglass.

A new attack on the bridges over the Touques and Risle rivers was carried out by the mediums of the 9th in order to restrain the enemy's retreat.

St. Malo was captured. Thirty-five P–38 Lightnings of the 370th Fighter Group, on their way to bomb the citadel, diverted their attack after delivering two napalm bombs on the citadel. They went to the Île de Cézembre where they dropped the rest of their napalm bombs.

Lightnings of the 474th Group attacked pinpoint targets in a Gestapo headquarters near Châteauroux. Despite the overcast, considerable damage was inflicted.

The first rocket-equipped Thunderbolt of the 8th Air Force launched an attack on rolling stock at Braine-le-Compte. The pilot was Lt. Col David Schilling of the 56th Fighter Group. He was not very pleased with the results, and like him the pilots were of the opinion that they could do more with their guns and bombs than with the rockets in those large tubes which had a detrimental effect upon the performance of the aircraft.

290

Friday, 18 August

8th Air Force Liberators flew a mission to the airfield at Nancy/Essey. Lightnings of the 479th Fighter Group flew escort and their leader was Hubert Zemke who left his command of the 56th Group to lead this group, which would soon convert to the P–51. After the B–24s had bombed, Zemke took two flights down to strafe part of the airfield that had escaped the bombing. Spotting a large number of He–111s, he called the other aircraft of the group down and, in a well-conducted strafing attack, at least forty Heinkels were wrecked and many were damaged.

Fortresses of the 8th attacked a railroad bridge over the Meuse at Huy in Belgium as part of a general assault on tactical targets in France and Belgium.

Two Me–109s were shot down by fighters of the 357th Group flying a patrol near Paris. One Focke Wulf was shot up on Rosières-en-Santerre Airfield. Mustangs of the 4th Fighter Group were clobbering the airfield at Beauvais when all of a sudden 50–60 German fighters swooped down on them and destroyed nine P–51s.

Some twenty miles west of Soissons, one P–51 of the 355th Group was hit in the engine and the pilot made a belly-landing in a large hayfield. A Mustang, piloted by 2nd Lt. Royce Priest, made a landing near the bellied-in P–51. A German lorry appeared, but the other Mustangs circling the field took care of it. Priest, sitting on the lap of the other pilot, gave full throttle and after clearing a haystick at the boundary by six inches, both pilots returned to their base.

The German withdrawal across the Seine was in full progress and they succeeded in moving a considerable mass of men to the other side using all kinds of devices. All roads leading to the Seine were crowded, and pilots of the 9th every day claimed a mounting number of destroyed transport.

Seventeen IX TAC formations of Thunderbolts and Lightnings bore down on the Germans. Using their Thunderbolts as gun platforms, the pilots poured a concentrated stream of projectiles from their eight 50-mm. guns into barges and ferries. A pontoon near Les Andelys was blasted and 58 barges were destroyed.

Saturday, 19 August

The 8th Air Force attacked "Crossbow" targets on a limited scale. The tonnage dropped was less than 200, none of which was dropped on launching sites.

The Falaise pocket was closed as patrols of the 90th US Infantry Division met patrols of the Polish Armored Division operating with the Canadians.

291

Thunderbolts of the 405th Fighter Group destroyed barges in the Seine near Melun, where TUSA was nearing the river.

An American column near Dreux was in real trouble as it was the target of eighteen German divebombers. Immediately, assistance was called upon, and eight Thunderbolts of the 371st Group raced to the scene. They knocked down two of the enemy and the column could proceed undisturbed.

A squadron P-47s of the 406th Group was occupied with strafing an airfield near Pontoise when they were jumped by Luftwaffe fighters. Immediately, another squadron of Thunderbolts came to the aid; however, the Germans received considerable reinforcements as well. Five P-47s and an equal number of German fighters went down in the air combat. The third squadron of the same fighter group also became fully occupied when they were intercepted by a superior enemy fighter force in the vicinity of Paris. The trouble for the Americans was complete for they ran out of ammunition. The Thunderbolts dived for the deck and, owing to the great skill of the pilots, they succeeded, after hair-raising manoeuvering, in having two German planes crash. One P-47 failed to return.

Sunday, 20 August

The Falaise pocket was now securely closed. Of the 100,000 Germans trapped in the pocket, 10,000 were dead on the battlefield, 50,000 men were taken prisoner, and 40,000 had managed to escape, only to find a new trap when they reached the Seine.

TUSA crossed the Seine today at Mantes-Gassicourt.

Medium bombers of the 9th set course to Rouen where they bombed targets hidden in the forested bends of the Seine.

A squadron of the 362nd Fighter Group was out on an armed-reconnaissance flight in the afternoon and the fighters headed in the direction of Paris. On the way from Etampes to Paris, the eight Thunderbolts shot up two trucks. Nearing Paris, they ran into thirty-two Me-109s and FW-190s. With the first burst from the eight guns of one of the Thunderbolts, an Me-109 was hit and the fighter flew straight into his leader. The first two German aircraft dived into the ground. Another two German fighters fell to the guns of Lt. Joseph Z. Matte's Thunderbolt, giving him four kills for this single combat. In all, six German aircraft were shot down while two P-47s were lost.

A squadron of the same group was flying cover when they were vectored to a tank target by the 7th Armored Division. Taking a closer look at the target, the pilots spotted six well-camouflaged Panzers. Being very close to their own forces, the squadron leader stayed overhead and directed his pilots into the attack. When the last Thunderbolts pulled up, the Panzers were wrecked.

Other fighter-bombers of XIX TAC bombed and strafed ferries, tanks, machinegun nests, troop concentrations, and many other targets in support of the ground forces.

IX TAC fighter-bombers flew seven squadron-strength missions over the Seine, destroying thirteen barges. Among many other targets, at least 75 motor transport were bombed and strafed when they were revealed as military vehicles despite their "Red Cross" markings. They were parked near a ferry terminal. Many of them exploded.

Tuesday, 22 August

Tactical air operations continued after bad weather had made such operations impossible on the previous day. Most activity was in the Seine area.

An urgent call from ground forces that Me–109s were strafing was received by a flight of Thunderbolts, but when they arrived in the area of Vernon the Germans had left. One German aircraft was met and consequently destroyed in the area of Le Mans. More Luftwaffe aircraft were encountered by a flight over Mantes-Gassicourt where they mixed it up with twenty planes, of which two were shot down.

IX TAC aircraft attacked enemy airfields at Laon/Athies, Laon/Chambry, Juvincourt, Clastres, and Roye. In an air combat over Roye Airfield, nine German fighters were shot down while another ten aircraft were destroyed on the ground.

Sixteen P–51 Mustangs of the 354th Group were just in time to see enemy aircraft taking off from an airfield at Epernay. The Mustangs swooped down and eight were destroyed.

Thunderbolts of the 358th Group encountered twenty Me–109s when they flew a ground-cover mission. The Thunderbolts claimed four Messerschmitts. One P–47 was lost. The engagement took place near Chartres.

Germans were busy with the construction of a wooden bridge over the Seine when they were roughly disturbed in their job by the fighter-bombers partly demolishing it.

P–38 Lightnings of the 474th Fighter Group attacked a fuel dump. They were led by a Droop Snoot P–38 with a bombardier. It was the first of such flights undertaken by the 9th Air Force.

Wednesday, 23 August

Fighter-bombers of XIX TAC struck gun emplacements at Île de Cézembre.

Early in the day, P–38 Lightnings discovered tremendous quantities of German equipment and materiel massed along the Seine. All day long, the Lightnings of the 474th Fighter Group made sorties against this wealth of equipment. Heavy flak was met, especially near two bridges still partly in use. But at the end of the day, both bridges were destroyed and, along with many vehicles, two barges and a supply dump were either destroyed or damaged.

Thursday, 24 August

More than 1300 heavy bombers crossed the North Sea as they headed their way to the synthetic oil plants at Merseburg-Leuna, Ruhland, Brüx, Misburg, and Freital, and to the aircraft and ordnance plants in Brunswick and Hannover. Goslar and Kölleda were also bombed. This attack was coordinated with a mission of the 15th Air Force, sending 600 bombers to oil refineries in Germany and Czechoslovakia. Fighter opposition was slighter than had been anticipated and was mainly ineffective, though not for one bomber out of a formation heading for Weimar. It received a hit from the fire of a single jet and exploded in midair.

P–51 Mustangs of the 357th Fighter Group crossed the coast at Zandvoort on their way to central Germany. South of Brunswick, six Me–109s were sighted. Four managed to escape, but the other two were caught and sent down.

While strafing an airfield and shooting up Ju–52 transports, the 4th Fighter Group lost one of its skilled leaders, Major John Godfrey, probably shot down by flak. He was taken prisoner.

An armed trawler was damaged by Mustangs of the 359th Fighter Group.

Friday, 25 August

1191 heavy bombers of the 8th Air Force set out again on the long journey to the aircraft plants and component factories at Rostock, Neubrandenburg, Lübeck, Schwerin, and Wismar, and to the synthetic oil plant at Pölitz. Also the experimental establishments at Peenemünde and Rechlin received a bombload. From this force, one Fortress and two Mustangs landed in Sweden.

The plant at Pölitz was heavily damaged just after it had resumed operation after the bombing in June. Also, the airfield and seaplane base at Rechlin was well covered with bombs from the 4th Combat Wing.

Paris was liberated. A task force from the 9th signal personnel took hold of the Eiffel Tower to have it serve as a relay link in the 9th Air Force radio network.

On recommendation of Intelligence, which was able to distinguish from the chatter between German pilots and ground controllers when the time was opportune to visit the German airfields, bases in the St. Quentin-Laon area were selected as the promising targets. Several missions were flown by the Lightnings of the 367th and 474th Fighter Group. And there were plenty of German fighters.

After the P–38s of the 367th Group had divebombed and strafed the airfields at Clastres, Peronne, and Rosières, they ran into some fifty enemy fighters and a violent air battle developed. When, after 40 minutes, the battle was over, eight P–38s were left on the fields below. However, the Americans claimed twenty German aircraft destroyed. Much the same experience was the 474th Fighter Group's, working over the airfields at Tergnier, Laon-Chambry, and Herpy. Eleven Lightnings went down, but the group claimed twenty-one German fighters shot down.

Thunderbolts of the 365th Group proceeded to the airfields near Cognac and Dijon. It was known that the Germans had many Ju–88s on those fields, using them for air evacuation. After persistent strafing attacks, thirty-three German aircraft were transformed into scrap; thirty of them were Ju–88s.

P–51 Mustangs of the 354th Fighter Group meanwhile disregarded the guns around the airfields at Beauvais and Rheims and, after several strafing attacks, the pilots claimed thirteen aircraft on the ground. One squadron became engaged in a fight with some 25 FW–190s heading for the front. Ten Focke Wulfs were picked off.

In the afternoon, a squadron of the same group had an engagement with the Luftwaffe fighters east of Paris, while at the same time a second squadron, out on a sweep east of Rheims, bounced fifteen enemy fighters, but they were in turn attacked by another thirty German aircraft. The third squadron did not meet a German plane on both missions in the morning and afternoon. Six Mustangs were lost by the group, claiming 36 victories against a numerically superior enemy.

When P–47 Thunderbolts appeared over the partly repaired rail bridge at Oissel, the pilots looked at a long row of vehicles: trucks going bumper to bumper across it. The 368th Group P–47s peeled off and swooped down. When the last Thunderbolt climbed away from the target, the bridge had received its final blow. The row of vehicles blocked by the demolished bridge extended for many miles into the countryside.

The total claims of destroyed aircraft by IX and XIX TAC today amounted to 77 in the air and 46 on the ground.

278 B–26 Marauders from nine groups attacked the fortifications at Brest. VIII Corps opened the assault on the city.

Saturday, 26 August

The I. G. Farbenindustrie oil-chemical complex at Ludwigshafen was bombed by 8th Air Force heavies, but the results were poor. Two minor oil refineries near the Dutch border were bombed with more success, one of them at Gelsenkirchen.

Apart from this mission, heavy bombers of the 8th turned to nine targets on the Brittany peninsula where they attacked coastal installations which prevented the occupation of the city. Two Fortresses were lost in a mid-air collision over England.

Mediums of the 9th headed for the Seine where they would attack troops hidden in the wooded bends near Rouen. They also looked for enemy dumps east of the river.

Fighter-bombers continued their attacks on enemy airfields and on many other tactical targets. On one of these patrols, Mustangs of the 354th Fighter Group flew to the area of Rheims where they found many FW–190s refuelling on the airfield at Beauvais. The Mustangs came down to twenty feet above the ground and made two passes over the field, clobbering the Focke Wulfs. When they pulled off, fifteen German aircraft were shot up.

Sunday, 27 August

The 8th Air Force had planned a big assault on Berlin with 1202 heavy bombers, but it had to be cancelled because of high clouds on the route. Bombs were dropped on Heligoland.

9th Bomber Command dispatched its aircraft against German troop concentrations in the woods along the Seine near Rouen, and against some dumps east of the river. As part of the "Crossbow" campaign, the mediums dropped 47 tons of bombs on an electrical installation near Boulogne.

Eight P–47s of the 404th Group flew in the Coulommiers area looking for targets. Top-cover was provided by eight Thunderbolts of the same group, flying at 12,000 feet. Suddenly, some twenty Me–109s and FW–190s jumped the low formation and all four Thunderbolts of the second flight were shot down. In the ferocious fight that ensued eight German fighters were downed.

Meanwhile, the commander of the 404th, Colonel McColpin, was out flying on his own when he heard the battle over the radio. He immediately shoveled some coal to the fire and turned in the direction of the battle. However, he ran into four FW–190s approaching from his right. The Focke Wulfs split into pairs when he turned into them, with one flight passing over him and attacking from the left. In whatever direction he pulled his Thunderbolt, he was greeted with a hail of fire. Only by reducing his speed and by great skill did he manage to maintain a tight turn until they flew in a five-plane lufberry.

Colonel McColpin kept his Thunderbolt right on the deck, gaining gradually on the Focke Wulfs in their tight circles. Making use of the treetops, he made a sharp bank, just skimming between two rows of trees. The Focke Wulf directly behind him failed to make it between the trees and crashed into the ground. McColpin then tightened his turn and reduced speed to 120 mph, at the edge of stalling. Ten more circles and he was almost on the tail of the last Focke Wulf when a second German fighter stalled and crashed. Then, all of a sudden, the Focke Wulf in front of the P–47, perhaps caught in the prop wash of the other German fighter, did a snap roll, flipped on its back, and slammed into the ground. The last German fighter gave up and disappeared, so when McColpin landed at his base, he had destroyed three enemy aircraft without firing a shot.

Twelve Thunderbolts operated in coordination with heavy artillery when they silenced one of the batteries of the Brest fortress.

A heavy daylight attack on the oil plant at Homburg was this time carried out by RAF Bomber Command, despatching 200 Halifaxes with a fighter escort of 200 Spitfires. Only one Me-110 was sighted, and no losses were sustained. From now on, the RAF would send its bombers more often to German towns in daylight since, at this stage of the war, the daylight raids were evidently less expensive than nightraids.

Monday, 28 August

The rapid advance in France made it extremely difficult to provide the front armies with the necessary supplies, and although C–47s established a kind of air bridge, it could not possibly fulfill the demands. Therefore, B–24s of the 492nd Bomb Group and some 200 Liberators of the 2nd Division were diverted to the transport role.

During the morning, forty–two Thunderbolts of the 353rd Fighter Group bombed and strafed ground targets in the area of Trier. They encountered a variety of enemy aircraft, and two He–111s, a Ju–88, and two Fi–156s were shot down. Another He–111 was destroyed by strafing an airfield.

The group flew a second mission in the afternoon with forty-two P–47s. Operating in the area of Mons, they met a Me–410, a Me–109, and a Me–110 successively. Two Me–410s were wrecked on the ground. Mustangs of the 8th Air Force were also out on strafing missions. Mediums of the 9th turned again to the dumps east of the Seine.

Weather hampered operations of XIX TAC. Yet Thunderbolts of the

405th Fighter Group carried out a very successful attack on the marshalling yards at Neufchâteau, south of Toul. They destroyed three locomotives, while a train loaded with Ju–88 fuselages was strafed.

Tuesday, 29 August

Rheims was taken by TUSA.

The German dumps east of the Seine were again subjected to an attack by medium bombers of the 9th.

Early in the morning, 44 Thunderbolts crossed the Belgian coast at an altitude of 9,000 to 14,000 feet to carry out a bombing and strafing mission in their assigned area. Northeast of Brussels, the P–47s arrived over an airfield where at least thirty-five aircraft were spotted. One after the other, the Thunderbolts peeled off and started their strafing run. Eighteen aircraft were shot up; one exploded at the moment that a Thunderbolt passed overhead. The jug caught fire and crashlanded. A second Thunderbolt recieved a direct hit from flak when they strafed an airfield near Chièvres and the plane blew up. Two aircraft were destroyed on the ground.

In the evening, Thunderbolts of the 78th Fighter Group, 8th Air Force, attacked ground targets at Termonde near Brussels. Eight Thunderbolts of the same group flew top-cover. Suddenly, they spotted an aircraft flying very low and the pilots at first mistook it for a B–26. Noticing the speed of the aircraft, they realized that it could not be a Marauder and one of the P–47s dived from 11,000 feet to chase the aircraft. Catching up with it, the pilot soon recognized it as a new twin-engined jet. The jet pilot saw the Thunderbolt gaining on him and tried to take evasive action. Just before the P–47 pilot pressed the gun button, the jet crashed in a field. The first Me–262 was destroyed in action.

Wednesday, 30 August

There was no strategic bombing on the three previous days. However, today 637 B–17 Fortresses were back on the old track to the U-boat and shipyard targets at Kiel. And the results they achieved here were better than at Bremen where a load was delivered on the aircraft and motor plants.

The 8th Air Force heavies made their last contribution in the "Crossbow" offensive and flew 173 sorties in which they dropped 454.5 tons of bombs on the V-weapon targets. The 8th made 89 missions against the "Crossbow" targets this month.

Medium bombers of the 9th renewed their visits to the enemy dumps east of the Seine.

298

Thursday, 31 August

The combined assault against Île de Cézembre started. 255 B–26 Marauders dropped 465 tons of bombs and a heavy attack was launched by RAF Lancasters. Meanwhile *H.M.S. Warspite* poured its 15-inch armor-piercing shells into the fortress. Ground artillery joined in the bombardment, and the icing of the cake was provided by 33 P–38 Lightnings of the 370th Fighter Group, dropping napalm bombs on the target.

TUSA crossed the Meuse at Commercy and St. Mihiel. The commanding general of the German Seventh Army was taken prisoner by the British when they entered Amiens.

Mediums of the 9th paid their daily visit to the dumps east of the Seine.

This month 6554 medium and light bombers of the 9th made attacks, dropping 10,470 tons of bombs at a cost of thirty-four bombers. IX TAC flew 12,305 sorties in 378 missions, losing 123 aircraft. XIX TAC made 12,292 sorties and lost 114 aircraft.

The two night fighter squadrons, the 422nd and the 425th, flew some nightly defensive operations with the Northrop P–61 Black Widow during which operations the 422nd Squadron claimed the destruction of three bombers.

August, 1944—date approximate. Havocs of the 410th Bomb Group in formation. (Photo from *Air Combat 1939–1945*)

299

August, 1944—date approximate. Havocs of the 410th Bomb Group in formation. (Photo from *Air Combat 1939–1945*)

This month, and the first thirteen days continuously, RAF Bomber Command flew 5745 heavy bomber sorties against "Crossbow" targets, dropping 25,328.8 tons of bombs, which meant 27.7 percent of the total number of sorties and 30.8 percent of the tonnage of bombs dropped during the month. Yet it remained doubtful if all this effort did diminish the German V-operations and it was more probable that it could be regarded as having failed to achieve the objectives.

This night, 603 heavy bombers of the RAF dropped 240.7 tons of bombs on targets which were thought to be connected with the V-2 production. Since the 12th of June, 6716 missiles were plotted. Modified launching sites, as was obvious by then, could be built faster by the Germans than they could be destroyed by Allied air power.

9

SEPTEMBER

Friday, 1 September

Kent had the dubious honor of receiving the last V–1 fired from a launching site in France.

Heavy bombers of the 8th attacked targets in the area of Paris.

138 Thunderbolts of the 8th Air Force, representing all of its four groups still equipped with the type, shot up all that moved on road or rail between Brussels and Antwerp, and before the day was out they had reaped a rich harvest. Thunderbolts of the same force bombed and strafed ground targets in the Liège and Metz areas.

Medium bombers of the 9th Air Force set out with 115 aircraft to bomb Brest to contribute in the daily attacks of the fighter-bombers.

XIX TAC flew several missions in a further effort to immobilize German troops. One of the groups, the 36th Fighter Group, started its operations against enemy convoys at 0645 hours. They attacked three columns during the day and their claims amounted to over 500 vehicles.

September 1, 1944. Bombs dropped by Marauders and Havocs burst on the bridge connecting the peninsula with the mainland of Brest. (Official USAF Photo)

The heavy bombers of the 8th had been dispatched to Frankfurt but after crossing enemy territory, the bombers were recalled due to bad weather.

Saturday, 2 September

Île de Cézembre surrendered. Most probably this surrender was more induced by shortage of water than by bombed-out pillboxes.
TUSA crossed the Meuse at Verdun.

Sunday, 3 September

Weather conditions continued to be very unfavorable for 8th Air Force operations during the first days of September. However, today, 325 B–17 Fortresses managed to get through to Ludwigshafen. They achieved only moderate results when they delivered their load on the synthetic oil plant. Another attempt to bomb the Germans out of Brest was made by heavy bombardment units attacking sixteen coastal batteries. Thunderbolts of the 8th strafed and bombed rail and road targets in the Aachen area.

A mass of retreating Germans was caught between the converging VII and XIX Corps at Mons. Troops of some twenty enemy divisions were trapped along a distance from Mons extending to Compiègne. The 9th Air Force took a very heavy toll of the troops and vehicles, and as the pocket ceased to exist, over 25,000 Germans were made prisoners of war. The largest amount of all kinds of vehicles was destroyed in a single day with the 368th Fighter Group's having a prominent part in the destruction.

Thunderbolts of the 405th Fighter Group operated east of TUSA in the Saarbrücken-Strasbourg-Basle area, where three of its squadrons harassed German troops and transportation.

Monday, 4 September

The British Second Army liberated Brussels and reached Antwerp.

Tuesday, 5 September

Ludwigshafen was bombed again, and this time the results achieved by the 277 Fortresses were better than after the visit to the synthetic oil plant on the 3rd. 200 Fortresses of the 3rd Division dropped 1000-lb. bombs and incendiaries on the Daimler-Benz aero-engine plant at Stuttgart. No enemy fighters were encountered, but the flak was heavy and accurate. One Fort diverted to Switzerland. Other formations turned to Karlsruhe.

While escorting the heavy bombers to the Stuttgart area, 55th Fighter Group Mustangs encountered a flock of primary trainers. Seventeen of them were shot down. Another engagement took place when the Mustangs bounced three Me–109s, one of which was shot down while the other two could make a landing although they were badly shot up. But there was not much jubilation about the claims, when it was learned that the Messerschmitts were Swiss.

Meanwhile, 8th Fighter Command continued to harass German airfields, many of them being surprisingly poorly defended. In two missions to airfields in the Hanau and Gieszen areas, the 56th and 479th Fighter Groups claimed 143 German aircraft destroyed and 90 damaged. Four P–47s of the 56th Group were shot down, while another three made a crashlanding in France. One Thunderbolt of the 479th Group was shot down; another one made a crashlanding in France.

An 8th Air Force reconnaissance Spitfire XI, flying over Stuttgart, was suddenly hit by cannonshells. The engine caught fire. At the same moment, an Me–262 passed, climbing away at high speed. Probably this Spitfire was the first victim of the new jets.

9th Air Force fighter-bombers were in strength over Brest: twelve groups out of the total of eighteen groups flew 544 sorties while 310 B–26 Marauders delivered their bombs on the German strongpoints. B–26 Marauders of the 391st Bomb Group dropped leaflets over Ostende, Dunkirk, Calais, Boulogne, and many other towns.

Every day, the P–51s of the 10th Photo Reconnaissance Group were out to direct artillery fire.

British troops entered Antwerp and reached Ghent.

September 5, 1944. A B–17 of the 452nd Bomb Group flies through a curtain of flak during the bomb run. With its bomb doors open, the Fortress was about to release its load on Ludwigshafen. (Official USAF Photo)

Wednesday, 6 September

Forty-six P–47 Thunderbolts of the 353rd Fighter Group carried out fighter sweeps and strafing attacks in the area of Arnhem in the afternoon.

9th Air Force Thunderbolts of the 48th Fighter Group dropped leaflets in the Maastricht-Tongeren area.

A new type of aircraft joined the Marauders of the 9th in their attack on Brest. It was the A–26 Douglas Invader, of which eighteen were attached to the 386th Bomb Group. All told, 545 bombers dropped on the fortifications.

Thursday, 7 September

FUSA entered Sédan, while TUSA began its attack on the Metz forts. Antwerp was taken by the British Second Army.

Thirty-six P–47 Thunderbolts of the 406th Fighter Group took off at 1505 hours and headed for the Châteauroux area where a large enemy convoy was reported. Racing to the spot, the Thunderbolts found the road from Châteauroux to Issoudon cramped with all kinds of vehicles, horse-drawn and armored vehicles, artillery and troops.

The P–47s came in on the deck and worked it over, up and down, with bombs, rockets, and gunfire. The road became blocked with the remnants of vehicles for a distance of at least fifteen miles. The Thunderbolts only turned back to refuel and to rearm, and then they hurried back to continue their mauling. Even when rain started to fall and the return flight threatened to be in darkness, the P–47s remained over the convoy and went on with their job as long as possible. The remnants of the column were taken prisoner by the French.

Two days earlier, the British Chiefs of Staff had agreed that all bombings against "Crossbow" targets should cease, convinced that "there should shortly be no further danger." And today Duncan Sandys of the War Cabinet announced to the press that the "Battle of London" was over, except "possibly . . . a few last shots." Again, history was to repeat itself, and this time they had only to wait till the next day to see the proof.

Friday, 8 September

The V–2, a twelve-ton rocket missile was fired for the first time in combat. Traveling at more than five times the speed of sound, the rocket descended without making any noise on its target, a suburb of Paris. A few hours later, at dinnertime in the early evening, the first one to strike England exploded at Chiswick, and only six seconds later the next one came

304

down at Parndon Wood, Epping. Before the end of hostilities, another 14,000 were fired against targets in England and on the continent (against approximately 16,000 V–1s).

The scientific achievement apparent in the V–2 was much more spectacular than its military value. It even caused less blast damage than the much cheaper and more primitive V–1 (see 13 June).

The 8th Air Force dispatched more than a thousand heavy bombers against the oil-chemical works at Ludwigshafen, and against factories at Mainz involved in armored vehicle and tank production. Fighters of the 8th escorted the bombers and they also carried out bombing and strafing missions. One of the many fighter groups in action was the 353rd Group, operating in the area of Koblenz with forty-three Thunderbolts.

Two Focke Wulfs were shot down and a third FW–190 was damaged by Captain King of the 359th Fighter Group. One pilot of the same group lost the canopy and side panels of his Mustang in a screaming dive behind a Messerschmitt from 32,000 to 10,000 feet. The Messerschmitt was shot down.

In spite of heavy German resistance, TUSA started to force a crossing over the Moselle between Metz and Pont-à-Mousson.

Saturday, 9 September

When the bombers of the 8th Air Force approached their target, the Rheinmetall Borsig arsenal at Düsseldorf, they ran into one of the deadliest flak-barrages the crews had ever met. Especially the 390th Bomb Group was the victim of this concentrated mass of fire, and only one minute before release point, three Fortresses, out of a formation of eleven aircraft, exploded immediately. One minute later, another Fort blew up. Two other bombers peeled off and were last seen spinning into the undercast. The bombs were scattered wide of the target.

Ludwigshafen was again the target for a concentrated attack.

Sunday, 10 September

1145 heavy bombers of the 8th Air Force set out on a mission to a variety of targets in the cities of Nürnberg, Gaggenau, Sindelfingen, and Stuttgart. The bombers were heavily escorted by the fighters of the 8th.

Two bombers of the force heading for Gaggenau collided when one bomber suddenly pulled up and cut the Fortress flying overhead in half just to the rear of the radio compartment. Only two men of this bomber escaped, the others being trapped in the wreckage. Both parts spun down to crash near St. Quentin. The bomber that caused the crash was still airwor-

305

thy and it even returned to base. Yet three men had bailed out in the assumption that this bomber was also doomed.

In another case, a bomber was severely hit by flak over Gaggenau. After continuing its flight for some time, the pilot ordered his crew to bail out. Unknown to him, the alarm bell installation was also shot out, and none of the men in the aft section was aware of the fact that they were alone in the aircraft. Only when the aircraft started to perform extraordinary manoeuverings did the top-turret gunner, at that time in the waist of the aircraft due oxygen trouble and alarmed by this strange pilotage, make his way forward to find the cockpit empty. He hoisted himself into the co-pilot's seat and, despite one engine on fire, he flew the plane for one hour and a half until the crew concluded that they might be well over France (which, in fact, they were) and they all bailed out.

Returning from escort, the fighters strafed targets of opportunity near Kassel and many other places.

Luxembourg was liberated by FUSA. The Germans launched repeated counterattacks when TUSA crossed the Moselle between Metz and Pont-à-Mousson. The crossing was supported by strong fighter-bomber cover, hitting targets immediately in front of the American forces. One unit of the 406th Fighter Group, XIX TAC, attacked a concentration of fifteen tanks in the town of Array. The Thunderbolts made forty individual passes and all fifteen tanks were put out of action.

An ammunition dump near Amanvillers was hit by twenty bombs dropped by fighter-bombers while, on request of ground forces, enemy troops in the same region were strafed. A fortification, tanks, trucks, and a large variety of other targets received the full attention of the P–47s.

One enemy aircraft was shot down by Mustangs of the 354th Fighter Group during a sweep in the Saarbrücken area.

The 404th Fighter Group, IX TAC, distinguished itself by its achievements on three armed-reconnaissance missions in support of ground forces in the Aachen area, destroying a large number of rolling stock, a factory, communication centers, and many more targets they came across.

A strong garrison in several strongpoints covered by thick woods was defending the region in the western outskirts of Nancy. Heavy attacks against these strongpoints were carried out by B–26 Marauders and A–20 Havocs.

Night-intruder missions were flown by P–38 Lightnings to interfere with the enemy's nocturnal movements.

Monday, 11 September

It promised to become an eventful mission when 1131 heavy bombers, with all of the 8th Air Force fighter groups, were heading into Germany to

306

deliver a full-scale attack on the synthetic oil plants at Ruhland, Böhlen, Brüx, Merseburg-Leuna, Lützkendorf, Misburg, and Magdeburg, a military vehicle plant at Chemnitz, engine works at Hannover, and an ordnance depot at Magdeburg.

The German Air Force rose in great strength to meet the attacking forces. In fact, the Germans hadn't sent so many fighters into the air since 28 May, and the American crews counted some 400 enemy aircraft. Large numbers of them appeared along the penetration route at the Rhine and in the target area near Leipzig. The escorting fighters were soon entangled in violent dogfights. 125 German fighters broke through the protective fighter screen and within five minutes they sent down eleven heavy bombers out of a lagging low group near Annaberg. A twelfth bomber of the same ill-fated 100th Group crashlanded in France.

The 92nd Bomb Group also received a severe blow and lost eight B–17s. Part of the 339th Fighter Group came to the rescue of the 100th, and in the fierce battle they knocked down fifteen Luftwaffe fighters. Numerous battles raged from 25,000 feet to the deck. The 55th and the 359th Fighter Groups claimed respectively 28 and 26 enemy fighters, and the 4th Group claimed eleven German fighters shot down near Halle. The Germans paid dearly for their victory over twenty bombers and fifteen Mustangs. They lost ninety-seven fighters.

Several American fighters made emergency landings in France. One Mustang was reported to be shot down by an Me–262, although most of the jets refused to do combat as soon as the P–51s turned into them. The 25 German jets merely kept zooming about at a terrific speed, easily outdistancing the Mustangs. However, the menace for the future was clear enough.

In many cases, the bombers inflicted much damage. 75 B–17 Fortresses and 64 P–51 Mustangs of the 20th Fighter Group, after attacking the military vehicle plant at Chemnitz, continued their flight to land in Russia.

FUSA crossed the German frontier. Here, too, the Luftwaffe reacted in force, and air battles developed above the Vaterland in two encounters with 70 German fighters and 9th Air Force formations of the 365th, 368th, and 474th Fighter Groups. Six German fighters were claimed by the pilots of the 406th Group, losing two of their number in a skirmish over Landau. In the Bonn-Düren area, four Luftwaffe fighters attacked twelve Thunderbolts of the 365th Fighter Group. All four German fighters were shot down. Over Eupen, five Me–109s were destroyed by a squadron of the 368th Fighter Group, losing one P–47.

Seven groups of 9th bombers set course to enemy positions from north of Thionville to south of Metz. After this bombing operation in the morning, four groups headed to the same targets in the afternoon.

Tuesday, 12 September

888 heavy bombers of the 8th Air Force made a visual attack on the oil targets at Ruhland, Brüx, Magdeburg, Böhlen, Misburg, and Hemmingstedt, and on an aluminium plant at Lauta. And again the Luftwaffe did not intend to let the bombers pass unharmed. In violent battles, twenty-three Fortresses were shot down. Bomber gunners claimed 108 German fighters and, although this figure was obviously exaggerated compared with the German figure of 41, it gave good testimony of the ferocity of the air battle. In all, 45 bombers failed to return.

Thionville was captured by TUSA.

Only a fraction of the mediums dispatched was able to attack enemy positions in the Siegfried Line in front of VII Corps. 9th Bomber Command A–20s and B–26s carried out a concentrated attack against the strongpoints in the Forêt de la Haye, in the western outskirts of Nancy.

9th Air Force fighters had only a short engagement with German fighters, although many had been sighted. Thunderbolts of the 405th Fighter

September 12, 1944. 2nd Division Liberators of the 489th Bomb Group leave the oil plants as Misburg belching huge clouds of smoke when they turn home. (Official USAF Photo)

308

Group covering ground forces near Pont-à-Mousson were jumped by German fighters. Two Thunderbolts went down, whereas the Germans lost five aircraft. P–51 Mustangs of the 354th Fighter Group visited airfields in the Frankfurt-Limburg area, and in a strafing attack they demolished nine planes.

Forty FW–190s with Me–109 top-cover attacked fifteen Mustangs of the 354th Group, but it cost the Germans twenty-four aircraft for no loss to the Mustangs. Again the Germans demonstrated that aggressiveness was no substitute for lack of experience.

Fighter-bombers also attacked obstructions barring the advance to Aachen.

P–38 Lightnings of the 474th Fighter Group flew their night-intruder mission in order to attack German movements.

Wednesday, 13 September

That the Luftwaffe had not vanished from the skies was again demonstrated today when more than 150 fighters rose to intercept the 748 heavy bombers of the 8th Air Force heading for the aero-engine factories at Stuttgart, the synthetic oil plants at Ludwigshafen, Merseburg, and Lützkendorf, and for the ordnance depot at Ulm.

South of Nordhausen, the rear of the bomber formations was attacked by some twenty Me–109s when forty-eight Mustangs arrived on the scene. One squadron intercepted the Germans, breaking off their attack. Eight Messerschmitts were shot down. Again on the way back, the same Mustang group encountered some 50–60 Me–109s on their way to the bombers. The Mustangs dispersed their formation, sending five of them earthwards.

Eight Me–109s were met at 35,000 feet over Kassel. One Messerschmitt was shot down. Five Mustangs were lost by the group in the day's battles. Thanks to very efficient fighter protection, the bomber losses were light this time. Twenty-three German fighters were shot down.

Five enemy aircraft were destroyed on Nellingen Airfield when P–47s of the 353rd Fighter Group went down to strafe the airfield. The fighters formed part of the escort of the Stuttgart bomber force. Escorting the bombers to Ulm, the 4th Fighter Group claimed eleven German aircraft destroyed on the ground.

The 75 Fortresses and 64 Mustangs of the 8th Air Force which landed in Russia on the 11th left Russian territory, bombed steelworks at Diosgyör in Hungary, and landed in Italy.

Thunderbolts of IX TAC strafed an airfield at Seligenstadt, claiming eleven on the ground.

309

Thursday, 14 September

FUSA liberated Maastricht and penetrated the outer defenses of the Siegfried Line south of Aachen. By this time TUSA was grinding to a stop, not from enemy resistance but from lack of fuel (quotation of the 12th Army Group's report). Troop carriers had flown over 5200 sorties in the past ten days, delivering 15,000 tons of freight including nearly 2,500,000 gallons of gasoline. But the supply priority of the First Army already had an average daily consumption rate of 571.000 gallons and the demands of the Third Army exceeded 1,000,000 gallons.

The intensity of ground operations along several army fronts was reflected in the establishment of a new Tactical Air Command: XXIX TAC, composed of older combat units of IX TAC and XIX TAC. The XXIX TAC Fighter Groups were the 36th, 366th, and the 373rd, all equipped with the P–47 Thunderbolt. XXIX TAC was to give air support to the Ninth US Army (NUSA), which would be moved from the Brittany Peninsula to take position between the British and Canadians in the north in Holland, and FUSA in front of Aachen.

A mother-plane B–17 guided an explosives-loaded B–17 by radio control to a target at Hemmingstedt. Thirteen Thunderbolts escorted the Fortresses. However, the missile-bomber struck 150 yards from the target.

Friday, 15 September

The Allied average daily strength during this month was:

	TOTAL	OPERATIONAL
8th Air Force bombers:	2710	2045
fighters:	1234	904
9th Air Force bombers:	1111	734
fighters:	1502	968
2nd Tactical Air Force bombers:	293	254
fighters:	999	879
RAF Bomber Command:	1871	1480

The frontline ran generally along the Albert and Leopold Canals, then south along the eastern boundaries of Belgium and Luxembourg, continu-

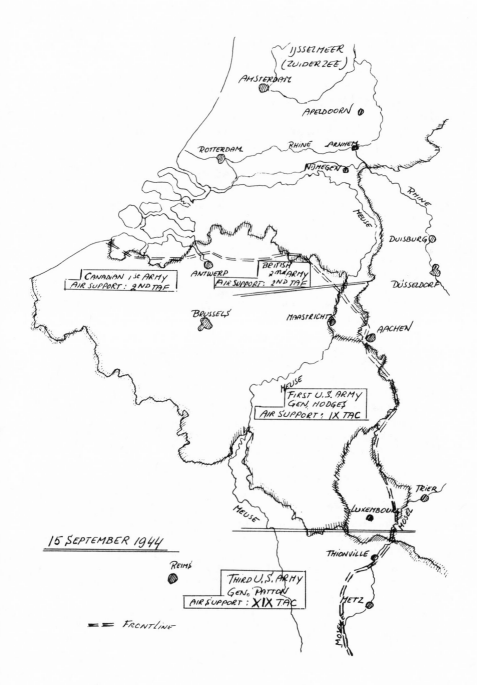

IJSSELMEER
(ZUIDERZEE)

AMSTERDAM

APELDOORN

ROTTERDAM

RHINE ARNHEM

NIJMEGEN

RHINE

MEUSE

DUISBURG

CANADIAN 1st ARMY
AIR SUPPORT: 2ND TAF

ANTWERP

BRITISH
2nd ARMY
AIR SUPPORT: 2ND TAF

DÜSSELDORF

BRUSSELS

MAASTRICHT

AACHEN

MEUSE

FIRST U.S. ARMY
GEN. HODGES
AIR SUPPORT: IX TAC

TRIER

LUXEMBOURG

MOSEL

MEUSE

THIONVILLE

15 SEPTEMBER 1944

REIMS

THIRD U.S. ARMY
GEN. PATTON
AIR SUPPORT: XIX TAC

METZ

MOSEL

=== FRONTLINE

311

ing roughly along the Siegfried Line from Aachen to Trier, and accordingly along the Moselle to the Mont Beliard–Lure region southeast of the Belfort gap.

The left of the Allied front was formed by the 21st Army Group under Field Marshal Montgomery. Direct air support was provided by the 2nd TAF.

To the right of Montgomery was Bradley's 12th Army Group with direct air support by the 9th Air Force. Its fighter force was divided as follows:

Simpson's Ninth Army: XXIX TAC (provisional because the Ninth Army was at this time still largely engaged in the reduction of German forces in Britanny. After the move to the German frontier where it would take position at 1 October, the XXIX TAC became an independent command).

Hodges' First Army: IX TAC.

Patton's Third Army: XIX TAC.

South of Bradley's 12th Army Group was the 6th Army Group of General Devers (Patch's Seventh Army and the French First Army of General Lattre de Tassigny). Air support was formed by XII TAC (moved into southern France from the Mediterranean front) and the French First Air Force (organized and equipped by the Americans in the MTO).

The strategy to be followed was laid down in the directives of General Eisenhower with the latest amplification of 13 September. Montgomery's 21st Army Group was to push north to secure the approaches to Antwerp or Rotterdam and then forward to the Rhine, supported on the right flank by Bradley's forces, which wer₂ to drive with the center toward the Rhine, trying to obtain bridgeheads near Cologne and Bonn. The First Allied Airborne Army was to be ready to assist.

Montgomery, whose drive thus had been given priority, had issued a directive on the 14th. The ground phase of operation "Garden" was to be a rapid advance of the British Second Army along a narrow front in the direction of the Rhine and the Zuider Zee via Eindhoven, Veghel, Grave, Nijmegen, Arnhem, and Apeldoorn, and the possession of the area between Arnhem and the Zuider Zee to start the thrust across the river Ijssel via the eastern part of the Netherlands into Germany.

Operation "Market" was to pave the way by seizing bridges between Eindhoven and Arnhem, and this would be the task of the US 82nd and 101st Airborne Divisions, the British 1st Airborne Division, the Polish 1st Independent Parachute Brigade, and some smaller units of specialized troops. The American 101st Division was to seize Eindhoven and the bridges near Veghel, St. Oedenrode, and Son. The American 82nd Division was to seize the bridges at Nijmegen and Groesbeek. The British First

312

Division, together with the Polish paratroopers, were to capture the bridges at Arnhem.

One route for the Airborne fleet would pass over Schouwen Island. This was the more direct route, which meant a flight of eighty miles over enemy-held territory. A more southerly route, which meant a flight of about sixty miles over enemy-held territory, would also be maintained to eliminate the danger of congestion in air traffic.

The date was set for Sunday, 17 September.

All 8th fighter groups were relieved from 8th Fighter Command and were assigned to the three bombardment divisions.

9th Air Force fighter-bombers carried out attacks against barges on the Rhine.

Saturday, 16 September

Nancy was entered by TUSA.

Thirty-three Lightnings of the 370th Fighter Group flew in the vicinity of Aachen when more than fifty German aircraft jumped the formation. Seven Thunderbolts of the 404th Fighter Group joined the melee and knocked down four Luftwaffe fighters for no losses, whereas the Lightnings claimed two Germans for the loss of one P-38.

Twelve Focke Wulfs attacked a squadron Thunderbolts of the 50th Fighter Group ending up badly for the German fighters which lost six of their number with no losses for the Thunderbolts. All this increased Luftwaffe activity near Aachen was meant as a support for the Wehrmacht to stop the American forces in front of Aachen.

Seventy-seven medium bombers of the 9th carried out missions in support of the British/Canadian forces. They attacked a viaduct near Arnemuiden, while 73 bombers from two groups dropped their loads on an embankment, rail tracks, and a highway.

The last full-scale Carpetbagger mission was flown (see 4 January).

Sunday, 17 September

It was a bright Sunday morning when Operation Market was launched. During the night, 282 heavy bombers of the RAF carried out attacks on flak defenses along a northern route within striking distance of the drop zone. The targets attacked were Moerdijk bridge, and airfields at Leeuwarden, Steenwijk, Havelte, Hopsten, and Salzburg. The bombers were preceded by six RAF and five USAAF aircraft with radio-jamming devices.

Early in the morning, coastal batteries in the Walcheren area and shipping near Schouwen Island were attacked by 100 RAF bombers, escorted by 53 fighters.

Later in the morning, the 8th Air Force arrived with 852 B-17 Fortresses escorted by 153 fighters. 112 anti-aircraft positions along the carrier route were attacked. Two B–17s and one fighter were shot down by flak. One of the B–17s that dived into the ground at Weert carried the air commander. So far, no enemy fighters had shown up.

At noon, the carriers and gliders arrived above the drop and landing zones: 1546 troop carriers and 478 gliders were despatched of which 1481 carriers and 425 gliders dropped and landed on the right spots. Thirty-five carriers and thirteen gliders were lost.

1075 fighter sorties were flown to escort the airborne armada: 371 by fighters of the RAF, 538 by the 8th Air Force, and 166 by the 9th Air Force. Four American fighters were shot down. 200 Thunderbolts of the 56th, 78th, 353rd, and 356th Fighter Groups had the unenviable task of neutralizing gun emplacements in the drop zone. They flew over the transport route to Nijmegen and Arnhem at 2000 to 2500 feet and, as soon as the ground batteries opened up, one element peeled off and attacked with 260-lb. fragmentation bombs, and then came back to strafe. Nearly all the guns had been suppressed by the time the carriers arrived.

The Luftwaffe made between 100 and 150 sorties without much effect.

Paratroops of the 101st Airborne Division came down between Veghel and Eindhoven. They quickly took hold of positions near Son. A few German tanks tried to interfere, but they were knocked out by fighter-bombers of the 2nd TAF. The bridge across the Wilhelmina Canal was found to have been destroyed by the Germans. The US 82nd Division landed about fifteen miles farther north, southeast, and southwest of Nijmegen. A bridge over the Maas at Grave was captured, as were two bridges over the Maas-Waal Canal. However, their attempts to seize the bridge at Nijmegen failed.

British troops of the 1st Airborne Division which landed west of Arnhem were welcomed by the 9th and 10th SS Panzer Divisions, the presence of which Intelligence had given insufficient warning. Clear information from the Dutch underground movement about the presence of these German forces had been disregarded by Allied Command. The Germans, well aware of the Allied intentions, and also soon in possession of the complete operational plan, took all measures to annihilate the paratroops.

One hour after the landing, the Guards Armored Division started its move out from the bridgehead across the Meuse-Escaut Canal and, although supported by heavy artillery fire and fighter-bombers of the 2nd TAF, the division met such stiff resistance that by nightfall it had only proceeded about six miles, to the village of Valkenswaard, and thus Montgomery's army was not able to make contact with the main elements of the 101st Airborne Division.

314

Supporting Mustangs of the 4th Fighter Group knocked down five FW–190s near Bocholt.

Monday, 18 September

The uprising of the patriot army in Warsaw had started on 1 August after receipt of what was regarded by the Poles in Warsaw and London as authentic radio orders from Moscow. The Soviet armies approached the city but, after the uprising, halted mysteriously and stayed at a distance of ten kilometers for the next three months. However bravely the Poles fought, they were beaten down by powerful, vengeful, and cruel German forces, destroying Warsaw stone by stone. Help was bitterly needed in the beleaguered city and steps were undertaken to carry out a supply-dropping mission.

This couldn't be done by England-Warsaw-England flights, the distance being too large. Also, flights from Italy to Warsaw were very difficult to undertake, and thus a shuttle mission to Russian bases was obvious. But then the Russians announced that the Warsaw forces were reckless adventurers who had risen prematurely and without Russian incitement, and refused the use of Russian bases to American forces in behalf of Warsaw missions. Appeals even from President Roosevelt and Prime Minister Churchill were fruitless.

Volunteer aircrews of the Italian-based 205th Group of the Royal Air Force sent seven extremely difficult and costly missions to Warsaw dropping supplies by night and then returning to their base in Italy. But at last the Russians gave their approval, and the first supply mission by the 8th Air Force was carried out today.

For one hour, 107 Fortresses of the 13th Wing circled over Warsaw dropping 1284 containers with machinegun parts, small arms and ammunition, hand grenades, incendiaries, food, and medical supplies. Possibly 250, but probably no more than 130, of the containers fell into Polish hands—all the others into German.

Despite 64 Mustangs of the 355th and 361st Fighter Groups providing escort, twenty German fighters managed to break through the fighter screen and attack the bombers. One Fortress of the low 390th Group exploded, while the pilot in another B–17 was killed. One B–17 made an emergency landing at Brest-Litowsk; the rest landed at the Russian bases Poltava and Mirgorod. (A second mission of this kind would be refused by the Russians on 2 October.)

Poor visibility at English bases in the morning prevented the take-off of a new armada with reinforcements and supplies for the heavily engaged paratroopers near Arnhem. But at noon, the sky cleared and, during the remainder of the day, 1306 aircraft and 1152 gliders, escorted by 674 RAF and 8th Air Force fighters, accomplished their mission, at a cost of 22 aircraft and 21 gliders. Thirteen fighters failed to return.

Two hundred forty-six B–24 Liberators of the 8th, escorted by 192 fighters, dropped supplies for the American paratroops. Seven bombers and 21 fighters were shot down, nearly all victims of murderous flak, though the German fighters appeared in larger numbers than on the previous day. Sixteen of the fighters that fell to flak were of the 56th Fighter Group.

In atrocious weather, both the 56th and 78th Fighter Groups arrived before the B–24s to deal with the anti-aircraft emplacements. With horizontal visibility seriously limited by haze and an overcast in some places down to 500 feet, the fighter pilots had great difficulty locating the gun positions, whereas the German gunners saw the Thunderbolts sooner. Allied fighters were already at a great disadvantage compared with the flak crews because they were only allowed to attack when fired upon because of the danger of attacking their own troops.

A low-altitude battle north of Maastricht between sixty Me–109s and FW–190s and the Mustangs of the 357th Fighter Group had fatal consequences for the Luftwaffe fighters. Twenty-six were shot down for the loss of

September 18, 1944. A Liberator flies over Son, near Eindhoven, while a military column is passing through the village. (Official USAF Photo)

316

two Mustangs. Another battle between thirty-five Focke Wulfs and Mustangs of the 359th Group gave an equal score: two for two.

The Luftwaffe was still very active over Aachen and a squadron Thunderbolts of the 365th Fighter Group was intercepted by some 36 German fighters. Four Thunderbolts were shot down, however the Germans lost an equal number of their fighters.

Tuesday, 19 September

Formations of the 8th Air Force heavy bombers attacked the marshalling yards at Soest, Hamm, and other targets in Germany.

The 13th Wing Fortresses that landed on the previous day at Russian bases took off again and, after dropping a load of Russian bombs on a rail center at Szolnok in Hungary, they landed at the Italian base, Foggia.

An unfavorable turn of the weather made it very difficult to provide air support for the paratroops. Large-scale operations were out of the question. No sufficient interdiction of enemy reinforcement routes was possible, and this enabled the Germans to cut American lines of communication with Montgomery's forces and to encounter these forces in strength. Not until today were Montgomery's Guards able to make contact with the American 82nd Airborne Division.

Notwithstanding the appalling weather conditions, a ferocious battle raged in the skies around Arnhem where German, British, and American fighters were entangled in numerous dogfights. In the confusion, several times it occurred that Spitfires bounced the Mustangs, and one Mustang was actually shot down by a Spitfire.

Today saw the capitulation of Brest. After the capitulation, Simpson's Ninth Army took a position along the German frontier between the First and Third Armies. Shortly thereafter it would move to a position between the British Army and Hodges' First Army.

Wednesday, 20 September

8th Air Force fighters flew patrols near Nijmegen and Arnhem. However, very poor weather conditions made air support for the hard-pressed paratroops in this area practically impossible.

Thursday, 21 September

The bombers of the 8th were dispatched against various targets in western Germany, including Mainz.

Very low clouds enabled only the 56th and 353rd Fighter Groups to operate with their Thunderbolts over the Arnhem battle area. And they were kept very busy because the weather that similarly hindered the Luftwaffe was obviously not bad enough to keep them grounded; on the contrary, they were out in force to intercept the transports, gliders, troop carriers, and supply aircraft flying into Holland. And the efforts of the German fighters paid off, for most of the thirty-five RAF and AAF transport aircraft lost this day would fall to their guns.

The 353rd Fighter Group caught several German aircraft making passes at the transport Dakotas, and six Luftwaffe fighters went down for the loss of one Thunderbolt in the vicinity of Nijmegen. Northeast of Nijmegen, the 56th Fighter Group, flying at 3500 feet, spotted about twenty FW-190s below them. Dave Schilling took his group down and, in a surprise attack, they sent fifteen Focke Wulfs into the ground. Three Thunderbolts were lost in the dogfights.

9th Air Force fighter-bombers were directed to concentrate on a large scale upon the German rail system west of the Rhine.

Friday, 22 September

With a strength of more than 600 heavy bombers, the 8th Air Force flew a mission to the great Henschel complex at Kassel. Clouds obscured the target, and bombing had to be done by radar. More than 1600 tons of bombs caused considerable damage.

Fighter-bombers of IX TAC flew patrols along the Rhine and to a considerable depth east of the river, chalking up a number of rolling stock.

Saturday, 23 September

One-third of the Junkers engines were turned out by the Junkers aero-engine factory at Magdeburg and, in an attempt to diminish the output, the 8th Air Force heavy bombers concentrated their efforts on this target.

Considering the hopeless situation, the British 2nd Army authorized the paratroopers to withdraw from Arnhem. A fierce battle raged over this area, with the 353rd Fighter Group having the brunt of the fighting. At 1745 hours, they ran into more than fifty Me-109s and FW-190s. They met the Messerschmitts head-on and then became engaged in violent dogfights with the Focke Wulfs, ranging from 5000 feet to the earth. The group lost three Thunderbolts, whereas the American pilots claimed eleven FW-190s and eight Me-109s.

With the battle of Arnhem coming to a close, the 8th fighters could count their losses: the toll they paid was heavy, and forty-five of the lost aircraft were Thunderbolts.

Formations of the 8th Fighter Command flew fighter sweeps and patrols.

318

Sunday, 24 September

It was bitter fighting in Arnhem, where totally exhausted British and Polish troops tried to withdraw over the Rhine; it was bitter fighting, too, for the American Airborne forces trying to consolidate and enlarge their position or to keep their communication lines open, which were constantly cut by enemy attacks. There was not sufficient relief from Montgomery's army because it lacked the strength to push forward to support the paratroops.

All missions of the 9th Air Force against rail and road junctions, marshalling yards, etc., in the area of Aachen which had been planned for today had to be cancelled due to unfavorable weather.

Despite the appalling weather, with rain from a very low ceiling, the Thunderbolts of the 405th Fighter Group took off when a request was received to give air support to the 4th Armored Division east of Nancy. The Germans had started a counteroffensive near Château-Salins. After a fruitless effort to climb above the overcast, the two squadrons flew through the murk on instruments. One squadron was guided by the ground controller on the last leg to the target.

Under 800 feet, in heavy rain and intense ground fire, the Thunderbolts raced to the spot and plunged into the middle of a tank battle. They managed to destroy a number of tanks. The other squadron failed to locate the tank battle, but ran into an enemy convoy of reinforcements which they attacked with their bombs and gunfire.

In the afternoon, a request was received to attack a fort offering heavy resistance. Still in the same abominable weather, the third squadron took off and succeeded in finding the target where they scored many direct hits. Despite the rain and heavy ground fire, the Thunderbolts made several runs and silenced all opposition.

Monday, 25 September

Heavy bombers of the 8th Air Force proceeded to a number of targets in western Germany. Bombs were dropped on the marshalling yards at Mannheim and Frankfurt, while 364 aircraft attacked the important railyards at Ludwigshafen serving the military movement to Saarbrücken where the Germans were tangling with TUSA between Metz and Nancy. The bombs were dropped through a dense undercast so results could not be observed. Several aircraft were hit by intense flak.

At night, the withdrawal of the remnants of the British and Polish paratroops near Arnhem was accomplished.

A new order was issued giving cuttings of all rail lines within a predetermined tactical boundary first priority, to hamper enemy's transport of troops and equipment to the battle area.

No missions in the Aachen area were possible because of poor weather conditions.

Effective today, 9th Bomber Command was redesignated the 9th Bombardment Division.

Tuesday, 26 September

The immensity of the air operations from 17–26 September may appear from the following figures as they are given in the *Official History of the Army Air Forces* (part III, page 610):

	Despatched	Successful	Losses
IX Troop Carrier Command			
Aircraft (including 246 B–24s, see 18 Sept.)	4242	3880	98
Gliders	1899	1635	137
RAF 38, 46 Groups			
Aircraft	1340	1200	55
Gliders	699	627	2
RAF Bomber Command	392	392	2
8th Air Force	4269	3943	58
9th Air Force	501	385	2
Air Defense Great Britain	1746	1677	12
Second Tactical Air Force	898	860	13

Data of photo and weather-reconnaissance flights, dummy dropping flights, etc., were not mentioned.*

Heavy bombers of the 8th set out to strike on targets in Germany. 381 B–17 Fortresses headed for the Focke Wulf plants at Hemelingen and Hastedt, while other formations turned to Bremen and also dropped a bombload on the marshalling yards at Osnabrück. One Fortress was shot

---

*Material from *The Army Air Force in World War II*, edited by Wesley Frank Craven and James Les Cate, © copyright 1951, used by permission of the publisher, University of Chicago Press, Chicago, Illinois.

down by flak over Osnabrück. The bombing of the Focke Wulf plants was not very successful, and inflicted no damage of any importance.

Two squadrons of Lightnings and one squadron of Mustangs, together forming the 479th Fighter Group, roamed the German countryside on a sweep to the area east of Münster and Haltern. Hubert Zemke, leading the group, received a call to proceed to an enemy formation. The thirty-one P–38s and twelve P–51s soon caught sight of a large batch of Me–109s. They tore into the German formation and, in a ferocious battle, the Lightnings scored one of their last victories in 8th Air Force service. Twenty-nine Messerschmitts were shot out of the sky.

Again, poor weather conditions made tactical assaults in the Aachen area impossible.

Wednesday, 27 September

The large Henschel complex at Kassel was again the target for the bombers of the 8th Air Force, and more than 600 heavies would have to make a blind bombing attack because of the thick undercast. 315 Liberators of the 2nd Division flew over a solid cloudcover with 37 aircraft of the 445th Bomb Group leading in the second combat wing.

A navigational error brought this group on the wrong heading, separating them from the main bomberstream. They made their attack by pathfinder means, and what they thought to be Kassel was in fact Göttingen, where the bombs fell outside the town some twenty miles from their target. Turning around and taking a course for home, they were placed far apart from the rest of the 2nd Division.

The German ground controller, always alert, was immediately aware of the advantageous situation and within minutes, a few miles from Eisenach, the first FW–190s appeared from 6 o'clock in line-abreast formation with, in their wake, two gruppen of Me–109s. Within three minutes, 25 Liberators were sent to earth.

Urgent calls for help made the Mustangs of the 361st Fighter Group race to the scene, but all they found were the battered remains of a bomber group, a sky full of smoke, blazing aircraft, debris of battle, tumbling aircraft, and parachutes. The plea for help was also heard by the 4th Fighter Group returning from their escort. They hurried back to the bombers and they were able to destroy five Me–109s.

Several other targets were visited by the 8th bombers, such as the marshalling yards at Cologne and an ordnance depot at Mainz.

One pilot of the 361st Fighter Group, Lt. William R. Beyer, picked off five Focke Wulfs in quick succession when the Mustangs were escorting the bombers to Kassel and caught sight of some forty enemy fighters.

Beyer bore onto a flight of eight FW–190s and scored his victories using his new K–14 gunsight.

Thursday, 28 September

Early in the morning, a large bomberstream left England to head for targets in Germany. One of the targets to be visited by 600 heavies was again the Henschel factory at Kassel, where heavy destruction was inflicted after the three bombings within a week. A heavy flak barrage was thrown up when the bombers neared their target. Clouds forced the bombers to carry out a blind bombing attack.

As on the previous day, the German Air Force was up in great strength. Again the German fighters succeeded in breaking through the escorting fighter formations, and this time it was the 303rd Bomb Group that got the brunt of the assault. Eleven Fortresses of this group heading for Magdeburg were shot down. Another group lost six B–17s near Magdeburg in a twelve-minute-long attack by some fifty Me–109s and FW–190s.

Merweburg was visited by Fortresses of the 3rd Division. The oil production there was now 40 percent of its normal output, which meant back to 20,000 tons a month. Rated second on the priority list, it was likely to be visited regularly. This time towering clouds protected the target, and many bombers dropped in the fields near Leipzig.

In all, forty-nine heavy bombers failed to return, though it was assumed that more than half of this number fell to anti-aircraft guns. American claims were ninety German fighters shot down (fifty-five according to the Germans).

The P–38 Lightnings delivered their last battle in the 8th Air Force, as the 479th Group came to blows with the Luftwaffe fighters near Halberstadt.

P–47 Thunderbolts of the 358th Fighter Group, XIX TAC, armed with 100-lb. GP-bombs and 150-gallon napalm bombs, proceeded to the notorious fortifications near Metz where they delivered their loads. Three airfields in the Mainz-Frankfurt area were strafed by Mustangs of the 354th Fighter Group, destroying seven aircraft and a glider.

The 9th Bombardment Division dispatched four groups to bomb the Forêt de Parray in support of the ground forces. Only 37 planes managed to unload over the target.

Friday, 29 September

The ADGB, 2nd TAF, 8th, and 9th Air Forces were released from further support to operation "Market," and herewith ended the hope of an early victory over Germany. The air-ground operation had ended in a failure.

The tactical boundary indicating the area embracing all rail lines open to attack from fighter-bombers was extended farther to the east, many of them even about forty to fifty miles east of the Rhine. The 2nd TAF was to operate in the northern sector and concentrate on cutting rail lines. This was on special request from the 9th Air Force which could then concentrate on the communication lines in front of the central and southern army groups. This request was made necessary because the boundary was now so far to the east that it was nearly out of range of the fighter-bombers.

Weather had improved and 243 medium bombers of the 9th attacked marshalling yards at Prüm, where considerable damage was inflicted, and also struck fortified positions and communication targets. The 416th Bomb Group attacked the marshalling yards at Bitburg in the morning. Murderous anti-aircraft fire was met, and two Havocs went down. In the afternoon, three more Havocs were shot down over the marshalling yards at Jülich.

It was also a very busy day for the fighter-bombers—attacking artillery, enemy troops, villages, and also many times assisting when a tank battle raged. They also destroyed fifteen barges in the Rhine, together with a tug.

The 406th Fighter Group was out on a rail-cutting mission near Landau when they were bounced by thirty German fighters. The Thunderbolts dropped their tanks, and in the ensuing battle they sent six Luftwaffe fighters into the ground for the loss of two P–47s.

Saturday, 30 September

8th Air Force heavy bombers crossed the North Sea and headed for the marshalling yards at Münster and Bielefeld, and for many other targets in western Germany. The assigned target at Bielefeld had been an ordnance depot but 9/10ths cloud forced the bombers to unload their 600 tons on the marshalling yards.

During late spring and summer, German fighters had only occasionally interfered with the bomber fleets, but although for many months the German Air Force had been looked upon as a beaten arm, German industry had succeeded in raising their monthly production, month by month from 1016 single-engine fighters in February to 3013 in September. The total number of fighters of all types produced this month even amounted to 4103, September being the peak month of the war for the German aircraft production.

Fortunately for the Allies, the Germans lacked sufficient pilots and gasoline to use fighters in such numbers. Allied air leaders were not aware of this, but worried chiefly about the jets.

323

It had been a busy month for the fighter-bombers of the 9th Air Force. IX TAC made 9708 sorties and XIX TAC made 7791 sorties. They claimed the destruction of 102 enemy aircraft in the air and 58 on the ground.

The 9th Bombardment Division flew 5103 sorties and lost 12 bombers.

September, 1944—date approximate. Mustangs of the 4th Fighter Group preparing to take off from their base at Debden for another mission. (Photo from *Air Combat 1939–1945)*

324

10

OCTOBER

Sunday, 1 October

The Canadian First Army opens its campaign to clear the Schelde Estuary. This included the seizure of the south bank of the Schelde, Zuid Beveland, and Walcheren.

Monday, 2 October

Heavy bombers of the 8th repeated their attack against the Henschel works at Kassel when they were out in strength to bomb targets in western Germany. Among the fighter groups that accompanied the bombers was the 353rd Group, flying their first mission with the P–51 Mustang. The group took the air with sixteen P–51s and forty-two P–47s. The bombers were forced to drop by pathfinder means. Several delivered their loads on targets of opportunity, such as Geseke.

The First Army under Hodges renewed its offensive in the direction of Aachen and Bonn.

The 9th Bombardment Division dispatched 363 medium bombers. The results, however, were of little help to the ground armies. Only thirty bombers attacked the designated targets. Faulty preliminary planning, navigational errors, and, to a certain degree, the weather underlay this very poor showing. No agreement was reached between demands for saturation and pinpoint bombing, and the resulting pattern of requests dissipated the forces over too large an area.

This poor navigation had tragic consequences for the small Belgian town of Genk where one medium group delivered its entire bombload, resulting in 79 casualties and a lot of damage to civilian property.

An urgent call for assistance from the 30th Infantry Division was received by fighter-bombers of the 370th and 474th Fighter Groups. When the Lightnings arrived, they found a number of pillboxes in a wooded area. They dropped their fire-bombs in a dive-attack, setting the woods afire and destroying several pillboxes. The ground report stated: "Bombing excellent."

Several gun positions at Fort Driant were silenced when Thunderbolts of the 405th Fighter Group, XIX TAC, made an attack in support of Patton's army.

The 9th Air Force had its first encounter with the new German jet, the Me–262. It took place twenty miles southwest of Münster when a squadron Thunderbolts of the 365th Fighter Group came across four Me–262s, flying at 9000 feet. The Thunderbolts turned ino them. One of the Messerschmitts made several passes at a P–47 in a dogfight that brought both planes on the deck. Suddenly, the engines of the jet quit and before the rapidly closing Thunderbolt could press the fire-button, the jet sideslipped too much, hit the ground with a wing, and exploded.

Tuesday, 3 October

The 8th heavies set out on a mission to bomb targets in the Nürnberg area and airfields in the lower Rhine Valley. Part of the escort was formed by the Mustangs of the 353rd Fighter Group, while the Thunderbolts of the same group accompanied the bombers to Mayen.

A squadron of the 405th Fighter Group was vectored to two trains, observed south of Trier. The Thunderbolts picked up both and hit hard. One Thunderbolt squadron, out on a rail-cutting mission, reported the destruction of eleven locomotives.

Thursday, 5 October

Marshalling yards and airfields in western Germany were attacked by the bombers of the 8th Air Force. Among the targets that received a load were the yards at Münster and Cologne, while the airfield Münster/Handorf was also bombed. Heavy fighter escort was provided by Thunderbolts and Mustangs.

Friday, 6 October

Large formations of the 8th Air Force headed into Germany to continue their campaign against the aircraft industry. A mission to Hamburg took the bombers over the Klochner Humboldt-Deutz engine works where much damage was brought about.

326

Fortresses of the 1st Division headed to the large synthetic oil plant at Pölitz. However, the target was covered by clouds, and bombs were dropped on secondary targets like Stargard.

Large forces of Fortresses of the 3rd Division destroyed the Arado assembly plant at Neubrandenburg, inflicted heavy damage to ordnance plants and depots around Berlin, and hit all major buildings at the Bayerische Motorenwerke near the city. From 26,000 feet, the explosives descended on the Bosch Aero-engine works at Spandau.

Just at the moment that a squadron of a high group of the last combat wing became somewhat separated, thirty-five Luftwaffe fighters came diving out of the clouds one thousand feet above the bombers. They approached from the rear, closing in rapidly and, before the escort could interfere, the entire high squadron was shot out of the sky. Mustangs raced to their aid, but before they arrived, eleven bombers were downed, mainly from the 385th Bomb Group. The Mustangs knocked down five FW–190s and two Me–109s.

Returning from the escort to Hamburg, a pilot of the 353rd Fighter Group spotted two jets preparing to land on the Rheine airfield. He took his Thunderbolt into a steep dive and pursued one of them, closing in

October 6, 1944. Liberators of the 489th Bomb Group unloading over an aircraft factory in Hamburg. (Official USAF Photo)

quickly. The Me–262 tried to take evasive action, but when it filled the sight of the P–47, the pilot gave a burst from his eight guns and pieces flew off the jet. He then quickly pulled away because the second jet was on his heels. The Me–262 crashed into the ground, the second to be destroyed by the 8th fighters.

Heavy bomber formations also struck workshops and hangars at a jet airfield near Wenzendorf.

Medium bombers of the 9th Bombardment Division attacked marshalling yards at Düren, while in the same area an ammunition dump and barracks were bombed.

Fighter-bombers of IX TAC flew numerous sorties in close support of the ground forces, attacking troop concentrations, artillery, defended road junctions, and various strongpoints. Thunderbolts of the 368th Fighter Group carried out a sweep east of Aachen. This took them to the enemy airfield at Breitscheid, where they found fifty Me–109s on the field. The Thunderbolts came down and, in strafing attacks, they destroyed twenty-two Messerschmitts. Another two Messerschmitts made an attempt to land, but they were promptly intercepted and shot down.

Saturday, 7 October

There was evidence that by the end of September only three oil installations were in full production and that the oil production had fallen to less than 300,000 tons from all sources. But with the many bad flying weather days of autumn, it was very well understood that it would be very difficult to keep the balance that way.

It was also understood that the Germans were capable of reconstructing their bombed plants at a much faster rate than the Allies had even considered possible. Besides, the synthetic oil plants had been dispersed in a same way as they had done with their aircraft industry. All that the Germans needed were a few weeks of unflyable weather to raise their production to 60 per cent of normal. And thus the 8th Air Force carried out missions in weather that was considered as unflyable a year before.

However, today the weather gods were with the 8th Air Force, and 1422 of its heavies took off early in the morning to visit Pölitz, Ruhland, Böhlen, Lützkendorf, Merseburg-Leuna, Magdeburg, and other targets connected with the oil production.

The Luftwaffe demonstrated its existence as a fighting power, and eighty fighters rose to intercept the bombers. Near Leipzig, disaster struck the 4th Wing when, all of a sudden, a mass of enemy fighters of JG 3 dived out of the clouds and, within eight minutes, twelve Fortresses of the wing were lost.

328

Nearing their target at Pölitz on the bomb run, and about one minute before release, a tremendous flak barrage was thrown up and most aircraft of the lead squadron were hit. Two bombers went down, one of them taking the commander of the 457th Bomb Group, who led the wing, into imprisonment. A third aircraft landed in Sweden. Two more bombers of the same group also failed to return, making the total loss for the Pölitz force 25 planes.

Flak over Böhlen was meager this time when the Fortresses of the 3rd Division arrived over the plants. Haze and a smokescreen made visual bombing virtually impossible, and the bombers dropped by pathfinder means. Some bombers turned to a target of opportunity, and a load was delivered on Bielefeld.

The German aircraft industry was again on the target list, and 118 B–17s attacked the Basser aircraft repair factory at Zwickau where several buildings were demolished. The Henschel factory in Kassel was not overlooked either, and three of the five large workshops were left in ruins.

Twenty-five jets were sighted by the American flyers. Three Mustangs of the 364th Fighter Group trapped an Me–163 and they sent it down under their combined fire. Another Mustang of the 361st Group spotted two Me–262s taking off from Achmer. From its advantageous position, the Mustang swooped down and gained fast on the two Messerschmitts, which had no time to accelerate beyond its range of fire, and both were sent into the ground. Another Me–262 was destroyed when the jet found itself suddenly in the stream of fire from a 78th Group Thunderbolt.

As on the previous day, many tactical targets in the region of Aachen were attacked by the medium bombers of the 9th Bombardment Division. Six warehouses supplying German divisions, standing near the marshalling yards at Trier, were demolished, and four were severely damaged by A–20 Havocs from three groups.

By now two Jäger-Erpröbungskommandos of Me–262s had been formed under the leadership of Major Walter Nowotny. The unit was composed of some thirty aircraft and was based at Achmer and Hesepe, near Osnabrück.

Sunday, 8 October

Marshalling yards, rail and road junctions, four railway bridges, and a highway bridge between Aachen and Metz were plastered with bombs dropped by the medium bombers of the 9th Bombardment Division. Six flights from two groups dropped their loads on the important rail and road junction at Jülich, while one flight unloaded on the marshalling yard at Geilenkirchen.

Monday, 9 October

8th Air Force heavies were on their way to bomb targets in the Merseburg and Wiesbaden areas. 329 Fortresses turned to the notorious ball-bearing works at Schweinfurt. Although the plant received 820 tons of bombs causing much damage, production was not hampered seriously. As before, the target proved to be a very stubborn one. The bombers also visited the Gustavsburg assembly plant; results, however, were disappointing.

Tuesday, 10 October

The commander of V!I Corps issued an ultimatum to the defenders of Aachen to surrender, which, however, was rejected.

Five Gloster Meteor MK I jets arrived at Debden so the pilots could discuss tactics to fight these kind of aircraft.

Wednesday, 11 October

Fifty-seven Fortresses of the 8th obtained good results when they bombed the oil plant at Wesseling.

The artillery and air bombardment of Aachen started. Fighter-bombers, usually in response to special requests, dropped their bombs, including many incendiaries, on the city. Armed-reconnaissance aircraft flew over the city and, when ground forces had no immediate target for attack available, they unloaded their bombs in designated areas.

Thursday, 12 October

The 8th Air Force bombers were dispatched against aircraft targets and 238 Fortresses went to the Focke Wulf plant at Hastedt, while another 238 Fortresses headed to the Focke Wulf components factory at Bremen where accurate bombing inflicted great damage.

54 P–51 Mustangs, led by Lt. Charles Yeager, rendezvoused with the bombers of the 3rd Division southeast of Zwolle at 1045 hours. Nearing Steinhuder Lake, twenty-two Me–109s were sighted. Turning into the Messerschmitts, Yeager destroyed five of them in quick succession. Three other Messerschmitts were shot down in the engagement for the loss of one P–51. (In post-war years, Charles ''Chuck'' Yeager became famous as the first man to exceed the sound barrier in level flight.)

The heavy artillery and air bombardment of Aachen continued. The ground forces were supported by strong forces of IX TAC fighters. A notable success was booked when Thunderbolts of the 373rd Fighter Group, together with three squadrons of other groups, succeeded in breaking up strong enemy counterattacks. Of the 38 missions flown by IX TAC, thirty were in support of the ground forces near Aachen.

The Luftwaffe was again very active in this area and this led naturally to vicious combats with the American fighters. Thunderbolts of the 365th Fighter Group were vectored to forty German fighters. Without loss to themselves, the American pilots claimed the destruction of four enemy planes. Thirty-six Me–109s jumped eight P–38s. The Lightnings picked off two Me–109s, but lost two of their own. P–47s of a 368th Group squadron interfered with the battle and shot down three Messerschmitts for the loss of one Thunderbolt. Then the Lightnings of the 474th Fighter Group arrived on the scene and plunged into the scrap over Aachen. And another three Me–109s went down with no losses for the 474th Group.

Gun positions near Fort Driant were successfully attacked by Thunderbolts of the 406th Group, XIX TAC. One squadron of P–47s of the 362nd Group made an attack and consequently destroyed four command posts southeast of Château-Salins.

One hundred forty Liberators with P–47 and P–51 escort flew from Peterborough to Colchester. Gloster Meteors carried out mock attacks. The results of these simulated combats were discussed afterwards at Debden.

Friday, 13 October

Until nightfall, Aachen was subjected to constant heavy artillery fire and attacks from the air.

Fifty German aircraft were sighted in the Düren area, and twenty-eight Lightnings of the 474th Fighter Group were put on an intercepting course. In the encounter that followed, the Lightnings claimed seven enemy aircraft for the loss of three P–38s. When the Lockheeds returned to their base, two of them spotted a formation of sixteen FW–190s. They managed to shoot one down.

Another air battle raged as nine Thunderbolts of the 368th Fighter Group met ten Me–109s. Three Thunderbolts were shot down for a claim of one German fighter.

Aircraft of XIX TAC carried out one of the most successful attacks on bridges of the war when they destroyed the one at Hermeskeil.

Successful rail-cutting missions were flown by XXIX TAC in the vicinity of Cologne-Düren.

Saturday, 14 October

A variety of targets in western Germany was looked after by the bombers of the 8th Air Force. Marshalling yards and other targets connected

331

with transportation, as at Cologne and Saarbrücken, received a heavy bombload. Escorting fighters became entangled in several dogfights with gaggles of German fighters.

Southeast of Aachen, where American troops of the First Army were hard pressed by strong German counterattacks, fighter-bombers of IX TAC received a request for help from elements of the 9th Infantry Division to overcome the German pressure. The German attacks were launched from the town of Udenbreth. Undisturbed by flak, twenty-three Thunderbolts of the 368th Fighter Group worked the town over until hardly a house was left not destroyed or damaged.

Again, successful rail-cutting missions were flown by Thunderbolts of XXIX TAC in the Cologne-Düren area, where they achieved a temporary interruption of all traffic on several lines.

Sunday, 15 October

The oil plants at Düsseldorf and Monheim were the assigned targets for the bombers of the 8th Air Force. At Düsseldorf, only minor damage was

October 15, 1944. A direct flak hit over Cologne blew off the nose of this B–17, killing the bombardier. With his instruments and oxygen system knocked out, 1st Lt. Lawrence de Lancey managed to bring his ship back to Nuthampstead. (Official USAF Photo)

done, whereas at the latter target, a heavy blow was dealt by 64 B–24 Liberators. Other bomber formations turned to several targets in western Germany. Clouds covered the five marshalling yards at Cologne and the Fortresses dropped by pathfinder means.

Fighter-bombers of the IX TAC were active all day in support of the ground forces near Aachen. Of the twenty-four missions flown during the day, eighteen were in the ground-support role. Towns, gun positions, and entrenched troops were constantly harassed by the fighter-bombers. One squadron of Thunderbolts, on its way home, was called upon to attack some thirty German tanks leading a counterattack. The Thunderbolts strafed on the deck through heavy enemy fire, making good use of the bombs they still carried. The spearheading tank formation was totally broken up.

Monday, 16 October

Aachen was completely surrounded.

Tuesday, 17 October

The marshalling yards at Cologne formed a very important rail center for traffic to and from the Ruhr. Flak was intense but not very accurate when the Fortresses of the 1st and 3rd Divisions arrived again over the city. It was one of the many targets to be visited by the 8th heavies with their fighter escort. Again cloud conditions forced many bombers to drop by pathfinder means.

Wednesday, 18 October

In their campaign against ordnance targets, the bombers of the 8th turned to the Ford factories at Cologne where they delivered 232 tons of bombs. A large force proceeded to Kassel to visit the Henschel aero-engine plants. Many bombers dropped on the city as a secondary target because clouds obscured the plants.

As for locomotives, it was reported that 42 percent of the locomotives operational in 1939 had been made unserviceable.

Thursday, 19 October

The 8th heavies arrived once more over the Gustavsburg assembly plant, and again they achieved no encouraging results. Cologne, Ludwigshafen, and several other targets were bombed. Other formations turned to Mannheim to attack the Daimler-Benz plants. However, complete cloud covered the city and targets of opportunity were hit.

Friday, 20 October

In the morning, Thunderbolts of the 362nd Fighter Group, XIX TAC, carried out an attack on the earth and masonry dam at Dieuze with 1000-lb. GP bombs. Ten bombs hit the bull's-eye. A third squadron arrived in the afternoon to find that the morning attack had cut a channel through the dam. They placed four additional hits. The purpose of the attack was to deprive the Germans of the opportunity to cut off the troops of TUSA and to flood them by blowing the dam while they crossed the Seille River.

Luftwaffe fighters were met on a number of occasions. Lightnings of the 367th Fighter Group had three encounters with the German fighters near Brühl and Düren. The Lightnings downed nine enemy fighters for the loss of seven P–38s.

Near Bonn, a formation of thirty-two P–38s was bounced by thirty Luftwaffe fighters. When the fight was broken off, two enemy planes had been shot down for an equal number of P–38s lost. Eleven Thunderbolts of the 368th Fighter Group were embroiled in a vicious fight with twenty enemy planes near Koblenz. The Thunderbolts knocked down six German fighters for the loss of two of their number.

Saturday, 21 October

Aachen surrendered unconditionally.

Thunderbolts of the 365th Fighter Group were out on a fighter sweep. Two squadrons flew abreast at some distance from each other, while the third squadron flew top-cover one thousand feet above and ahead of both other squadrons.

It was near Koblenz that they met a formation of thirty FW–190s head-on. A feint attack of the top squadron forced the Germans to pass between the other two squadrons, resulting in a severe mauling of the Luftwaffe fighters.

After this encounter, the Thunderbolts re-formed again when another thirty enemy fighters were sighted, approaching the Thunderbolts at 24,000 feet. Although the Thunderbolts were low on fuel, they didn't waste this second chance and the same story was to repeat itself. When the P–47s finally returned to base, they had shot down twenty-one enemy planes for the loss of three Thunderbolts.

334

Sunday, 22 October

8th Air Force heavy bombers attacked targets in Germany, including the ordnance depots at Hannover and Brunswick. 352 heavies went to the important marshalling yards at Münster, again in full operation after the bombardment on the 5th. Most bombers dropped by pathfinder means, so the results could not be observed. This was also the case at Hamm where Liberators tried to hit the marshalling yards through the clouds.

Headquarters of XXIX TAC was established at Maastricht.

The 366th Fighter Group returned to IX TAC, while the 48th and 404th Fighter Groups were assigned to XXIX TAC.

Tuesday, 24 October

Fighters of the 8th Air Force ranged over western Germany flying fighters sweeps and patrols in the Hamburg and Brunswick areas. Ground targets were attacked. An FW–190 was shot down over Nordhausen by a P–51 of the 359th Fighter Group.

Wednesday, 25 October

Heavy bombers of the 8th Air Force crossed the North Sea and headed into Germany to strike on the crude oil refineries at Hamburg. Each of the refineries received 800 tons of bombs dropped on pathfinder indication. The results could not be observed. Flak was heavy and took its toll of the bombers. Thunderbolts and Mustangs escorted the bombers.

Thursday, 26 October

A large force of heavy bombers of the 8th Air Force was heading toward west German industries at Bremen, Bielefeld, Münster, Hannover, and many other cities.

A bomber force dispatched to attack the oil refinery at Misburg found heavy clouds over the target and continued on to unload on Hannover where a military depot was the objective.

Saturday, 28 October

The marshalling yards at Münster and Hamm were among the targets to receive a considerable bombload from the 8th Air Force heavies. A multilayered cloud front concealed the important communications center at Hamm when 184 Fortresses of the 3rd Division appeared over the city.

Most of the flak was encountered while crossing southern Münster, but none of the B–17s of this force was lost.

XXIX TAC Thunderbolts flew at 16,000 feet, waiting for a rendezvous with the bombers over Andernach, when the pilots spotted three waves of some thirty, new, long-nosed FW–190D's, flying at 8000 feet. The Thunderbolts swooped down and in a short engagement they destroyed five of the Focke Wulfs.

Three hundred twenty-one fighter-bombers of IX TAC carried out heavy attacks on rail lines and bridges west of the Rhine. Cuts in rail lines were made on eleven different places.

Sunday, 29 October

Three hundred three fighter-bombers were dispatched to strike interdiction targets: rail lines and bridges. With yesterday's operations, five bridges were destroyed, four on the Remagen-Ahrdorf lines, and one on the Modrath-Nörvenich line west of Cologne. Eight other bridges were damaged. At eighteen points, cuts were made in rail lines.

Near Bockingen, 35 P–51s of the 354th Pioneer Mustang Group were bounced by 75 Me–109s. Thirty German fighters, providing top cover, joined the melee which lasted for 35 minutes. Although the Germans were very aggressive, the experienced American pilots of the old-hand 354th claimed the destruction of 24 enemy aircraft with two probables for a loss of only three Mustangs.

Monday, 30 October

Two hundred tons of bombs descended on each of the two crude oil refineries in Hamburg, dropped by the 8th Air Force bombers in a blind attack. The bombers also turned to the oil refineries at Buer-Scholven where 246 tons were unloaded, to Merseburg, and again to the marshalling yards at Münster and Hamm. Cloud tops extended above 30,000 feet. Together with the heavy contrails, it made formation flying impossible and some groups on the way to Merseburg were called back to base.

Two hundred sixty-four P–51 Mustangs and 179 Thunderbolts of the 8th Air Force crossed the North Sea in weather conditions contrary to those predicted by the forecasters. In fact, the rapidly spreading clouds contained a fury of elements that made the formations scatter all through the clouds.

Colonel Hubert Zemke, leading the 479th Fighter Group, was thrown onto his back and the Mustang started a power dive. One wing folded back and came off. Zemke managed to abandon the tumbling aircraft, and parachuted into imprisonment. He was not the only one who didn't return;

three others, including a squadron commander, were struck by an enemy against which skilled tactics could not help.

Tuesday, 31 October

Fighter-bomber activity this month was largely concentrated on rail lines and bridges, although almost every day the marshalling yards were attacked, while the pilots kept a daily watch for targets along the highways. As a rule, the rail-cutting missions were carried out in group strength. 217 Railcuts were claimed by IX TAC and 315 by XIX TAC, most of them in the vicinity of Trier and Koblenz in the north, Kaiserslautern and Landau in the east, and Pirmasens, Saarbrücken, and Strasbourg in the south. Thirty-three bridges were attacked, of which seventeen were claimed to be destroyed.

Medium bombers paid most attention to marshalling yards and rail bridges. 721 mediums attacked rail bridges and 140 turned to the marshalling yards. In addition to these targets, many other tactical objectives were bombed.

IX and XIX TAC together claimed the destruction of 393 miliary transport, 316 armored vehicles and tanks, 493 locomotives, and 1755 railway cars.

9th Air Force losses for the month were 177 aircraft, almost entirely victims of flak. Yet the month's claims for enemy aircraft shot down were 172.

The 8th Air Force this month lost 117 heavy bombers.

Meanwhile, Simpson's Ninth Army had been shifted to Hodges' First Army's left flank, with XXIX TAC operating consequently north of IX TAC.

Directives had been issued to start a new offensive:

British 21st Army Group:	to move in a southeasterly direction between the Rhine and the Meuse, with possible starting date 10 November.
First US Army:	to push to the Rhine.
Ninth US Army:	to cover the First Army in an assault to the Rhine and cooperate in the encirclement or capture of the Ruhr; date: 5 November.
Third US Army:	to advance in a northeasterly direction on the right flank of FUSA, starting north and south of Metz to form ultimately a bridgehead over the Ruhr near Darmstadt; date: 10 November (actually the assault started on 8 November).

Devers' two armies and Bradley's right flank were to force crossings over the Rhine after breaching the Siegfried Line.

The principal task of the 9th Bombardment Division was to destroy bridges over the Moselle and those west of the Rhine between Euskirchen and the Moselle.

The 2nd Tactical Air Force was to destroy bridges over the Ijssel.

IX And XXIX TACs were to concentrate on rail bridges, rail and road junctions, and viaducts in support of the intended advance of the Ninth and First Armies; more specifically, in a region west of the Rhine between Cologne and Düsseldorf.

Assistance from heavy bombers was discussed in view of the expected weather, because rain and snow might hamper the operations of the fighter-bombers.

11

NOVEMBER

Wednesday, 1 November

8th Air Force heavy bombers continued their missions in connection with the oil campaign and dropped nearly 700 tons on an oil plant at Gelsenkirchen. Little opposition was met and the bombers were on their way home via Holland when a single Me-262 appeared.

Flying at 38,000 feet, the Luftwaffe pilot nosed his jet into a dive toward a section of Mustangs of the 20th Fighter Group, flying top-cover. He lined up behind one of the Mustangs and sent it down in flames. He continued his dive through the Fortress formations with the Mustangs in hot pursuit.

At 1000 feet he leveled out and then climbed in a northerly direction toward the Zuider Zee. He then made the fatal mistake of staying above a cloud layer instead of disappearing into it. Mustangs and Thunderbolts of three different fighter groups were on his heels and cut him off. After receiving hits from both Mustangs and Thunderbolts, it was a P–47 of the 56th Fighter Group that gave him the final blow, and the Messerschmitt burst into flames and spun down. The pilot managed to bail out.

Thursday, 2 November

One thousand heavy bombers of the 8th Air Force set off on a mission to Germany, a mission destined to leave a deep impression on the Air Force leaders, not because of the bombing results, but because a supposedly beaten Luftwaffe was capable of mustering 400 fighters into the air to intercept the bomberstream.

683 B–17 Fortresses followed a somewhat erratic course to the synthetic

oil plants of the I.G. Farben Industrie at Leuna, three miles from the center of Merseburg. The erratic course was meant to bring the German fighter defense off-balance, but when the leading 3rd Division, with its escort of more than 400 Mustangs and 30 Lightnings of the 9th Air Force, arrived at their destination, it left no doubt that the Luftwaffe was in no uncertainty as to the intended objectives to be visited.

About 100 Me–109s and FW–190s made towards the bombers, but the escort managed to disperse them, shooting down nineteen fighters for the loss of one P–51. Some fifteen Me–163 jets avoided the Mustangs, and nine made passes at the bombers, however, without success.

Twenty minutes later, the 1st Division Fortresses were faced with the strongest opposition so far encountered. More than 200 Mustangs escorted this force. First, some fifty German fighters were sighted heading for the bombers, but within minutes larger forces followed and a violent air battle developed, ranging all over the sky. In spite of the German efforts, the bombers were able to drop their loads on the target, and 1400 tons descended on the oil plants.

Two groups of B–17s had gone off course and were trailing the main bomberstream. And, as usual, this didn't pass unnoticed by the Luftwaffe; in fact the largest force of enemy fighters, some 200, concentrated on these groups and before the Mustangs could interfere, sixty plus German fighters closed in on the formation and started the assault.

Nine Fortresses from the 457th and twelve from the 91st Bomb Groups tumbled down. The 20th Fighter Group came to the rescue. Twenty-six of the forty bombers destroyed were shot down by fighters, while also eight Mustangs were lost. But the Luftwaffe came near to disaster: 134 fighters were claimed to be shot down.

Other bomber formations unloaded more than 700 tons of bombs on the oil plants at Castrop and Sterkrade. They escaped without much attention from the German Air Force.

Dense contrails over Merseburg caused some formations of the 3rd Division to bomb the secondary target, the city of Halle, where the bombs were released by pathfinder means.

For the first time, Me–262s made use of air-to-air rockets when a flight of these jets fired its missiles at the B–24s near Minden. Their aim was, however, not accurate, and none of the Liberators was hit. Thunderbolts of the 56th Fighter Group intervened and the jets disappeared.

Friday, 3 November

Medium bombers of the 9th Bombardment Division, escorted by fighters of the 9th, attacked rail bridges preparatory to the new ground offensive.

Saturday, 4 November

The 8th Air Force dispatched its bombers again on a mission to oil targets in Hamburg, Harburg, Hannover, Bottrop, and Gelsenkirchen. Also, a benzol plant at Neunkirchen was bombed by the Fortresses of the 3rd Division, led by pathfinder aircraft.

The escort of Mustangs and Thunderbolts was attacked by the Me-262s of Kommando Nowotny. Their first appearance was over the Zuider Zee, and they continued their activity by trying to find isolated elements. Two escorting fighters, a Mustang and a Thunderbolt, failed to return.

Including yesterday's operations, medium bombers made 131 sorties with fighter escort, attacking rail bridges at Konz-Karthaus and Morscheid, and the Kaiserslautern overpass.

Sunday, 5 November

The heavy fortifications in the Metz salient formed a serious obstacle for the coming offensive, and therefore three forces of heavy bombers of the 8th Air Force took a course to the Metz-Thionville fortifications only to find them completely covered by cloud. The bombers continued to secondary targets deep in Germany. The marshalling yards at Frankfurt and the oil plant at Ludwigshafen were bombed. Also, Offenbach received a heavy load of explosives.

Monday, 6 November

Heavy bombers of the 8th struck two crude oil plants at Hamburg and Harburg, and also attacked benzol plants at Duisburg and Minden. Liberators dropped 434 tons of bombs on the oil plant at Sterkrade.

The B-24s were escorted by four groups of Mustangs, and near Minden the Me-262s made their appearance. In scattered combats, two jets were shot down. One of these was destroyed near Osnabrück by Captain Charles Yeager of the 357th Fighter Group.

A force of B-17s of the 3rd Division went to an airfield at Neumünster which had become increasingly important as a repair depot for FW-190s and He-111s. Heavy clouds fouled a successful attack.

Pilots of the 416th Bomb Group, 9th Bombardment Division, returned from England with their brand-new A-26B Douglas Invaders after a conversion training on this new type. The group was now equipped with forty of these aircraft, which had a longer range, could carry more load, and had a higher performance than the A-20s which the 416th had ferried back from France to England on the 4th. Since glass-nosed A-26C Invaders were not yet available in England, the group retained its glass-nosed A–20J and A–20K Havocs to lead the boxes and flights.

Wednesday, 8 November

The oil plant at Merseburg-Leuna received 477 tons of bombs, dropped by the heavies of the 8th. Osnabrück was also bombed, but many bomber formations were recalled due to weather.

In encounters with the Me–262s, at least one Mustang was shot down by the jets. However, the jets lost at least three aircraft, including the leader of Kommando Nowotny, Major Walter Nowotny. Who shot him down remains a mystery. It was known that he attacked a B–17 formation and that he was intercepted by Mustangs. His Me–262 came down in a vertical dive and crashed in flames six kilometers north of Bramsche, taking one of the most successful German fighter pilots to his death. It also meant the end of the Kommando. General Adolf Galland gave the order to dissolve it for reorganization. The unit had been credited with the destruction of twenty-two Allied aircraft during the period from October 1st to November 8th.

Two Mustangs of the 357th Fighter Group, one of them with engine trouble, were on their way back to England when they approached a group of approximately thirteen Fortresses, also on their way home but without escort. The Mustang pilots decided to stay with the bombers. At the same time, a Me–262 made its second pass on the bombers, but when it turned to start a third attack, one of the Mustangs scored several hits on the jet. Shortly thereafter, the pilot, Lt. Franz Schall of Kommando Nowotny, bailed out. The P–51 with engine trouble didn't make it home and crashlanded near Brussels.

All enemy resistance in the Schelde Estuary ceased.

Operation Madison, the attack on the Metz fortifications by TUSA, had started. The offensive had been preceded by a tremendous artillery barrage and was supported by fighter-bombers of XIX TAC. Troop concentrations, command posts, gun positions, bridges, rail and road traffic, and airdromes were attacked with bombs and gunfire, and also with thirty-one tanks with napalm. Five troop concentrations received hits and four command posts were destroyed. The headquarters of the 17th SS Panzer Grenadier Division was demolished, disorganizing the operations of this division for a considerable period. Even airfields as far as Wiesbaden and Darmstadt were attacked. Forty Me–109s jumped sixteen P–47 Thunderbolts, but in the ensuing fight they lost eleven aircraft for downing three Thunderbolts.

In the course of the morning, the weather became worse and worse, and all medium bomber operations in the afternoon were recalled or cancelled, while fighter-bomber operations were drastically reduced.

342

TUSA crossed the Seille River in three places and captured eight villages.

Thursday, 9 November

Widespread attacks on a large-scale were carried out in support of the advance of TUSA.

The 8th Air Force arrived over the battle zone with 1223 heavy bombers. The first force was to deliver its load in the Thionville area, however clouds made visual bombing impossible. Only 37 bombers dropped 104 tons of bombs in the assigned area; 308 bombers went to their secondary target; the marshalling yards at Saarbrücken. The second and third forces of bombers had the fortifications at Metz as their primary targets. 689 heavies dropped 2386 tons of bombs in the area; 86 aircraft bombed targets of opportunity. Bombing was done both visually and on instruments. Although the accuracy of the bombing was low, the density of worthwhile targets was such that vital objects were always hit.

576 fighters of the 8th accompanied the bombers, thirty fighters acted as weather scouts, and another 208 fighters of the 8th bombed and strafed ground targets, including airfields east of the Rhine. Five Bombers and three fighters were lost.

The 9th Bombardment Division sent 514 mediums to four forts near Metz, to defensive installations, troop concentrations, and to dumps in the wooded areas nearby. When the bombers arrived, the targets were covered by clouds, and only 74 bombers were able to make attacks on road junctions, an artillery camp and ordnance arsenal at Landau, and on military barracks at Dieuze.

Fighter-bombers of XIX TAC operated in close support of the ground forces, attacking enemy troops, armored vehicles, marshalling yards, flak positions, and many other targets, including all road movements. Thirty-four tanks of napalm started large fires at Bezange and Manderen. Ground forces succeeded in making two crossings over the Moselle.

Friday, 10 November

8th Air Force bombers were on the way to Wiesbaden. On request of the ground forces, they tried to limit German air activity from the important airfield there by means of a large amount of explosives. Weather was very poor and many bombers turned to secondary targets. Many fighter groups accompanied the heavies and, apart from their escort duties, the fighters flew patrols and sweeps over western Germany.

343

Saturday, 11 November

B–24 Liberators of the 8th put the oil plant at Bottrop entirely out of action by dropping 344 tons of bombs on the mark. 236 tons of bombs descended on the oil plant at Gelsenkirchen, while other formations turned to Wiesbaden.

A lone Me–262 made a pass at four Mustangs patrolling over Holland. Making use of its superior speed, the jet disappeared before the Mustangs had a chance to tackle.

November 11, 1944. B–24s of the 492nd Bomb Group climb to altitude. (Official USAF Photo)

Thursday, 16 November

1204 heavy bombers of all three divisions of the 8th Air Force formed a tremendous bomberstream when they droned on toward their targets—Eschweiler, Langerwehe, Weisweiler, Durwiss, and Helrath. The first bombs which started to fall at 1113 hours formed the prelude to operation "Queen." Within one and a half hours, 4120 tons of fragmentation bombs were unloaded to soften up the defenses in front of the major Allied offensive by FUSA starting at 1245 hours by VII Corps in the direction of Eschweiler-Düren-Cologne.

344

482 8th Air Force fighters rode along with the bombers. 1188 heavy bombers of RAF Bomber Command dropped 5640 tons of bombs on Düren, Jülich, and Heinsberg. 275 fighters of the RAF escorted the bombers.

Jülich, Eschweiler, and Düren were almost completely destroyed, together with several fortified villages. Yet the defenses directly in front of the ground forces were not sufficiently softened up because the bombers refused to bomb "short," well remembering the tragedy at St. Lô, although this time, radio aids, normally used for instrument landings at USAAF bases, had been placed along the frontline of the troops, giving an indication on a dial in the cockpit at the moment the bomber passed that line. It was in fact the most useful device among the many to prevent bombers from dropping on friendly troops.

The complete destruction of towns and villages, strongpoints, and road intersections was the aim of the 9th Bombardment Division. However, bad weather at the bases and at the front enabled only 119 mediums to take off, of which number only eighty bombed four fortified positions. The mediums were escorted by fighters of the 8th Air Force. Weather at the bases had prevented some 300 heavy bombers, more than 500 mediums and a far larger number of fighters and fighter-bombers, from taking off.

212 fighter-bomber sorties were flown by IX TAC, attacking specified targets.

XXIX TAC made 137 sorties against towns and villages, road junctions, and many other targets in support of XIX Corps of NUSA, starting its offensive simultaneously with FUSA.

Prior to the launching of the ground offensive, P–38 Lightnings of IX TAC attacked targets marked by smoke. 47 P–38s of the 370th and 474th Fighter Groups hit three targets near Huertgen and three targets southeast of Eschweiler with excellent results. 45 Lightnings of the 367th Fighter Group struck only one of their assigned targets, the others being hidden by clouds.

Anti-aircraft fire was meager and only ten planes out of the attacking 2809 were lost. Four of these were of the 8th Air Force.

Friday, 17 November

In support of TUSA's slow movement eastward, XIX TAC fighter-bombers flew 317 sorties against rail and road transportation systems, since air reconnaissance had revealed intense transportation activity on the lines leading to the front.

Less favorable weather conditions made only 129 sorties possible for IX TAC against Huertgen and four other defended areas in the line of the advance of FUSA, an advance initially measured in yards because of stiff enemy resistance, weather, and short days, limiting air-ground support considerably.

Only 78 aircraft of XXIX TAC could take off in support of NUSA, which was chiefly occupied with repelling counterattacks.

Led by its glass-nosed A–20J and A–20K Havocs, the 416th Bomb Group flew its first A–26 Invader mission to a stores depot at Hagenau, about fifteen miles north of Strassburg. Weather over the target was very bad and the bombardiers in the A–20s dropped down to 8000 feet. At this altitude, they picked up the target in their bombsights and they placed their eggs with damaging results. The 416th was the only group of the six dispatched by the 9th that actually bombed.

Bad weather also restricted the number of missions of the 67th Tactical Reconnaissance Group, IX TAC. Although the six missions flown did not bring in results of primary targets, several pilots reported steady vehicular traffic of mainly motor transport and ambulances between Jülich and Düren. The 10th Photo-Reconnaissance Group of XIX TAC reported after 24 missions considerable rail activity near Merzig, St. Wendel, Worms, and Mainz, and scattered road traffic between the Rhine and the Moselle.

Saturday, 18 November

355 P–51 Mustangs and 47 P–47 Thunderbolts of the 8th Air Force visited the jet airfield at the Lechfeld development center. Dropping down on the deck, the fighters of the 4th and 353rd Fighter Groups shot up fourteen jets. The 357th Group picked off four Me–109s in the air, and scored an a additional ten aircraft on the ground while strafing Mengen Airfield.

XIX TAC aircraft kept hammering on the enemy's transport lines heading to the front of TUSA. They made 347 sorties. Heavy rail activity was reported by the pilots at many places.

Numerous marshalling yards on both sides of the Rhine contained a large amount of rolling stock. Many rail lines were occupied with flat cars loaded with trucks, ambulances, and possibly tanks. One group dropped napalm bombs on trains near Wittzingen and, after many strafing attacks, the pilots of the group claimed fifteen locomotives as part of a total of 74 locomotives and 456 railway cars destroyed by the command.

IX TAC aircraft set out on 32 missions. Pilots reported heavy rail movements east and west of the Rhine in the vicinity of Hamm, Münster, and Wuppertal, and between Koblenz and Mayen, and in numerous other localities. Many suspected canvas-covered objects were noted in a field near Golzheim. At several places, camouflaged motor transports were observed. (All this increased German activity was preparatory to the coming Ardennes Offensive which would be unleashed on the 16th of December. It remains a mystery how the Allies could have been taken by surprise.)

346

XXIX TAC fighter-bombers flew many times in the armed-column-cover role. Thunderbolts of the 48th Fighter Group made 24 such missions in the course of the day.

In the afternoon, mediums of the 9th Bombardment Division attacked a number of villages in support of FUSA's VII Corps. A Marauder was shot down over a supply depot at Gey, southeast of Aachen, while attempting to make a second run.

Sunday, 19 November

Metz was encircled and bypassed by TUSA.

Aircraft of XIX TAC flew 403 sorties against enemy transport. Claims of the last three days amounted to a huge number of locomotives, railway cars, motor transports, and armored vehicles. Among the railyards attacked were those at Hartgarten and Saargemünd. Over one hundred gun positions were destroyed. Pilots reported intense rail activity throughout the day, with crowded marshalling yards on both sides of the Rhine.

Forty-three reconnaissance missions were flown by IX TAC aircraft. Pilots reported very heavy rail activity between the Rhine and the front, and great activity on roads and marshalling yards, notably at Koblenz and Siegburg. Suspicious-looking haystacks were reported, possibly camouflaged tanks or other vehicles.

East of Aachen, a squadron Lightnings of the 367th Fighter Group was jumped by 25 FW–190s. Another squadron of the same group came to their aid. Seven Focke Wulfs were shot down in the encounter, without loss to the Lightnings. The Thunderbolts also came to grips with the Luftwaffe as a squadron of the 368th Fighter Group ran into some 20 German fighters. The Americans claimed four aircraft for no loss.

In the last two days, 1737 fighter-bombers of both IX and XXIX TACs attacked a large variety of targets, while 293 mediums made sorties. Today the mediums turned again to villages in front of VII Corps. The ordnance depot at Merzig was the target for B–26 Marauders of three groups plus 41 A–26 Invaders led by eight A–20K Havocs. The Marauders launched their attack from 5000 feet, while the light bombers came in at 6000 feet. In spite of occasionally heavy flak, the bombing was very accurate and all bombers returned to base.

Monday, 20 November

Fighters of the 8th Air Force flew patrols and fighter-sweeps.

Fighters of XXIX TAC broke up two enemy counterattacks. The Thunderbolts struck within 400 yards in front of their own ground forces to pave the way for the advance of the troops near Koslar, which town was

347

seized shortly thereafter. Several attacks were made on tanks, of which a number were destroyed.

Tuesday, 21 November

More than 700 heavy bombers of the 8th Air Force, with an escort of 650 Mustangs, headed toward Germany in compliance with their efforts to deprive the Germans of their precious oil. 475 tons of bombs were dropped by the Fortresses on the oil plants at Merseburg-Leuna, and about the same tonnage was delivered on the plants at Hamburg-Rhenania.

Heavy clouds made some formations abandon their oil targets, and this was the reason that bombs also hailed down on the rail lines near the airfield at Gieszen.

The German Air Force only occasionally brought up its fighter arm, but when it did it was mostly in large numbers. This new tactic was unquestionably mainly a consequence of a desperate shortage of gasoline.

It was always unpredictable as to when a large German fighter force would be met, but today happened to be one of those days. Some 400 Luftwaffe fighters intercepted the bombers in the Leipzig area. Mustangs succeeded in shielding all formations but one. This formation was jumped by hordes of German fighters. Five Fortresses went down. One unit of FW-190s was caught while assembling, and they didn't even drop their belly tanks when the Mustangs tore into them. The inexperience of the German pilots was going to take a heavy toll of them. The fight raged all through the heavy clouds, and when the final tally was made up, 73 German fighters had been shot down. Only two Mustangs failed to return.

9th Air Force operations were limited by the bad weather.

Fifteen Thunderbolts of the 366th Fighter Group received a call to intercept some sixty Me-109s near Düsseldorf. The encounter ended up with another mauling for the Luftwaffe. Ten Messerschmitts were claimed for no losses.

Wednesday, 22 November

Weather conditions were so abominable that no air operations of the 9th Air Force in support of the ground forces were possible.

Thursday, 23 November

Persistent bad weather conditions foiled 8th Air Force operations against a number of oil targets. It also limited air operations of the 9th Air Force.

Friday, 24 November

Foul weather precluded all 8th and 9th Air Force operations.

Saturday, 25 November

The 8th Air Force dispatched its heavy bombers again on a mission to the oil plants at Merseburg-Leuna. This time, 1390 tons of bombs hailed down on the plants.

Pilots of IX TAC flying reconnaissance missions reported heavy rail traffic on the east bank of the Rhine near Cologne, and between Cologne, Wahn, Bonn, and Koblenz. Road traffic was especially heavy at Zülpich, Hergarten, and Rheder.

November 26, 1944. Streaming heavy contrails, these Fortresses proceed to railway targets at Bielefeld. (Official USAF Photo)

Sunday, 26 November

Oil installations in the Hannover area and the rail yard at Hamm were the destinations of a large stream of nearly a thousand Fortresses and Liberators.

One of the largest Luftwaffe forces so far encountered took to the air, and between 400 to 500 fighters were all set up to deal with the bombers in the target area. The Liberators of the 2nd Division, which dropped 860 tons of bombs on the last operative plant at Misburg, received the brunt of the Luftwaffe assault. Diving out of the clouds in line-abreast formation, the Germans struck deadly blows, and twenty Liberators were shot down, including an entire squadron. The 491st Bomb Group lost fifteen B–24s.

266 B–17 Fortresses bombed the fourth-most-important communications target at Hamm. Bombs were dropped through the clouds. Flak brought down one Fortress in the target area.

All told, 25 heavy bombers were lost. However, the German fighter force was decimated by the fighter escort, and 110 were claimed by the Mustang pilots.

The same intense rail traffic as on the previous day was observed by reconnaissance pilots of IX TAC, as well as heavy road traffic between Düren and Zülpich.

Eleven P–61 Black Widows of the 422nd Night Fighter Squadron encountered the Luftwaffe on their nocturnal mission and they sent two aircraft down. They also destroyed a V–1.

Monday, 27 November

Large forces of 8th Fortresses and Liberators were on their way to targets in Germany such as Bingen and Offenburg, when they were intercepted by the largest number of German fighters seen on any day. An estimated 750 Luftwaffe aircraft intended to strike a tremendous blow at the bombers.

But then, some 200 Germans made a gross error. Near Magdeburg, they mistook a huge force of P–51 Mustangs of the 357th and 353rd Fighter Groups for a bomber formation, and when the Luftwaffe pilots were aware of their blunder, it was too late to rectify.

The 357th Group attacked one of the novice formations. As if paralyzed, the Germans clung together while the Mustangs knocked down one after the other. Within 35 minutes, the group had shot down thirty aircraft. The 353rd Fighter Group ran into the same situation with a German formation merrily continuing its way ignoring the fights that were going on to its rear. Twenty-one German fighters went down for the loss of two Mustangs.

350

The only loss of the 357th Group was a Mustang shot down by another Mustang just as he was lining up behind a German fighter to make his third victim of the day. The pilot never made his third kill, but instead became a POW.

Mustangs of other fighter groups had joined the aerial shooting. The German losses were frightful: 98 were claimed by the Mustang pilots, losing eleven of their number.

IX TAC pilots flew their reconnaissance missions to keep an eye on the heavy rail and road traffic. Heavy road traffic was observed at Vossenack, Soller, Blatzheim, and a number of other villages.

Tuesday, 28 November

Road traffic west of the Rhine had increased on a scale that impressed the pilots of reconnaissance aircraft. Some twenty-five ambulances were observed going from Blatzheim in a southwesterly direction. About fifteen tanks were noted leaving a road and moving into a wood. An undetermined number of German tanks, all camouflaged, were observed near Hürtgen.

Fourteen Thunderbolts of the 365th Fighter Group were flying a ground support mission when they ran into 39 Luftwaffe fighters east of Düren. After the scrap, all Thunderbolts were able to assemble again, whereas the Luftwaffe had its rows depleted by four aircraft.

Wednesday, 29 November

After they had visited Misburg on the 26th, the heavy bombers of the 8th turned again to the oil plant today to complete the job. 400 B–17 Fortresses totally wrecked the plant with 1152 tons of bombs. 294 Fortresses returned to Hamm to bomb the heavily loaded west-bound sorting. As usual, clouds covered the target and the Fortresses were led over the target by pathfinders.

Thursday, 30 November

More than 1200 heavy bombers were sent out to attack Merseburg-Leuna and several other oil targets. The enormous bomberstream was led by the 1st Division, heading towards its assigned target, the synthetic oil plant at Zeitz. Merseburg, some twenty miles to the north, was the objective for the 3rd Division.

Both divisions followed the same route on the stretch to Osnabrück. Here they had to separate to continue on to their respective targets. At least, so it was planned. However, the 1st Division overshot this point, also caused by haze, and the 3rd Division followed. When the error was detected, the 3rd Division was many miles south of its correct course and beyond the turning point. Their new route to the target would have taken the bombers over the heavy concentration of eighty-six guns defending Zeitz. A try was made to cross over the narrowest points of the defended area during the bomb run.

Strong headwinds prolonged the torture, and the 3rd Division found itself subjected to the strongest anti-aircraft barrage it had ever experienced. And most of the 29 bombers that failed to return fell to these guns. Seven of the victims were of the 390th Bomb Group.

1015 tons of bombs were unloaded on the oil plants, while Böhlen, Zeitz, and Lützkendorf received respectively 166, 320, and 419 tons of bombs.

German oil production in November was estimated at 31 percent of the average monthly production in the spring.

At this stage of the war, the situation of the 9th Air Force was as follows: the 9th Bombardment Division occupied fields in the general area of Paris, and it would remain there throughout the winter; XIX TAC occupied fields in the northeast corner of France, south of the Belgian and Luxembourg borders; IX and XXIX TACs in the north, east of Brussels, and in part of Holland (Limburg).

Operation "Queen" could be considered as ended without attaining much progress. VII Corps had moved some ten miles at the most, but elsewhere the front of FUSA hadn't changed much. NUSA had pushed its front line forward in the vicinity of Würselen, Bourheim, and Aldenhoven. On the whole, a discouragingly small progress had been made in November.

TUSA captured all but four of the forts at Metz. The Siegfried Line had been reached.

A heavy effort had been put in the attacks on the German railway system by all air forces, and there was a clear indication that the Germans suffered from exhaustion of locomotive reserves and strain of servicing and repair facilities. In spite of this, vital military traffic was still moved over the rails, and at this time at a large scale, especially west of the Rhine.

Reconnaissance aircraft also noted many flats loaded with tanks. Some twenty flats loaded with Tiger tanks were seen on the Euskirchen-Münstereifel railroad. More of those flats with tanks were observed near Euskirchen, and two squadrons of Thunderbolts raced to the spot and dropped their loads on the train. Much damage was done and several tanks were destroyed.

Marshalling yards on both sides of the Rhine were crowded. A considerable increase in road and rail traffic west of the Rhine was noticed. All sorts of vehicles were observed in towns, villages, on roads, and isolated farmsteads and numerous other places.

352

During this month, IX TAC flew 5015 sorties. They destroyed 37 enemy aircraft in the air and claimed the destruction of one on the ground. The command lost 45 aircraft. XIX TAC flew 3509 sorties, and claimed 23 enemy aircraft in the air and 50 on the ground. XXIX TAC made 4501 sorties and claimed one German aircraft in the air and none on the ground. The command lost 18 fighters.

The 354th Fighter Group, which had introduced the P–51 Mustang to combat in Europe, had had to give up its Mustangs this month and was re-equipped with the P–47 Thunderbolt.

The 8th Air Force this month lost 174 aircraft.

November, 1944—date approximate. 2nd Division B–24s thunder onwards above the clouds. (Official USAF Photo)

12

DECEMBER

Friday, 1 December

Atrocious weather made flights by the 9th Air Force, 67th Reconnaissance Group, impossible, but the 10th Photo-Reconnaissance Group was able to confirm the increased tempo of preparations of the enemy.

Saturday, 2 December

Heavy bombers of the 8th Air Force were on their way to Koblenz in very bad weather conditions. Near Koblenz, some twenty Me-109s jumped the escorting Mustangs from out of the cloud layer. Yet they might better have stayed behind the clouds, for they lost six of their number.

The Mustangs continued their mission, when their path was crossed by a Ju-88 nightfighter, nose and wings bristling with antennas. The Junkers was promptly shot down.

For the first time in months, the Luftwaffe made a serious effort to defend their troops west of the Rhine. A formation of Liberators was intercepted by some 150 fighters and eight B-24s were downed.

IX and XIX TACs aircraft kept watch on enemy movements with their increasing rail and road transport.

In very bad weather, Lightnings of the 370th Fighter Group set out to strike a heavily fortified strongpoint in Bergstein, standing in the way of TUSA when clearing the Huertgen Forest. The Lightnings were greeted with concentrated anti-aircraft and small arms fire. Yet they managed to deliver their napalm bombs right on the target, setting fire to the entire village and inflicting heavy casualties among the enemy troops. After the attack, ground forces captured the village.

354

Sunday, 3 December

Reconnaissance aircraft observed very heavy rail movements east of the Rhine, particularly heavy between Siegen and Cologne and Limburg and Cologne. Between the latter two cities, 170 flat cars were seen, carrying, for the most part, tanks and motor vehicles. In another area near Koblenz, 72 cars were observed with the same cargo.

Many trucks and half-tracks were seen moving in a southwesterly direction, with all trucks bearing the American white square panel markings.

Some sixty Me–109s attacked positions along the FUSA front in support of the defenders. This resulted in a number of encounters with the fighter-bombers of IX TAC. At least nineteen German fighters were shot down.

Monday, 4 December

Many targets such as Kassel, Giessen, and Mainz, were attacked by the bombers of the 8th Air Force. Some formations bombed the railyard at Friedberg as a target of opportunity, while barges in the Rhine were also subjected to an 8th Air Force treatment.

The 56th Fighter Group, returning from a strafing and support mission, ran into very thick clouds extending from the ground to several thousand feet. Many aircraft became lost and for nine aircraft, the pilot either bailed out or made a belly-landing.

More and more rail activity was observed west of the Rhine. Very heavy road transport was moving in the Schmidt area.

Tuesday, 5 December

The heavy bombers of the 8th once again went to Berlin. That a strong Mustang escort was still not an excessive luxury was demonstrated when some 300 German fighters tried to intercept the bombers. But they paid a heavy toll for their ambitious intentions, and ninety of them were claimed by the American fighter pilots. Twenty-two of these were shot down by the Mustangs of the 357th Fighter Group, escorting the Fortresses of the 3rd Division. Near Berlin, some 100 FW–190s made efforts to attack the bombers, but the Mustangs prevented the execution. The group lost two Mustangs. Four bombers failed to return from the mission.

Atrocious weather precluded all reconnaissance flights by IX TAC. XIX TAC reconnaissance pilots reported very heavy rail traffic near Frankfurt and Hanau. These pilots also reported many flats with canvas-covered tanks and trucks.

Pilots of the 422nd Night Fighter Squadron of IX TAC reported an unusual number of hooded lights along roads on both banks of the Rhine, which could hardly be interpreted as other than road convoys.

Wednesday, 6 December

Even after the many attacks in the previous months, the oil plants at Merseburg-Leuna were in partial operation. Therefore, the 8th Air Force continued its offensive against this important target, and today the bombers struck the plant with a load of 1075 tons of bombs.

The 48th Fighter Group flew a mission to a heavily defended area north of Jülich in support of the 9th Army. A heavy overcast forced the Thunderbolts to fly at a very low level. Arriving at their destination, the P–47s circled around at zero altitude to locate enemy forces. Several planes were damaged by intense flak and small ground fire.

After the Thunderbolts had bombed and strafed enemy troops, strongpoints, defended buildings, and entrenchments, NUSA was able to move forward again.

Again the pilots of the 422nd Night Fighter Squadron, IX TAC, reported numerous lights on the roads further west of the Rhine. Pilots of the 425th Night Fighter Squadron, XIX TAC, reported same experiences. Apart from the usual objects, they also observed fifty searchlights in the Kaiserslautern area.

Thursday, 7 December

Bad weather made reconnaissance flights in connection with the movement of German forces impossible.

Friday, 8 December

The many transports of the enemy, reported by the reconnaissance pilots of IX TAC, now included several hospital trains, west of the Rhine. The reports also made clear that all kinds of traffic movements were taking place nearer to the front.

Saturday, 9 December

The 8th Air Force dispatched its bombers on a mission to targets involved in aircraft production such as the aircraft factories at Stuttgart/Böblingen. There a destructive load was dropped by the Fortresses of the 1st Division.

In spite of bad weather conditions, the 9th Bombardment Division flew missions in support of the ground forces. The defended village of Tholey was bombed, but results could not be observed.

Sunday, 10 December

Koblenz was one of the targets to receive a punishment from the 8th Air Force heavies.

Every reconnaissance mission flown by IX TAC reported numerous trains on almost every line on both sides of the Rhine, with more and more congestion near the front.

Monday, 11 December

The Reich was visited by the largest force of heavy bombers ever dispatched by the 8th Air Force. 1467 Fortresses and Liberators attacked many targets without interference from German fighters. Much damage was brought about in places like Giessen, Frankfurt, and many others. Marshalling yards were among the objectives to be visited, while other formations turned to targets of opportunity such as Koblenz.

Tuesday, 12 December

Oil targets and marshalling yards were the main objectives for the bombers of the 8th Air Force. 1000 tons descended on the plants at Merseburg-Leuna, while other formations of heavies bombed the marshalling yards at Giessen, Frankfurt, Darmstadt, and several other cities.

461 Fortresses of the 3rd Division dropped a bombload on the rail center at Darmstadt in a visual attack. Built-up areas, including the Merek chemical works, were severely hit.

Pilots of XIX TAC returned with reports of continuing heavy transport movements.

An attempt by medium bombers of the 9th Bombardment Division to attack the defended village of Blumenthal, prior to a ground assault, was prevented by weather, and the bombers returned with their bombloads. One bomber became uncontrollable due to icing, and crashed. The Marauder came down southwest of Liège, killing the entire crew.

Thursday, 14 December

IX TAC Reconnaissance pilots reported numerous trucks and a 200-yard-long infantry column in the vicinity of Monschau. Near the front in

357

the vicinity of Einruhr, twenty to twenty-four dual-purpose guns were seen on a hill. They were not even camouflaged.

XIX TAC Reconnaissance pilots reported the same congestion on the roads as their northern colleagues. And like so many times before, numerous stacks of large boxes were noticed along the roads.

Friday, 15 December

Escorted by a heavy fighter force, the bombers of the 8th Air Force headed for a number of targets in Germany, chiefly marshalling yards. Kassel was again visited, and also Hannover received a share of the bombload.

In spite of the persistent bad weather, which seriously hampered fighter-bomber operations during the first half of the month, many towns and villages had been attacked to destroy troops, equipment, and stores.

Reconnaissance aircraft observed more than 120 vehicles proceeding south from Heimbach as part of numerous other traffic movements.

Saturday, 16 December

A large offensive was planned by the Allies to reach the Rhine in an all-out effort before the year was out. But it turned out to be very different, and the offensive was on the German side.

In the early morning hours, the Germans started Operation "Greif," the Ardennes Offensive, under Field Marshal von Rundstedt. With an overwhelming force, the Germans launched their attack on an approximately 75-mile front, extending from Monschau to Echternach. Involved were eight Panzer grenadier divisions and ten infantry divisions, supported by 500 tanks, 350 assault guns, 1300 artillery pieces, and 1376 fighters and bombers.

The German plan was to drive through the Allied lines, only weakly held by battle-worn American divisions, through the hilly, heavily wooded Ardennes, to the Meuse. After crossing the river, they were to race for Antwerp.

Surprise was a main factor for success, and this was fully realized. Both the Allied command and its battle-weary troops were completely taken by surprise. Why they were taken by surprise remains amazing (to say the least), because reports from air reconnaissance and ground intelligence gave mounting information regarding the enemy's preparations and concentrations of troops and all kinds of materiel and equipment in the area opposite the Ardennes. This information started to come in in the latter half of November, and piled up until this day. Sure enough, there must

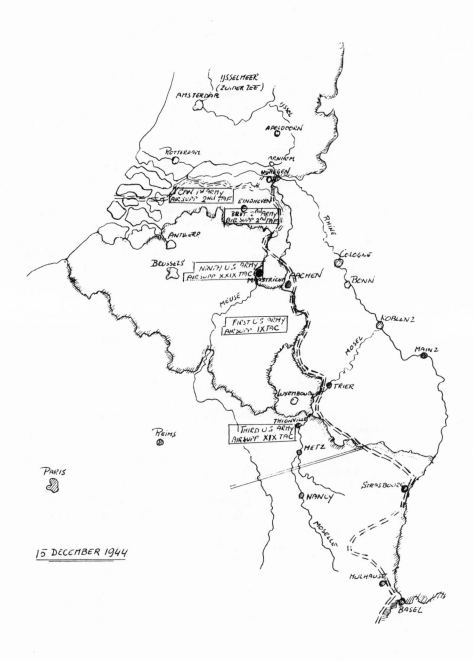

IJSSELMEER
(ZUIDER ZEE)

AMSTERDAM

IJSSEL

APELDOORN

ROTTERDAM

ARNHEM

NIJMEGEN

CAN 1st ARMY
AIR SUPP 2ND TAF

EINDHOVEN

BRIT 2nd ARMY
AIR SUPP 2ND TAF

ANTWERP

RHINE

BRUSSELS

COLOGNE

NINTH U S ARMY
AIR SUPP XXIX TAC

MAESTRICHT

AACHEN

BONN

MEUSE

FIRST U S ARMY
AIR SUPP IX TAC

KOBLENZ

MOSEL

MAINZ

LUXEMBOURG

TRIER

REIMS

THIONVILLE

THIRD U S ARMY
AIR SUPP XIX TAC

METZ

PARIS

NANCY

STRASBOURG

MOSELLE

15 DECEMBER 1944

MULHAUSE

BASEL

359

have been a total misinterpretation of incoming information and a fault in organization, for the failure was complete.

The attack was well prepared, and it had to be launched during a protracted period of bad weather, so as not to give the Allied air forces a chance to interfere. Hitler and Goering assured the ground commanders that air support of the tactical air arm could be provided with some 3000 aircraft. However, Luftwaffe Command West knew that such irresponsible promises could only harm the operation and informed the Commander-in-Chief West that the fighter strength was at most 1700 aircraft, of which number about half might be operational. This first day, Luftwaffe fighters made only 120 sorties in support of their army.

The weather limited the operations of IX and XXIX TACs aircraft to slightly over 100 sorties. Many villages and numerous woods with enemy troops were attacked. In spite of low clouds, the fighters aimed at bridges or tried to cut rails.

The weather was slightly better in the XIX TAC zone of operation, and in 237 sorties, the fighters were able to gather a high score on the crowded railroads and highways. Especially between Koblenz, Homburg, and Trier, the pilots obtained lucrative results.

Meanwhile, Stuttgart was among the targets to receive a bombload from the 8th Air Force heavy bombers.

P–61 Black Widows of the 422nd Night Fighter Squadron destroyed five enemy aircraft.

Sunday, 17 December

Countermeasures against the German offensive were taken as quickly as possible with the following purposes:

1. To strengthen the American forces on the northern and southern flanks of the penetration, to make this penetration as narrow as possible;
2. To defend key communications centers on the axis of the German advance as long as possible, in particular the road centers of St. Vith and Bastogne;
3. To establish a strong line of defense along the Meuse;
4. To regroup forces in preparation for a counteroffensive. All action of Allied forces north and south of the German attack area in the direction of the Rhine had to be halted.

Weather still prohibited the use of the bombers of the 9th Bomb Division.

360

Fighter-bombers operated in strength, making 647 sorties, most of them on the Ardennes front in direct support of FUSA troops.

The Luftwaffe showed its power to strike, flying between 600 and 700 sorties in support of the German advance. Most Luftwaffe attacks were concentrated in the St. Vith area.

Many encounters between the German fighters and Allied fighter-bombers took place, forcing the fighter-bombers to jettison their bombs and start a dogfight. That was why many assigned targets could not be reached, and one of these targets escaping a treatment was the Hangelar airfield. A Thunderbolt squadron of the 404th Fighter Group, intending to carry out this task, was jumped by some fifty Me–109s and FW–190s. A second squadron of the same group joined the scrap and six Messerschmitts were downed.

In the afternoon, a squadron of the 404th Fighter Group came to the aid of P–38 Lightnings which were heavily engaged in a struggle with FW–190s near Bonn.

After an encounter in the morning with sixteen Me–109s north of Trier, Lightnings of the 474th Fighter Group mixed it up again with the Luftwaffe after bombing two bridges and strafing a train. Two Lightnings were lost, one of them making a belly-landing near Luxembourg. Four Focke Wulfs were shot down by the Lightnings.

In all, the American flyers claimed 68 German aircraft for a loss of sixteen of their number.

Reconnaissance aircraft kept an eye on enemy movements in the Ardennes and eastward towards the Rhine. Fighter pilots who took part in the battle in the Ardennes-Eifel region, reported columns of vehicles on roads all around the area, often bumper to bumper.

At night, the 422nd Night Fighter Squadron attacked the marshalling yards at Rheinbach, Gemünd, and Schleiden. Some uneventful intruder missions were flown.

Monday, 18 December

The 8th Air Force struck with 963 heavy bombers on the marshalling yards at Koblenz-Lützel, Cologne-Kalk, Ehrang, and Mainz. Also, road chokepoints between Luxembourg and the Rhine were bombed.

Two Mustangs of the 359th Fighter Group, flying at 10,000 ft. and heading for home, became mixed up with 60-plus German fighters. In the ensuing air battle, the Mustang pilots shot down five German aircraft. At the end of the battle, light flak opened up and one of the Mustangs was set ablaze. The pilot was thrown clear of the aircraft when it exploded. His clothes were on fire, but the pilot managed to beat out the flames before pulling the ripcord. He was taken to a hospital by nearby flak troops. The other Mustang pilot also bailed out. He also suffered from severe burns, but eventually recovered.

The German 5th SS Panzer Army passed to the east of Malmedy and rushed to Stavelot, while the 6th SS Panzer Army reached St. Vith. In the south, Wiltz was captured and the Germans were heading for Bastogne.

It was the first day in the Ardennes battle that the weather enabled the 9th Bombardment Division to put its weight into the scale, and 165 medium bombers dropped over 274 tons of bombs on a number of defended villages.

The fighter-bombers were also active, and now that the Germans were coming more into the open, they offered very profitable bombing and straf-

December 18, 1944. Oil facilities at Regensburg under attack. (Official USAF Photo)

ing targets. But, as on the previous day, many a fighter pilot had to jettison his bombs before reaching his targets because the Luftwaffe showed up in force, resulting in many air fights. The German Air Force flew 450 to 500 sorties.

The fighters of IX TAC encountered deteriorating weather in the afternoon and accomplished only 300 sorties. One of these sorties took the 365th Fighter Group Thunderbolts, assisted by three squadrons from two other groups, over an armored column stretching out from Stavelot, La Gleize, to Stoumont. The fighters were called to their target by reconnaissance aircraft. The Thunderbolts came in very low, forced down by the exceedingly low ceiling. In persistent attacks, from one end to the other they created havoc, and 32 armored vehicles and 56 motor vehicles were destroyed, and many others damaged.

Road and rail traffic from München-Gladbach in the north to Euskirchen and Schleiden in the south were treated likewise. This all didn't pass unnoticed by the Luftwaffe, and in several air combats, the American flyers claimed 34 German aircraft for a loss of four.

Reconnaissance sorties were flown throughout the day.

At night, the defended villages of Harperscheid and Dreiborn were bombed by nightfighters, flying twelve sorties, most of them uneventful night patrols.

Tuesday, 19 December

The 8th Air Force directed its efforts to tactical targets and Gemünd was one of them. Escorting fighters became entangled in dogfights with Luftwaffe fighters. Heavy bombers of the RAF were escorted by XIX TAC aircraft when they attacked communications centers at Trier, Bonn, and Cologne.

Major elements of twenty-one American divisions were engaged in an attempt to halt the German offensive. With no reserves left, it was decided that Patton would deliver two corps for a swiftly executed attack northwards against the flank of the enemy salient. TUSA's right flank was taken over by the Seventh Army of General Patch (American component of Devers' Sixth Army Group).

The Luftwaffe's support to the ground forces was limited to some 250 sorties. The weather was very bad, which also made only a few fighterbomber missions possible.

A low ceiling over bases, and rain and snow in the battle area, limited the IX and XXIX TAC's operations to close-support missions, attacks on troops and armored vehicles at the front, and bombing of defended villages.

Wednesday, 20 December

General Eisenhower decided to split the battlefield through the middle of the enemy salient, the dividing line running approximately from Givet on the Meuse to Prüm in Germany. All forces north of this line, including the entire US Ninth Army and virtually the whole US First Army, came temporarily under the command of Field Marshal Montgomery. This also implied that IX TAC and XXIX TAC were temporarily transferred to the operational control of the 2nd Tactical Air Force.

Foul weather prohibited flying of the fighter-bombers and also forced the Luftwaffe to stay on the ground.

Thursday, 21 December

The Germans threw more infantry and tanks into the battle. Considerable progress was made in the south where the key road center of Bastogne was encircled. St. Vith had fallen into German hands.

The weather permitted only a few fighter-bomber sorties. The Luftwaffe was grounded all day.

At night, heavy bombers of RAF Bomber Command were escorted by fighters of XIX TAC on a mission to communications centers at Trier, Bonn, and Cologne.

Friday, 22 December

General Patton launched his drive northward against the German Seventh Army.

Fighter-bomber operations were not possible because of bad weather in the American zone. However, above the 2nd Tactical Air Force bases, the weather lifted and some eighty sorties were flown between Aachen and Trier.

The Luftwaffe made about 100 sorties, mainly in the area of Bastogne.

Saturday, 23 December

For the first time in days the weather broke and the Allied air forces used it to good advantage. The 8th Air Force sent 417 heavy bombers to the marshalling yards at Homburg, Kaiserslautern, and Ehrang, to the communications centers at Junkerath, Dahlem, and Ahrweiler, and to many targets of opportunity.

The German Air Force tried to interfere and 78 fighters made an attempt to attack the bombers, but 433 escorting fighters took care that such efforts

364

became a costly enterprise and 29 Luftwaffe fighters were shot down. The Americans lost two bombers and six fighters.

Another 183 fighters of the 8th Air Force carried out a freelance sweep over the tactical area. It was during this sweep that fifty-six Thunderbolts of the 56th Fighter Group were vectored to the vicinity of Bonn. Two large formations of German fighters were circling over the airfield at Euskirchen. Colonel David Schilling sent two squadrons to attack one formation, while he himself took the third squadron to close in on the other formation, simulating another staffel. The trick worked and his Thunderbolts were close enough to attack before they were recognized. The combat lasted for 45 minutes and raged from 28,000 feet to the deck, and when the fight was at its close, the Thunderbolts had accomplished one of the most successful actions of the war, claiming 37 Luftwaffe aircraft shot down for the loss of only four Thunderbolts. Schilling personally shot down three Me–109s and two FW–190s, being his last victories in this war. The fighter sweep eventually led to the destruction of 46 German fighters, whereas nine American fighters failed to return.

Three P–51 Mustangs of the 353rd Fighter Group flew an escort mission for two photo-reconnaissance Lightnings, when they engaged in two Me–262s. One of the Lightnings was shot down.

Four Mustangs of the 357th Fighter Group flew escort for an RAF PRU–Spitfire. While the Spitfire was taking its pictures, the Mustangs mixed it up with two Me–109s. Both Messerschmitts were destroyed.

The Allied tactical air forces were up in full strength, much to the regret of the Germans. The Luftwaffe made 800 sorties, but half of that number was now assigned to the defensive role.

The 9th Bombardment Division had its busiest day since Normandy and dispatched 624 bombers. They went for many targets, such as railroad bridges at Mayen, Eller, Euskirchen, and Ahrweiler, a railhead at Kyllburg, a road bridge at Saarburg, and the marshalling yard at Prüm. In addition, a number of communications centers were bombed. All targets were situated directly behind the front line.

However, the mediums also ran into the stiffest resistance of enemy fighters they had ever met, and before the day was out, they were to lose the largest number of aircraft in a single day. Among the 465 bombers that attacked their targets were the mediums of the 391st and 386th Bomb Groups. Flying their morning mission to the railroad viaduct at Ahrweiler, both groups, with the 391st composed of thirty Marauders in the lead, were unable to make contact with their fighter escort. The bombers continued on without escort.

Nearing Ahrweiler, the anti-aircraft fire became very heavy and the two pathfinder aircraft went down, but the bombers started their bomb run. At this moment, some sixty German fighters tore into the bomber formation of the 391st Group, concentrating on the second box. Meanwhile, the first box failed to identify the target and wheeled around to start a second run. This time they placed their bombs on the mark. Under heavy attacks, the second box dropped its bombs on the first run.

But then the Germans directed their assault on the first box also, and sixteen Marauders of the 391st Bomb Group were blown out of the sky. The 386th Bomb Group, trailing the 391st, fared better and, although it had to sustain heavy flak for almost one hour, only some aircraft were damaged and none was lost.

Notwithstanding the heavy losses in the morning, the 391st Bomb Group was out on a mission again in the afternoon. With 21 B–26s, course was set to the defended village of Neuerberg. This time they suffered no losses.

The 387th Bomb Group was out on a mission in the morning to the important railroad bridge at Mayen, connecting the rail line from Koblenz to the front. The first and the second boxes of the group, involving some forty Marauders, became separated over a considerable distance. This left the second box without fighter protection. While nearing the target, the bombers met some twenty German fighters. Their pilots immediately observed the situation and took good advantage of it. In a short, savage attack, they destroyed four Marauders.

Very heavy flak could not disturb the bomb run, and an accurate bomb pattern destroyed the bridge. Two Marauders went down, a pathfinder lead plane and one of the flight leaders. Two other B–26s were so heavily damaged that they didn't make it home either, but their crews survived.

Trailing the 387th Group over the target were 33 Marauders of the 394th Bomb Group. They also delivered their bombs on the target and added to the damage. The 387th Group was not the only group that failed to pick up its fighter escort. Unescorted, the 397th Bomb Group neared the target, the rail bridge at Eller. Heavy and accurate flak met the bombers and three Marauders were shot out of the formation. But their suffering was not yet at an end. After dropping the bombs, which severely damaged the bridge, some 25 German fighters arrived on the scene. When the Me–109s withdrew after vicious attacks, they had finished off seven Marauders, leaving only five aircraft of the 397th undamaged.

Another bridge target for the mediums was the railroad bridge at Euskirchen. Here the 322nd Bomb Group met 20 to 30 Me–109s and FW–190s. The Germans attacked with vigor and tenacity, but the Marauders continued on to their objective. Both approaches to the bridge were hit, although the bridge itself was not demolished. Two Marauders went down in the target area; one of them was the lead plane. A third Marauder crashed near Sédan after the crew had bailed out.

A highway bridge near Saarburg was attacked by the 416th Bomb Group with their A–26 Invaders and A–20s as lead planes. The first flight could not identify the target and didn't bomb. The others delivered their charges with very good results. One of the A–20s started the bomb run with one engine pouring black smoke, yet the pilot kept his kite steady on course. On the way back, the Havoc crashlanded near Rheims.

In the afternoon, the 9th Bombardment Division flew out on many missions to a large variety of targets. 26 Marauders of the 387th Bomb Group attacked communications targets at Prüm without suffering losses. Marshalling yards at the same town were bombed by the 394th Group. One Marauder was hit by flak. The plane flipped over onto her back and then straightened out again, dropped the bombs, next slipped out of formation, and crashed.

The village of Zülpich was the target for the 322nd Bomb Group. However, weather interfered and only a few bombers were able to drop. Unfortunately, six of them unloaded near Malmedy, within their own lines, but no serious damage was done.

A–20 Havocs of the 97th Wing bombed communications targets.

The break in the weather also enabled the fighter-bombers to unfold their massive air power in devastating attacks against the German ground forces. IX TAC fighters flew close-cooperation sorties in the Marche–St. Vith area, and armed-reconnaissance missions in the northern sector of the penetration area. Three groups of IX TAC fighter-bombers escorted 260 C–47 Dakotas on a supply mission to the beleaguered troops in Bastogne. Flak was heavy and eight Dakotas were brought down.

In the early morning, P–47s of the 406th Fighter Group took off to support the surrounded troops at Bastogne, and from the moment they arrived until the evening of the 27th, the 406th Thunderbolts would cover the troops in Bastogne from dawn till dusk.

While two groups of XXIX TAC had to stay on the ground because of poor weather over the base, the other two groups, the 48th and 373rd, were heading toward the Bonn-Hangelar and Wahn airfields. Flying a few feet above the field, the Thunderbolts destroyed nine aircraft on the ground, while seventeen buildings and two hangars were demolished and a number of other installations were damaged.

Fighter-bombers under 9th Air Force control flew 696 sorties in which 91 enemy aircraft were claimed to be destroyed for a loss of nineteen aircraft.

Road targets in the Malmedy–St. Vith area and a large number of road junctions, especially at Kall and Gemünd, were heavily attacked by the fighter-bombers and mediums of the 2nd Tactical Air Force of the RAF. RAF Bomber Command took part in the daylight attacks with 500 Lancasters, striking on transportation targets.

At night, thirteen sorties were made by the two nightfighter squadrons attacking several towns in the area of Nohfelden. A railhead at St. Vith

367

and transport on the roads were strafed. One P–61 Black Widow was lost.

Today the three reconnaissance groups made 113 sorties. The 9th Bombardment Division lost 35 mediums and one light bomber. 182 aircraft received damage in various degrees.

For their extraordinary exploits of the day some medium groups received Distinguished Unit Citations.

Sunday, 24 December

A bright winter sky invited the 8th Air Force to send the largest bomber force into Germany that ever crossed its border. 2034 heavy bombers set off to attack airfields and communications centers. The large-scale enemy fighter opposition of the previous day asked for countermeasures to neutralize its aircraft and bases.

The enormous bomber column was led by the 3rd Division with, in its wake, the Fortresses of the 1st Division, droning on toward the airfields of Giessen, Ettinghausen, Kirch Göns, Nidda, Merzhausen, Rhein-Main, Zellhausen, Gross Ostheim, Badenhausen, Griesheim, and Biblis, all situated east of the Rhine. The rear of the bomberstream was brought up by the 2nd Division, briefed for fourteen communications centers. The last of the 2nd Division Liberators left England as the first Fortresses arrived over Germany.

Take-off of the escorting fighters was delayed due to ground haze and as it happened the Luftwaffe was up quite unexpectedly with 800 fighters to

December 24, 1944. B–24 Liberators of the 458th Bomb Group taxi to the runway to take part in the biggest mission the Eighth ever launched. (Official USAF Photo)

368

December 24, 1944. Havocs are made ready for another mission at Coulomiers Airfield. (Photo from *Air Combat 1939–1945*)

meet the bombers with one Gruppe already over the Allied lines. Near Liège, the first Me-109s started their passes at the head of the bomberstream. Four Fortresses of the 487th Bobm Group were shot down and five were so badly damaged that they had to make emergency landings in Belgium.

One of the victims carried the leader of the bomber force, Brigadier General Fred Castle. When his Fortress was on fire, he took over the controls and refused to jettison the bombs for fear that he might hit Allied troops. He ordered his crew to bail out. Still under attack, he continued his flight until a burst of cannonfire severed the burning wing. The Fortress went into a spin, taking the general to his death.

Shortly thereafter, the 726 fighters arrived to accompany the 1400 Fortresses to the many airfields where the bombers distributed a load of 3506 tons of bombs. Thirty-one bombers and twelve fighters failed to return, whereas 84 German fighters were claimed destroyed.

634 Liberators unloaded 1530 tons of bombs on the communications centers west of the Rhine: Wittlich, Eller, Bitburg, Mayen, Ahrweiler, Gerolstein, Euskirchen, Daun, and a number of targets near the front. Eight German fighters were claimed to be shot down for the loss of thirteen American aircraft. The marshalling yards at Koblenz received a bombload from Fortresses both in the morning and in the afternoon.

369

Yet the plastering of German airfields was not only allotted to the 8th Air Force. 800 Lancasters and Halifaxes of the RAF joined in the all-out effort to disrupt enemy airfields.

376 medium bombers of the 9th Bombardment Division went to the railroad bridges at Konz-Karthaus and Trier-Pfalzel, and to the Nideggen and Zülpich communications centers. It was a considerable relief to the crews that it was all accomplished without a single loss, after the many losses on the previous day. They dropped 686 tons on these targets and on targets of opportunity. Escorting Thunderbolts of the 373rd Fighter Group and Lightnings of the 474th Fighter Group strafed motor transport at Rochefort and Hotton, and in the Malmedy–St. Vith area.

Fighter-bombers of all three tactical air commands flew 1157 sorties and gathered an impressive amount of destroyed tanks, armored vehicles, motor transport, railway cars, gun positions, and dumps, and on rail-cutting sorties, rails were cut in 31 places.

The three reconnaissance groups flew 161 successful sorties. Very heavy road activity was reported leading to the German armies. Total Allied claims for shot-down German aircraft amounted to 125.

160 Aircraft of IX Troop Carrier Command resupplied the beleaguered forces at Bastogne.

December 24, 1944. A Havoc drops its bombs, also from under-wing shackles. (Photo from *Air Combat 1939–1945*)

December 24, 1944. Back from another mission, the CO
of the 647th Squadron, 410th Bomb Group, walks away
from his Havoc. (Photo from *Air Combat 1939–1945*)

Nightfighters flew fourteen patrols in an area between the Meuse and Monschau.

German ground forces had reached a point within five miles of the Meuse.

Monday, 25 December

The Luftwaffe again made a serious effort to oppose the 8th Air Force bombers which were well protected by their fighter escort. During these last three days, most bombers had fallen to anti-aircraft fire and only thirteen heavies were lost due to fighter interference, whereas there was reason to believe that the 220 German fighters shot down during these days, as claimed by the American crews, was not too exaggerated when compared with German figures.

422 heavy bombers of the 2nd and 3rd Divisions were on the way to communications centers and rail bridges west of the Rhine. The Luftwaffe was kept at distance by escorting fighters, although near St. Vith a few German elements slipped through the umbrella and managed to bring down three bombers of the 467th Bomb Group.

With an engine on fire, one Liberator pilot ordered his crew to abandon the aircraft. However, the sign was not heard by men in the rear and nose section of the aircraft, and after a while they were astounded to find the flightdeck deserted. The fire, meanwhile, subsided and the bombardier took control and brought the bomber on a course to the Allied lines. Over France, they bailed out, but the empty bomber continued her flight across the Channel to make a perfect belly-landing in a Welsh marsh.

Other bomber formations headed for Fulda and Kassel, and escorting Mustangs ran into heavy enemy resistance.

A rail bridge at Morscheid was demolished by 3rd Division Fortresses in a pinpoint attack from 25,000 feet.

Weather over many bases in England was bad. This not only limited 8th Air Force operations, but also precluded resupply missions to Bastogne.

However, most of the continental bases were in the clear, and so the 9th Bombardment Division could make 1920 sorties on this Christmas Day. 629 bombers dropped 1237 tons of bombs on rail and road targets like the rail bridges at Konz-Karthaus and Nonnweiler, and road bridges at Taben and Keuchingen. An additional number of communications centers were among the primary targets. Opposition was met near Koblenz. Three bombers were lost and 223 were damaged, chiefly by heavy concentrations of flak.

Many fighters escorted the bombers, and among them were the Mustangs of the 352nd Fighter Group. The group had taken off from their advanced base at Asche, Belgium, where the Mustangs had taken station on the 23rd. Near Koblenz, the Mustangs became engaged with the German fighters and one of the most successful fighter pilots of the 8th Air Force, Major George Preddy, scored his 26th and 27th, though also his last, victories. After the fight, with two other Mustangs he headed to Liège, where Luftwaffe fighters were reported. Approaching the area, they spotted a Focke Wulf at 1500 feet. Preddy chased the Focke Wulf, flying at zero feet when he passed the American positions near Liège. The anti-aircraft fire opened up. The German fighter flew through the barrage, but Preddy's Mustang received several hits and before he could free himself from the aircraft, it crashed into the ground. The top-scoring Mustang pilot had fallen to friendly fire.

Fighter-bombers flew almost 1100 sorties. The 48th and 404th Fighter Groups of XXIX TAC were grounded by weather but both other groups, the 36th and the 373rd, made 170 sorties on armed-reconnaissance flights near St. Vith and Stavelot, and in the areas of Euskirchen and Ahrweiler. The Thunderbolts paid special attention to the airfield at Bonn-Hangelar, which was successfully strafed and bombed.

IX And XIX TACs fighter-bombers operated in their respective northern and southern areas, ranging out as far east as the Rhine, delivering heavy blows to road transports. The day's claims of all three commands amounted to 99 tanks and armored vehicles, 813 motor transports, and a whole stock of other targets. Twenty-four enemy aircraft were claimed shot down for a loss of eighteen, mostly to flak.

371 aircraft of the 2nd TAF, 83rd Group, were out on armed-reconnaissance flights between Düren in the north and Prüm in the south, and westward to Stavelot. Their attacks added to the rubble on the roads near St. Vith, with six armored vehicles and 170 motor transports destroyed or damaged. Thirty-six mediums of 83rd Group, RAF, attacked the communications center at Junkerath.

Nightfighters flew defensive patrols in the areas St. Vith-Monschau-Kall-Dahlem-Euskirchen.

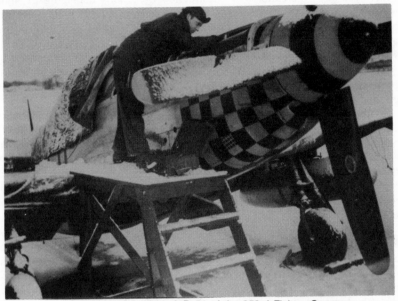

December 25, 1944. A P–51 of the 353rd Fighter Group being prepared by a mechanic for the next mission. (Photo from Air Combat 1939–1945)

Tuesday, 26 December

The RAF and 8th Air Force heavy bombers attacked marshalling yards, the road center at St. Vith, and several communications targets. Bomber formations of the 8th dropped a load on the yards at Koblenz, while 151 heavies attacked the marshalling yards at Niederlahnstein, Neuwied, and

Andernach, and the railroad bridges at Sinzig and Neuwied. St. Vith, with its surrounding area, was the target for 274 aircraft of RAF Bomber Command.

Rail and road bridges were bombed by the mediums of the 9th Bombardment Division, while fighter-bombers of all three TACs continued to take a high toll of German tanks, armored vehicles, motor transports, and many other tactical objects in close cooperation with the ground forces on armed-reconnaissance flights or freelance fighter sweeps throughout the battle area as far as the Rhine.

Much traffic was canalized through small streets of numerous villages, and by bombing these points, traffic was blocked by the rubble in the streets for days thereafter. The destruction or serious damaging of highways, railroads, and road and rail bridges, and the loss of huge quantities of transport all added to the enormous supply difficulties of the Germans, and it started to show its effects on the offensive. The 2nd Panzer Division was halted a few miles from the Meuse and would soon be surrounded by American troops. The German armor and transport had completely run out of gasoline and were brought to a standstill near Celles. Their fate was sealed, and the 2nd Panzer Division was smashed to pieces.

With yesterday's operations, 879 sorties were flown by the mediums against communications centers at La Roche and Houffalize, railheads at Kall and Pronsfeld, and rail bridges at Ahrweiler, Bad Münster, Eller, Konz-Karthaus, and Nonnweiler. With a few exceptions, the rail bridge attacks yielded only fair results.

289 sorties were flown by IX TAC aircraft, mainly armed-reconnaissance with some groups escorting the medium bombers, as on the mission to Houffalize and La Roche, which centers were severely hit.

Three fighter groups of XIX TAC, the 362nd, 406th, and 405th Groups, furnished close support to the ground forces, and the two other groups, the 354th and 367th, flew armed-reconnaissance missions with the special task of striking enemy reinforcements brought to the front, and more specifically to Bastogne. The beleaguered garrison at Bastogne was relieved by the 4th Armored Division after a determined drive north. Troop carrier transports were again flown to this town. Thunderbolts of the 354th Fighter Group provided escort. The 361st Fighter Group was also on escort duty, and accompanied the medium bombers.

XXIX TAC efforts were chiefly directed against rail and road transports in the 6th SS Panzer Army's sector, and in the area of the right flank of the Fifth Panzer Army. Successful attacks were carried out against traffic on the roads near St. Vith, Malmedy, Clerf, Houffalize, and St. Hubert, and along highways leading to the Ardennes. They formed very profitable hunting grounds.

374

Wednesday, 27 December

To attain a more equal division of air power between Montgomery's and Bradley's forces, three fighter groups, the 365th, 367th, and 368th Groups, were transferred from the IX TAC to the XIX TAC, and both commands were reinforced with a P–51 group from the 8th Air Force (the 361st and 352nd Fighter Groups).

The 8th Air Force dispatched its bombers to strike tactical targets like rail bridges, rail centers, and marshalling yards such as the rail yard at Fulda and the railroad bridge at Gerolstein. Fighters of the 8th flew patrols and fighter sweeps in the area of Koblenz and Trier. Many Luftwaffe fighters were engaged by the 364th Group, escorting the bombers to the Rhineland. IX TAC aircraft flew 301 sorties in support of the ground forces of the First Army.

At the request of ground forces, several towns and villages were hit. A considerable amount of enemy vehicles on the roads between Prüm, St. Vith and Houffalize was transformed into scrap. While escorting the medium bombers, the 352nd Fighter Group became entangled in a number of air combats with the Luftwaffe fighters in the vicinity of Euskirchen, Mayen, Bonn, and Prüm. Forty-five German aircraft were claimed by the Americans, losing five aircraft to enemy fighters and six to flak during the last two days.

Since early morning of the 23rd, the Thunderbolts of the 406th Fighter Group had flown 529 sorties in 81 missions in support of the troops in Bastogne. They had had to carry out their attacks against heavy anti-aircraft fire. Recognition of enemy targets was especially difficult because the Germans used Allied equipment, uniforms, and identification marks. During these five days, the Thunderbolts had destroyed thirteen aircraft, 610 motor transports, 194 tanks and armored vehicles, 226 gun positions, 59 fortified buildings, 43 horse-drawn vehicles, twelve bridges, and thirteen ammunition and fuel dumps. For its outstanding work, the 406th Fighter Group would receive the Distinguished Unit Citation.

The 361st Fighter Group was occupied with medium bomber escort.

XXIX TAC fighter-bombers continued their work of the previous day and when the evening fell, they could claim the destruction of 191 motor transports, 49 tanks and armored vehicles, and 207 buildings. Rail and road cuts had been made in respectively 23 and 53 places. Enemy air opposition was negligible, but heavy flak took a toll of eleven aircraft.

XIX TAC aircraft provided support to Patton's counterthrust with three fighter-bomber groups. The other five groups were reaping a rich harvest of all kinds of enemy transport, especially near Bastogne where the enemy was concentrating large forces. In these last two days, the claims amounted to 690 motor transports, 90 tanks and armored vehicles, 44 gun positions, 143 rail cars, two bridges, while also 55 highway cuts and 33 rail cuts were made. The fighters claimed 25 German aircraft shot down for a loss of four aircraft in the air and thirteen by flak.

Five German aircraft fell to the guns of the P–61 Black Widows of the 422nd Night Fighter Squadron during a night patrol.

Thursday, 28 December

While the 8th Air Force bombers ranged over western Germany to attack a large variety of targets, notably at Bonn and Koblenz, the bombers of the 9th Air Force were grounded. Deteriorating weather over a large part of France and Belgium made the mediums nonoperational and also kept the fighter-bombers on the ground.

One of the means to impede German traffic was to fill the roads with rubble by destroying buildings. Therefore, six villages were assigned to be annihilated. One of them was Stadtkyll, but when the bombers of the 8th arrived, they found the village covered by a thick carpet of clouds. Instead they turned to Koblenz.

Friday, 29 December

The heavies of the 8th Air Force turned to marshalling yards and rail bridges. The rail complex at Frankfurt was among the targets to be bombed by the 3rd Division, while the Fortresses of the 1st Division also dropped a load on an ordnance depot at Bingen.

The continuing bad weather enabled only six bombers of the 9th Bombardment Division to make an attack, although more bombers had been dispatched. Fighter-bomber operations were only possible on a very limited scale.

Saturday, 30 December

Large formations of heavy bombers of the 8th Air Force were heading toward Germany to add to the destruction of the transportation system by wrecking the marshalling yards. This time the yards at Kassel, Kaiserslautern, and many others were plastered with bombs.

9th Air Force aircraft were for the greater part tied down by weather over part of France and Belgium.

Sunday, 31 December

B–17 Fortresses and B–24 Liberators thundered off the runways all over southern England and assembled for a massive raid on targets in Germany on this last day of the year, a year that ended with massive attacks on five successive days in which 5516 heavy bombers of the 8th Air Force struck rail centers, marshalling yards, communications centers, and bridges, escorted there by 2883 fighters.

This time the Fortresses of the 3rd Division headed for the oil targets at Misburg and Hamburg, and also for a jet aircraft factory. The B–17s ran into heavy German fighter resistance, and though the Mustangs of the 364th Fighter Group knocked down many of the attackers, the Germans extracted their toll from the Fortresses and fourteen were sent down.

Heavy and accurate flak was encountered, and another ten B–17s tumbled down. One Fortress received a direct hit and dived out of control onto another one, which was last seen heading for the coast.

An extraordinary collision at 19,000 feet occurred when two B–17s remained stuck together, one on top of the other. The crews from both aircraft bailed out, save for the two pilots in the top aircraft. Flying on the three engines of the lower Fortress and finding that some control was left, they decided to try a belly-landing with the combination, which they successfully accomplished. Only after the impact did the Fortress on top slide off the lower one.

Half the loss of this division was again borne by the 100th Bomb Group: twelve of its Fortresses were knocked down by fifty enemy fighters.

The 1st and 2nd Division Fortresses and Liberators continued their campaign against the German communications, including the marshalling yards at Koblenz. Eupen was also bombed, while the Fortresses of the 1st Division also looked after airfields such as Krefeld/Uerdingen.

The 78th Fighter Group scored the 400th and last victory with the Thunderbolt before the group converted to Mustangs, leaving the 56th Fighter Group as the sole P–47 group in the 8th Air Force.

The 8th Air Force Mustang groups were increased from seven groups in June to fourteen groups in December by converting seven P–38 and P–47 groups during this period. Many of the old P–38s and P–47s were sent to the 9th Air Force for replacement. The pilots of the 9th were not happy at all about it, and complained about the poor quality and even unserviceability of many of these aircraft.

Over Viviers, Mustangs of the 352nd Fighter Group spotted an AR–234 turbo-jet–powered reconnaissance aircraft, flying in a northeasterly direction. Down came the Mustang in a perfect dive and ended up behind the tail of the jet. However, the other Mustangs overhead caught sight of another Arado, lining up on the attacking Mustang. Calling the pilot to break, Lt. Colonel John C. Meyer immediately chased the jet. Near Bonn, he caught up on the jet and scored several hits. For a moment the plane was swallowed up in the clouds, but when it appeared again it was heading straight down to the ground. The Ar–234 did not have the superior speed of the Me–262.

Mediums of the 9th Bombardment Division were still grounded by weather over France and Belgium. Fighter-bomber operations were only possible on a limited scale.

Three B–24 Liberators of the 856th Squadron of the special duty "Carpetbagger" 492nd Group flew on a northerly course, one B–24 going to drop supplies in Norway, while the other two were going to drop over Denmark. Till March 5, 1945, forty-one sorties to these countries would be undertaken.

Total 8th Air Force heavy bomber losses this month: 96.

378

Part IV

1945

1

JANUARY

Monday, 1 January

Operation "Bodenplatte" called for a simultaneous attack with well over 1000 aircraft on the Allied airfields at Volkel, Eindhoven, Antwerp/ Deurne, Le Culot, St. Trond, Metz/Frascaty, and on the airfields in the area of Brussels and Ghent. Originally planned to precede the offensive on the ground, it was delayed by bad weather.

Since the first briefing on 14 December, many aircraft had dwindled from their rows after the many battles during the previous weeks. But to the German Command it was clear that if the Ardennes Offensive stood a chance, and with it Germany itself, the scourge of their armies had to be eliminated, and this could only be accomplished by a mass attack on the Allied airfields close to the front.

The German fighter-bombers took off in sections of four in line-abreast with many sections following, all in line-astern formation. By 0900, the first were airborne. In all, about 800 aircraft took the air, almost all of them Me–109s and FW–190s. Those heading for the Brussels and Ghent area passed the southern part of the Zuiderzee, Rotterdam, and the tip of Zuid-Beveland. The fighters, their destination the area round Eindhoven, came from the north over the Zuiderzee, while the other waves, heading for the American bases, came in from due east.

The Allies were completely taken by surprise. The most successful attack was made on Eindhoven airfield, just as the Typhoons of Nos. 438 and 439 Squadrons of the Royal Canadian Air Force were taxiing out for a fighter-bomber operation. The Germans came in, skimming the ground and attacking with their cannon and machine guns. Almost all the Typhoons were destroyed or seriously damaged, while other units on this base suffered heavy losses as well.

But not all the attacks were as successful as the one on Eindhoven. Great confusion was caused over some airfields when the attackers got in each other's way. Sometimes the German formations failed to find their objectives altogether. Over the airbase at Asche, eight Thunderbolts of the 366th Fighter Group had just assembled when the Luftwaffe fighters came roaring in. Jettisoning their bombs, the Thunderbolts swooped down on the Germans and a vicious air battle raged on tree-top level over the airfield.

Twelve P–51 Mustangs of the 352nd Fighter Group, temporarily based on the same field, took off in the midst of the fight and in the face of the German attacks. Led by Lt. Col. John C. Meyer, the Mustangs knocked down twenty-three German fighters. The Thunderbolts accounted for twelve out of a total of fifty attacking, while another seven were shot down in flames by the anti-aircraft batteries joining in the melee. Not a single Mustang was lost and only one P–47 crashed (the pilot came racing back on a bicycle).

Yet the Allies received a severe blow: some thirty AAF and one hundred twenty RAF aircraft were destroyed on the ground, and a further sixty-two were heavily damaged. However, the Luftwaffe came to disaster. 226 German aircraft were shot down: 129 by anti-aircraft guns and 97 in air combat.

A feature not included in the German planning materialized when it appeared that the operation had been held a secret to such an extent that not all of their ground batteries had been informed, and so it occurred that many German fighters surviving the Allied guns were shot down by flak across the Scheldt estuary and by several other batteries. More than 200 went down.

Eventually the losses to the Allies were, from a military point of view, negligible, whereas the German Air Force lost, apart from many aircraft, some of its last capable pilots and experienced squadron leaders. The first day in the new year had become the worst single day for aircraft losses the Luftwaffe had ever experienced.

A variety of tactical targets were visited by the heavy bombers of the 8th Air Force, including the marshalling yards at Kassel, and rail and road bridges between Koblenz and Cologne.

Two of the three Konz-Karthaus bridges were damaged by the medium bombers of the 9th Bombardment Division. Fighters of IX TAC escorted the bombers.

Thunderbolts of the 366th Fighter Group, earlier in the day involved in the scrap over Asche, destroyed two Me–109s south of Malmedy.

The 365th Fighter Group suffered heavily from the German assault in the morning, losing twenty aircraft, yet the group managed to dispatch forty-four Thunderbolts on an armed-reconnaissance mission. In this mission, they destroyed four locomotives and twenty-five rail cars, while eight railcuts were made.

Night fighters of the 422nd Squadron brought down two Ju–88s during a night patrol. An Me–110 was destroyed by aircraft of the 425th Night Fighter Squadron.

To ease the pressure on their retreating troops, the Germans launched a new offensive in the area of the 6th Army Group in the direction of the Alsatian plain, north and south of Strasbourg.

January 1, 1945. A 500-lb. bomb hung up over the target. It fell off and exploded when this P–47 of the 366th Fighter Group touched down at its base at Asche. Miraculously, the pilot escaped with only minor injuries and temporary deafness. (Official USAF Photo)

Tuesday, 2 January

Heavy bombers of the 8th Air Force turned again to the Rhine bridges between Cologne and Koblenz. In two days, a total of 569 bombers attacked the rail and road bridges at Koblenz-Lützel, Koblenz-Engers, Neuwied, and Remagen. Formations of Fortresses delivered a bombload on the marshalling yards at Mayen, while other formations placed hits on a railroad bridge and nearby factories at Kaiserslautern.

In addition to their escort missions, the fighters of the 8th flew sweeps and patrols.

Aircraft of the 9th Bombardment Division scored a success when they destroyed the bridge at Bad-Münster.

Wednesday, 3 January

In heavy snow and extreme cold, VII Corps opened its offensive between the Ourthe and Marche, supported on its flanks by an airborne corps and the British 30 Corps. In poor visibility and on slippery roads, only very slow progress was made against a stubborn German resistance.

Bombers of the 8th Air Force set out to many targets, including Aschaffenburg, Fulda, Aachen, and the bridges at Cologne.

The 56th Fighter Group, the sole group in the 8th Fighter Command still using the P–47D, received the new model Thunderbolt, the P–47M. The aircraft was fitted with a new engine that increased speed in level flight by 40 mph, and various other performance advantages were incorporated.

Friday, 5 January

Heavy snowstorms harassed bases in England and caused several crashes when bombers of the 8th Air Force took off for a mission against rail targets at Hanau and Frankfurt, where a mixed load of high explosives and incendiaries was distributed. Bombs were also dropped on Koblenz. Flak was heavy and two bombers made an emergency landing in France on the return flight.

Fighter-bombers of XXIX TAC raised a heavy toll of enemy traffic, notwithstanding the worsening weather. Aircraft of IX TAC provided cover for the mediums, out on a bombing mission.

Saturday, 6 January

The bombers of the 8th carried out a heavy attack on the road and rail bridge at Bonn, and two rail bridges at Cologne, along with many other targets such as Kempenich and Darmstadt.

Flak over Stuttgart was intense, and the bombers of the 3rd Division had to divert from their assignment. The lead plane was hit and aborted the mission. In the confusion that followed, the bombers turned to targets of opportunity like Kusel, where the railyard was bombed, together with chokepoints, a bridge, and industrial buildings. Another town that received a load was Siebeldingen.

The Luftwaffe flew approximately 150 to 175 sorties in support of their Alsace offensive.

Weather still hampered operations of the three TACs.

Sunday, 7 January

Weather over the continent, that kept so many 9th Air Force aircraft grounded, didn't stop the 8th Air Force bombers from renewing their visit to the road and rail bridges at Cologne. Apart from these targets, the heavies turned to many other objectives such as Altenkirchen, Bitburg, and Rüthen.

An attempt to knock out the three-span Rodenkirchen Bridge, leading into Cologne, failed. Twelve bombers dropped through dense clouds by instrument.

Wednesday, 10 January

8th Air Force heavies droned on toward western Germany to strike transportation and communications targets. Ostheim was one of the towns to receive a load.

And again the bombers appeared over the bridges at Cologne. A break in the clouds enabled Fortresses of the 3rd Division to bomb the road bridge over the Rhine between Düsseldorf and Neuss. As usual, many fighter groups accompanied the bombers.

One of the places where the bombs hailed down was the airfield at Euskirchen. One bomber had an engine on fire. Over Belgium, the pilot ordered his crew to bail out. When he freed himself from the doomed aircraft, he was too low for his parachute to have a chance to open.

Apart from escort, fighters of the 8th also flew fighter sweeps and patrols.

Saturday, 13 January

Fortresses of the 8th Air Force set course to the Maximiliansau Bridge over the Rhine, south of the Ruhr. The bombers arrived there at an altitude of 21,000 feet. Flak was heavy and one Fortress received a direct hit and blew up. The bombs hailed down, covering the bridge, and the main span was knocked out.

Mainz was another target, and Fortresses of the 3rd Division unloaded on the Gustavsburg Bridge by instrument. The built-up area of a suburb, Kastel, was severely hit, while bombs also descended on the main railway line leading to Frankfurt and Darmstadt. Railway tracks and buildings at Euskirchen were also among the many targets.

IX TAC fighter-bombers flew close-support missions in the St. Vith–Houffalize area. Both other TACs carried out very active fighter operations as well.

Sunday, 14 January

A force of 841 heavy bombers of the 8th was dispatched on a mission to oil targets, still high on the priority list. The formations flew over Schleswig Holstein in a bright, clear winter sky. After some time, they took a southeasterly course and proceeded in a direction toward Berlin. The leading groups of the 3rd Division went to the oil refineries at Derben, while other groups headed for a synthetic oil plant at Magdeburg and a benzol plant in the Ruhr.

Ahead of the bomberstream of the 3rd Division flew the 357th Fighter Group. The Mustangs had rendezvoused with the first three combat groups of Fortresses off the North Frisian Islands, making landfall at Cuxhaven at noon. It was in the vicinity of Brandenburg that the Mustangs spotted a large concentration of enemy fighters preparing for an assault on the leading bomber formation. The high group of the German fighters was flying at 32,000 feet and consisted of some sixty Me–109s, and the low group was at 28,000 feet, made up of more than seventy FW–190s.

The Focke Wulfs came flashing in on the bomberstream in company-front formation in waves of eight aircraft each. But they were intercepted by the Mustangs and, although heavily outnumbered, it became an entirely one-sided affair. In a fight that raged for thirty minutes, the much more experienced Mustang pilots sent 56 German fighters into the ground for a loss of only three P–51s.

Other fighter groups also became engaged with the Luftwaffe fighters. The 20th Fighter Group, escorting the Fortresses flying in the wake of the formations escorted by the 357th Group, claimed the destruction of nineteen enemy fighters. Other Luftwaffe formations encountered the bombers, but in most cases the escorting fighters made the Germans pay dearly for their efforts.

One squadron of the 390th Bomb Group was lagging behind because of supercharger trouble of the lead aircraft of this squadron. Moreover, the squadron was some 2000 feet below the rest of the group, and here the Germans had more luck. All eight Fortresses were brought down, one after the other.

The bombing results could be considered as good. A crude oil refinery at Hemmingstedt was destroyed, while a synthetic oil plant at Magdeburg and a benzol plant in the Ruhr were severely hit.

Returning from escorting the Fortresses of the 3rd Division over the target at Derben, Mustangs of the 353rd Fighter Group picked up the B–17s in the Hamburg area to escort them home. When the P–51s neared the bombers, they spotted some fifty Me–109s with a top-cover of sixty FW–190s, preparing to launch an attack on the bombers. The Mustangs sneaked behind the Germans' tails and in the ensuing melee they sent three Me–109s and three FW–190s into the snow-covered ground.

Escorting the bombers out over Bergen in Holland, the Mustangs witnessed P-51s of the 4th Fighter Group chasing a number of FW-190s. One of the escorting Mustangs turned into their path and picked off one of the Focke Wulfs.

A flight of the same 353rd Group, flying at 20,000 feet, caught sight of two Me–262s flying at 10,000 feet. Diving down, the Mustangs built up speed and closed in on the tails of the jets rapidly. Both jets were shot down.

Other elements of the same fighter group strafed barges in the Elbe Canal, east of Hannover. They also shot up a locomotive, strafed a marshalling yard where they destroyed six locomotives and a number of railway cars, and passing an airfield, the fighters went down and, skimming the ground, they clobbered the field with their guns.

Heavy flak near the bridges at Cologne damaged many Fortresses when they made a renewed attack on these targets.

On the return flight, the bombers were also escorted by the fighters of IX TAC. On several occasions the Luftwaffe tried to interfere, which cost them three aircraft, shot down by the fighters of the 366th.

Losses for the day were nine Fortresses, thirteen Mustangs, and three Thunderbolts. The Americans claimed 161 German aircraft.

IX TAC fighter-bombers not only escorted the heavy bombers, but also the mediums when they flew a bombing mission to tactical targets. In the St. Vith–Houffalize area, the aircraft of IX TAC were mainly occupied with close-support missions. The fighter-bombers took advantage of the improved weather conditions and many armed-reconnaissance missions were flown, the main targets being again enemy traffic, strongpoints along

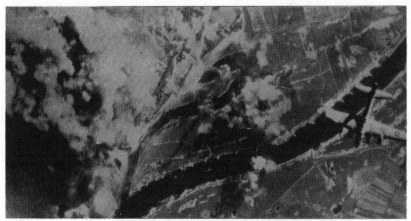

January 14, 1945. A 3rd Division Fortress wheels for home after bombing the oil storage depot at Derben. (Official USAF Photo)

roads, in villages and towns, dumps, and troop concentrations.

A large stock was collected by XXIX TAC aircraft operating in their specified area of responsibility between Lieurneux and Houffalize in the west and Wahlen and Pelm in the east.

XIX TAC fighters concentrated on rail and road traffic, gun positions, troop concentrations, and many other targets in the Bastogne area and on the southern flank of the German penetration.

Monday, 15 January

Bombers of the 8th Air Force were winging over western Germany, and among the many targets that received a bombload were Leipheim Airfield and Ingolstadt.

The 9th Tactical Air Command flew many missions, harassing the armies of the enemy. German towns and villages north and south of the Moselle were attacked, close-support missions were flown for Patton's forces in the Ardennes, while XIX TAC fighter-bombers included airfields and bridges in their numerous strafing and bombing attacks.

Tuesday, 16 January

The 8th Air Force dispatched its bombers on a mission to strategical targets in Germany and a force of nearly 1000 heavies set course to the synthetic oil plants at Magdeburg, Ruhland, and Salzburg, and to tank plants at Bitterfeld and Buckau. After escorting the Liberators to Magdeburg, Mustangs of the 353rd Fighter Group strafed an airfield near Nürnberg, destroying an Me–163 and a FW–190 on the ground.

South of Berlin, Cottbus and Jüterbog airfields were worked over by Mustangs of the 4th Fighter Group, returning from a B–24 escort to Ruhland. The group claimed 25 aircraft wrecked.

Out of a force of approximately 400 Liberators, 133 dropped their bombs on the marshalling yards at Dresden from an altitude of 22,000 feet.

Hodges' and Pattons' forces established contact in the town of Houffalize. By this, the western tip of the German penetration had been eliminated. No German troops of a force worth mentioning were trapped, and they continued to withdraw their troops in good order.

The Luftwaffe exploited a large activity in supporting the withdrawal of the ground forces. This led to many clashes with the fighters of the tactical air commands and it resulted in the loss of fourteen fighters. On the American side, five aircraft were written off.

To strengthen IX TAC in support of a new offensive action of the First Army, two Thunderbolt groups of XXIX TAC, the 48th and 404th Fighter Groups, were transferred to this command, leaving the XXIX TAC only two Thunderbolt groups, the 36th and the 373rd. Consequently, its area of responsibility was shifted farther to the North, covering a territory approximately between the Roer and the Rhine from Gemünd to Neuwied in the south, and Erkelenz to Düsseldorf in the north.

The withdrawal of German forces in a northeasterly direction presented the fighter-bombers with lucrative targets. During the greater part of the day, IX TAC fighters flew close-support missions, and in addition they escorted the medium bombers. XIX TAC aircraft also set out on close-support and armed-reconnaissance missions.

At this point, Fighter Group assignments to Tactical Air Commands were as follows:

XXIX TAC: 36th, 373rd
IX TAC: 48th, 366th, 370th, 404th, 474th
XIX TAC: 354th, 362nd, 365th, 367th, 368th, 405th, 406th

Wednesday, 17 January

Oil refineries at Hamburg and Harburg were bombed by the 8th Air Force with only fair results. Along with the oil refineries, the heavies dropped a load on Paderborn and struck the Blöhm und Voss U-boat yard in Hamburg. Although previous bombing campaigns against U-boat pens offered only negligible results and high air circles still regarded efforts in that direction as a waste of power and bombs, the U-boat targets were still on the priority list, though at the fifth place.

However, there was enough evidence that the German submarine fleet had grown into a formidable weapon again and that it might even be capable of bringing back 1942 conditions in the Atlantic (as judged by Winston Churchill).

The bombing of the Blöhm und Voss yards could hardly be considered as successful.

Thursday, 18 January

The 8th Air Force dispatched its bombers to Karlsruhe and some other places in the Reich.

The First US Army was put again entirely under control of General Bradley. The Ninth US Army still remained under control of Montgomery.

IX TAC had consequently returned to General Vandenberg's command.

Saturday, 20 January

B-17 Fortresses struck the synthetic oil plant at Sterkrade. The bombers also turned to the marshalling yards at Rheine, along with many other targets such as Mannheim, Heilbronn, and Ludwigshafen.

Near Heilbron, escorting Mustangs caught sight of a lone Me-262, flying at 18,000 feet. Aware of the danger, the German pilot pulled his jet away and tried to land at Lechfeld. But here a Mustang caught him and he was shot down. One of the Mustangs received a hit from flak and crashed too. The pilot managed to bail out.

Near Münster, another Me-262 made the mistake of turning within firing range of one of the pursuing P-51s, and the jet was promptly shot down.

Sunday, 21 January

The pounding on German targets continued and today Aschaffenburg was one of the victims. The 8th bombers carried out a blind-bombing attack on a tank factory, while 66 Fortresses delivered their bombs on the marshalling yards in this town. 3rd Division Fortresses made a blind-bombing attack on the marshalling yards at Mannheim.

Weather above the bases in England was also abominable, and when one bomber in trouble returned to its base, it was sent out over the North Sea again to drop the bombs before landing. The bomber was never seen again. . .

Fighter-bombers of IX TAC flew armed-reconnaissance missions, attacking road and rail traffic, especially along routes leading east from the Gemünd, Schleiden, and Prüm area in the direction of Hillesheim, Munstereifel, Euskirchen, and accordingly to the Rhine crossings at Cologne, Bonn, Remagen, and Koblenz.

Agents were dropped in Germany by the 856th Bombardment Squadron of the 8th Air Force, based at Lyon.

Monday, 22 January

The 8th Air Force dispatched the bombers to oil targets in Germany, along with many other objectives. Sterkrade was one of the unlucky places where a heavy bombload came down.

During a morning mission, the 362nd Fighter Group discovered more than 1500 vehicles. It was a portion of the 6th Panzer Army, heading east into the Prüm area. Other fighter groups, also from IX TAC, hurried to the scene.

390

Meanwhile the 9th Bombardment Division was in the air with 304 medium and light bombers, heading toward three railroad bridges, the railhead at Blankenheim, the marshalling yards at Gerolstein, and the highway bridge at Dasburg.

Two groups of Marauders, the 387th and the 394th, were assigned to attack the Dasburg bridge, crossing the river Our. At noon the 27 Marauders of the 387th Group arrived over their target and dropped their bombs very accurately. Ten minutes later when the 22 Marauders of the 394th dropped their charges from 12,000 feet, there was no longer a bridge at Dasburg left over which the 6th Panzer Division could withdraw. The result was a terrific congestion of traffic on all exit routes in the area of Clerf, Dasburg, and Vianden.

And while the XIX and IX TAC fighter-bombers raised havoc in the Prüm area, Thunderbolts of the 368th Fighter Group, XIX TAC, rushed to the area west of the Our, where they found all roads choked with every sort of vehicle, bumper to bumper, more than 1500 of them. Lightnings of the 367th Group came to their assistance.

Constantly the P–47s and P–38s raced over the columns from one end to the other, strafing, bombing with high explosives and incendiaries, and firing rockets. Motorized flak hammered at the roaring juggernauts in a vain effort to ward off the devastation. One Thunderbolt and one Lightning were shot down.

In the Prüm area, five Thunderbolts of the 362nd Group dived down and none of the planes taking part in the shooting left the ravage unscathed. However, 1233 vehicles were destroyed and 536 damaged by the XIX TAC, including twenty tanks and ten armored vehicles, which were claimed destroyed.

Claims of IX TAC were 409 motor transports, eight tanks, twenty armored vehicles, eight horse-drawn vehicles, and thirteen gun positions destroyed and many more damaged. The results of the attacks even surpassed the destruction in the Falaise Gap of August, 1944. IX TAC had lost six aircraft during the operations of the day.

Thunderbolts of both fighter groups of XXIX TAC were operating in the area of Düren, where rail traffic drew their special attention.

Tuesday, 23 January

The marshalling yards at Neuss received a bombload from the 8th heavies. Haze covered the target and many bombers dropped on the built-up area.

Just before noon, six Invaders of the 416th Bomb Group took off to carry out another attack against the German transportation concentrations near Dasburg. Only one plane was able to attack, dropping its bombs from

391

3000 feet. After releasing its bombs, the Invader dived down to strafe the columns. Very heavy flak kept the other five Invaders at a distance; some of them received serious hits, while others failed to identify the target. Two Invaders crashlanded in friendly territory.

Again six Invaders of the same 416th Group raced along the runway and set course to their assigned target. Soon after one of the A–26s lifted from the runway, it failed to retract its landing gear. The plane touched down again, but the landing gear collapsed and the bomber came to a halt beside the runway.

Two Invaders failed to find their target in the heavy clouds and returned. Only the formation leader picked up the target area, but he was welcomed with such intense flak that his plane was instantly hit, knocking out the hydraulic system. Without making an attack, he pulled his stricken plane away from the area and managed to land his A–26 at Laon.

The fifth Invader dropped its bombs near Berk, but heavy flak wounded the pilot and the A–26, with an unconscious pilot at the controls, dived down. At 1000 feet, the pilot regained consciousness and he pulled the bomber on a level flight again.

The sixth Invader found a rail junction near Blankenheim and unloaded from 3000 feet. Accordingly, the pilot swooped his aircraft down on the deck and attacked a mass of vehicles with his guns. Although severely hit by flak, he brought his plane back home.

The 409th Bomb Group also dispatched six A–26s. Five of them failed to identify the target. The only Invader left bombed vehicles near Arzfeld. After releasing his bombs, the pilot brought his plane down on the deck and attacked a gun emplacement and strafed a village. With the rudder of his aircraft damaged, the pilot machinegunned some vehicles and then he pulled his bomber up. By then the left engine was on fire, but he lined his A–26 up on the gun emplacement again and started another run. Next he strafed nearby troops. At this moment, his right engine was also on fire, but he attacked three more trucks before turning away to land his plane on a hillside.

Six A–20 Havocs of the 410th Bomb Group unloaded on columns of vehicles near Blankenheim.

XIX TAC fighter-bombers were also on their way to the profitable hunting grounds near Dasburg. Although many fighter groups were grounded by the weather, four groups, the 354th, 362nd, 365th and the 368th Groups, chalked up again a considerable amount of vehicles of all sorts, and this time without suffering a single loss. The four groups flew 183 sorties.

IX TAC aircraft hammered at traffic congestions throughout the day, making 408 sorties. The 366th and 474th Fighter Groups operated in the Blankenheim, Dasburg, and Prüm areas, while the 48th, 370th, and 404th

Fighter Groups roamed the area Blankenheim-Ahrdorf. Five aircraft were shot down and two came back with damage beyond repair.

XXIX TAC aircraft concentrated again on targets in the Düren area. 159 sorties were made by the group, resulting in a further depletion of German transportation. One aircraft of the 373rd Fighter Group failed to return.

Wednesday, 24 January

The weather grew worse and worse, and hampered 8th Air Force operations. The deteriorating weather also hampered 9th Air Force operations considerably, yet further actions were undertaken to eliminate the German columns. Weather in the southern area was better and permitted operations on a larger scale than was possible for the XXIX TAC. Only eight aircraft were dispatched by this command.

IX TAC fared better, and its 366th Group obtained the highest score of the day, claiming the destruction of 159 motor transports. Three P–47s were lost.

XIX TAC fighter-bombers continued to attack the southern flanks of the German withdrawing forces, and kept on harassing several towns and villages in Luxembourg and Germany.

Thursday, 25 January

Medium bombers of the 9th flew missions with a fighter escort of IX TAC aircraft. The three Tactical Air Commands made 581 sorties to deliver a final blow to the German columns. IX TAC had a loss of two aircraft, while 25 were damaged. XIX TAC lost one aircraft.

Since the first columns were observed near Prüm on the 22nd, the Germans had lost a disastrous amount of 6618 motor transports destroyed or damaged, 159 tanks, and many other vehicles.

Friday, 26 January

Operations were still possible in the XIX TAC's operational territory. Farther north, fighter sorties were impeded by poor weather that grew worse and worse, with snow showers from a very low ceiling. XIX TAC fighters continued to furnish close support to Patton's forces and maintained pressure on enemy strongpoints in Luxembourg and Germany, strafing all kinds of vehicles on road or rail.

Sunday, 28 January

Marshalling yards at Cologne and Recklinghausen were bombed by the Fortresses of the 8th Air Force. 115 Liberators appeared over two benzol plants in the Ruhr. B–17s of the 3rd Division attacked the rail bridge at Duisburg, serving the armies facing the British front. Haze partly concealed the snow-covered earth, but many bombers could make a visual bomb run and two direct hits were placed.

Monday, 29 January

The Henschel tank works at Kassel were once again visited by 93 Fortresses of the 8th Air Force. Aside from hits on buildings in the plant, a considerable amount of explosives came down on the nearby marshalling yards. Flak in the target area was meager this time.

Those 93 Fortresses formed part of a larger force turning to a variety of targets, including ordnance plants at Siegen and at Niederlahnstein.

Wednesday, 31 January

The American ground forces were almost everywhere back on the positions they occupied before the Germans launched their Ardennes offensive on December the 16th; the battle that would go into history as the "Battle of the Bulge" had ended.

For the Germans it had been a terribly costly adventure, both in manpower and in materiel, the latter losses for the greater part inflicted by the air forces. Total claimed losses: 11,378 motor transports, 1161 tanks and armored vehicles, 507 locomotives, 6266 railroad cars, and 472 gun positions.

9th Tactical Air Command aircraft made 11,657 sorties for a loss of 107 planes (including the losses on the ground on January the 1st). The fighter-bombers claimed 70 German aircraft shot down and eleven destroyed on the ground. The 9th Bombardment Division despatched 2515 bombers (though there were only eighteen operational days during the month). Thirteen bombers were lost.

The 8th Air Force this month lost 93 bombers and 44 fighters. The 8th fighters claimed 315 enemy aircraft and the bombers 41 German planes shot down or destroyed on the ground.

Also worth mentioning is that the British 2nd Tactical Air Force flew 75 fighter-bomber missions this month against V–weapon targets, thereby dropping 100 tons of bombs.

394

2

FEBRUARY

Thursday, 1 February

Seven hundred heavy bombers of the 8th Air Force opened the month's bombing with an attack on railway targets in Mannheim and Ludwigshafen. Bombing had to be done by radar. The bombers also attended to the bridges over the Weser. The road bridge at Wesel was attacked by pathfinder means, but without success.

Aircraft of the 9th Bombardment Division carried out attacks in the interdiction program, bombing railroad bridges, communications centers, and defended villages.

The first night attack by a 9th Air Force bomb group took place. The 410th Group had trained for more than a month in night operations. Equipped with all-black B–26s, A–20J and Ks, and A–26s, the group had been

February 1, 1945. Fortresses of the 401st Bomb Group high up in a wintery sky on their way to Mannheim. (Officials USAF Photo)

395

instructed by a squadron leader of the Royal Canadian Air Force, detached to the group because of his great experience in night bombing operations.

This night 25 Havocs took off and set course to Hillesheim communications center. Very unfavorable weather conditions were predicted and the decision was made to recall the mission. 22 bombers received the recall message, but three didn't and they continued on to the target. When they arrived there, the Havocs dropped their bombs, but they were unable to observe results. All returned to their base.

Friday, 2 February

The 9th Bombardment Division continued its activities against their specific targets as a preparation for the coming assault of the land forces in the direction of the Rhine.

The three Tactical Air Commands of the 9th were mainly occupied with armed-reconnaissance flights and ground-support missions. On one of these missions, Thunderbolts of the 362nd Fighter Group XIX TAC encountered and destroyed a Ju–88.

Sixteen Thunderbolts of the 406th Group carried out a low-level attack on an enemy airfield. With their gunfire and rockets, they destroyed ten enemy planes and damaged five others. One P–47 was hit by flak and crashed.

IX TAC fighter-bombers kept a special eye on the lines leading toward Bonn and Cologne, and especially the lines Sinzig-Ahrweiler-Dumpelfeld and Bonn-Euskirchen-Kall offered extremely profitable targets.

Saturday, 3 February

At a conference at Malta on 30 January, just prior to the Yalta Conference, it had been decided to support the massive Russian advance in the east by the full weight of the Allied heavy bomber fleets. This support was to be attained by bombing transportation centers through which the Germans transferred their armies from west to east and thus prevent the Germans from reinforcing their crumbling eastern front.

Many German towns in the eastern part of the Reich were already overcrowded by the refugees fleeing in advance of the Russian troops, and it might very well be possible to raise panic and confusion in those cities by heavy bombardment and eventually hamper the movement of reinforcements. Second on the priority list (with oil still in the first place) came cities like Berlin, Leipzig, Dresden, Cottbus, Chemnitz, and several others.

The first city to undergo a treatment by massive air power was Berlin.

Always attractive for Allied bombardment, it was now especially important because it served as a major transportation center and moreover, it was believed that the Sixth Panzer Army was passing through the city on its way to the eastern front.

1003 B–17 Fortresses of the 1st and 3rd Divisions arrived over the city, flying at an altitude of 24,000 to 27,000 feet. Visual bombing was possible and the Fortresses dropped their loads on marshalling yards and several railway stations throughout the city. The government district was also plastered with bombs. Severe damage was inflicted, and not only on the targets but also on the whole area in which the targets were situated. Civilian casualties were exceedingly high.

German flak was murderous and the bombers had to take evasive action. Twenty-one Fortresses were blown from the sky. The German fighters were unable to interfere because of very effective protection from escorting Mustangs. Apart from their escort work, the P–51s strafed railway cars and shot up locomotives.

For the Germans, it was difficult to make out the difference between the spilling of bombs and terror-bombing, and it was also difficult for AAF leaders, who had always steadfastly opposed indiscriminate attacks on civilians. Now they were confronted with civilian casualty figures amounting to 25,000, and the question now was—if the planned bombardments on German cities that served the eastern front did not deviate from the policy of only attacking legitimate military objects.

At the same time that the Fortresses bombed Berlin, 400 Liberators turned to oil targets and railway centers around Magdeburg.

Four Mustangs of the 55th Fighter Group were shadowing two locomotives southeast of Hamburg when one of the pilots caught sight of three large aircraft heading in the opposite direction at a low altitude of 800 feet. The Mustangs manoeuvred to approach them from the rear, and when they closed the distance, the pilots were very astonished to see that they formed a composite: an Me–109 on top of a Ju–88.

The first assembly crashed after a Mustang nearly severed the tail of the Ju–88. One Me–109 tried to release the bomber, but it was too late to escape. The third combination was also shot down. Shortly thereafter, the Mustangs spotted another three composites at a mile distance. But the Messerschmitts also saw the P–51s and they immediately released the bombers. One of the Messerschmitts had no chance to escape and was shot down.

The 9th Bombardment Division attacked bridges, railroad centers, and communications centers in connection with the planned offensive that would soon start in the north.

The 410th Bomb Group flew its second night mission when 26 A–20s, eight B–26s, and two A–26s were dispatched to bomb the motor transport depot at Mechernich. With the B–26s and A–26s serving as pathfinder and marker aircraft, eighteen Havocs unloaded with good results. The other eight Havocs found their target in the dark and proceeded to a secondary where they dropped their bombs on the Arlos rail junction. One A–20 was damaged and was destroyed in the landing.

Eight P–61 Black Widows of the 422nd Night Fighter Squadron had a busy night trying to intercept enemy aircraft, mostly without success. However, at 0120 hours, they contacted a Ju–87 Stuka at an altitude of 4000 feet and the once-so-notorious divebomber made its last dive.

Tuesday, 6 February

Poor weather had kept the bombers of the 8th Air Force grounded on the two previous days, and today it caused a diversion from the synthetic oil plants to the marshalling yards at Chemnitz and Magdeburg. These attacks complied with Russian wishes. 800 tons of bombs descended on each city, resulting in considerable damage to both targets and towns. Gotha, Böhlen, Schmalkalden, and several targets of opportunity received a bombload.

The 9th Bombardment Division dispatched its medium bombers against ammunition dumps, communications centers, and defended villages.

The three TACs operated in their designated areas. Two Me–210s were damaged when Thunderbolts of the 368th Fighter Group attacked an airfield at Giebelstadt.

Wednesday, 7 February

The 1st Division dispatched 300 Fortresses. En route to Germany the bombers were recalled because weather scouts, flying ahead of the formations, met a high front over the continent. One bomber which was separated from the formation did not receive the recall sign and continued on toward Germany alone. With no interference from fighters or flak, the lone Fortress arrived over Essen, unloaded its three tons, and returned to base.

Starting this month, the 2nd TAF flew over 3000 sorties in one week in preparation for the coming assault, attacking road and rail traffic, bridges, supply and communications centers, depots, and various other targets to harass the German defenses. More than 700 heavy bombers of RAF Bomber Command unloaded over 2000 tons of bombs on the defended towns of Kleve and Goch. Nightfighters of the 2nd TAF swarmed over a wide area, attacking all movements on road and rail leading to the intended assault area.

Thursday, 8 February

As on the day before, worsening weather conditions made it necessary to recall the heavy bombers of the 8th, already on their way to Germany.

The Canadians on the left flank of Montgomery's forces opened the offensive in a southeasterly direction from their positions in the vicinity of Nijmegen. They had to clear the area between the Rhine and the Meuse as far as Geldern and Xanten. The Second British Army of General Dempsey was temporarily to hold its front line from Boxmeer to Roermond along the Meuse river.

The offensive started after much preparatory work by the tactical air forces against rail and road networks west and east of the Rhine. Heavy support was furnished by fighter-bombers and medium bombers. Aircraft of the 9th Bombardment Division attacked marshalling yards, communications centers, rail bridges, depots, and many other objectives.

The 416th Bomb Group flew its 200th mission, and on this mission the group was equipped solely with the A–26 Invader, since sufficient glass-nosed Invaders were available to lead the six flights. 37 A–26s attacked the defended village of Elton, where 739 fragmentation bombs were delivered. One plane did not return to its base because it ran out of gas and crashed twelve miles short of its base, killing the pilot and seriously wounding the gunner.

IX TAC Thunderbolts on a patrol along the lines leading to Cologne and Bonn found very fruitful targets on the rail lines east of the Rhine between Cologne, Bonn, and Koblenz.

In order to provide the Ninth Army with its three Corps and two armored divisions with a fighter group for each unit, three more groups were added to the strength of XXIX TAC: the 373rd of IX TAC, and the 405th and 406th Groups of XIX TAC. XXIX TAC thus had a strength of five fighter groups: the 366th, 370th, 373rd, 405th, and 406th.

General Nugent requested an additional two fighter groups, but this was turned down because Nugent's command was under operational control of the 2nd TAF and thus under the control of the 21st Army, and it was well known that whatever came under the control of Field Marshal Montgomery was difficult to get back.

Fighter-bombers of the 2nd TAF flew 1211 sorties in direct support of the ground forces and on armed-reconnaissance sorties.

RAF Bomber Command's heavy bombers dropped a considerable amount of explosives on Kalkar, Udem, and Weeze.

Friday, 9 February

A large stream of heavy bombers of the 8th Air Force droned on toward Germany. 1296 bombers with their enormous fighter escort were on their way when weather intervened again and only the assigned targets of Lützkendorf and three viaducts could be reached. The majority of the bombers turned to targets of opportunity such as an ordnance plant at Weimar, an aero-engine plant at Eisenach, and an oil-storage depot at Dülmen.

The damage inflicted was considerable, and when the bombers came off their target at Lützkendorf, they had wrecked the place completely. This oil plant was wiped from the target list.

For many weeks, there had been no encounters with the German jets, but now, shortly before noon, about nine Me–262s approached the bomber formations near Fulda. Making use of their superior speed, they made wide S's around the formations to evade the gunners, but by doing so they were not in the right position to make a pass at the bombers, except their formation leader, who turned into a box of Fortresses and sent one down in flames. The Mustangs chased the jets and made efforts to force them into combat. They claimed two jets probably destroyed.

The 9th Bombardment Division dispatched its aircraft against marshalling yards, rail bridges, communications centers, and many more targets in support of the ground forces.

February 9, 1945. Jersey Jerk and companions returning from a bomber escort to Lützkendorf. (Official USAF Photo)

Saturday, 10 February

Weather permitted only a minor operation, and the targets selected for the bombers of the 8th were the oil depot and the marshalling yards at Dülmen.

The 9th Bombardment Division kept hammering on a large variety of tactical targets.

The Germans opened the flood gates of the Ruhr dams in the area of the First US Army. The large-scale offensive of the Ninth Army to cross the Ruhr had to be postponed.

Sunday, 11 February

The oil depot at Dülmen was the only objective to be visited by the heavies of the 8th.

The Canadians captured Kleve.

Tuesday, 13 February

As on the previous day, the 8th Air Force was grounded by weather, and all planned missions were scrubbed.

Mediums of the 9th Bombardment Division concentrated again on bridges and dropped an additional load on motor depots.

The three tactical commands flew armed-reconnaissance missions. On one of these missions, twelve Thunderbolts of the 36th Fighter Group, IX TAC, flying in the vicinity of Bonn, were bounced by two formations of twelve FW–190's and twelve Me–109's flying top-cover. The furious fight raged only for four minutes because the Thunderbolts were very low on fuel and broke off the fight, dived for the deck under the overcast, and raced for home. But not without leaving three of their number behind, the Germans losing one FW–190.

Fighter-bombers of the 367th Fighter Group attacked an airfield and destroyed a Ju–88 on the ground.

A small force of the Canadian First Army reached the Rhine opposite Emmerich. Elsewhere on the front, progress was also made, and by now the entire Reichswald was cleared of German troops.

Wednesday, 14 February

Railway centers which were believed to serve the German armies on the Eastern front were the objectives for the heavy bombers of the 8th Air Force. When the 311 B–17 Fortresses neared Dresden, smoke towered

401

15,000 feet high into the sky as a macabre monument of the terrible bombardment by the RAF on the previous night. 771 tons of bombs descended on the unlucky city. The attack was made by instrument.

294 Fortresses turned to Chemnitz where 718 tons were unloaded on the city, which also had to endure two bombardments within the space of a few hours. Some of the bombers could not pick up the target and turned to an airfield at Cheb, Czechoslovakia, and to Plauen. One of these Fortresses was shot down by flak. Meanwhile, 340 B–24 Liberators appeared over Magdeburg and dropped 811 tons on the city.

782 medium bombers of the 9th were dispatched during the morning and afternoon, of which number 622 struck rail targets, defended villages, depots, communication centers, bridges, troop concentrations, and supply dumps. Eight mediums were known to be shot down, while another six also failed to return. Six bombers crashlanded and 316 aircraft were damaged in various degrees.

9th TAC fighters strafed enemy airfields near towns like Darmstadt and Frankfurt. One Thunderbolt was shot down by flak, however many German aircraft were either damaged or destroyed.

Twelve Thunderbolts of the 362nd Fighter Group had a strange encounter when they bounced three enemy-operated Thunderbolts. The Germans used the P–47's to attack allied ground forces. They chased the two olive-drab and one silver-colored P–47s, but the Americans had to break off and return to base.

Today was a busy day for the 2nd TAF, flying 1890 sorties. The Luftwaffe reacted with over one hundred sorties, by both conventional and jet fighters, although no serious attempts were undertaken to interfere with the Allied air forces.

Thursday, 15 February

It was obvious that if the oil campaign had to be kept up-to-date, a renewed attack on these important targets had to be undertaken. Therefore, more than 1100 heavy bombers of the 8th Air Force set out to look after the execution. However, visibility was very poor and only one primary target could be bombed. The synthetic oil plant at Magdeburg was this time on the receiving end of 900 tons of bombs. 435 Fortresses turned to marshalling yards instead, and more than 1000 tons descended on Cottbus in a blind-bombing attack.

Another blind-bombing attack was carried out by 210 Fortresses on Dresden. Results were unassessable because bombing had to be done through a solid overcast.

402

Friday, 16 February

A large force of heavy bombers of the 8th Air Force was heading forward into Germany to deal another blow to targets in the western part of the Reich, principally the oil refineries at Dortmund and Salzbergen, and benzol plants at Gelsenkirchen and Münster. Other formations attacked marshalling yards at Hamm and Osnabrück.

The Ruhr Valley, which was considered notorious for its defenses by the heavy bomber crews, flying at an altitude of at least 20,000 feet, was now going to be penetrated by the medium and light bombers of the 9th, flying at around 12,000 feet. The targets included the jet aircraft parts plant at Solingen, and an ordnance depot at Unna, near Dortmund. The latter target was going to be attacked by three bomb groups involving 63 A–26 Invaders, 33 B–26 Marauders, and eight A–20 Havocs.

As could be expected, flak was murderous, and when the bombers neared the target, three aircraft of the 409th Group and a Marauder of the 386th Group went down. The pathfinder Marauder leading the 416th Group was badly hit and dropped the bombs off the target. Most of the Invaders of the 416th dropped their bombs on release of this aircraft. The Marauder and one Invader of the group failed to return. Another A–26 made a crash-landing.

American fighters had several encounters with the Luftwaffe. Just reconverted to P–51 Mustangs, the 354th Fighter Group destroyed four Me–109s during a brief combat in the afternoon. The 367th Fighter Group, which had just started to operate the Thunderbolt together with the Lightning, ran into German fighters. Two Me–109s were damaged. Strafing an airfield, the group destroyed an He–111, while P–47s of the 404th Group destroyed a Ju–88 on the ground.

At night, Mosquitoes of the 425th Night Fighter Squadron, XIX TAC, flew intruder missions.

Saturday, 17 February

Two of the three forces dispatched by the 8th Air Force were recalled due deteriorating weather. The third force continued to the marshalling yards at Frankfurt and Giessen. Only moderate flak was met.

Weather also hampered 9th Air Force operations, and only one fighter group took to the air. Sixteen Mustangs of the 354th Group were out on a fighter sweep, fifteen on armed reconnaissance, and two made a weather-reconnaissance flight. The fifteen Mustangs on their reconnaissance mission were busy attacking Zelligen with their bombs when, all of a sudden, two Me–262 jet fighters arrived on the scene. They made an unsuccessful attack on the P–51s only to receive several hits, whereupon the jets with-drew.

Monday, 19 February

Prohibitive weather kept the 8th Air Force grounded on the previous day. Now weather permitted only shallow penetrations into the Reich, and the bombers set out to strike at many targets in western Germany including the marshalling yards at Osnabrück, Dortmund, Münster, and Rheine, a bridge over the Weser, and a tank plant and benzol installations at Gelsen-kirchen.

In order to keep the German transportation system in alarming condition, medium and light bombers of the 9th kept pounding bridges and other rel-evant targets.

Fighters of the 9th Air Force were out on many missions. One of the fighter groups was the 362nd, going with sixteen Thunderbolts to Frickho-fen where they attacked the marshalling yards with bombs and rockets. Accordingly, the P–47s headed for Westerburg where the marshalling yards received a treatment by strafing. Pulling up after the attack, the formation was suddenly jumped by thirteen Me–109s and eight FW–190s hurtling down on them from out of the clouds at 16,000 feet. But again, aggres-siveness alone could not make up for lack of experience, as was clearly demonstrated when three Messerschmitts and three Focke Wulfs were shot down and another ten Me–109s were damaged for no loss to the Ameri-cans.

Tuesday, 20 February

If the citizens of Nürnberg had cherished the hope that their town might be overlooked by the 8th Air Force for the duration of the war, they were to be cruelly disappointed. Many supply trains formed the invitation for large forces of heavy bombers, and 2000 tons of bombs were unloaded.

The German railways were also visited by the fighters of the 55th Fighter group, and with yesterday's operations included, the group attacked 170 locomotives.

The 367th Fighter Group, XIX TAC, was exclusively operating the P–47 Thunderbolt by this point, after converting from P–38s.

Wednesday, 21 February

Railways and industrial centers in Nürnberg received a severe blow when 1800 tons of bombs were dropped by the heavies of the 8th. Fighters of the 8th Air Force swept the area.

The 386th Bomb Group of the 9th Bombardment Division had completed its conversion to the A–26 Invader. The group flew its first mission with this type as part of a force of 348 medium and light bombers going to rail bridges and communications centers. One of the rail bridges was at Vlotho. Flak was heavy and one of the attacking Marauders was shot down. One of the two boxes wandered off-course, and when they were near Münster, some twenty Me–109s and FW–190s jumped the formation. Three Marauders went down and four were heavily damaged.

Fighter-bombers of the 9th paid much attention to airfields. A lone Me–109 was met and sent into the ground.

Goch was cleared of German troops by the Canadian First Army. German resistance was increasing day by day.

Thursday, 22 February

Plans were ready to resume the offensive toward the Rhine by the Allied armies and, as a part of it, it was decided to launch an attack by all available British and American air forces on German communications. Flying at low altitude, the bombers and fighters would range simultaneously over most of Germany, attacking all sorts of transportation targets, many of them located in small towns and villages which had never been bombed before. A day with clear skies was all that was needed to make visual bombing possible, and today these conditions promised the best of results for operation "Clarion."

1411 heavy bombers of the 8th Air Force left England on a mission to numerous towns in the north and middle of central Germany. This time no large formations, but small attacking units flew at an altitude of 10,000 feet instead of the customary 20,000–25,000 feet. Twenty-five different targets were attacked by the 1st and 2nd Divisions.

The 3rd Division found low clouds over most of the eight primary targets in the southern part of Germany and Czechoslovakia. Most of its bombers looked for targets of opportunity such as the marshalling yards at Schwenningen and at Villingen.

In spite of the low altitude at which the big bombers were flying, only seven were lost. One was shot down by a Me–262, the other six by flak.

All the fighters of the 8th Air Force were aloft. Their main effort was strafing and bombing, although sufficient protection was given to the bombers to ward off about seventy German fighters trying to interfere. Thirteen 8th Fighters were lost, chiefly due to groundfire, though one Mustang had to belly-in after being hit by another P–51. This Mustang was strafing an airfield when all of a sudden the other fighter crossed its path.

A squadron of the 479th Fighter Group was flying near Berlin when the Mustangs were suddenly bounced by sixteen Me–262 jets. Both sides were of the same strength and a violent combat developed. Every trick in the book, and many more, were tried, but the Me–262s were also in experienced hands. The fight ended when the Mustangs got low on fuel and broke off. The Messerschmitts made no attempt to follow. On both sides there were no losses.

Hearing the call from the bombers that jets had been sighted in the vicinity of Brandenburg, a squadron of the 353rd Fighter Group, out on a freelance mission, headed in the given direction. They soon caught sight of the jets and, after giving them chase that would bring them over the heart of Berlin, one of the Mustangs got one of the jets in firing range and, with a few bursts, he sent it down. A lone flying Me–262 was encountered and shot down by the group leader.

The operational area of the tactical air forces was western and northwestern Germany. 503 medium and light bombers of the 9th were dispatched against fifty separate targets. After bombing, the aircraft dropped down and strafed on the deck any target that was connected with transportation. Forty-five of the assigned targets were hit, including eight bridges. Three bombers were shot down, and three others limped home, damaged beyond repair.

Only on one mission were the bombers brought in contact with the German fighters. It occurred on one of the three missions flown by the 397th Bomb Group ("Bridge Busters"). The 26 Marauders had bombed the Rheda bridge and a rail bridge, and were flying in the Münster-Dülmen area when two Me–109s appeared. But the gunners were on guard and one of the attackers was shot down while the other one was damaged. One of the Marauders failed to return. Another Marauder that didn't make it back belonged to the 322nd Bomb Group (the "Annihilators").

Leading his two flights in a strafing attack, the squadron C.O. of the 450th squadron was hit by flak. The bomber crashed and exploded. One of their Marauders had already crashed on take-off, taking with it another Marauder resting in a hardstand when the B–26 blew up.

The targets attacked by the 322nd Bomb Group were Lang Göns, Butzbach, Niedernhausen, Montabaur, and Fredeburg.

Railway bridges at Wehrstapel and Nuttlar, and the defended village of Dülmen were attacked by the 387th Bomb Group ("Tiger Stripe Group"). This implied for its Marauders a flight to the northern part of the Ruhr Valley. One of the Marauders was badly damaged. Yet the crew managed to fly the plane back and left the bomber over its base where it would continue to fly for several minutes before diving into the ground.

A marshalling yard at Simmern and several bridges were bombed by the Invaders of the 416th Bomb Group. Thereafter, the A–26s dropped down and carried out strafing attacks.

1082 sorties were flown by the three tactical air commands. In addition to the usual reconnaissance and support missions, the fighter-bombers flew escort for the mediums. They carried out strafing and bombing missions to assigned targets and targets of opportunity. Near Saarlautern, three Me–109s tried to intercept nine Mustangs of the 354th Fighter Group. But the Germans had to pay dearly for their efforts, and all three were shot down.

Three Me–262s made a pass at Thunderbolts of the 493rd Squadron, 48th Fighter Group, without firing at them. They just pulled away in level flight. However, the Thunderbolts hit and damaged two of them.

A squadron of the 365th Fighter Group received reports of Me–262s attacking American positions northwest of Düren. Two flights of Thunderbolts hurried to the position and they spotted one Me–262. Neglecting the heavy flak, the P–47s closed in on the jet, one flight at 11,000 feet, the other flight at about 8000 feet. At the moment the jet made for home, the high flight chased it, reaching in the dive a speed of 530 mph, and before the German pilot was aware of his situation, he was shot down.

Northeast of Aachen, a P–47 of the 366th Fighter Group encountered an Ar–234 and sent it down. In the afternoon, many dogfights took place between the Thunderbolts and the German fighters, which, in most cases, ended up very unfavorably for the Germans. P–38 Lightnings of the 370th Fighter Group strafed Fritzlar Airfield and destroyed one aircraft on the ground.

In combination with the 8th and 9th Air Forces' attacks, 700 heavy bombers of the 15th Air Force, with an escort of 350 fighter-bombers, made attacks over a wide area in southern Germany. Heavy bombers of the RAF turned to objectives in the Ruhr area.

Although allied flyers were supposed to maintain a safety distance from Swiss borders of fifty miles for visual and 150 miles for blind-bombing, Schaffhausen was accidentally bombed.

At night, the 410th Bomb Group of the 9th was over the communications center at Blatzheim. Seven Marauders dropped flares, two Invaders dropped target indicators, and accordingly thirty-one Havocs delivered their loads and, notwithstanding very heavy flak, the bombing was very accurate. One A–20 turned to a secondary target, and six A–20s aborted the mission. Only five aircraft received minor damage.

Friday, 23 February

The success of the other day seemed to justify a repetition of the operation, so that, again, a large force of heavy bombers of the 8th thundered on to targets in the same area of operations as on the previous day. Meiningen, Hildburghausen, and the Treuchtlingen and Nordhagen railyards were among the twenty-six targets the 1193 bombers were heading for.

To be prepared for heavy resistance of the Luftwaffe, which was definitely expected after yesterday's operations, the full 8th fighter force with its fifteen fighter groups went along with the bombers. But what no one had expected occurred—not a single Luftwaffe fighter interfered, and the only German fighters that were seen refused combat. Even the jets didn't show much eagerness to become involved. Only two bombers were lost; one of them ditched in the North Sea.

Escorting fighters strafed targets of opportunity. After the Fortresses had dropped their bombs on Kitzingen Airfield, the Mustangs of the 353rd Fighter Group came in at zero feet and destroyed four enemy aircraft.

At 0300 hours, after 45 minutes of intense artillery bombardment, the Ninth US Army (NUSA) commenced its drive to the Rhine, while south of this army the First US Army (FUSA) began its offensive across the Roer. Both XXIX TAC and IX TAC gave full support to their respective armies. XXIX TAC aircraft flew 613 sorties. The 405th and 373rd Fighter Groups launched heavy attacks in cooperation with XIII and XIX Corps against communications centers and the defended areas of Lövenich, Titz, and many others.

Armed-reconnaissance flights by the other fighter groups resulted in large numbers of destroyed locomotives (52), railroad cars (755), motor transport, tanks, armored vehicles, and gun positions. Rails were cut in many places. IX TAC aircraft made 661 sorties.

Meanwhile XIX TAC was fully occupied with supporting the Third US Army (TUSA) in its advance to the Rhine. The fighters enjoyed a very successful day, especially when German traffic became congested when TUSA reached the Prüm River. Their claims amounted to 269 tanks and armored vehicles, 1308 road cars and 724 motor vehicles destroyed or damaged.

The Germans here were disorganized. They tried to hide trains loaded with tanks in tunnels. Near Ehrang, Thunderbolts of the 371st Fighter Goup found a train ducked in a half-mile-long tunnel. However, 25 cars stuck out on the north and five cars on the south. They were all destroyed.

XIX TAC was credited with 527 sorties. Sixteen P–47 Thunderbolts of the 368th Fighter Group were attacked by fifteen longnosed FW–190s and five Me–109s. The Germans had numerical advantage and had no lack of spirit, but they surely lacked experience—and three of them went down. One P–47 was lost. In all, the command lost six fighter-bombers during the day.

The 9th Bombardment Division flew the same pattern as on the day before, attacking marshalling yards, rail centers, rail and road bridges, and many other targets mainly connected with transportation.

408

The Luftwaffe attacked bridges in the vicintiy of Linnich. Two were destroyed before the Thunderbolts of the 405th Fighter Group arrived to keep cover over the bridges in spite of a low ceiling at 1500 feet.

The 15th Air Force dispatched 455 heavy bombers from Italy to strike targets in southern Germany. RAF Bomber Command made a heavy daylight attack on Gelsenkirchen and Essen.

Saturday, 24 February

The sky was filled again with the thunder of thousands of engines, this time from the 1090 heavy bombers of the 8th out on a mission to targets in northwestern Germany. Heavy clouds were met, even worse than anticipated, and bombing had to be done by radar.

Oil refineries at Hamburg were the targets for the 1st Division. The 2nd Division turned to the marshalling yards and an oil refinery at Hannover, while the Fortresses of the 3rd Division concentrated on a submarine pen in Bremen, two bridges near Minden, a bridge at Wesel, and the industrial area of Osnabrück.

Bombing was not very successful. Fortunately, the anti-aircraft fire was not very accurate either, and only two bombers failed to return.

The three tactical air commands operated all day in support of the ground forces, attacking all movements of the enemy, bombing and strafing towns, defended villages, and all sorts of other tactical objectives.

Chief targets for the 9th Bombardment Division were again communications centers east and west of the Rhine.

At about 2000 hours, the 410th Bomb Group arrived over its target, the marshalling yard at Hillesheim. Seven B–26 Marauders opened the attack and dropped 103 flares. Next came two A–26 Invaders dropping fourteen target indicators from minimum altitude, and then the thirty-four A–20 Havocs came in between 5000 and 8500 feet to drop 204 500-lb. GP bombs. Considerable destruction was caused. Only light flak was met. One German nightfighter showed up and made an attack on the master bombers' Invader. No damage was done to either plane, and the German broke off the attack. All bombers returned safely to their base.

Sunday, 25 February

Although the weather was not favorable, the 8th Air Force was out again on a mission with a heavy force of 1177 bombers, accompanied by eleven fighter groups. Course was set to southern Germany where they were going to visit the area of Bavaria.

A tank factory at Friedrichshafen received only minor damage, but on

409

the other hand a tank assembly plant at Aschaffenburg was practically destroyed while severe damage was done to an oil storage depot at Neuburg. The marshalling yards at Munich and Ulm underwent an equal treatment, and various jet airfields were plastered. Five bombers and five fighters did not return from the mission.

The best chance to deal with the jets was to destroy them on the ground or to shoot them down as they attempted to take off or land. In air combat, it became increasingly difficult when the jet was in the hands of an experienced pilot.

Mostly one squadron of Mustangs flew high in the air as top-cover for another squadron strafing the jet airfield. If a jet tried to escape or tried to interfere, another flight of Mustangs was loitering in the area to get these jets.

Today the 55th Fighter Group of the 8th Air Force had luck when the Mustangs flew in the vicinity of Giebelstadt Airfield and they spotted several Me–262s taking off. The P–51s came roaring down and closed in rapidly on the jets. Their guns belched fire and steel into the Messerschmitts and six jets slammed into the ground. A pilot of the same group caught another Me–262 attempting to land at Leipheim Airfield. A squadron of the 364th Fighter Group got on the tail of an Ar–234 in the landing circuit near Steinhuder Lake. The jet had no chance and was shot down.

Several Arado Ar–234s attacked US forces near Jülich, but they were intercepted by the Thunderbolts, whereupon the jets withdrew, three of them damaged.

9th fighter-bombers had several encounters with the German jets, though only one group got involved in an air combat. It was the 365th Fighter Group, its Thunderbolts mixing it up with some fifteen jets. The jets withdrew, but not until after four of them had been damaged. This took place early in the morning and the encounter was near Düren. This same morning, another formation of the same group ran into two Me–262s over Aachen. One of the jets was damaged.

Six Thunderbolts of the 36th Fighter Group were flying an early Sunday morning mission when they were jumped by twenty-five FW–190s and Me–109s. In the ensuing battle, one Thunderbolt went down, but the American pilots claimed two FW–190s destroyed and some probably destroyed.

Fifteen P–38 Lightnings were busy bombing a marshalling yard and a factory near Wuppertal when more than fifty Me–109s interfered. The battle ranged from 20,000 feet to the deck. Two Lightnings and four Messerschmitts went down.

FUSA captured Düren.

410

Monday, 26 February

Berlin was on the receiving end of 2879 tons of bombs, dropped by 1102 heavy bombers of the 8th. Each of the three divisions turned to a main target: the Schleisischer railway station, the North railroad stations, and the Alexanderplatz station in the Horst Wessel District. Only the Schleisischer railroad station received a severe mauling. Much damage was inflicted to buildings in the city, including the Reichstag building where a wing of the Ministry of Propaganda was destroyed.

The bombers had no encounters with the German fighters, and of the five bombers and five fighters that failed to return, most had fallen victim to flak.

Very poor weather conditions kept the 9th Air Force grounded.

Enormous fires lightened the clouds above Berlin and guided the Mosquitoes of the RAF to their target on their regular nightraid.

February 26, 1945. The Shack, a B–24 of the 458th Bomb Group revving up prior to take-off on the Group's 200th mission. (Official USAF Photo)

Tuesday, 27 February

Nearly 1100 heavy bombers of the 8th Air Force, escorted by the full fifteen fighter groups, were on their way to the Leipzig-Halle-Chemnitz area. The weather proved to be even worse than anticipated and visibility was so poor that only a few of the objectives could be bombed. Railway targets at Halle and Bitterfeld didn't escape the treatment however, and neither did a central transportation point in Leipzig.

Returning from their target escort, Mustangs spotted over fifty aircraft on Rohrensee Airfield. The P–51s worked it over systematically and when they withdrew, 37 enemy aircraft lay in ruins.

411

Wednesday, 28 February

The general plan for an assault by land forces included the isolation of the Ruhr. This was to be done by cutting at least one viaduct or vital bridge on every line of communication in an area extending from Bremen down to Koblenz. Involved were eighteen bridges or viaducts, of which six were assigned to the strategic air forces. Next, all important marshalling yards between the eliminated bridges and the Ruhr had to be ruined.

The only part of Germany where visibility allowed accurate bombing was in the west, so the targets to receive attention from the 8th Air Force were all in connection with the transportation program in order to isolate the Ruhr.

The bombing of marshalling yards was in many cases very accurate, even though it had to be done through overcast. One of the yards to receive a bombload was at Soest, another at Schwerte, while 364 Fortresses attacked the Henschel tank factory and marshalling yards at Kassel. The plant was very heavily damaged, as was a castings factory at Meschede.

February, 1945—date approximate. The railyard at Limburg after 9th Air Force aircraft paid their visits. (Official USAF Photo)

412

Many German fighters were destroyed on the ground by the fighters returning from their escort duties.

Carrying out a fighter sweep in the Schwerin area, Mustangs of the 8th Air Force came upon a large airfield crowded with aircraft. It turned out to be the airfield at Lubuck/Blankensee, northwest of Berlin. One after the other, the flights of P–51s came racing down and strafed the field in ever-increasing flak that kept the Mustangs on the deck even after passing over the edge of the field. And so it happened that some Mustangs, skimming the ground at zero feet, encountered two locomotives on the same level. Both were damaged.

Fighters of the 9th Air Force met the Luftwaffe on several occasions and in the engagements they downed six German fighters. In addition, they claimed two enemy aircraft on the ground after strafing airfields.

During this month, the three tactical air commands had lost 95 aircraft.

As for the RAF aircraft of the 2nd Tactical Air Force, they made 100 sorties against V-weapons during February, dropping 75 tons of bombs.

The 8th Air Force had left the practice of flying with a 36-plane formation and flew with a 27-plane formation instead. This was the result of the heavily increasing flak, now that the Germans were defending an ever-decreasing area.

3

MARCH

Thursday, 1 March

The first mission by the 8th Air Force this month was directed against targets in southern Germany, mainly marshalling yards. 1219 heavy bombers formed the armada that set out on one of those missions that day after day pounded the German transportation system and that deprived the German armies of their supplies on an ever-increasing scale.

Many yards such as at Göppingen and Heilbronn were plastered with bombs, yet many primary targets were hidden under a solid overcast and in several cases secondary targets were chosen. Though not at Ulm where 418 heavies bombed through heavy clouds by pathfinder means and unloaded more than 1300 tons on every factory and rail target in the city.

Several jets made passes at the bombers aiming more specifically at the lead formation, but swarms of protecting fighters made their attacks unsuccessful.

Meanwhile, the Allied ground advance continued and Venlo was entered by forces of NUSA. In the early morning hours, Thunderbolts of the 406th Fighter Group, in close cooperation with the ground forces, were about to bomb enemy strongpoints when they were jumped by some fifteen enemy fighters. Flying at 3500 feet, the squadron jettisoned its bombs and a violent battle developed.

One Me–109 poured its gunfire into another Me–109 and the stricken plane limped away only to be shot down by a Thunderbolt. At least five enemy fighters were destroyed for no losses.

Three P–61 Black Widows of the 422nd Night Fighter Squadron encountered several German aircraft on their nightly patrol. First a Me–110 was attacked and damaged, and a few minutes later a Ju–87 was shot down. Another Ju–87 Stuka was met some ten minutes later, but this one could only be claimed as probably shot down.

414

Friday, 2 March

Large formations of German fighters were cruising in the Berlin area where they expected a mass attack by American bombers. But they waited in vain and the 1210 heavies of the 8th headed for other destinations. Escorted by all fifteen fighter groups, the bombers turned to the synthetic oil plants at Magdeburg, Ruhland, and Böhlen, and to marshalling yards in Dresden and Chemnitz. At the head of the enormous bomberstream went the 305th Bomb Group, today flying its 300th operation. 36 B-17 Fortresses of this group had the task of silencing the battery of some ninety heavy guns near Böhlen. In this they succeeded, helped by excellent visibility. Three Fortresses of the 1st Division were shot down; two of them were of the 305th Group.

Bombing was very heavy and accurate. Part of the significant tonnage that descended on Magdeburg was caught by a tank plant.

After having circled over Berlin for some time, 75 German fighters set course to Dresden where they picked up the B–17s of the 3rd Division, still nine minutes flying time away from the city. Thirty-five jets started the assault on the head of the formation, attacking from all positions and levels. When the jets withdrew through lack of fuel, six B–17s of the leading bomb group had been destroyed. Conventional types of fighters meanwhile attacked the rear groups in an attempt to decoy the escorting fighters.

When the 406 Fortresses arrived over the city, their bombs were distributed over a large part of the city, and the only noteworthy success was the sinking of the steamer *Leipzig,* after its stern had been blown off by a stick of bombs. For the German fighter force the battle ended disastrously. The overwhelming fighter escort accounted for half of the attackers shot down.

One Fortress pilot was forced to return with engine trouble shortly after take-off. He and his crew transferred to another bombed-up B–17 and took off again in the hope they might catch up with the formation, being only five minutes behind. They spotted a large mass of aircraft heading east but when they drew nearer, they discovered that they were following RAF Lancasters. With no hope of joining up with the others, the Fortress followed the Lancasters, bringing up the rear of the formation, heading for Cologne. The Fortress bombed and returned with the Lancasters. After this event, the Fortress was named "RAFAAF."

After the air battle with the German fighters, the escorting Mustangs came down to carry out low-level strafing attacks. They passed over a grass airfield and found it crammed with more than 200 aircraft. The Mustangs started their strafing runs, racing over the field from one end to the other. When the P–51s pulled away, they left many burning aircraft behind. Another airfield to endure a strafing attack was at Kamenz where ten aircraft were destroyed.

In the afternoon, thirty Marauders of the 394th Bomb Group attacked an ordnance depot at Giessen. Some ten FW–190s and Me–109s appeared to intercept the bombers. They made persistent coordinated attacks and one of the B–26s went down while two others had to make a crashlanding.

The 354th Fighter Group had its first engagement with the German jets. Out on a mission in close cooperation with the ground forces of TUSA, moving east from Prüm, two pilots spotted four Me–262s flying near their airbase at Kassel. The Mustangs dived from 12,000 feet and one of them caught a jet at 1500 feet and sent it down. The other Mustang closed in behind the second jet at 4000 feet and, after several bursts, the German pilot bailed out, his plane crashing into the ground.

Meanwhile, a pilot of the same group spotted a Me–262 making a bomb run near Osthofen. The Mustang swooped down to 1000 feet and closed in behind the tail of the jet. The pilot of the Mustang fired a few bursts, but was then out of ammunition. He brought his fighter alongside the jet, opened his canopy, and fired his pistol at it. However, the jet had already been hit and the plane started to smoke, whereupon the German pilot made a belly-landing.

München-Gladbach and Neuss were captured by NUSA. At Walbeck, NUSA linked up with the Canadian First Army.

Saturday, 3 March

Widely scattered targets in central and western Germany were the objectives for 1048 heavy bombers of the 8th. Bombs were dropped on the synthetic oil plants at Magdeburg, Ruhland, and Chemnitz, and refineries at Dollbergen and Misburg, while in Brunswick bombs were dropped on tank plants and on the Wilke Werke, making equipment for refineries and synthetic oil plants. The bombers also unloaded on several marshalling yards in the Ruhr. This time the dreaded jets were up in force; more than fifty Me–262s and Me–163s attacked the bombers, encircling the Mustangs and keeping them at a distance by their superior speed without apparent difficulty.

Six Mustangs were shot down and three bombers underwent the same fate before the jets were driven off by the Mustangs. One Me–262 was shot down in the Leipzig area by a Mustang of the 359th Fighter Group.

At night, thirty Me–410s crossed the English coast and set course to the American bomber bases in Norfolk and Suffolk. However, their attack by bombing and strafing was not successful.

416

Sunday, 4 March

Nearly 1000 bombers were dispatched by the 8th Air Force. Nine B–24 Liberators, separated from their formation through heavy clouds, made a gross navigational error and dropped their bombs on Basle while six others attacked Zürich in Switzerland. A break in the clouds made a town visible which both squadrons mistook for Freiburg, 25 miles from Basle and 45 miles from Zürich. General Spaatz went to Switzerland to make formal apologies.

Most of the 8th Air Force bomber formations encountered bad weather and diverted from their primary targets to attack targets of opportunity. Reutlingen was one of the targets; however, the only successful bombing occurred at Ulm, where an ordnance depot received 657 tons of bombs.

Krefeld was cleared of German troops by NUSA. Patrols of FUSA reached the Rhine south of Cologne.

The German Me–410s repeated their attacks of the previous night against American bomber bases in England, and again their effort was insignificant.

Colonel Aber, commanding the 406th Special Leaflet Squadron (former 422nd Squadron) from the start, was shot down over England by "friendly" flak while returning from a mission to the Netherlands.

Monday, 5 March

Exceptionally poor visibility made the 500 heavy bombers of the 8th Air Force divert from their originally planned oil objectives to low-priority targets where they attacked blindly without decisive results. The only exceptions were attacks on an oil refinery at Hamburg and one at Chemnitz.

Foul weather conditions made the 9th Air Force inoperative.

Tuesday, 6 March

Weather conditions were so poor that both the 8th and 9th Air Forces were grounded all day.

Meanwhile, NUSA controlled the west bank of the Rhine from Neuss to Rheinberg, and was now in a position to assist the British Second Army.

In support of the army's advance to the Rhine, starting 1 February, XXIX TAC flew almost 7080 sorties, during which the amount of destroyed targets rose rapidly. Claims accounted for the destruction or serious damage to 77 tanks and armored vehicles, 838 motor transports, 2808 railroad cars, 89 gun positions, 1323 buildings, and 22 bridges.

Wednesday, 7 March

The 8th Air Force dispatched 926 heavy bombers to the important oil and transportation targets in the Ruhr. When the bombers neared their objectives, they found them again hidden under a solid overcast. Yet their attacks on an oil refinery at Dortmund and on benzol plants at Dortmund, Giessen, and Castrup were fairly successful, contrary to the much less effective bombing of the railway targets. A new benzol-producing plant at Datteln received a bombload from the B–17s of the 3rd Division. One of the marshalling yards to be visited by the heavies was at Siegen. There were no losses for the 8th bombers on this mission.

The 9th Air Force was still grounded due to weather.

The entire city of Cologne was captured by FUSA. Units of the 9th Armored Division of FUSA, driving hard along the west bank of the Rhine, found a big surprise waiting when they arrived at the Ludendorff Bridge at Remagen and found it left fully intact by the withdrawing enemy. A last-minute demolition attempt had only caused some slight damage. The bridge had been scheduled for attack by the 36th Fighter Group of IX TAC this same morning, but weather had prevented the mission.

The unexpected prize was seized immediately, and all available forces, infantry and tanks, raced across the bridge to form a bridgehead over the Rhine. The Germans were taken completely by surprise.

Thursday, 8 March

Clouds covered western Germany, but that didn't keep the 8th Air Force from sending a very large force of 1340 heavy bombers to this part of the Reich. 3773 tons of bombs were dropped by pathfinder indication on the marshalling yards at Frankfurt and many other places, and five different benzol plants and oil plants in Gelsenkirchen and Bottrop. A new benzol plant at Langendreer was bombed through 10/10 cloud, while another attack was carried out on Hüls.

The Canadian First Army captured Xanten. This was one of their goals when they started their offensive on 8 February. The bridgehead across the Rhine at Remagen had been enlarged to about a mile and a half in both depth and width. Resistance of the Germans, initially very slight, increased considerably. Poor weather conditions with a low cloud cover made fighter-bomber support impossible.

Notwithstanding the adverse weather, the 9th Bombardment Division dispatched some 300 bombers to carry out blind-bombing attacks on the marshalling yards at Altenkirchen and Bergisch Gladbach, and communications centers at Eitorf, Troisdorf, Siegburg, and Geistingen. At Buschdorf, near Bonn, bombs were dropped on an autobahn overpass.

418

Friday, 9 March

Breaks in the clouds over the continent invited more than 1000 heavy bombers of the 8th to revisit the great tank plant at Kassel. The bombers struck with such a blow that the plant was abandoned after the mission. A castings work at Frankfurt, the Deutsche Metallwerke, producing Jumo engine castings for the Me–262, and several marshalling yards on the transportation list, received significant tonnages, causing heavy damage.

FUSA captured Bonn.

The Germans were pounding the bridgehead at Remagen with long-range artillery and with attacks from divebombers coming in from below the cloud cover. However, their attempts to destroy the bridge failed.

For the first time, the fighter-bombers could fulfill their assignment of interdicting enemy reinforcements. The 474th Fighter Group flew cover missions over the bridge. But they could not prevent a sudden attack by a Focke Wulf diving out of the overcast. Its bombs missed by 200 yards, but before any of the Lightnings could interfere, the German fighter had pulled up into the overcast again.

The area south of Remagen was subjected to heavy attacks by medium bombers of the 9th Bombardment Division. The marshalling yards at Wiesbaden, Butzbach, and Niedernhausen, and armored vehicle store depots at Wiesbaden and Dotzheim, were the targets for today. Weather forced the mediums to blind-bombing, and only the marshalling yards at Wiesbaden and the store depot at Dotzheim received a thorough treatment.

At 1133 hours, 31 B–26 Marauders dropped their loads on the marshalling yard at Niedernhausen. Some eight FW–190s and Me–109s hurried to the spot and made attacks from astern. One of the German fighters was shot down; three Marauders were damaged.

The 391st Bomb Group arrived with 19 Invaders over the marshalling yards at Wiesbaden. At 1238 hours, they dropped their bombs, and at this very moment six Me–109s made their appearance. But only one made an attack without causing much damage.

Nearly half an hour later, thirty Invaders of the 386th Bomb Group were attacked by thirty Me–109s over the same target, and this time the German fighters did not intend to let the bombers go unpunished. They made violent attacks, head-on and from behind. A number of German fighters went down in flames, but three Invaders were also lost, while two were forced to make a crashlanding.

The 370th Fighter Group of XXIX TAC had converted from the P–38 Lightning to the P–51 Mustang.

Saturday, 10 March

Germany's railway troubles were further increased after a visit by 1358 of the 8th heavies. Escorted by ten fighter groups, the bombers made instrumental attacks on numerous transportation targets in western Germany, including those at Hamm, Soest, and Dortmund.

Meanwhile the Germans, hard-pressed by the Canadians from Xanten, the British Second Army, and NUSA, withdrew across the Rhine, blowing up the bridge behind them.

The 9th Bombardment Division set out on a mission to a variety of targets in the Remagen area. Only blind-bombing was possible.

Several German aircraft attacked the Ludendorff Bridge at Remagen. The Lightnings were unable to make contact on account of the low ceiling.

Sunday, 11 March

With protective clouds still covering western Germany, the 8th Air Force made no attempts to aim at the primary goals, but there did still exist a U-boat menace, and therefore, the efforts of today were directed against the yards at Kiel, Bremen, and Hamburg.

Each of the three divisions of the Bomber Force was dispatched against one of these targets. The bombs were dropped by means of H2X and the damage brought about remained doubtful, as was always the case with these well-concealed targets.

Also, at Hamburg, the 475 bombers found the target hidden by heavy clouds and they unloaded on the Rhenania plant.

RAF Bomber Command was more and more employed in daylight operations, and today a mission involving 1079 heavy bombers was underway to Essen. The largest tonnage of bombs ever dropped in a single mission descended on the town when the 4738 tons were delivered.

A number of airfields from which the Germans undertook missions against the Remagen bridgehead were subjected to attacks by the 9th Bombardment Division. The number of German planes trying to destroy the bridge at Remagen was increasing.

Monday, 12 March

With the Russian armies forcing their way into eastern Germany, the port of Swinemünde became increasingly important to the Germans as a seaborne reinforcement port. A last-hour request of the Russians called for an attack on this target by the 8th Air Force.

Planes were withdrawn from other planned missions and a total of 671

420

heavy bombers arrived over Swinemünde. The port was completely hidden by 10/10 cloud, but since it could be easily detected on the radar screen, the nearness of the Russian lines caused no objection to a heavy bombardment by radar. 1609 tons descended on ships, quays, slips, buildings, and industrial areas.

The results could not be observed, and therefore, the Americans would afterwards request the Russians to provide them with photographs. Only after several weeks did the answer of the Russians come, a brief note minimizing the results. However, British photographs taken later revealed considerable damage.

Flak was not heavy and not accurate. One bomber was severely hit, but managed to reach Sweden.

Other formations of the 8th headed for Dillenburg and two rail targets back of the bridgehead at Remagen. One of them was Siegen where the bombs were dropped through a complete undercast.

RAF Bomber Command surpassed its record of the previous day when 1107 heavy bombers added ruins to ruins in the city of Dortmund by dropping 4899 tons of bombs. For the first time, 12,000-pound Tallboy bombs were used, dropped by the RAF on the Bielefeld and Arnsberg viaducts, which hitherto had escaped fairly unscathed.

After many earlier efforts by German aircraft, two Me–262s arrived in the afternoon to make an attack on the bridge at Remagen.

Tuesday, 13 March

The 9th Bombardment Division turned again to airfields like Lippe and Breitscheid from which it was possible for the Germans to operate against the Remagen bridgehead.

But now IX TAC fighters took full advantage of a break in the weather to encounter the German aircraft making desperate attacks to destroy the bridge. Nine were shot down. The activity over Remagen lasted all day, and many air combats took place.

In the morning, the Germans dropped anti-personnel bombs and strafed the area. Weather prevented the Lightnings of the 474th Fighter Group from intercepting until just before noon, when contact was made with some seven FW–190s, coming in at zero feet, singly and in pairs, determined to destroy the bridge. The first Focke Wulf was shot down.

At 1400 hours, a squadron of Thunderbolts of the 36th Fighter Group came down in a screaming dive from 17,000 feet to end up behind the tails of some twenty Me–109s flying at 10,000 feet. A vicious battle raged and five German aircraft went down. Also the Me–262s made their appearance, but no contact was made. Three Lightnings were lost.

A squadron of Thunderbolts of the 365th Fighter Group had an engage-

421

ment with four Me–262s northeast of Cologne. One of the jets exploded.

Wednesday, 14 March

Weather permitted the execution of a visual bombing mission by the 8th Air Force, and the opportunity was seized by 1246 heavy bombers. Many high-priority targets were attacked, such as the oil refineries near Hann-over, where severe damage was brought about. The Panther tank works in this city were completely wrecked. At Hildesheim, the bombers struck with devastating effect on a jet castings plant. Marshalling yards at Löhne, Seelze, Osnabrück, and at many other places, and also bridges in the Ruhr, were damaged. Two Fortresses collided when one was caught in propwash and slammed into the other.

Lancasters of the RAF attacked the Bielefeld viaduct with 22,000-lb. Grand Slams, and the viaduct was wrecked. For several months, B–24s of the 8th Air Force had gone to this important rail link with the Ruhr, but all their efforts to destroy it had been fruitless.

The 8th Air Force, well aware of the limitations of its bombs, had been experimenting with a kind of rocket-propelled bombs, the so-called Disney bombs. Released from normal altitude, the rocket would start at 5000 feet, giving the bomb a 2400 ft/sec–speed on impact. It meant that the bomb could pierce through twenty feet of concrete before exploding. The lengthy bombs could only be slung under the wings. Weight: 4500 lbs.

The first attack had been a trial run on the captured concrete structures of the launching site at Watten. Today the second experimental attack was launched against the concrete E-boat pens at Ijmuiden. The results were not encouraging. Nine Fortresses of the 92nd Bomb Group made the at-tack.

An Ar–234, making an attempt to destroy the Ludendorff bridge at Re-magen, was shot down by an 8th Air Force fighter of the 352nd Fighter Group. Another Ar–234 was chased by Mustangs in the Bielefeld area. One of the Mustangs lined up in the right position to fire, but the German pilot didn't wait for the coupe de grâce and went over the side. Two Ar–234s and an Me–262 were shot down by Thunderbolts of the 56th Fighter Group.

The 353rd Fighter Group of the 8th Air Force flew a patrol in the Mag-deburg area intended to draw enemy fighters. And they did not have to wait long. One of the squadrons closed in on some fifteen Me–109s. When the fight was broken off, eleven Messerschmitts had been destroyed. The Mustangs emerged with only one plane moderately damaged.

TUSA's XII Corps suddenly started a move to the south in a combined offensive with the Seventh US Army. They crossed the lower Moselle.

In the vicinity of Frankfurt, fifty-plus Me–109s and FW–190s tore into two formations of Thunderbolts of the 368th Fighter Group. Again the force with its inexperienced pilots, had to pay the toll, and ten German fighters were shot down.

IX TAC fighter-bombers flew cover missions. Thunderbolts of the 36th Fighter Group discovered, on a well-hidden airfield at Lippe, over fifty German aircraft, mostly Ju–87 Stukas, all bombed-up and ready to take off for a mission to Remagen. The P–47s started their attack at 1100 hours, using bombs, rockets, and guns, and when they left after forty minutes, twelve P–47s of the 404th Fighter Group came in to continue the demolition for another quarter of an hour. Two Thunderbolts collided and exploded in midair. In the afternoon, the 36th Fighter Group returned to the field, scattered with smoking ruins.

Three Me–262 jets prepared for a second bomb run on the bridge at Remagen when they were intercepted by Lightnings of the 474th Fighter Group. All three were damaged.

As of this date, the bridge had been attacked by 372 German planes, of which eighty had been shot down by anti-aircraft fire alone.

March 14, 1945. A flight of P–51s of the 4th Fighter Group returning to their base after an escort mission to Hannover. (Photo from *Air Combat 1939–1945*)

Thursday, 15 March

More than 1340 heavy bombers of the 8th left the English coast behind them when they set out on a mission to two different targets, both in the Berlin area. All fifteen fighter groups rode along with the bombers.

Half of the bomberstream took a heading to Zossen, about twenty-eight miles from Berlin. The headquarters of the German High Command was to be the tempting objective here. Normally considered as invulnerable, there was now a chance to strike a blow because the Oberkommando der Wehrmacht was evacuating. Visual bombing was possible and 1400 tons of bombs descended on the target area, destroying most of the buildings.

The other half of the bomberstream proceeded to Oranienburg. 1327 tons of bombs were placed on the railways and the city itself, creating additional piles of rubble in the streets.

Jets were encountered at several points en route and, although they occasionally fired rockets at the formations, they made no attempt for an organized mass attack. The Germans were obviously still experimenting with formation flying and tactics with their jets. A Mustang pilot spotted two Me–163s in the Wittenberg area and he managed to destroy one of them. It would be the last claim against the Me–163 rocket fighter.

The Seventh US Army started its offensive in a northerly direction in order to break through the Siegfried Line and to advance to the Rhine. The German forces facing SUSA were already being attacked from the rear by TUSA's XII Corps.

The 9th Bombardment Division sent its eleven groups to pound the area in front of the advance of the Seventh Army.

Friday, 16 March

It was a very busy day for the 362nd Fighter Group, XIX TAC, flying missions from sunrise to sunset in support of Patton's Army in the Moselle-Rhine area. Enemy strongpoints, artillery, and armor, as well as all kinds of transportation targets were bombed and strafed by the 175 Thunderbolts dispatched by the group. Three enemy aircraft were shot down; two Thunderbolts were lost, one of them in a fight with the German aircraft.

For these and many other actions accomplished today, many times through dense defensive fire, the group received its second Distinguished Unit Citation.

424

Saturday, 17 March

In much worse weather than anticipated the bombers of the 8th made their blind attacks on the oil plants at Ruhland and on the synthetic oil plant at Böhlen. Many bombers turned to secondary targets like marshalling yards and power stations. Also, an ordnance depot at Altenburg was bombed.

During the past week, the Germans had made desperate attempts to concentrate the main elements of eleven divisions against the Remagen bridgehead, but they had been unable to mount a counterattack.

Sunday, 18 March

The mission for today was to be available on request and in support of the Russian armies. The intended mission of a small penetration into western Germany was cancelled and instead a heavy attack on Berlin was projected. And so it turned out to be a mighty force of 1327 heavy bombers that crossed the North Sea shortly after daybreak on their way to the German Capital.

The three bomber divisions converged to one bomberstream near Egmond and, with the 1st Division in the lead position, the bomber column crossed the Zuider Zee and Dümmer Lake to continue to a point northwest of Berlin. Fourteen fighter groups accompanied the bombers, all Mustangs.

The only 8th fighter group to fly the P-47 Thunderbolt did not join the circus because it was converting its P-47D to the P-47M series. With its new P-47M, the 56th Fighter Group possessed a fighting machine that was, with its 465 mph at 32,000 feet, faster than the Mustang. The 56th would go on to fly the Thunderbolt, and they were loath to have it replaced by any other aircraft.

Meanwhile, the biggest daylight raid ever made on the city was nearing Berlin. Flak became heavy and accurate, and more than half of the bomber force would return in some way or other damaged, but the greatest threat today came from the so-long-feared mass attacks of the German jets.

The Me-262s concentrated first on the rear of the 1st Division. Taking advantage of the heavy contrails of the bombers, some 10–20 jets approached the bombers unseen. At the last moment, they emerged behind the bombers and pressed home their attacks. Two Fortresses went down.

The 3rd Division Fortresses were attacked by an equal number of jets and, more specifically, the 100th Group low squadron received the blow in the vicinity of Salzwedel. Twenty-four bombers and five fighters were shot down and another sixteen Fortresses and Liberators made force-landings behind Russian lines. At least eight of the B-17s shot down fell to the four

30-mm. cannons of the jets, which also displayed a far greater range of interception than the Americans had expected.

More than 3000 tons of bombs were dropped on H2X indications from an altitude of 25,000 feet. Transportation targets and industrial areas were the objectives, but considerable damage was done throughout the whole city. Bombing by radar was necessary because heavy contrails and haze hampered visibility.

Mustangs of the 359th Fighter Group flying over the eastern suburbs of Berlin chased two unidentified aircraft heading in an easterly direction. Catching up with them near Zäckerick Airfield, they recognized them as Soviet Yak–9s. At that moment, they spotted four FW–190s strafing the airfield, and the Mustangs destroyed one. On this occasion, Yak's and Mustangs waggled their wings, but somewhere near Berlin a Mustang had to belly-in behind Soviet lines, most probably damaged by the fire of some La–5s. Soviet knowledge of aircraft recognition made a meeting in the air always a precarious affair.

After strafing Prenzlau Airfield some 45 miles from Berlin, a Mustang of the 4th Fighter Group received a hit in the engine from flak. The pilot bailed out and landed in a meadow. Another Mustang made three attempts to land, and on the last one the pilot made it. The other pilot ran for the Mustang, but he was not the only one; the Germans too were rushing in the same direction.

March 18, 1945. The P–47M Thunderbolt, taken at Republic's Farmingdale plant. (Courtesy Fairchild-Republic Company)

426

The P–51s circling overhead came down and kept the Germans flat on the ground. Both pilots discarded their parachutes and, with one pilot sitting on the lap of the other, cramped in the cockpit, the Mustang took off to land two and a half hours later at Debden.

Flak was very heavy when the mediums of the 9th Bombardment Division arrived over Worms. 67 bombers went to the communications center. Five of them were brought down, while thirty-two were damaged. 128 bombers turned to the marshalling yards. One was shot down and 34 were damaged.

When the 322nd Bomb Group set out to attack the marshalling yard at Wetzler, they lost three aircraft shortly after take-off. While assembling, one bomber collided with another and the ensuing explosion of both bombers blew a third one out of the sky. There was only one survivor. One other bomber aborted the mission and 32 continued to their target.

Monday, 19 March

Almost 1000 heavy bombers of the 8th Air Force, with their escort of fourteen fighter groups, droned on to the high-priority oil and jet targets in the Leipzig area. Many German jets took to the air to meet the bombers. They tried to force the escorting fighters to jettison their fuel tanks. But the Mustangs of the 78th Fighter Group, flying ahead of the 1st Division Fortresses, turned into the oncoming jets without dropping their precious tanks. The jets disappeared.

Shortly thereafter, the 48 Mustangs encountered an equal number of Me–109s, and the time that the outcome would have hung in the balance had already passed long since. Thirty-two German fighters were claimed by the American flyers, losing five Mustangs. Two jets which came too near to the melee were included in the number of Luftwaffe fighters shot down.

A dense haze hung over the area and the bombing results were not very successful. Part of the bombers turned to secondary targets like the marshalling yards at Fulda-Plauen. One of the bombs that came down on the yard hit a train standing on a siding and the explosion that followed left no doubt that an ammunition train had been hit.

Some forces turned to Jena to bomb the Carl Zeiss optical works; however, many bombs came down too far south and fell in the small town of Burgau. On the other hand, an attack on jet airfields at Leipheim and Neuburg and on jet components plants fully justified the mission. Three Fortresses of the 3rd Division were shot down.

A special assignment was reserved for the 367th Fighter Group of XIX TAC, and the Thunderbolts of all three squadrons set off to carry out an attack on the headquarters of the German Commander-in-Chief West at

Ziegenburg. This headquarters served as the nerve center for all operations in the west, and was, therefore, well protected by anti-aircraft guns. Moreover, it was situated in a rugged type of terrain that made it very difficult to attack from the air.

Despite guns, terrain, and a ground haze that veiled the target, the Thunderbolts came roaring in at close intervals and placed their bombs right on the mark. After releasing their bombs, the Thunderbolts wheeled around and worked the place over with their guns. When they left without losses, the headquarters was in ruins.

TUSA captured Koblenz.

Tuesday, 20 March

Protected by 10/10 clouds, Germany permitted only shallow penetrations, and therefore, the 8th Air Force turned to targets like Hamburg and Heide-Hemmingstedt. 415 bombers struck at U-boat yards and oil refineries at Hamburg. The bombs were scattered over a wide area in the environs of the docks.

More success was attained at the refinery at Hemmingstedt, where considerable damage was done. Some forty German jets appeared and, after having been entangled in combats with the Mustangs, they managed to destroy two Fortresses of the 1st Division, 303rd Bomb Group.

West of Dümmer Lake, two FW–190s led by a Me–109 made the fatal mistake of joining up with a Mustang formation on the assumption that they were Luftwaffe aircraft. Only one German pilot survived the error.

Plodding slowly through the Siegfried defenses, SUSA captured Saarbrücken and there was all reason to believe that the German resistance on the entire western end of the front was crumbling and collapsing. Corps of SUSA and TUSA linked up in Neunkirchen.

The three tactical air commands rendered invaluable support to their assigned ground forces. In preparation for the intended Rhine crossing in the Ninth Army sector, Thunderbolts of the 373rd Fighter Group of XXIX TAC concentrated on communications targets and also on the German Air Force. In six consecutive missions, they had not only delivered a devastating blow to the enemy's transport, rolling stock, highway and railway system, but in attacks on three vital airfields they had destroyed or damaged 119 enemy aircraft and, moreover, they rendered the fields completely unserviceable. All Thunderbolts returned to their base.

A P–61 Black Widow flying a nightpatrol spotted a Do–217. The nightfighter sneaked in on the tail of the German bomber and, when the P–61 opened fire, the Dornier exploded and tumbled down in flames.

428

Wednesday, 21 March

In close connection with the great airborne and land assault over the Rhine, the Allied air forces concentrated their efforts in an enormous operation lasting four days to isolate the Ruhr completely and to smash the German defenses. Of paramount importance was the neutralization of German airfields from which it would be possible to interfere with the airborne armada of the First Allied Airborne Army. The 8th Air Force started the campaign with 1254 heavy bombers and in a clear sky, course was set to Rheine Salzbergern and nine other airfields.

One hundred seven Fortresses headed for central Germany to visit a tank plant at Plauen. Hidden by high cirrus clouds, the German jets drew nearer and, near Wittenberg-Torgau, some twenty minutes from Plauen, they pounced upon the 96th Bomb Group, third in the column.

Within five minutes, the lead Fortress was blown out of the sky. The 490th Bomb Group encountered a larger number of jets and in persistent attacks, lasting for ten minutes, three B–17s went down. Another Fortress that would never make it back was from the 100th Bomb Group. Escorting Mustangs of the 78th Fighter Group claimed six Me–262s.

West of Darmstadt, the P–51s of the 354th Fighter Group intercepted fifteen FW–190s and managed to send five into the ground. Half an hour later, at 1500 hours, the same squadron jumped on the tail of an Me–262, flying at 500 feet. After several hits, the jet made a belly-landing, with smoke pouring out of the aircraft.

After the B–24 Liberators had bombed Achmer/Bramsche Airfield, the escorting fighters dropped down and strafed the airfield, destroying thirty-three aircraft, including twelve Ar–234 jets. Another eighteen aircraft were damaged. Four Mustangs were shot down.

One of the airfields that was severely hit by the heavies was the Handorf Airfield near Münster. In fact, seven out of the nine airfields attacked were rendered unserviceable.

582 medium and light bombers of the 9th Bombardment Division set out on a mission to six communications centers and one marshalling yard. The bombers suffered no losses, though 89 were damaged, one to such an extent that it was written off after landing at its base.

Hitherto this month, 10,948 Allied heavy and medium bombers had dropped 31,635 tons of bombs on the transportation system within the Ruhr alone. The Ruhr's rail and road transportation systems had also been the chief targets for the fighter-bombers of the 2nd TAF and XXIX TAC, flying 7311 sorties between the 11th and 21st against these targets.

Thursday, 22 March

The 8th Air Force dispatched more than 1200 bombers on missions against five airfields, defended villages, military encampments, and depots in the vicinity of the intended Rhine crossing. A clear sky with splendid visibility gave the 8th the possibility of wiping the objects completely from the target list.

German jets tried to interfere, but they were warded off by the escorting fighters. Three Me–262s were claimed by the 78th Fighter Group, one of the many groups that escorted the bombers to targets, such as the airfields at Alhorn, Dorsten, and Twenthe.

Finding the jet airfield at Alhorn hidden by smoke from the preceding bombardment, some bombers dropped on the marshalling yard at Oldenburg, which by this time was loaded with traffic.

One hundred fifty Mustangs of the 8th Air Force formed the escort for Fortresses of the 15th Air Force bombing the oil refineries at Ruhland. Just when FW–190 fighter-bombers took off from an airfield near Berlin to make for the Russian lines, the Mustangs of the 4th Fighter Group, forming part of the B–17 escort, arrived overhead. Five of the Focke Wulfs were shot down and, before the day was out, they had added another six to their score.

Patton's forces crossed the Rhine at Oppenheim after a speedy drive from their bridgehead at the Moselle. Aerial support was furnished by XIX TAC, hammering on interdiction targets from Limburg to Mannheim. Mainz was captured.

The intended assault across the Rhine kept the XXIX TAC in the air daily whenever weather permitted, attacking rail and road objects, escorting medium bombers, and striking airfields. Today, very successful attacks were carried out against the airfields at Münster and Handorf. At Münster, more than fifty aircraft were sighted on the field and, after bombing and strafing, the Thunderbolts of the 406th Fighter Group claimed seventeen Me–109s and three Me–410s destroyed and many damaged, including two four-engine aircraft. Substantial destruction was inflicted at Handorf.

798 medium and light bombers of the 9th attacked principally communications centers. Three medium bombers failed to return.

RAF Bomber Command's heavies dropped 2869 tons of high explosives and incendiaries in a daylight attack on the towns of Bocholt, Dorsten, Dülmen, and Hildesheim, and delivered an additional load on the Bremen-Arndorf bridge.

Friday, 23 March

1240 heavy bombers of the 8th thundered along toward a large number of marshalling yards in the Ruhr and surrounding areas. All of these were strategically situated in view of the expected site of the crossing. The yards at Recklinghausen, Schwerte, Coesfeld, and Holzwichede, and many others, received several hits. An Ar–96 was destroyed by Mustangs of the 359th Fighter Group.

Meanwhile, TUSA had a bridgehead over the Rhine eight miles wide and five miles deep.

Marauders of the First Tactical Air Force operated even as far north as Heidelberg, where they bombed the crowded marshalling yards. The 9th Bombardment Division despatched 842 aircraft, of which 804 strike on communications centers. Two bombers were lost.

South of Frankfurt, Mustangs of the 354th Fighter Group, XIX TAC, had an early morning meeting with three FW–190s at an altitude of 15,000 feet. As soon as the Mustangs attacked at least fifty Me–109s and FW–190s tore into them. A second Mustang squadron of the same group raced to their assistance, and a vicious battle raged all over the sky. When the fight was broken off, the P–51s claimed seven enemy aircraft.

Sixteen Mustangs of the same group were flying area cover when they were vectored to nine Me–109s entering the Hanau area at 12,000 feet. The Mustangs were flying at 15,000 feet when they caught sight of the Messerschmitts. The P–51s swooped down and, in a short engagement, they brought down eight of them. The 354th Fighter Group Mustangs all returned to their base.

During the last fourteen days, the three tactical air commands had delivered a severe blow to the German armor and transport: 896 tanks and armored vehicles were either destroyed or damaged, as were 969 locomotives, 19,019 rail cars, 10,220 motor transports, and many other military items.

Sixteen P–61 Black Widows of the 425th Night Fighter Squadron flew nine intruder and patrol missions. One Black Widow was put on the tail of a Ju–87 Stuka, flying at 2500 feet. The Stuka was shot down. One P–61 failed to return.

At 2100 hours, the British Second Army commenced the assault. A tremendous artillery barrage preceded the operation. 1900 heavy and medium guns pounded away at positions across the Rhine.

Saturday, 24 March

At 0930 hours, medium bombers, light bombers, and fighter-bombers of the 9th Air Force and 2nd Tactical Air Force started their mass attacks in the area of the selected drop and landing zones. The whole area was carpeted with fragmentation bombs in order to knock out flak batteries that might have escaped the previous days' attacks. At 0953 hours, seven minutes ahead of schedule, the first pathfinder aircraft arrived over the target and behind this aircraft followed the airborne armada.

And so, at 1000 hours, Operation Varsity started: the big airborne assault of the British 6th and US 17th Airborne Divisions across the Rhine north and northwest of Wesel.

Escorted by 676 fighters of XXIX TAC and 213 fighters of the 2nd TAF, 2029 aircraft and gliders of IX Troop Carrier Command and 832 aircraft and gliders of the RAF flew in an enormous 2½-hour-long column over the Rhine. Around the target area was the 2nd TAF with a screen of 900 aircraft providing front-line cover, escort, and patrol.

Heavy flak took its toll, and 39 of the 46 aircraft lost by IX Troop Carrier Command fell to the anti-aircraft guns. One aircraft was lost by accident, and the cause of the other six losses was unknown. Seven aircraft of the RAF were shot down by flak.

Not a single German aircraft interfered with the airborne operations, though some 150 Luftwaffe fighters made sorties.

The three tactical air commands flew 2039 sorties. Fighter-bombers of XXIX TAC made 716 cooperative missions in connection with "Varsity" and made anti-flak patrols for NUSA's assaulting troops. They attacked flak positions, troop concentrations, dumps, airfields, villages, and rail and road traffic.

IX TAC fighter-bombers operated on the southern flank of the battle area. They were also occupied in escort missions.

In the eastern sector of the area, 1253 fighters of the 8th Air Force guarded against German intruders. Seventy Mustangs of the 4th Fighter Group patroled an area near Osnabrück.

Meanwhile, more than 1400 heavy bombers of the 8th Air Force struck many airfields such as Twenthe, near Enschede, and Steenwijk/Havelte in Holland. Sixteen different air bases were smashed, like Ziegenhain Airfield, east of the Rhine, and Vechta.

The 9th Bombardment Division made 688 sorties and its bombers, along with those of the 2nd TAF, attacked communications centers, marshalling yards, bridges, troop concentrations, and flak batteries. Three bombers failed to return, all three from attacks on rail bridges.

The British Second Army was planned to strike across the Rhine between Wesel and Rees, and thence to drive north and northeast between Münster and Rheine. NUSA commenced its assault at 0200 hours and had to attack in an easterly direction toward Münster and Paderborn, after crossing the Rhine south of Wesel. The hard lessons of Arnhem had been learned, and the airborne troops were dropped after the main assault forces had crossed the river. They landed in close proximity to these forces and the river, within range of covering artillery fire from the west bank.

In all, 14,365 troops, 109 tons of ammunition, 645 vehicles, 113 artillery weapons, and large amounts of other equipment and supplies were transported across the river.

432

The opposition of the Germans was light, and firm footholds were established directly after the landing. By afternoon, contact was made between airborne troops and the British 2nd Army. Moreover, a link-up had been effected with NUSA whose two divisions also formed a strong bridgehead south of the Lippe Canal.

237 B–24 Liberators flew supply missions for the airborne troops. This implied a low-level flight and, as had been anticipated, murderous fire from small arms and light cannon was met. Most of the fourteen Liberators that failed to return fell victim to these guns. In the afternoon, the Liberators took off again to pound on enemy airfields.

Twenty-two P–51 Mustangs flew a patrol west of Kassel heading north. Flying at an altitude of 7000 feet, the pilots spotted at least fifteen bombed-up FW–190s with a top-cover of an equal number of Me–109s, heading west, some 4000 feet below.

The Mustangs came hurtling down, and in the next moment a battle raged all over the sky, from 8000 feet to the deck. When it was all over, 17 Mustangs assembled again. One of the five lost P–51s had crashed into an Me–109 while taking evasive action. Both planes had gone down, with a part of the Mustang's wing embedded in the cockpit of the Messerschmitt. German losses amounted to more than twenty fighters.

Mustangs of the 357th Fighter Group out on a patrol over the Ruhr Valley had a similar encounter with some twenty German aircraft, flying at zero feet and heading for the front. Here, too, the outcome was disastrous for the Germans. The Mustangs tore into their formation and picked off sixteen of them.

Sunday, 25 March

Two additional crossings over the Rhine were made by Patton's forces on the assumption that the German forces were already too much tied up by the Remagen bridgehead to be able to offer effective resistance. One crossing took place at Boppard and the other near Lahnstein. Darmstadt was captured and also three crossings over the Main were realized.

Resupply by air for the forces near Wesel was not required.

The 9th Bombardment Division continued its pressure on German communications and, of the 701 bombers dispatched, 641 attacked in nineteen group-strength missions—seven against the communications centers and twelve against three marshalling yards. One bomber failed to return.

Monday, 26 March

A repeated visit to the tank plant at Plauen by the bombers of the 8th Air Force was sufficient to put it out of operation. The marshalling yards at Fulda, along with several other targets, also caught significant tonnages.

SUSA crossed the Rhine, and it was effected at several places near Worms. Fighter-bombers of the First Tactical Air Force swarmed over the area, and the Thunderbolts and Spitfires of this force even operated as far north as Koblenz.

Tuesday, 27 March

Fighters of the 8th Air Force escorted bombers of the Royal Air Force to Paderborn.

Weather prevented large-scale operations by the tactical air forces, and only XIX TAC was able to sent its fighter-bombers on missions. The 362nd and 368th Fighter Groups again took a tremendous toll of German rolling stock. The 362nd Group Thunderbolts had a meeting with the Luftwaffe in the air, and a FW–190 was sent down.

Wednesday, 28 March

The last V-weapons that reached Antwerp were fired, and both a V–1 and a V–2 descended on the city.

Four hundred B–17 Fortresses set out on a mission to the suburban areas of Berlin to deliver a load on tank and armaments plants, notably at Spandau and Stendal. Heavy clouds prohibited visual bombing, and the damage inflicted remained doubtful. The Fortresses also bombed the marshalling yards at Hannover, while a substantial load was dropped on the town itself.

By this point, FUSA had advanced some sixty miles eastward, and today elements of this army swung northward in a drive to Paderborn to link up with the advancing NUSA.

Thursday, 29 March

The last V-weapon to strike London was fired. It was a V–2. Since September 1, 1944, 831 V–1s and 1115 V–2s reached England, a considerable decrease in operations as compared to the 6716 V–1s plotted in the summer of 1944.

Foul weather grounded both the 8th and 9th Air Forces.

Friday, 30 March

Weather had improved sufficiently to allow the 8th Air Force to send the bombers out on a mission to northwestern Germany. The targets to be attacked were the Schindler storage facility (handling 468,000 tons of oil per

434

year) holding large quantities of crude oil from Hungary, and the low-priority U-boat targets at Hamburg, Wilhelmshaven, and Bremen. Approximately 2500 tons of bombs descended on the target areas, and luck was with the bombers at Wilhelmshaven when spilled bombs hit nineteen ships in the harbor. Thirty German jets were sighted around Hamburg, but they didn't compose themselves to interfere with the bombers.

Major Hans Fay, an acceptance-test pilot for Me–262s, took off from Neuburg in a new Me–262 and landed at Frankfurt to surrender to the Americans.

Fighters of the 9th Air Force continued to harass the German Air Force on the ground. Many airfields were attacked, among them Gutersloh, where 58 Thunderbolts of the 405th Fighter Group created havoc against the Luftwaffe and claimed the destruction of ten Ju–88s, seven Me–109s, five He–111s, four Me–410s, three FW–190s, and one FW–200.

Saturday, 31 March

During this month, the second largest amount of bombs in the entire oil offensive had been dropped: 36,000 tons descended on refineries and storage dumps. And today the offensive was continued by 1338 heavy bombers of the 8th, going to oil storage tanks at Derben, the oil plant at Zeitz, and many other places in central Germany and Brandenburg. They also attacked targets of opportunity, such as the marshalling yards at Halle, Aschersleben, and Erfurt.

Large forces of German jets rose to meet the bombers, but they attacked only one formation. One Liberator of this formation was fatally hit and plunged down to earth. One jet was caught by an escorting Mustang and, after a chase, it was shot down in flames.

Another Mustang of the same 353rd Fighter Group spotted an Me–109 about to land on an airfield. The Messerschmitt never reached the field.

During March, the 8th Air Force made 30,358 sorties in 26 days. In the same time, the fighters of the 8th shot down 43 jets in air combats. The 9th Bombardment Division flew 13,642 sorties.

Thunderbolts of the 371st Fighter Group were escorting medium bombers when suddenly one of the fighters peeled off and plunged down in a screaming dive to line up behind the tail of an Me–262 at 900 feet. The Messerschmitt had just taken off. A few bursts were enough to destroy the jet.

In the Ninth Army's sector of the front, the 2nd Armored Division forced a breakthrough from the bridgehead, and advanced some 35 miles eastward.

4

APRIL

Sunday, 1 April

NUSA's 2nd Armored Division made contact with FUSA's 3rd Armored Division at Lippstadt, trapping some 400,000 German troops in the Ruhr. Paderborn was also taken by FUSA.

Patton's Third Army's offensive with the armored divisions in the lead competed again with its dashing drive of the previous summer, rushing in northeasterly and southeasterly directions. Kassel was cleared of German troops.

Poor weather kept the bombers of the 9th Bombardment Division grounded. A Ju–88 was shot down by Mustangs of the 354th Fighter Group.

Monday, 2 April

Heavy bombers of the 8th Air Force, already nearing their target, were recalled due to weather. The same atrocious weather kept the bombers of the 9th Bombardment Division grounded again.

Two P–51 Mustangs of the 354th Fighter Group, XIX TAC, were out on a weather reconnaissance mission when they encountered two FW–190s near the airfield at Erfurt. Both German fighters were shot down. Continuing their flight, the Mustangs came across a lone FW–190 near Gotha Airfield. This one, too, was sent into the ground. But then they encountered more than ninety FW–190s and Me–109s flying in eight-plane formations with belly-tanks, at 3000 feet. The Mustangs closed in on the tails of the last aircraft, shot down two, but then hurried home because they were nearly out of fuel.

In the afternoon, it was the 354th again that ran into the Luftwaffe. One

436

Me–109 was shot down and, shortly thereafter, another flight of four P–51s encountered sixty German fighters. In the ensuing battle, the Americans claimed five FW–190s and two Me–109s.

Tuesday, 3 April

Heavy bombers of the 8th Air Force carried out an attack by instrument on the naval dockyard at Kiel. In spite of the attack's being done by instruments, most of the 2200 tons were placed in the target area.

By now, the largest concentration of enemy ships ever seen in Kiel made the port area an inviting target. The pocket battleship *Admiral Scheer*, the cruisers *Emden* and *Admiral Hipper*, six liners, thirty merchant vessels, and a flotilla of submarines were present. These vessels also formed the special targets for the RAF's heavies with their 10,000-pound bombs.

The encirclement of the Ruhr Valley was now a fact.

At midnight, NUSA, temporarily under the command of Field Marshal Montgomery, was restored to General Bradley's command.

Wednesday, 4 April

Fifty German jet fighters rose to meet nearly 900 heavy bombers of the 8th Air Force out on a mission to the Hamburg area where they were to attack airfields from which jets may have operated. Also, a visit to the U-boat yards at Hamburg and Kiel was on the program, while an additional load would be delivered on Fassberg and on an ordnance depot at Rotenburg.

Overwhelming fighter escort prevented a general slaughter among the bombers, yet five heavies went down, three of them from the 448th Bomb Group.

When the Me–262s launched their attack, one group commander flying in a Mosquito beside the bombers for formation monitoring purposes was shot down by one of his own Liberator gunners. In his excitement, he mistook the Mosquito for a jet.

A Fortress of the 95th Bomb Group landed in Sweden. It would be the last bomber of the 8th Air Force to land in this neutral country. Since the *Georgia Rebel* had come to Sweden on July 24, 1943, nearly seventy B–17s had force-landed there.

Near the airfield at Parchim, three jets were shot down by Mustangs of the 4th Fighter Group.

When, early in the morning, F–6 Mustangs flew a tactical reconnaissance mission, they had several encounters with the German fighters and in

April 4, 1945. This Liberator of the 448th Bomb Group is
shot completely in half. (Official USAF Photo)

consecutive skirmishes they destroyed seven of them.

The French First Army seized Karlsruhe, after initial stubborn resistance.

Thursday, 5 April

The heavy bombers of the 8th Air Force took off before dawn in darkness to carry out one of the few strategic missions that could still be executed before the war had come at a stage in which there were no longer targets available for this kind of warfare. One bomber had an engine on fire as soon as it cleared the runway. The bomber crashed and blew up.

As the fighters were taken off strafing tasks, except strafing of airfields, because the chance of hitting friendly troops or prisoners had become too real, the full fighter force was available for bomber protection, a luxury not superfluous in view of the increasing jet menace.

Flying through heavy clouds, 450 heavies set course to ordnance depots in central Germany, while other formations turned to the marshalling yards in Nürnberg and Bayreuth, and also struck airfields, including one at Ingolstadt. A tank arsenal at Nürnberg also received a bombload. One Fortress was lost, shot down by a few Me–262s in an attack on the leading 1st Division.

438

Escorting fighters passed over Weiden airfield where the pilots observed about twelve aircraft. A squadron of Mustangs from the 353rd Fighter Group went down onto the deck. After strafing the field, the Mustangs continued their mission, leaving behind them seven aircraft shot up.

The 9th Bombardment Division was grounded due to weather.

Supporting NUSA in their assault to cross the Weser, the 406th Fighter Group dispatched 58 Thunderbolts on seven missions. The Hameln marshalling yards, enemy troops, transport, and various other targets were bombed with GP and napalm bombs. Rocket and strafing attacks added to the devastation. Shortly after noon, the Thunderbolts were jumped by four Me–109s. The Messerschmitts made only one pass and then climbed back into the protecting clouds.

F–6 Mustangs flying a tactical reconnaissance mission ran into enemy aircraft on a number of occasions. Six German fighters were claimed in the air and one Me–109 on the ground. One Mustang failed to return.

TUSA seized Mulhouse, Gotha, and Eisenach in its drive eastwards.

Friday, 6 April

Six hundred fifty heavy bombers of the 8th concentrated their efforts on transportation centers in central Germany. Leipzig and Halle carried the heaviest burden of the attack.

The main purpose of these attacks was to prevent the Germans from retreating with their supplies to the "National Redoubt" in southern Bavaria and Austria. 215 heavy bombers attacked the main rail station of Leipzig through 10/10 cloud. Four planes were lost by the 8th Air Force.

NUSA established a bridgehead over the Weser.

Saturday, 7 April

One of the last desperate attempts of the Luftwaffe to blow the American bombers from the skies was launched by 130 conventional and 50 or more jet fighters. Near Dümmer and Steinhuder Lakes, they tried to intercept the stream of more than 1200 bombers by making frenzied, suicidal attacks. The German pilots were of the "Sonderkommando Elbe," and their main purpose was to ram the American bombers with their Me–109s. The jets flew cover.

Some 300 pilots had been selected out of volunteers, and at Stendal they had received a ten-day course in ramming. Most of the lectures, however, consisted of getting them into the right frame of mind by films and Nazi indoctrination. If possible, they were allowed to bail out at the last moment, but usually it was not possible. After the course, eighty pilots equipped with Focke Wulfs went to Prague to practice against the 15th Air Force. The remainder were given Me–109s to face the bombers coming from the west.

The heavy bombers of the 8th headed for northwestern Germany where their attacks were directed against airfields at Lüneburg, Parchim, Kaltenkirchen, and many others, against ammunition plants, dumps, and oil storage depots. About forty fighters of the "Raubvogel" unit and a dozen jets managed to attack the leading bomber formations on their way to Kaltenkirchen Airfield.

Exhorted by a woman's voice broadcasting slogans like "Deutschland über Alles" and "Remember our dead women and children. . ." and patriotic music, the German pilots, who were unable to say anything back because the radio transmitters had been removed from their planes, deliberately rammed the bombers and four Fortresses tumbled down. A fifth B–17 was shot down by an Me–109. Another Fortress was damaged by a ramming fighter, destroying the German aircraft, but the B–17 continued on its way. Two Fortresses went down under the cannonfire of the jets.

The 2nd Division Liberators heading for ammunition plants at Lüneburg encountered the "Ramstaffel" when an Me–109 slammed into the nose of a leading B–24. The bomber crashed into another Liberator and both went down. A German fighter crashed into the tailsection of a B–24, but the crew managed to bring the bomber over friendly territory where they bailed out.

The enormous fighter escort of some 850 Mustangs prevented further losses, with disastrous consequences for the Luftwaffe. American claims passed 100 German fighters and, although this figure was a little exaggerated, it indicated that a few more of these blows would mean the end of the German Air Force. Eighteen bombers and three fighters were lost on this mission.

In late afternoon, 34 Marauders of the 391st Bomb Group attacked the marshalling yards at Göttingen. Although they were bounced by some ten FW–190s and Me–109s, they suffered no losses.

Two F–5 Lightnings of the 30th Photo-Reconnaissance Squadron were lost. One of them was making a photo run over a strip of the autobahn near Seesen when two Me–262s closed in on the Lightning. With his engines and instruments shot out, the pilot freed himself from the doomed aircraft and was taken prisoner.

F–6 Reconnaissance Mustangs operating in the Ruhr pocket destroyed many locomotives, railway cars, tanks, motor transports, and other vehicles. The pilots spotted an Me–109 trying to ram a P–38 Lightning. The Mustangs raced to assistance and destroyed the Messerschmitt. Five more German aircraft underwent the same treatment.

P–61s of the 422nd Night Fighter Squadron set out on an intruder mission. They downed an Me–410, and thereafter a Ju–88.

440

The RAF discontinued area-bombing after a warning of Portal that further destruction of German cities would magnify the problems of the occupying forces.

Sunday, 8 April

The heavies of the 8th were again en route to northwestern Germany to strike a variety of targets of the same nature as on the previous day, including an ordnance depot at Halberstadt. In order to stop supplies from

April 8, 1945. The last 91st Bomb Group Fortress to go down. (Official USAF Photo)

441

reaching the "National Redoubt," the marshalling yard at Eger in Czechoslovakia was attacked, while a bombload also came down on Stendal.

F–6 Reconnaissance Mustangs mixed it up with Luftwaffe fighters in several encounters. The Germans lost eleven aircraft, including four Ju–87s and an He–111.

P–61s of the 422 Night Fighter Squadron brought down a Ju–88 on their nightly patrol.

The last oil target to be bombed was Lützkendorf, and RAF Bomber Command carried out the final attack in the oil campaign.

Monday, 9 April

This time the 8th Air Force directed its bombers to airfields and marshalling yards in a southerly direction. 1212 heavy bombers attacked München, Memmingen, Lechfeld, Neuburg, Fürstenfeldbrück, Oberpfaffenhofen, and a number of other cities. On the airfield of München alone, some seventy enemy aircraft were counted. Bombs worked over the control tower, workshops, hangars, and other buildings. Bombs were also salvoed on warehouses, docks, and rail facilities at Ingolstadt. After bombing the airfields, the escorting fighters dropped down to strafe the fields.

Reconnaissance revealed an accumulation of 1550 locomotives in south central Germany's smaller rail yards.

729 aircraft of the 9th Bombardment Division attacked oil storage facilities at Bad Berka, an ordnance depot at Amberg-Kummersbruck, the ordnance and armored vehicle storage depots at Naumburg, and the marshalling yards at Jena and Saalfeld.

And today the first German jet was shot down by the bombers of the 9th. It occurred when forty Marauders of the 387th Bomb Group attacked the ordnance depot at Amberg-Kummersbruck. Shortly after 1000 hours, two Me–262s approached the bombers from behind. One jet made a second pass through the formation. It was fatally hit and went down in flames. The pilot bailed out. One Marauder failed to return.

In the afternoon, a Mustang pilot caught sight of an Me–262 flying at 24,000 feet in the München area. Two other Mustangs also chased the jet, but after some time they gave up. After losing him for a moment, the first Mustang pilot discovered the jet approaching Munich/Riem Airfield. After a hot pursuit, the Mustang caught the jet at 50 feet over the perimeter track and opened fire. The Messerschmitt bellied-in in a cloud of dust and flying debris.

A Ju–52 fell to the guns of a P–61 Black Widow of the 422nd Squadron during their nightly intruder mission.

Tuesday, 10 April

The largest amount of American bombers to fall prey to the German jets in a single mission was lost today. Some fifty Luftwaffe jets succeeded in bringing down ten heavy bombers, five of the 1st Division and five Fortresses of the 3rd Division, shot down in the Berlin area near Brandenburg. The attack by 1232 heavies of the 8th was directed against airfields, jet assembly plants, ordnance depots, an ammunition factory, and marshalling yards, all situated in the area of Berlin. The airfield Burg near Magdeburg and Rechlin/Lärz were among the airfields which were very successfully bombed.

A mass of 8th Air Force fighters was circling over the German airfields, waiting for the jets to return. And they didn't wait in vain. Eighteen of the twenty Me–262s shot down fell to the guns of the Mustangs. One of the jets made a head-on pass at a Mustang, but was shot down in flames. The pilot bailed out, but his chute failed to open.

A huge number of aircraft was destroyed by strafing airfields, notably at Neuruppin, some 40 miles north of Berlin. The 8th fighter pilots found an estimated 150 aircraft dispersed in the woods north of the field.

The 391st Group of the 9th Bombardment Division had converted from B–26 Marauders to A–26 Invaders, and today the group flew its first mission with the type.

At 0100 hours, a Ju–88 was set afire by the Black Widows of the 422nd Squadron. When it hit the ground, the Junkers exploded. It was their first victim this night, and within half an hour two Ju–52 transports were shot down as well. The last one to go down in flames was again a Ju–52.

Hannover was captured by NUSA.

Wednesday, 11 April

1300 Fortresses and Liberators ranged over Germany in a clear sky inviting them to turn to many targets like the marshalling yards, airfields, and oil storage and ordnance depots at Regensburg, Freyhan, Landshut, and many other places. All bombers returned from the mission.

In the expectation that the Germans might develop a last desperate resistance in the mountainous areas of South Germany and Austria, the so-called "National Redoubt," the 9th Bombardment Division changed its target priorities. The elimination of ordnance depots, motor transport, and tank factories, and the sealing off of the National Redoubt were believed to speed up the disintegration of the enemy. In the light of this campaign, a heavy blow was dealt to the motor transport assembly plant at Bamberg by the medium bombers. Half of the plant was wrecked.

A lone Me–109 was attacked and shot down by Thunderbolts of the 368th Fighter Group. Another Me–109 was shot down by Mustangs of the 354th Fighter Group, busy with strafing motor transport. At about 1900 hours, fourteen Mustangs of the same group ran into some 25 Me–109s and a few FW–190s. The ensuing fight ended up in a terrible punishment for the Luftwaffe fighters, losing 19 Me–109s and one FW–190, with no loss for the Mustangs. One P–51 Mustang was shot down while strafing an airfield.

Thunderbolts of the 373rd Fighter Group were working over an enemy airfield when sixty FW–190s appeared resulting in a vicious air battle that raged for one hour. And again, the inexperienced Luftwaffe pilots had the worst of the battle. The P–47 pilots claimed seventeen aircraft for the loss of one Thunderbolt.

The attacks on German airfields brought in claims of at least seventy aircraft destroyed.

At night, P–61s chased many German aircraft. The nightfighters claimed three Ju–52s and one Ju–88.

Meanwhile, NUSA reached the Elbe, south of Magdeburg.

Thursday, 12 April

NUSA captured Brunswick, and Devers' Sixth Army Group captured Schweinfurt after the terrific resistance of its garrison and heavy bombardments by B–26s on the 10th. After nine days of bitter fighting, Heilbronn was seized. In the south, Baden-Baden was captured by the French First Army, while TUSA captured Erfurt.

The 9th Bombardment Division's medium bombers caused much damage to the ordnance depot at Kempten. Further attacks were carried out to sever the "National Redoubt." Autobahn bridges, rail junctions, and marshalling yards were the favorite objects for the mediums.

It was undoubtedly a big day for the 36th Fighter Group, with a number of enemy aircraft destroyed unequalled by one group on one day. Only eleven Thunderbolts were on a mission to strafe airfields in the Köthen area. The first target was Schneuditz, where fourteen He–111s and three Do–217s were scrapped from the German inventory list, along with a hangar. But the next step brought the Thunderbolts over Leipzig/Mockau Airfield, and here the pilots could hardly believe their eyes when they spotted some 300 aircraft dispersed about the field.

Blasting away with everything they had, the Thunderbolts raised tremendous havoc among the many aircraft of all different types, even a captured Thunderbolt. Total claims for both missions were 73 aircraft. At 1050 hours, all Thunderbolts returned to their base.

Fighter-bombers continued their operations in close cooperation with the ground forces. On the north side of the Ruhr, factories, a fuel dump, buildings, troop concentrations, and all kinds of transportation targets were bombed and strafed by 78 Thunderbolts of the 366th Fighter Group, pounding away on the enemy in nine missions from early in the morning until the evening. No Thunderbolts were lost, although three were damaged.

Friday, 13 April

The 8th Air Force dispatched a small force of heavy bombers against marshalling yards. Neumünster was one of the targets.

Thunderbolts of the 56th Fighter Group worked over the crowded airfield at Eggebeck, near Kiel. The Thunderbolts returned with claims of 95 destroyed. The 56th was the first 8th Air Force group to reach the magic 1000 figure for destroyed enemy aircraft.

A last directive by General Spaatz and Air Marshal Bottomley gave first priority to direct assistance to the ground forces by the strategic air forces.

The 9th Bombardment Division were grounded on account of weather.

Weimar was captured by the southern flank of Patton's Third Army, driving speedily in a southeasterly direction.

At 0303 hours, the P–61s of the 422nd Squadron shot down their last victim, a Ju–52.

Saturday, 14 April

More than 1200 heavy bombers of the 8th Air Force dropped their 2000-pound demolition bombs, incendiaries, and napalm bombs on a very stubborn German garrison at Royan, near Bordeaux. Although no enemy aircraft interfered and flak was negligible, disaster struck the 389th Liberator Group when fragmentation bombs, dropped by the B–17s of the 3rd Division on their second run, hit five of their aircraft. Two B–24s plunged down immediately and two others crashlanded at airfields in France, while the fifth struggled back to England.

The 9th Bombardment Division was only able to dispatch eighteen bombers, due to weather. Mustangs of the 354th Fighter Group had an encounter with the German jets. Near Lonnewitz Airfield, a Mustang closed in on an Me–262 flying at an altitude of approximately 3000 feet. After a few bursts, the jet slammed into the ground. The same afternoon, a Mustang caught an Me–262 near Riesa and the second jet went down.

By now, the Ruhr pocket was split into two parts.

445

Sunday, 15 April

8th Air Force bombers set out again to the area near Bordeaux. Twenty-four Liberators bombed a coastal battery at Pointe de Grave. A high degree of accuracy was achieved by the 467th Bomb Group when all bombs fell within 1000 feet of the target, and half of them within 500 feet. A large number of napalm bombs was unloaded. Fortresses of the 1st Division dropped in the Rochefort area.

Thirty-four Marauders of the 394th Bomb Group made a mission to the marshalling yards at Günzburg. Near Lake Constance, three Me–262s made a pass at the bombers, but no damage was sustained. A–26 Invaders flew a mission to Ulm. They were escorted by Mustangs of the 8th Air Force.

The leading 9th Air Force fighter ace, Lt. Bruce WK. Carr, downed an He–111. He was a pilot of the 354th Fighter Group.

The southern flank of Patton's Third Army took Bayreuth.

Monday, 16 April

General Spaatz sent out a personal message to Doolittle and Twining:

> The advances of our ground forces have brought to a close the strategic air war waged by the United States Strategic Air Forces and the Royal Air Force Bomber Command. It has been won with a decisiveness becoming increasingly evident as our armies overrun Germany.
>
> From now onward our Strategic Air Forces must operate with our Tactical Air Forces in close cooperation with our armies. All units of the U.S. Strategic Air Forces are commended for their part in winning the Strategic Air War and are enjoined to continue with undiminished effort and precision the final tactical phase of air action to secure the ultimate objective: complete defeat of Germany.
>
> The above is order of the day number 2 and is to be released by this Headquarters at 2200 hours tonight.

Bordeaux was again the target for the bombers of the 8th Air Force in a renewed effort to smash the German garrison. The Liberators and Fortresses of the 2nd and 3rd Division dropped incendiaries and napalm bombs, while the Fortresses of the 1st Division delivered the GP bombs. Three groups of this division circled the area to bomb any anti-aircraft activity,

446

April 16, 1945. German aircraft burn after a strafing attack by Mustangs of the 353rd Fighter Group. (Official USAF Photo)

and four Mosquitoes were around to curtail radar of flak batteries by dropping chaff.

The heavy bombers of the 8th also headed for targets in the area of Münich and Regensburg. Along with many other objectives, the Fortresses of the 1st Division attacked a railroad bridge at Regensburg.

The 8th fighters shifted their attention to southeastern Germany and Czechoslovakia, only to find airfields crowded with aircraft. With the number of airfields decreasing virtually every day, the number of aircraft occupying the remaining fields increased. Never before had such a harvest been reaped, and claims mounted to 752.

Mustangs of the 353rd Fighter Group claimed 131 German aircraft after strafing crowded airfields at Pocking, Bad Aibling, and several others. They also strafed an autobahn and one squadron of the group was working for thirty minutes over two airfields before climbing for altitude to pick up the Liberators and escort them out to Stuttgart.

Three Mustangs of the group were lost. In all, the 8th Air Force fighter losses for today mounted to 34 Mustangs and one Thunderbolt.

Not only the fighters of the 8th, but also the fighter-bombers of the 9th Air Force swarmed over the enemy airfields, and today the largest number

447

of aircraft was destroyed on these profitable targets: 215 aircraft destroyed and 190 damaged.

Thunderbolts of IX TAC roamed the airfields in the Leipzig area, such as Pretzsch Airfield and Oschatz Airfield. Airfields near Magdeburg were pounded by Thunderbolts of XXIX TAC. The airfields at Marienberg and Michelsberg were visited by the P–47s of XIX TAC.

Besides these targets, close support was furnished to the ground armies. For instance, in the region of NUSA, 36 Thunderbolts flew three missions in the afternoon in cooperation with XIX Corps, now stationed along the Elbe and preparing to drive to Magdeburg. The destruction of the German Air Force didn't solely take place on the ground. Many encounters with the Luftwaffe resulted in 23 German aircraft shot down, most of them on account of the 354th Fighter Group, claiming fourteen.

Early in the afternoon, twelve Thunderbolts of the 368th Fighter Group were approaching an airfield when the pilots spotted a dozen Me–262s in the take-off. Before the superior speed of the Messerschmitts could take them far from the guns of the P–47s, two were shot down. In strafing attacks by the other groups, six more Me–262s were wrecked.

The ordnance depot at Kempten was again the target for the 9th Bombardment Division. After the last load had been delivered, the plant lay, for the greater part, in ruins.

The Russians opened an all-out offensive towards Berlin.

Tuesday, 17 April

Some thirty Me–262s tried to interfere with the 8th Air Force bombers, but very efficient fighter cover curtailed losses to one bomber. This B–17, *The Towering Titan,* of the 305th Bomb Group, was the last bomber of the 1st Division to be lost by fighter action. Many targets in southeastern Germany were attacked, including the marshalling yards at Dresden and Auszig.

Fighters of the 8th turned again to their hunting grounds in southeastern Germany and Czechoslovakia. Another 200 German aircraft were turned into scrap. One of the airfields attacked was Prague/Ruzyne, where over 100 aircraft were sighted.

One of the groups making a very successful strafing attack was the 339th Fighter Group. After having set fire to many aircraft parked on an airfield near Munich on the day before, the Mustangs returned to the field again. First they shot up the anti-aircraft defenses surrounding the field, and then worked over the field, leaving nearly forty wrecked German aircraft behind them. The strafing mission was skillfully led by Lt. Col. Joseph L. Thury, making nine passes over the field himself.

Many strafing fighters were shot down. One of them was piloted by the commander of the 55th Fighter Group. He managed to make a belly-landing and stepped out of his aircraft. Members of his group, flying overhead, saw him surrounded by a crowd of civilians. Nobody ever heard of him again, so it was believed that he had been lynched.

An armed-reconnaissance mission brought eight P–51s of the 354th Fighter Group near Karlsbad where one of the pilots manoeuvered his Mustang in the right position to have his gunsight filled by an Me–262. At 1500 feet altitude, he finished it off. Another jet to go down before the guns of a 9th Air Force fighter was the victim of a 371st Group Thunderbolt, flying a mission in support of ground forces preparing to cross the Austrian border.

Magdeburg was captured by NUSA.

Wednesday, 18 April

With the elimination of 21 German divisions and the surrender of over 300,000 troops, all organized resistance in the Ruhr Valley had ceased. Patton's Third Army reached the Czechoslovakian border.

Heavy bombers of the 8th were again en route to southeastern Germany and Czechoslovakia. Freising, Rosenheim, and the railyard at Straubing were among the many targets that caught a significant tonnage. The escorting fighters went down to strafe the airfields. Some Me–262s were met and a few were shot down by the P–51s. One Messerschmitt tried to land at Prague/Ruzyne airfield, but didn't make it.

The 9th Bombardment Division was on the way to rail and autobahn bridges, rail junctions at Falkenburg and Jüterbog, marshalling yards at Ulm and Neu Ulm, and to a rail center at Wittenberg. The bombers also flew a leaflet mission to the Ruhr.

Fighter-bombers of the three tactical air commands were piling up the number of demolished buildings, dumps, airfields with wrecked aircraft, destroyed transportation targets, and a large variety of other objectives. Thunderbolts of the 371st Fighter Group caught sight of a train loaded with tanks and many other vehicles. They had spent their bombs already in earlier attacks, but realizing that this was too beautiful a target to let pass unharmed, the squadron leader led his men into a kind of traffic pattern and, one after the other, the Thunderbolts came in, dropping their almost-empty belly tanks on the train. The P–47s made a wide turn and came back, strafing both train and belly tanks, and the train was set afire from head to tail.

Three German fighters were in the landing pattern at the airfield of Jüterbog. F–6 reconnaissance Mustangs witnessed this procedure and then dived down with the obvious aim of shortening the landing. One FW–190 with its landing gear down was sent straight into the ground. Another

Focke Wulf just touched down when, at the same moment, its right wing was cut off by concentrated fire. Number three, an Me–109, was caught at 500 feet and crashlanded north of the field.

Thursday, 19 April

Five Fortresses of the 3rd Division had the unfortunate distinction of being the last heavy bombers to fall to the German fighters. It also meant the last engagement of the heavies with the German jets.

The bombers were going again for the few remaining targets in southeastern Germany and Czechoslovakia, notably at Pirna and Falkenburg. Near Prague, a Me–262 made a head-on pass at a lead squadron of the 490th Bomb Group when the Forts were about to start the bomb run on the marshalling yards at Auszig. One Fortress went down. Suddenly, two Me–262s dived out of the clouds and shot down three B–17s. But then the Mustangs rushed to their aid and destroyed both Me–262s. Another Me–262 made a surprise attack on a high squadron, and a Fortress tumbled down.

Part of the 357th Fighter Group headed for Prague/Ruzyne Airfield, known to station jets. There the P–51s stayed orbiting the environs south of the field, concealed by the sun, waiting for the jets. And the Germans did not intend to disappoint them. After a short while, the Mustang pilots saw them coming, all Me–262s, tearing down the runway, taking off in pairs. Sixteen were airborne when the Mustangs attacked. Four were shot down, one crashing into a building in the outskirts of Prague.

Mustang pilots of the 364th Fighter Group flying near Lubben were very astonished when all of a sudden a Do–217 dived through their formation. The Dornier was promptly shot down. Four FW–190s, which they came across a short while afterwards, underwent the same treatment.

9th Bombardment Division mediums carried out missions in connection with the interdiction of the "National Redoubt." They also struck at jet airfields, communications centers, and defended cities.

The 394th Bomb Group attacked the marshalling yards at Ulm. Nearing the target, the low flight of the group was suddenly bounced by two Me–262s, but only one Marauder received some damage. In the afternoon, about ten Me–262s made for the bombers of the 322nd Group. The Marauders had just delivered their bombs on a secondary target, the Donauwörth rail bridge, when the jets came in from behind, concentrating on the second box with its flights still split up after the bombing. A few minutes later, sixteen Thunderbolts arrived in the midst of the fight. They were of the 404th Fighter Group, out on a bomber escort mission. Although some planes were damaged, there were no losses on either side.

FUSA captured Halle and Leipzig.

450

The last combat between 8th Air Force fighters and the conventional fighters of the Luftwaffe was fought over Letnany Airfield in Czechoslovakia when the 355th Fighter Group jumped a dozen Me–109s. Seven Messerschmitts were claimed to be destroyed for no losses.

8th Air Force bombers ranged over the daily decreasing territory of the Germans. Near Berlin, they struck Nauen, Brandenburg, and the marshalling yards at Oranienburg. Seddin also received its share of the bombardment.

Bombers of the 9th again made very successful attacks on rail junctions, marshalling yards, rail centers, bridges, and airfields. Heavy and concentrated flak saw to a hot reception for the mediums of the 322nd, 386th, and 409th Bomb Groups when they neared their target, the Wittenberg marshalling yards. One bomber went down and many received damage in various degrees.

The 323rd Bomb Group dispatched 48 Marauders on a mission to the marshalling yards at Memmingen. Nearing their target at 1100 hours, some fifteen Me–262 jets rushed to the bombers and made a concentrated attack in an attempt to wipe the bomber force from the sky. Three Marauders were shot out of the formation, and a fourth was so badly damaged that it was written off after landing. Two jets fell to the gunner of one of the Marauders. P–51s of the 370th Fighter Group engaged the jets, but after the fight, the Mustangs could only claim two probables. One P–51 had to make a belly-landing.

Six Marauders of the 394th Group flew a leaflet mission. Without knowing it, they were flying their last mission in this war.

NUSA had reached the Elbe and had, in fact, herewith accomplished its mission. From now on, it had only to remain in the defensive along the river. But also the primary mission of the XXIX TAC had come to an end, and the activities of the fighter-bombers were limited to uneventful airfield cover, patrol flights over frontline troops, and now and then a medium escort mission.

93 Thunderbolts of the 365th Fighter Group were in action from dawn till dusk to deprive the Germans of their vitally needed items to defend the area in central Germany against the advancing FUSA. Airfields, motor transport, and ammunition dumps were pounded, and this had many times to be done in murderous anti-aircraft fire. Disregarding the dangers of flying at low altitude over an ammunition dump under attack, the P–47s raced at zero feet through fire and smoke towering up to 8000 feet. No less than 88 ammo dumps were destroyed during this day, with an additionally large number of buildings and motor transports. In strafing attacks, the Thunderbolts wrecked three enemy aircraft. Two P–47s failed to return.

The 373rd Fighter Group took off from Venlo Airfield to strike two bridges crossing the Elbe near Wittenberg, a concrete road bridge and a railroad bridge. Despite intense flak, the Thunderbolts destroyed both bridges in their divebombing attacks.

After four days of house-to-house fighting, the Nazi holy city of Nürnberg was captured by SUSA.

Saturday, 21 April

Heavy bombers of the 8th set out to targets in southern Germany. Holzkirchen and Munich were just two of the selected unlucky objectives.

The 9th Bombardment Division sent 121 bombers to the Attnang Puchheim marshalling yards in Austria. Three Invader groups (the 386th, 391st, and the 416th) and the 410th Havoc Group bombed the yard with excellent results. No enemy fighters and not even flak disturbed the aiming. All bombers returned without a scratch.

Deteriorating weather enabled only the XIX TAC to make sorties. And they used it to good advantage. Many targets, including two airfields, were hard hit by the 367th Fighter Group, despatching forty Thunderbolts. They claimed 35 aircraft destroyed on the ground at Regensburg. By the end of the day, one P–47 did not return to its base.

Sunday, 22 April

Operations from the air were hampered by foul weather. Only XIX TAC aircraft made sorties.

Monday, 23 April

Stuttgart was seized by the French First Army.

Again, only the fighter-bombers of XIX TAC were able to take off, making 158 sorties during the morning.

Tuesday, 24 April

172 medium bombers of the 9th Air Force, composed of aircraft from five groups, attacked the Landau Airfield and a storage depot.

Thirty-two Thunderbolts of the 365th Fighter Group accompanied the bombers. One of the bomber groups was the 322nd, flying its last mission in the war, although at this stage this feature was still unknown to the crew.

Four Me–262s approached the bombers from the rear. Two flights of P–47s turned into them, breaking up their attack. One Me–262 was shot down and two others were damaged.

452

Wednesday, 25 April

Heavy bombers of the 8th Air Force flew their last mission against an industrial target. The end of the campaign was marked by 500 tons of bombs, well aimed at the Skoda works in Pilsen, Czechoslovakia. The laborers got an advance warning by radio and, although the Germans thus were informed about the coming raid as well, the Luftwaffe was no longer in a position to take advantage of such an opportunity. However, the flak was set for the scene, and when the 307 Fortresses arrived they were welcomed with murderous anti-aircraft fire. Six B–17s were knocked out of the sky.

While Fortresses of the 1st Division bombed Pilsen, a force of 282 Liberators visited the rail centers at Salzburg, Bad Reichenhall, Hallstein, and Traunstein. Clear visibility allowed accurate bombing.

Escorting Mustangs spotted an aircraft travelling at high speed below them. It was an Ar–234. With its altitude advantage, one of the P–51s swooped down to come up behind and below the jet. The Arado crashed into the ground near Reichenhall.

The 9th Bombardment Division dispatched 296 bombers to attack the Erding airbase and an ordnance depot. At 1745 hours, some eight Me–262s showed up near Erding, but they were intercepted by 38 Mustangs of the 370th Fighter Group. The jets were driven away from the bombers, though not until after one of them had been shot down. Four others were damaged.

Patrols of the 69th Division of FUSA established contact with the Russians at Torgau on the Elbe, and with this feature, Germany had been cut in two. This also meant virtually the end of combat operations for the IX TAC, which hereafter would be chiefly employed with airfield cover, an occasional escort mission, or strafing of one of the few remaining airfields. Today they flew 151 sorties.

Most activity was employed by XIX TAC, concentrating on a large number of tactical targets: buildings, gun positions, rolling stock, and many other objectives, including airfields. Here they claimed the destruction of 52 aircraft. Seven fighter-bombers were lost.

Mustangs of the 8th Air Force escorted RAF Lancasters over Berchtesgaden.

Thursday, 26 April

Two bombardment squadrons of the 8th Air Force, the 856th and 858th, operating from Dijon, were winging over Germany to drop secret agents. From 19 March onwards, 82 agents had been dropped at key locations in Germany.

125 A–20 Invaders of the 9th Bombardment Division, 391st, 409th, and

416th Bomb Groups, turned to the Plattling landing ground.

Six Me–262s with General Adolph Galland in the lead aircraft took off from München/Riem Airfield at about 1100 hours and climbed on a course that would lead them to two formations of B–26 Marauders of some thirty aircraft each. One Messerschmitt had to turn back with engine trouble; the other five continued their intercepting course.

Near Neuburg, on the Danube, contact was made and the jets attacked with cannonfire and rockets. The first Marauder exploded after a burst of cannonfire from Galland, and soon three more B–26s were to follow. Banking away from a second attack, Galland's jet was hit in the fuel tank by the bomber's gunfire. At the same moment, a Mustang caught him and sent a hail of fire into the engine and cockpit. The jet dived down and raced to Riem airfield, following the autobahn. When Galland put his jet down, the airfield was under low-level attack from P–47 Thunderbolts, but he escaped unseen.

The only ground claims were turned in by the aircraft of XIX TAC, being the only one to operate in a still-active area. The claims in the air, however, went to the IX TAC's 474th Fighter Group. Two Me–109s crossed the path of four P–38 Lightnings, and one of the Messerschmitts was shot down.

At 1635 hours, twelve Me–109s mixed it up with the Lightning formation. It cost the Germans two Messerschmitts, whereas only one P–38 received minor damage.

Patton's Third Army captured Regensburg.

Friday, 27 April

The 9th Air Force was only represented in the air today by the XIX TAC, making 125 sorties.

Saturday, 28 April

Weather kept the Air Forces grounded with the exception of sixteen P–47s of the 406th Fighter Group, flying a leaflet mission.

In the early morning hours, an Me–110 was shot down by an F–6 reconnaissance plane.

Sunday, 29 April

Indicative of the desperate situation of German transport was the number of destroyed horse-drawn vehicles. A total of 379 of such vehicles was chalked up by the three tactical air commands. The majority was credited to 69 Thunderbolts of the 362nd Fighter Group operating along the

Danube. In this region, the fighter-bombers also reaped a rich harvest of other transportation targets.

Monday, 30 April

Berlin was taken by the Russians. SUSA captured Munich, while in the north Bremen was seized.

9th Fighter-bombers made only a few sorites.

This month, the 9th Air Force flew 32,000 sorties, of which number only 7133 were made by the 9th Bombardment Division. Reconnaissance aircraft flew 3980 sorties, during which they collected very valuable information for air and ground forces on positions and movements of German troops and materiel. Weather limited the reconnaissance missions considerably during the first week of the month.

Where to bring its aircraft, since one airfield after the other had fallen into Allied hands, had become a big problem for the Luftwaffe. The few remaining airfields were crowded with aircraft and were consequently happy hunting targets for the fighter-bombers.

The Luftwaffe's operations were mainly concentrated in the area of the Third Army's front.

April, 1945—date approximate. A–26 Invaders of the 386th Bomb Group at St. Trond, Belgium. (Photo from *Air Combat 1939–1945*)

455

5

MAY

Tuesday, 1 May

396 B–17 Fortresses crossed the Dutch coast at 500 feet altitude, and this time no flak opened up. The first food supply mission was underway, after an arrangement between the Allies and the Germans through neutral sources that food would be dropped to the starving population in western Holland. Two airfields, a racetrack at The Hague, and an open space near Rotterdam, were the dropping zones, and 700 tons of food were delivered, a very satisfying task for the air crews.

Only a few operations were carried out by the fighter-bombers of the 9th Air Force.

May 1, 1945. One of the Fortresses flying above a drop zone, delivering food to the starving population in western Holland. (Photo Keystone)

Wednesday, 2 May

Today the campaign against V-weapons was formally declared to be ended.

About 400 aircraft of the 8th Air Force flew food-dropping missions to Holland.

Early in the morning, at 0630 hours, a Fieseler Fi-156 liaison aircraft was shot down by an F-6 reconnaissance Mustang pilot. Five minutes later, an Me-109 turned into his eyesight near Parchim. The Messerschmitt was also shot down. About two hours later, he encountered a Ju-88, but he was only able to damage it.

Thursday, 3 May

B-17 Fortresses of the 8th continued their food-dropping missions to Holland.

No food was carried by the bombers of the 9th when 130 Invaders of the 386th, 391st, 409th, and 416th Bomb Groups, plus eight Marauders of the First Pathfinder Squadron, arrived over the Stod Ammon Plant in Czechoslovakia. When the last bombs dropped at 1202 hours, a load from Invaders of the 391st Bomb Group, the 9th Bombardment Division had accomplished its last mission in World War II.

Most of the 356 fighters that took to the air were of the XIX TAC, to carry out flights in support of the ground forces and clear the roads of enemy transport.

A different kind of target was attacked by two fighter groups of XXIX TAC. Fourteen P-47s of the 366th Fighter Group went to Flensburg where they poured their rockets into twenty-five ships. Hereafter, they strafed the vessels and left fourteen of them damaged behind, including seven 6000-ton vessels.

Nineteen Thunderbolts of the 406th Group fired their rockets at the shipping in Lübeck, leaving a large cargo vessel ablaze.

Friday, 4 May

Again the Thunderbolts of XXIX TAC turned to shipping targets at Kiel and Flensburg. Twenty-one P-47s of the 373rd Group dropped 42 bombs and strafed a freighter and two submarines. After fires had started on the freighter, the ship was beached. Also, a submarine was hit, while a second one received a near miss. Both were streaming oil.

Eight Thunderbolts of the 370th Fighter Group flew a fighter sweep. Ground claims were scored by both other TACs.

457

In all, 356 sorties were flown by the fighter-bombers.

Armed-reconnaissance missions were flown throughout the day. One enemy plane was shot down during one of these missions.

Fighter-bombers of the 405th Group brought down four German aircraft. Three Me–262s were encountered by Thunderbolts of the 365th Fighter Group. One of them was damaged after a chase over Prague/Ruzyne Airfield. The Thunderbolt that chased it was also damaged, caused by flak.

The same fighter group observed more than thirty Me–262s on an airfield, which was promptly strafed. Thunderbolts of the 404th Group ranged in the Prague area on what was to be their last mission.

The Fortresses of the 8th were unable to fly their mission of mercy to Holland because of the bad weather.

Saturday, 5 May

Food-dropping continued and the Fortresses of the 8th Air Force flew low over the Dutch countryside to observe various manners of appreciation by the population.

Only reconnaissance missions were flown by the tactical air commands.

Sunday, 6 May

The last food dropping by the 8th Fortresses over Holland took place.

One B–17 of the 95th Bomb Group had an engine on fire. The pilot ditched the aircraft in the North Sea. A swell broke the Fortress in two and only two crew members were picked up by A.S.R., of whom only one was to survive.

XXIX TAC flew its last mission with seventeen Thunderbolts of the 373rd Fighter Group. They carried out a demonstration mission.

Monday, 7 May

General Spaatz was among the air officers present to accept the surrender of the Germans at Rheims at 0141 hours. Formal hostilities had ceased.

But still the work went on, and fighter-bombers flew sweeps and also demonstration flights over prisoner-of-war camps.

The 368th Fighter Group flew its last mission when sixteen P–47s set out on a fighter sweep to the Chemnitz-Prague area.

F–6 Reconnaissance Mustangs had several encounters with the Luftwaffe. Four Focke Wulfs were met on different missions. One FW–190 was shot down in a dogfight.

458

Tuesday, 8 May

During the last month of operations, the 9th Air Force had claimed over 1400 planes destroyed on the crowded airfields. And the war was not over yet. IX TAC fighter-bombers flew 191 patrols and fighter-sweeps. Seven German aircraft were forced down to surrender. XIX TAC aircraft flew 194 sorties, patrolling over Linz and making demonstration flights over the P.O.W. camps. Again three enemy aircraft were forced down to surrender. One Thunderbolt buzzing a P.O.W. camp hit the water of Lake Trauen and the pilot had to make a belly-landing. It meant the last loss of the fighter-bombers.

94 F–6 reconnaissance Mustangs made sorties, and two F–5 Lightnings also flew their armed-reconnaissance mission.

At 0715 hours, two F–6 Mustangs encountered two FW–190s near Bischofteinitz in Czechoslovakia. The Mustangs turned into the Focke Wulfs and both German fighters dived for the deck. With both Mustangs in hot pursuit, one of the Focke Wulfs crashlanded after it had been hit in the tail. Seconds later, the other Luftwaffe fighter was destroyed.

During the afternoon, two more German fighters were shot down and it was at about 2000 hours that two F–6s of the 12th Tac. Recon. Squadron, flying a patrol along the Danube, were jumped by five FW–190s. The Mustangs managed to turn into them in a high-speed climbing turn and a few seconds after the leader settled his Mustang behind the tail of the trailing FW–190, the last German aircraft to be shot down by the 9th Air Force in the Second World War dived into the ground.

Four hours later, the war was over.

Wednesday, 9 May

The unconditional surrender of Germany became a fact when the ratification of the agreement at Rheims took place at Berlin shortly after midnight. All hostilities had ceased.

The cessation of hostilities also meant the end of the operations of the special 406th (originally 422nd) Bombardment Squadron or Special Leaflet Squadron. As such, they flew 2334 sorties during which they dropped about 1,758,000,000 leaflets. Losses were three aircraft and sixteen crew members, including Colonel Aber (see March 4, 1945).

The air forces had undoubtedly made a great contribution toward ultimate victory, but the inevitable toll they paid was terribly heavy. The 8th Air Force lost some 5200 heavy bombers and some 2100 fighters, while the 9th Air Force lost some 800 medium and light bombers and also some 2100 fighters. It had cost the lives of ten thousands of men. . .

Some 10,000 ground personnel were taken up in the bombers in the coming days on a sightseeing tour. The flights were called "trolley runs," and included personnel of bomber stations as well as fighter stations. So they all got an impression of the destruction they had helped to promote . . .

Bibliography

Craven W.F. and Cate J.L. *The Army Air Forces in World War II*, vols. 1-3. Chicago: The University of Chicago Press, 1948/51.

No Author. *Target Germany*. London: His Majesty's Stationery Office, 1944.

Peaslee, Col. Budd J. *Heritage of Valor*. Philadelphia and New York: J.B.Lippincott Company, 1946.

Irving, David. *The Destruction of Dresden*. London: Transworld Publishers, Ltd, 1966.

Galland, Adolf. *The First and the Last*. New York: Henry Holt and Co., 1954.

Freeman, Roger A. *The Mighty Eighth*. London: Macdonald and Company Ltd, 1970.

Rust, Kenn C. *The 9th Air Force in World War II*. Fallbrook, California: Aero Publishers, Inc., 1967.

Johnson, Robert S. and Caidin, Martin. *Thunderbolt*. New York: Ballantine Books, Inc., 1959.

Blakebrough, Ken. *The Fireball Outfit*. Fallbrook, California: Aero Publishers, Inc., 1968.

Blue, Allan G. *The Fortunes of War*. Fallbrook, California: Aero Publishers, Inc., 1967.

Rust, Kenn C. and Hess, William N. *The Slybird Group*. Fallbrook, California: Aero Publishers, Inc., 1968.

Olmsted, Merle C. *The Yoxford Boys*. Fallbrook, California: Aero Publishers, Inc., 1971.

Turner, Lt. Col. Richard E., USAF (ret). *Big Friend, Little Friend*. Garden City, New York: Doubleday and Company, Inc., 1969.

Hess, William N. *Fighting Mustang*. Garden City, New York: Doubleday and Company, Inc., 1970

Hess, William. *P-51 Bomber Escort*. New York: Ballantine Books Inc., 1971.

Constable, Trevor J. and Toliver, Col. Raymond F. *Horrido*. New York: Ballantine Books Inc., 1970.

Price, Alfred. *Luftwaffe*. London: Macdonald and Company Ltd., 1970.

Frankland, Noble. *Bomber Offensive*. London: Macdonald and Company Inc., 1970.

No Author. *The Story of the 390th Bomb Group*. Publisher unknown, 1947.

No Author *Log of Missions* The mission log appeared in six instalments of the issue of the 91st Bomb Group: "The Ragged Irregular," July 1968-January 1970.

No Author. *Royal Air Force Flying Review*, vols. 1952-1962 London: The Royal Air Force Review Ltd, 1952-1962.

461

Index

Groups and Squadrons of the United States Army Air Force and the Royal Air Force, as well as individual names of aircraft, geographical names and names of persons are listed separately.

390, 400, 403, 405–407, 410, 416, 419, 421–423, 425, 429, 430, 435, 437, 438, 440, 442, 443, 445, 446, 448–454, 458

Me-410, 109, 114, 171, 186, 192, 229, 240, 241, 249, 257, 280, 297, 416, 417, 430, 435, 440

Meteor MK I, Gloster, 330, 331

M.I.A.G. factories, 149

Ministry of Propaganda, 411

Mitchell B-25 North American, 56, 184, 225

Modified Sites, 199

Mosquito, 403, 411, 437, 447

Mühlenbau und Industrie A.G., 136

Mustang P-51: North American introduction, 105, 110; first sortie, 119; first escort sortie, 119; characteristics, 160, 197, 220; twin-seated P-51, 255; F-6 (Photo-reconnaissance P-51), 102, 437, 439, 440, 442, 449, 454, 457–459; operations *see* text; RAF operated P-51, 148, 161, 206

N

Napalm bomb, 262, 269, 290, 299, 322, 342, 343, 346, 354, 439, 445, 446

National Redoubt, 439, 442–444, 450

Nazi-indoctrination, 439

Nickling operations, 93

Ninth Air Force *see* Air Forces

Noballs, 118, 126, 139, 142, 144, 147, 153, 156, 161, 165, 170, 173, 174, 176, 196, 202, 239, 242, 257, 258

Nordisk Lettmetal, 63

Nye's Annihilators, 211, 257, 406

O

OBOE, 104, 108, 110, 113

Oil campaign, 204, 216, 238, 328, 352, 402, 442

"Omaha," 225, 227, 230

Operational Research Section, 176

"Overlord," 118, 119, 122, 148, 193, 238, 242

P

P-38 *see* Lightning

P-39 *see* Airacobra

P-40, 6

P-47 *see* Thunderbolt

P-51 *see* Mustang

P-61 *see* Black Widow

Panther tank works, 422

Pathfinder, 90, 103, 104, 106–108, 110, 113, 114, 121, 122, 124, 126, 225, 239, 257, 266, 325, 329, 333, 335, 341, 366, 395, 418, 431

Patriot army, 315

Persian Gulf Command, 242

Pilot training, 174, 231, 280, 289

Polish Armored Division, 291

Polish 1st Independent Parachute Brigade, 312

Potez aircraft factory, 9, 11

Poujean aircraft factory, 11

P.O.W., 350

P.O.W. camp, 152, 161, 203, 265, 458, 459

Predicted barrage, 25

Primary trainer, 302

Propaganda leaflets, 69, 93, 227

Q

"Queen," 344, 352

Queen Elizabeth, 26

R

Radar Equipment
    H2S, 77, 88–92, 106
    H2X, 88, 106, 111, 174, 212, 225, 246, 258, 259, 261, 277, 420, 426

Radar jamming device, 152

Radiation Laboratory, 88, 106

RAF *see* Royal Air Force

Ragged Irregulars, The, 166

Ramstaffel, 440

Rangers, 230

Raubvogel unit, 440

Rebecca, 133

Red Cross, 293

Reichstag building, 411

Renault motor factories, 38

Rheinmetall Borsig, 305

Rhenania, 348, 420
Rocket missile, 304
Rodeo (fighter sweep over enemy territory), 88
Royal Air Force
  Bomber Command, 77, 156, 159, 204, 205, 225, 229, 251, 258, 262, 273, 281, 282, 288, 297, 299, 300, 310, 313, 320, 345, 363, 364, 367, 370, 373, 374, 398, 399, 402, 407, 409, 411, 415, 420–422, 430, 434, 437, 441, 442, 446, 453
  Fighter Command, 226, 233, 316, 345
Royal Canadian Air Force, 381, 396
Russian bases, 241, 242, 244, 279, 282, 315, 317

S
Schindler storage facility, 434
Schleisischer railway station, 411
Scouts, 260, 265, 343, 398
Siegfried Line, 308, 310, 312, 338, 352, 424, 428
Skoda works, 453
Smoke marker, 89, 90, 268, 282
S.N.C.A. de l'Ouest aircraft factory, 59
Sonderkommando Elbe, 439
Sound barrier, 330
Soviet army, 315
Special Leaflet Squadron, 93, 94, 225, 227, 417, 459
S-phone, 133
Spitfire, 5–13, 16, 19, 21, 26–28, 32, 34, 35, 38–40, 44, 45, 51, 56, 57, 62, 66, 67, 70, 72, 73, 76, 77, 80, 85, 100, 102, 103, 148, 166, 167, 174, 226, 249, 297, 303, 317, 365, 434
Splasher beacons, 62
"Starkey," 73, 79, 86
Steyr Walzlagerwerke, 152
Stirling, 224
Stod Ammon Plant, 457
Stuka see Junkers Ju-87
Swiss Messerschmitts, 303
"Sword," 225

T
Tactical Air Force see Air Forces
Tallboy bombs, 421
Ted's Travelling Circus, 36
Thunderbolt P-47 Republic: introduction, 26; first operational sortie, 35; D-model, 52; characteristics, 35, 40, 102, 197, 220; tactics, 70, 113, 114, 171, 187, 262, 290; M-model, 384, 425, 426; German operated P-47, 402, 444; operations see text
Tiger Stripe Group, 406
Tiger tank, 352
"Tojo," 31
"Torch," 11
Transportation program, 192, 195, 221
Trolley runs, 460
Twelfth Air Force see Air Forces
Typhoon, 55, 56, 67, 161, 191, 217, 218, 244, 281, 283, 381

U
Unconditional surrender, 459
Underground movement, 133, 161, 177, 247, 257, 260, 275, 314
Unidentified bombers, 92, 238, 248
USSTAF (United States Strategic Air Forces in Europe), 134, 232
U.S. Strategic Bombing Survey, 156
"Utah," 224–226, 233

V
"Varsity," 432
Ventura, 32
V.K.F. anti-friction bearing plant, 154, 159
V-weapons, 77, 78, 80, 81, 104, 139, 199, 202, 235–237, 276, 277, 280, 284, 304, 305, 413, 434, 457
V-1, 77, 104, 139, 140, 191, 235–237, 254, 301, 350, 434; first launching, 235, 236
V-2, 235, 300, 304, 305, 434; first launching, 304, 305

W
War Cabinet, 77, 119, 304
"Warspite," 299
Wilke Werke, 416

Bomber and Fighter Groups of the Eighth and Ninth Air Force

Medium Bomber Groups

319th, 16

322nd, 35, 46, 49, 61, 66, 68, 70–72, 78, 80, 86, 88, 94, 102–105, 108, 116, 120, 145, 150, 158, 172, 173, 203, 211, 220, 257, 366, 367, 406, 427, 450–452

323rd, 61, 62, 66–69, 86, 96, 102, 116, 120, 122, 123, 163, 172, 220, 451

344th, 173, 220, 267, 271

386th, 61, 66, 68, 70–72, 77, 79, 82, 86, 94, 102, 116, 120, 123, 145, 173, 220, 229, 252, 304, 365, 366, 403, 405, 419, 451, 452, 455, 457

387th, 61, 74, 81, 86, 88, 96, 102, 116, 158, 173, 220, 366, 367, 391, 406, 442

391st, 147, 163, 173, 220, 256, 303, 365, 366, 419, 440, 443, 452, 453, 457

394th, 176, 192, 203, 220, 281, 282, 366, 367, 391, 416, 446, 450, 451

397th, 191, 214, 220, 287, 366, 406

Light Bomber Groups

409th 220, 392, 403, 451, 453, 457

410th, 220, 230, 299, 300, 371, 392, 395, 397, 407, 409, 452

416th, 159, 206, 220, 227, 249, 280, 323, 341, 366, 391, 392, 399, 403, 406, 452, 454, 457

Fighter Groups Eighth Air Force

1st, 5, 6, 9, 11, 12

4th, 10–13, 16, 19, 27, 28, 32, 35, 38–40, 43, 44, 46, 50, 68, 69, 73, 90, 107, 119, 121, 124, 129, 139, 141, 142, 145, 153, 157–162, 165, 171, 172, 174, 175, 177, 179, 181, 182, 184, 192, 197, 202, 212, 218, 226, 240, 241, 243, 254, 276, 280, 282, 291, 294, 307, 309, 315, 321, 324, 346, 386, 388, 423, 426, 430, 432, 437

14th, 11, 12

20th, 110, 116, 126, 129, 141, 143, 144, 147, 157, 182, 185, 193, 195–197, 217, 218, 265, 307, 339, 340, 386

31st, 5, 7, 8, 11

52nd, 11

55th, 102, 103, 106, 108, 110, 116, 121, 129, 143, 159, 184, 193, 195, 196, 218, 233, 264, 279, 302, 307, 397, 404, 410, 449

56th, 26, 27, 39, 40, 43–46, 52, 54, 55, 57, 59, 60, 69, 72, 73, 76, 77, 79, 80, 82, 90, 92–94, 97, 98, 100, 108–110, 112, 114, 116, 118–120, 124, 127–129, 134, 142, 144, 147, 149, 157, 158, 162, 166, 171, 174, 175, 177, 180, 182, 183, 187, 196, 202, 205, 208, 217, 218, 229, 231, 234, 235, 253, 255, 257, 265, 278, 290, 291, 303, 314, 316–318, 339, 340, 355, 365, 377, 384, 422, 425, 445

78th, 39, 40, 43, 45–47, 54, 59, 60, 69, 73, 90, 114, 129, 142, 182, 212, 218, 232, 274, 298, 314, 316, 329, 377, 427, 429, 430

339th, 218, 240, 307, 448

352nd, 91, 99, 115, 129, 141, 170, 201, 207, 209, 218, 232, 234, 241, 243, 266, 279, 372, 375, 377, 382, 422

353rd, 72–75, 81, 84, 88–90, 92, 93, 98, 99, 103, 104, 108–110, 113, 119, 121, 125, 127, 129, 135, 138, 140–145, 147, 151, 162, 170–172, 179, 187, 193, 196, 200, 210, 211, 218, 221, 224, 229, 232, 234, 236, 238, 240, 246, 248, 257, 276, 277, 297, 304, 305, 309, 314, 317, 318, 325–327, 346, 350, 365, 373, 386–388, 406, 408, 422, 435, 439, 447

355th, 91, 129, 181, 218, 226, 289, 291, 315, 451

356th, 102, 114, 129, 140, 207, 211, 218, 289, 314

357th, 117, 141, 147, 149, 151, 153, 155, 160, 162, 171, 186, 187, 192, 209, 210, 212, 217, 218, 235, 237, 249, 254, 269, 279, 291, 294, 316, 341, 342, 346, 350, 355, 365, 386, 433, 450

359th, 122, 129, 199, 209, 218, 232, 234, 271, 289, 294, 305, 307, 317, 335, 361, 416, 426, 431

471

361st, 129, 172, 201, 218, 249, 286, 315, 321, 374, 375
364th, 157, 218, 329, 375, 377, 410, 450
479th, 218, 272, 291, 303, 321, 322, 336, 405

Fighter Groups Ninth Air Force
36th, 220, 287, 301, 310, 372, 389, 401, 410, 418, 421, 423, 444
48th, 220, 304, 335, 346, 356, 367, 372, 388, 389, 392, 407
50th, 220, 248, 284, 313
354th, 110, 117, 119, 121–123, 128, 129, 134, 136, 141, 144–147, 149, 151, 155, 157, 159, 171, 181, 182, 187, 191, 195, 207, 214, 220, 235, 248, 249, 251, 255, 266, 277, 281, 283, 289, 293, 295, 296, 306, 309, 322, 336, 353, 374, 389, 392, 403, 407, 416, 429, 431, 436, 444–446, 448, 449
358th, 129, 220, 293, 322
362nd, 117, 220, 275, 281, 283, 292, 331, 334, 374, 389, 390–392, 396, 402, 404, 424, 434, 454
363rd, 125, 159, 160, 212, 220, 276, 281, 287
365th, 125, 199, 220, 230, 295, 307, 317, 326, 331, 334, 351, 363, 375, 382, 389, 392, 407, 410, 421, 451, 452, 458
366th, 171, 220, 230, 233, 248, 259, 281, 286, 310, 335, 348, 382, 383, 387, 389, 392, 393, 399, 407, 445, 457
367th, 220, 256, 295, 334, 345, 347, 374, 375, 389, 391, 401, 403, 404, 427, 452
368th, 220, 230, 239, 246, 248, 295, 302, 307, 328, 331, 332, 334, 347, 375, 389, 391, 392, 398, 408, 423, 434, 444, 448, 458
370th, 209, 220, 262, 290, 299, 313, 326, 345, 354, 389, 392, 399, 407, 419, 451, 453, 457
371st, 220, 232, 233, 248, 292, 408, 435, 449
373rd, 220, 281, 285, 288, 310, 330, 367, 370, 372, 389, 393, 399, 408, 428, 444, 452, 457, 458
404th, 202, 208, 220, 232, 238, 289, 296, 306, 313, 335, 361, 372, 388, 389, 392, 403, 423, 450, 458
405th, 220, 272, 284, 288, 292, 298, 302, 308, 319, 326, 374, 389, 399, 408, 409, 435, 458
406th, 220, 266, 270, 285, 292, 304, 306, 307, 323, 331, 367, 374, 375, 389, 396, 399, 414, 430, 439, 454, 457
474th, 195, 211, 220, 256, 290, 293–295, 307, 309, 326, 331, 345, 361, 370, 389, 392, 419, 421, 423, 454

Bomber and Fighter Squadrons of the Eighth and Ninth Air Force

Heavy Bomber Squadrons
67th, 19, 31
68th, 19
322nd, 18
323rd, 18
324th, 14
326th, 7
328th, 173
329th, 19, 25
330th, 17
342nd, 8
359th, 36
366th, 19
406th, 417, 459
412th, 8
422nd, 85, 93, 225, 227, 417, 459
563rd, 83
788th, 213
813th, 90, 103
850th, 213
856th, 133, 378, 390, 453
857th, 133

472

Bomber/Fighter Groups and Squadrons of the Royal Air Force

Individual Aircraft Names

Geographical Names

333, 336, 338, 344, 349, 355, 361,
363, 364, 382–385, 387, 390, 394,
396, 399, 415, 417, 418, 422
Commercy, 299
Compiègne, 157, 289, 302
Conches, 79, 80, 181, 255
Conflans, 217, 222, 235
Corbeil, 287
Corbie, 281
Corbronne, 239
Cordonville, 239
Cormeilles-en-Vexin, 204, 209, 210
Cornwall, 20
Contentin, 7, 16, 52
Cottbus, 186, 216, 388, 396, 402
Coulommiers, 184, 296, 369
Courcelles, 222
Courtrai, 9, 12, 46
Coutances, 262, 270, 272
Creil, 163, 165, 172, 173, 175, 178,
179, 191, 196, 203, 212, 217, 244,
248
Crequi, 147
Croisetter, 139
Cuxhaven, 53, 386
Czechoslovakia, 294, 402, 405, 442–
447, 449, 451, 453, 457, 459

D

Dahlem, 364, 373
Danube, 454, 455, 459
Danzig, 95
Darmstadt, 100, 337, 342, 357, 384,
385, 402, 429, 433
Dasburg, 391, 392
Datteln, 418
Daun, 369
Dawlish, 28
Debden, 10, 12, 35, 40, 157, 186, 243,
324, 330, 331, 427
Deelen, 153, 246
Delden, 124
Demouville, 264
Denain, 209
Denmark, 63, 95, 148, 152, 183, 378
Derben, 386, 387, 435
Dessau, 214, 216, 217, 289
Deurne, 381

Diedice, 242
Diepholz, 149
Dieppe, 7, 38, 73, 80, 226, 227
Dieuze, 334, 343
Dijon, 178, 195, 295, 453
Dillenburg, 421
Diosgyör, 309
Dollbergen, 416
Domfront, 236, 237
Donauwörth, 450
Dorsten, 430
Dortmund, 403, 404, 418, 420, 421
Dotzheim, 419
Douai, 198
Dover, 10
Dreiborn, 363
Dresden, 388, 396, 401, 402, 415, 448
Dreux, 229, 234, 235, 292
Drohobycz, 248
Drucat, 5, 36, 70
Duisburg, 341, 394
Dülmen, 400, 401, 406, 430
Dümmer Lake, 162, 166, 170, 197, 208,
257, 425, 428, 439
Dumpelfeld, 396
Düne Island, 47
Dungeness, 226
Dunkirk, 31, 32, 35, 40, 303
Düren, 93, 99, 103, 110, 307, 328, 331,
332, 334, 344–346, 350, 351, 373,
391, 393, 407, 410
Durwiss, 344
Düsseldorf, 192, 305, 332, 338, 348,
385, 389

E

East Prussia, 95
Echternach, 358
Eger, 442
Eggebeck, 445
Eglin Field (USA), 126, 200
Egmond, 425
Ehrang, 203, 361, 364, 408
Eifel, 361
Eindhoven, 312, 314, 316, 381, 382
Einruhr, 358
Eisenach, 321, 400, 439
Eitorf, 418

478

Maintenon, 256, 270, 290
Mainz, 305, 317, 321, 322, 346, 355,
    361, 385, 430
Maisons-Lafitte, 213, 214
Maldegem, 184
Malines, 191
Malmedy, 362, 367, 370, 374, 382
Malmö, 256
Malta, 396
Manderen, 343
Mannheim, 75, 187, 195, 213, 287, 319,
    333, 390, 395, 430
Manston, 57, 60, 74, 118
Mantes, 191, 198, 214, 217, 246
Mantes-Gassicourt, 200, 292, 293
Marche, 367, 383
Mardijck, 82
Marguenville, 191
Marienberg, 448
Marienburg, 95, 96, 183
Marigny, 139
Marquise, 208
Martinville Ridge, 237
Mayen, 326, 346, 365, 366, 369, 375,
    383
Mayenne, 281
Méaulté, 9–11, 45, 195
Mechernich, 398
Mediterranean, 74, 76, 312
Meiningen, 407
Melun/Villaroche, 110, 211, 218, 236,
    292
Memmingen, 442, 451
Mengen, 346
Meppel, 288
Merseburg, 205, 214, 217, 256, 264,
    271, 272, 294, 307, 309, 328, 330,
    336, 340, 342, 348, 349, 351, 356,
    357
Merville, 73
Merweburg, 322
Merzhausen, 368
Merzig, 346, 347
Meschede, 412
Metz, 135, 198, 211, 212, 301, 304–
    307, 319, 322, 329, 337, 341–343,
    347, 352, 381

Meulan, 217, 218
Meuse, 202, 203, 291, 299, 302, 337,
    358, 360, 364, 371, 374, 399
Meuse-Escaut Canal, 314
Mézières, 202
Michelsberg, 448
Mimoyecques, 110, 173, 208
Minden, 149, 340, 341, 409
Mirgorod, 242, 315
Misburg, 237, 239, 240, 294, 307, 308,
    335, 350, 351, 377, 416
Mockau, 148, 444
Modrath, 336
Moerdijk, 313
Molesworth, 29
Monceaux, 198
Monchy, 209
Monheim, 332
Mons, 297, 302
Monschau, 357, 358, 371, 373
Montabaur, 406
Montargis, 284
Mont Beliard, 312
Montdidier, 105, 209, 254
Montignies sur Sambre, 198
Montrichard, 285
Mont St. Michel, 285
Morlaix, 11
Morscheid, 341, 372
Mortain, 276, 279, 281, 284
Moscow, 315
Moselle, 305, 306, 312, 338, 343, 346,
    388, 422, 424, 430
Mulhouse, 203, 212, 277, 439
München (Munich), 172, 181, 193,
    258–261, 263, 273, 410, 442, 447,
    448, 452, 454, 455
München-Gladbach, 363, 416
Münster, 96, 97, 108–110, 124, 133,
    170, 174, 175, 200, 321, 323, 326,
    335, 336, 346, 390, 403–406, 429,
    430, 432
Münster/Handorf, 326
Münstereifel, 352, 390
Murmansk, 242

N
Namur, 184, 191, 193, 202
Nancy, 127, 212, 306, 308, 313, 319

486

Names of Persons